"Endicott Peabody's dying words, 'You know there's no doubt but that Roosevelt is a very religious man,' provide a good summation of America's thirty-second president. This remarkable and long-overdue biography traces Franklin Roosevelt's religious development from childhood through Peabody's Groton School to the presidency, during which FDR continued to serve as senior warden of St. James' Episcopal Church in Hyde Park. Roosevelt's self-description as a Christian and a Democrat comes alive in this excellent, thoroughly researched biography, a book that promises to reshape our understanding of the twentieth century's most consequential president."

— Randall Balmer, author of *Redeemer: The Life of Jimmy Carter*

"This timely, inspiring portrait of the role of Christianity in the life and presidency of Franklin Delano Roosevelt helps us better understand one of the influential leaders of the twentieth century. Woolverton has made a great contribution here that should lead us to reevaluate our view of the role of faith in the progressive movement, the Democratic Party, and American politics generally, while also stoking our imagination for how Christian principles might guide us today."

— Michael Wear, author of *Reclaiming Hope: Lessons Learned in the Obama White House about the Future of Faith in America*

"Historians have not taken Franklin Roosevelt's Christianity seriously enough when they analyze his response to the economic depression and then World War II. Thanks to John Woolverton's excellent new biography, they will not make this mistake again. Woolverton masterfully demonstrates that to understand the Roosevelt presidency, we need to understand how the president's Christian conceptions of faith, hope, and love shaped his policies and his views of the world."

— Matthew A. Sutton, Washington State University

"With James D. Bratt's deft revision, this study of Franklin Roosevelt's religious life by respected Episcopal historian John Woolverton arrives at just the right time. Woolverton's warm but frank spiritual biography describes a president who practiced a Christianity based on hope, charity, and faith and grounded in a deep sense of mutual responsibility. This book is a reminder that American Christianity might have followed an alternative trajectory into the twenty-first century."

— Alison Collis Greene, Emory University

"Rare is the opportunity to read a biography by someone who ran in the same circles as the author but who was not an acquaintance. Through a collective biography of FDR's many influences and their religious backgrounds, we learn that Franklin Roosevelt had the Social Gospel imprinted on his character. His boarding school teachers raised him with a strong sense of responsibility toward the less fortunate, which drove both his concern for the poor and his rejection of authoritarian methods of establishing justice. Woolverton and Bratt depict a man whose 'simple faith' drove his decisions in both domestic and foreign policy. It was this faith, they suggest, that helped save the prospects for democracy in the United States."

— Janine Giordano Drake, University of Providence

LIBRARY OF RELIGIOUS BIOGRAPHY

Mark A. Noll and Heath W. Carter, series editors

Long overlooked by historians, religion has emerged in recent years as a key factor in understanding the past. From politics to popular culture, from social struggles to the rhythms of family life, religion shapes every story. Religious biographies open a window to the sometimes surprising influence of religion on the lives of influential people and the worlds they inhabited.

The Library of Religious Biography is a series that brings to life important figures in United States history and beyond. Grounded in careful research, these volumes link the lives of their subjects to the broader cultural contexts and religious issues that surrounded them. The authors are respected historians and recognized authorities in the historical period in which their subject lived and worked.

Marked by careful scholarship yet free of academic jargon, the books in this series are well-written narratives meant to be read and *enjoyed* as well as studied.

Titles include:

*Sworn on the Altar of God: A Religious Biography of **Thomas Jefferson***
by Edwin S. Gaustad

*The Religious Life of **Robert E. Lee***
by R. David Cox

***Abraham Lincoln**: Redeemer President*
by Allen C. Guelzo

***Harriet Beecher Stowe**: A Spiritual Life*
by Nancy Koester

For a complete list of published volumes, see the back of this volume.

A Christian and a Democrat

A Religious Biography of Franklin D. Roosevelt

John F. Woolverton

with James D. Bratt

WILLIAM B. EERDMANS PUBLISHING COMPANY

GRAND RAPIDS, MICHIGAN

Wm. B. Eerdmans Publishing Co.
4035 Park East Court SE, Grand Rapids, Michigan 49546
www.eerdmans.com

Published 2019
Printed in the United States of America

25 24 23 22 21 20 19   1 2 3 4 5 6 7

ISBN 978-0-8028-7685-0

Library of Congress Cataloging-in-Publication Data

Names: Woolverton, John Frederick, 1926– author.
Title: A Christian and a Democrat : a religious biography of Franklin D.
    Roosevelt / John F. Woolverton with James D. Bratt.
Description: Grand Rapids : Eerdmans Publishing Co., 2019. | Series: Library
    of religious biography | Includes bibliographical references and index.
Identifiers: LCCN 2019005487 | ISBN 9780802876850 (hardcover : alk. paper)
Subjects: LCSH: Roosevelt, Franklin D. (Franklin Delano),
    1882-1945—Religion. | Presidents—Religious life—United States.
Classification: LCC E807 .W695 2019 | DDC 973.917092—dc23
    LC record available at https://lccn.loc.gov/2019005487

An earlier version of material in chapter 8 was published as "'Who Is Kierkegaard?':
Franklin Roosevelt, Howard Johnson, and Søren Kierkegaard," *Anglican and Episcopal
History* 80, no. 1 (March 2011): 1–32.

Contents

CONTENTS

PART III: INTERPRETATION

Foreword

John Woolverton changed my life.

During college, I signed up to take a course called "Significant Books in Western Religion," which had long been taught by a legendary and engaging professor in William and Mary's religion department. I was disappointed to arrive at the first day of class and learn that the professor was on sabbatical, and his substitute was a slightly stuffy-sounding, bow tie–wearing Episcopal cleric from a northern Virginia seminary. The substitute with the bow tie was John Woolverton. In that class we began a lifelong friendship.

I arrived at the College of William and Mary in Virginia with a fairly dark view of the world, after being held at gunpoint in my home my senior year of high school by a serial rapist and robber. Woolverton understood. Using the framing offered by Reinhold Niebuhr, Woolverton acknowledged that the world is dark and fallen—and challenged me to make it better. That is the only way to find meaning—and justice—in the face of sin and injustice.

With his encouragement, I focused my senior thesis on comparing and contrasting Niebuhr with an emerging force in American politics, the Reverend Jerry Falwell, founder of the Moral Majority, an organization urging evangelical Christians to become active politically. (Falwell's son followed in his footsteps; as of this writing, he is one of Donald Trump's strongest supporters.) Both Niebuhr and Falwell urged believers to participate actively in the life of their nation, but with very different approaches to our ability to discern God's will. Niebuhr urged caution and humility in claiming divine mandate for policy positions, teaching that pride infects all endeavor. Falwell, not so much.

It makes perfect sense that John Woolverton would become an admirer of Franklin D. Roosevelt and the way faith shaped FDR's life and leadership. Like FDR, Woolverton was raised in a world of Episcopalian privilege and duty. Although a generation apart, they attended the same college and elite boarding school, and were deeply influenced by the same headmaster, Endicott Peabody, to remember their obligation to serve those less fortunate. Woolverton came of age and served during World War II while watching Roosevelt try to live that obligation in a country in crisis and a world at war. Although Woolverton chose to serve the rest of his life wearing a clerical collar, he remained a student of the intersection of private faith and public duty, the place where FDR lived and died.

It also makes perfect sense that he would end this wonderful book comparing FDR and Abraham Lincoln, the two American presidents who dealt with existential, soul-searing challenges. They led the nation with a combination of confidence in their role and prophetic humility in their own limitations. Both were imperfect people who, with a keen sense of their own limitations, did great things for their country.

Were he still alive, John Woolverton would be deeply disturbed by the division in American society and the dark undercurrent of reaction and resentment that carried our current president into office, which to this day animates him and so many of his supporters. But he would not be entirely surprised by those developments.

As a student of history and human nature, Woolverton understood our weakness and the endless cycles we are prone to. As FDR did, Woolverton knew "the eternal trick of the demagogue who espouses 'doctrines that set group against group, faith against faith, race against race, class against class, fanning the fires of hatred in men.'" As he writes here, that demagoguery is toxic for the church, the state, and the world. But it is not new. And in that familiarity lies a certain comfort. We have been here before. We know what to do.

Were he still preaching, John Woolverton would likely say what he said to me so many years ago: Yes, things are a mess, but that only increases the urgency to step into the public square. We have an obligation to condemn the racism, misogyny, and lying at the center of our national life today. The sin deserves our active hatred—but our fellow Americans do not. We must approach them with Christian love and true humility as we try to heal our divisions. He would surely quote Lincoln, as he does in his book:

With malice toward none, with charity for all, with firmness in the right as God gives us to see the right, let us strive to finish the work we are in, to bind up the nation's wounds. . . .

John Woolverton inspired countless students to pursue lives of purpose and value in a troubled world. I am delighted that this book, with its compelling exegesis of the work and faith of Franklin Roosevelt, will enable him to continue to inspire.

—JAMES COMEY
Former Director, Federal
Bureau of Investigation

Preface

JAMES D. BRATT

In July 2014, David Holmes, a professor of American religious history at the College of William and Mary, sent me and some other colleagues in the field a tribute that he had written in honor of a friend, John F. Woolverton, who had died the previous month. I had never met Professor Woolverton, but I had admired his work on Episcopal Church history, especially his long and very able editorship of the flagship journal in the field, *Anglican and Episcopal History*. From David Holmes's tribute, it was obvious that John Woolverton had been a sterling teacher and pastor, a mentor and inspiration to many, and a most memorable personality besides. He was passionate about serious scholarship, social justice, and his Christian faith. That combination produced the book you have in your hands.

I read with interest, and real concern, in David Holmes's tribute that *A Christian and a Democrat* remained unpublished at Professor Woolverton's death, and so I volunteered to help get it into print. The message of this book, ever pertinent, is all the more timely, even urgent, in view of recent developments on the American political scene. How can it be that the most highly publicized arm of Christianity, white evangelical Protestantism, has overwhelmingly endorsed Donald Trump, the most forthright pagan ever to occupy the Oval Office? How is it that its version of social ethics, translated into public policy, so contradicts manifest Christian virtues? How will any Christian voice in politics survive the collapse—or, God forbid, the catastrophic denouement—of the Trumpian-evangelical alliance? In this context it is vital to recover the better heritage of Christian social witness in American history, to see another type of Christian faith active in the White House. John Woolverton provides just that in this memorable study of how the Christian triad of faith, hope, and love inspired Franklin Roosevelt's political vision.

Professor Woolverton was ably prepared for this task. He recounts his personal connections to the subject below; here we can summarize his professional qualifications. After graduating from Harvard, Rev. Woolverton was trained for ministry in the Episcopal Church at Virginia Theological Seminary (VTS). He served for three years as vicar of Trinity Church in Austin, Texas, then returned to academia, earning his PhD at Columbia University. Among the courses he took was one with Reinhold Niebuhr at neighboring Union Theological Seminary, which marked the beginning of a lasting friendship between the two. In 1958 he joined the faculty back at VTS, where he taught church history for the next twenty-five years. During that tenure he spent a year teaching at the Jesuits' Woodstock Theological College and another at William and Mary, where he was a colleague of his friend David Holmes.

Professor Woolverton's editorship of *Anglican and Episcopal History* spanned thirty years, from 1978 to 2007, and continued during his return to the pastorate as rector of Trinity Church in Portland, Maine. In 1989 he retired from that post to devote his energies to research and writing. His *Colonial Anglicanism in North America*, still the definitive study of the subject, had appeared in 1984; in retirement he devoted himself to biography. *The Education of Phillips Brooks* (1995) studied the formation of the man who became one of America's leading preachers and a powerful Episcopal churchman in the post–Civil War era. Ten years later he published a pioneering work on Robert H. Gardiner, the denomination's foremost ecumenical statesman in the early twentieth century. Professor Woolverton's biographical study of Franklin D. Roosevelt thus forms a capstone of his varied and multidimensional career.

David Holmes responded to my inquiries about the state of the Roosevelt manuscript by putting me in touch with Arthur Woolverton, John Woolverton's son, who had promised his father before he died that he would get the Roosevelt book published. David was among the colleagues of his father whose help Arthur sought to that end. Arthur and I soon came to agreement about changes the manuscript could use to increase its readership and impact, and upon Eerdmans Publishing Company's Library of Religious Biography as a good home for the book. Between my other academic obligations, I worked on editing the manuscript. It is approximately 75 percent of its original length. I trimmed some of the loving details that the author, as a fellow graduate with FDR of Groton and Harvard, had included; likewise some of his record of the tumultuous debates over American entry into World War II that Professor Woolverton, as a teenager in those years and a soldier at the very end of that war, recalled from that formative period in his political and ethical development. I also condensed some of the detail that the author included as a lifelong passionate participant in Episcopal Church politics, while simultaneously expanding the information provided on that church's distinctive history, teachings, and rites. Finally, I added detail and analysis of broader American religious history here and there to flesh out the Roosevelt family's non-Episcopal church background. The notes are largely as the author left them and do not pretend to be a comprehensive or entirely current scholarly record; I have added a few titles essential to the relevant topics. The account of FDR's death and funeral in chapter 9 is my own.

I am grateful to Arthur Woolverton personally and as the family's agent in this project for the trust he has shown in letting me edit his father's work by my best professional judgment. Our mutual wish is to make this book as accessible and compelling as possible to a broad readership. We hope that it is a fitting monument to the life and labors of his father, an important addition to Roosevelt scholarship in shedding light on an understudied aspect of FDR's life and motivation, and a hopeful reminder of the positive contribution that the Christian faith has made to American life in the past—and might again in the future.

Author's Preface and Acknowledgments

The idea for this book began in 2000 when I was editor of *Anglican and Episcopal History*, a scholarly publication of the Episcopal Church. At the time, I asked church historians involved with the journal briefly to describe three new or neglected subjects that in each one's estimation needed attention. The result was a compilation: "New Frontiers in American Episcopal History." To it thirteen church historians contributed their suggestions. One of the topics I myself put forward was the religion of Franklin Delano Roosevelt. I meant to cast a wide net, and by the word "religion" I included, along with Roosevelt's personal faith and practice, his ethics and morals, and the core convictions that inspired his political and social thought as well as his belief in democracy. The more I thought about such a study, the more I determined to put other matters aside and write it myself. Though Roosevelt's political legacy remained strong even in the midst of the counterreformation of the Reagan-Bush years, the kind of religious faith that motivated the thirty-second president has been less in evidence in the present century, overshadowed in part by the conservative Christian Right. Certainly it had never been given the contextual treatment it deserved. What then? Did Roosevelt's Christian faith inform his politics? He himself connected the two words "Christian" and "Democrat" featured in this book's title. But how did he connect them, and with what result? To answer these questions, I have chosen a combination of chronological and topical approaches.

I had more personal reasons for undertaking this book as well. I received my education at the same places as Roosevelt: Groton School and Harvard College. My wife was a student at Eleanor Roosevelt's and Marion Dickerman's Todhunter School, a private institution for girls in New York City. Frances Perkins was a close friend of my aunt Ethel Woolverton Cone. I came to know and appreciate Madam Perkins at an early age, even better as a graduate student. She once said to me, "If someone opens a door for you, go through," advice she no doubt gave to many other young people. She admonished me in other ways that are still vivid in my mind, one of which was the need in America for universal health care. As a boy I also felt the impact of FDR's revered headmaster (then retired), Endicott Peabody, with whom I had several conversations. Other people who appear in this study, not all of them admirers of FDR, became friends. One of them was William R. Castle, former undersecretary of state in the Hoover administration; the many kindnesses he and Mrs. Castle showed to me and my wife, Maggie, are memorable. So also is Major General Sherman Miles, a cousin who also became a friend and mentor.

My research was conducted in the Groton School Archives, the Harvard College Archives at the Pusey Library, the Archives of the Episcopal Church at Austin, Texas, the Archives of the Diocese of New York, and the president's papers at the Roosevelt Library and at St. James' Church Archives, Hyde Park, New York.

I wish to thank the following for their encouragement and criticisms of various chapters in this book: Joseph A. Conforti of the University of Southern Maine; Henry W. Bowden of Rutgers University; George W. Martin, biographer of Frances Perkins and of Charles C. Burlingham; Rebecca Sinkler, former book review editor of the *New York Times*; Vincent McCarthy of St. Joseph's University, Philadelphia; Alfred A. Moss Jr. of the University of Maryland; and John Morton Blum of Yale University. Their generosity of time and talent is greatly appreciated. Whatever weaknesses this book has are mine, not theirs.

Finally, I cannot but note with appreciation the information provided by the late Howard A. Johnson, my sometime colleague at the Virginia Theological Seminary. His account of an evening with the Roosevelts during which Johnson discussed the thought of the Danish philosopher Søren Kierkegaard is the core of chapter 8 below.

For their patience with my requests and the alacrity of their responses, I am much in the debt of the following: Douglas Brown, Groton School Archivist; Wayne Kempton, Archivist of the Episcopal Diocese of New York; Alicia Vivona, Archivist of the Franklin D. Roosevelt Library at Hyde Park; Gerald Morgan, son of FDR's friend of the same name; Robert Wilson, son of the Reverend Frank Wilson, rector of St. James' Church, Hyde Park; Gloria Golden, Archivist of St. James' Church; and the Reverend Harold T. Lewis of Calvary Episcopal Church, Pittsburgh. For their help with the intricacies of Dutch and German translations, I am grateful to Hansi Mead of Center Harbor, New Hampshire, and Caroline Snyder of North Sandwich, New Hampshire, respectively. My thanks as well to Gary McCool, Anne M. Lebreche, and Alice Staples of the Lamson Library at Plymouth State University, Plymouth, New Hampshire; Maggie Porter, Esq.; Mary Warnement of the Boston Athenaeum; Aura Fluet of the Episcopal Divinity School Library; Mitzi Jarrett Budde of the Virginia Theological Seminary Library; Dave Huether of the National Association of Manufacturers; Lynn Catanese of the Hagley Library; Margaret Peachey of the Harvard Law School Library; Anne Papen, Marion Blackshear, and Lois Brady of the Samuel Wentworth Library of Center Sandwich, New Hampshire; and Carol MacIntosh of the Lake Wales Public Library, Lake Wales, Florida.

Finally, I am grateful to my good friend and classmate G. Harold Welch and his talented wife, Betsy, for hospitality and a delightful weekend with John Morton Blum and his wife, Pamela.

—JOHN F. WOOLVERTON
Cumberland, Maine

Introduction

"The Strongest and Most Mysterious Force"

At one of his many press conferences, Franklin Roosevelt was suddenly asked about the source of his "political philosophy." Momentarily dumbfounded, he replied that he was a Christian and a Democrat. This study takes him at his word and explores how his faith contributed to his leadership of the American democracy through some of its gravest trials.

One of the people who knew him best—playwright, editor, and speechwriter Robert E. Sherwood—acknowledged that Roosevelt "could be a ruthless politician . . . utterly cynical, worldly, and illusionless"; yet, Sherwood continued, Roosevelt's "religious faith was the strongest and most mysterious force that was in him."[1] Others in a position to know recognized the same quality: his wife, Eleanor Roosevelt; his personal secretary, Grace Tully; another speechwriter and political aide, Samuel I. Rosenman; leading political advisers and cabinet members such as James A. Farley, Harold L. Ickes, and Frances Perkins; Tennessee Valley Authority director David E. Lilienthal; and federal relief administrator turned personal diplomatic emissary and White House lodger, Harry L. Hopkins. Though they would disagree on how reflective or complex Roosevelt's faith was, they all attested to its significance.

Historians' reports have been more mixed. Kenneth Davis, Thomas Greer, and George McJimsey have briefly followed up on Sherwood's observation. Ronald Isetti, Merlin Gustafson, Jerry Rosenberg, Kurt A. Klingbeil, and Gary Scott Smith have written notable articles on FDR's religious views, describing his practices of prayer, worship, biblical imagery, and contacts with clergy together with his churchgoing (in)frequency. Other historians, among them Richard Hofstadter and Geoffrey Ward, have largely ignored Roosevelt's relation to Christianity and to his church. Still others have acknowledged Roosevelt's religious views but not developed them. These have all had other fish to fry: politics, reform, diplomacy, and war. In terms of Roosevelt's presidency and of American or world history, these are naturally the main topics of interest. This book aims to show how his religious convictions were at work in these domains.

FDR enjoyed the worship of the church, sang hymns lustily, and in fact wanted to preach sermons. On the other hand, he was not a deep thinker or a mystic or a particularly pious man. There is no spiritual self-portrait to be found in the Presidential Library at Hyde Park. It was not his custom to speak of his personal faith. To a very few people— his wife, Eleanor; Perkins; Farley; and occasionally his son James—he sometimes remarked on their common faith, prayer, and so forth. Otherwise, outside of some biblical references and metaphors in formal addresses, the rhetoric of faith with Roosevelt is confined largely to expressions crafted by speechwriters. Those who look for more revealing material in the Presidential Library will be disappointed.

There are four significant exceptions, however. The first is an address, called "Lecture on Work," that FDR's father, James Roosevelt, delivered sometime in the early 1890s. In it the elder Roosevelt spoke of the human degradation and suffering he had seen among families doing sweatshop labor in the tenements of New York and London. He made it clear that such treatment went painfully against the grain of Christian faith. The lesson was not lost on his son. A second important resource is the neglected correspondence between FDR and the Reverend Frank Wilson, rector of St. James' Church, Hyde Park. From it we learn that Roosevelt was the senior warden (the chief lay officer) of that parish from 1928 until his death in April 1945. As such he performed his duties and maintained oversight of parochial affairs all through the Great Depression and World War II. The other two documents are more familiar. There is the State of the Union address of January 1939 with its extended discussion of religion and democracy. And there is the famous D-Day prayer of June 1944, which he delivered over the radio as American troops stormed ashore on Utah and Omaha beaches in Normandy. The prayer was written by Roosevelt, two family members, and an aide; the final draft with the president's personal emendations is reproduced for the first time in the text of this volume.[2]

This book itself divides into three parts. The first section details the close nurture that Roosevelt received at home and school, a nurture infused with the Episcopal variant of Protestant Christianity. Both of

Roosevelt's parents had moved to the Episcopal Church from other denominations and so had voluntarily entered into the clear and distinct role it set for itself in late nineteenth-century America.[3] Attracting the elite and upper middle class of a rising nation, the Episcopal Church aimed to be a genial, capacious house of faith on the one hand, but to assert a firm Christian tone for public life on the other. This entailed not just matters of correct personal conduct but standards of Christian ethics for collective life as well. Not accidentally, the Episcopal Church bred a disproportionate number of leaders of the Social Gospel, American Protestantism's contribution to the broader Progressive movement around the turn of the twentieth century. The Social Gospel preached the advance of God's kingdom in this world, with strong mandates for justice, peace, and holistic human well-being. Young Franklin heard this message at church and saw it modeled at home, but especially absorbed it in his impressionable teenage years at Groton School, where he came under the lifelong influence of the school's founder and headmaster, Endicott Peabody.

The second section of the book explores the heart of FDR's religion. Throughout his public life Roosevelt constantly referred to the three principles of faith, hope, and charity as set forth in Saint Paul's First Epistle to the Corinthians (13:1–13). Roosevelt quoted the passage often as president and always took the oath of office with his old family Bible opened to these verses. We can see one or another of these virtues coming to the fore at different periods of Roosevelt's career. *Hope* set the tone from the 1920s, when FDR had to endure his own trial in the wilderness after contracting polio, into the 1930s, when the nation plummeted into the Great Depression; FDR found in his own illness all too fitting an analogue for the nation's economic paralysis. On both levels, the personal and the national, he moved to restore hope by invoking an old pairing from Christian theology. He knew that faith and work, sometimes set at odds in various doctrinal systems, properly belonged together. Even as he, and then the American people, faced enormous challenges in their respective crises, they could move forward confidently in the knowledge that the future was in the hands of God. Trust bred action, and action, trust. With this common faith, he in his paralysis and they in theirs were called to take the next step toward regeneration, buoyed by divine providence.

After hope came *charity*, a theme that came to the fore in the New Deal years. The Greek *charis* means grace, favor, and benevolence, and the specific gifts of charity, *charismata*, called for social as well as personal expression.[4] The highest manifestation of *charis* was love or *agapē*, something far more than the noblesse oblige of giving Christmas boxes to the deserving poor that the young FDR had witnessed in his parents' social circle. In using this expanded meaning of the word "charity," Roosevelt had clearly absorbed the New Testament commentary of his youth in the late nineteenth century. What he took the Christian understanding of *agapē* to imply for social and political policy became clear in a major address he gave during his 1936 campaign for reelection. *Charis* in politics must entail economic security, decent wages, better health, education, recreation, and greater opportunity.

If charity predominated in the New Deal years, the *faith* of Saint Paul's formula became uppermost during the low point of Roosevelt's second term, 1937 through 1940. The rise of the European dictators and the threat of homegrown totalitarianism that FDR and many others perceived in the persons of Huey Long and Douglas MacArthur endangered democracy's future. In the wake of *Kristallnacht* (November 10, 1938), the first nationwide anti-Semitic outburst in Germany, FDR turned increasingly to the freedom to hold one's faith publicly as well as privately as a key ground and test of democracy itself. Nowhere is this more apparent than in his astonishing State of the Union address of 1939.

To understand Roosevelt's reasons for speaking of religious faith at such length at these moments, we will need to traverse some familiar historical ground. Equally pressing is the need to explain the hiatus between the 1939 speech and Roosevelt's inability to help Jewish people escape the horrors of Nazi criminality. More theoretically, the question arises of whether religion itself does not often breed tyranny. The answer is sometimes yes, sometimes no. A classic antidote to the possible threat was first offered for modern times by Jean-Jacques Rousseau in his proposal that Western societies cultivate a civil religion—that is, they use the language of Christianity without its "transcendental traffic" to turn religious loyalty to political purposes. This has been a common practice among American presidents; was it Roosevelt's too? This book, following legal historian John T. Noonan Jr., concludes the opposite. Roosevelt's D-Day prayer of June 1944 in particular shows clear evidence of Roosevelt's personal faith and of his broader reading of the Christian classics.[5] In short, this book argues that Roosevelt's was not a mere civil religion but a personal faith that had strong public resonance because of the neat fit between his Episcopal heritage and the broad contours of American political culture.

Roosevelt adopted a more prophetic tone amid the fear and rancor of the great national debate of 1939–1940 over the question of American involvement in World War II. Over against the anti-interventionist camp and its most notable spokesman, Charles Lindbergh, Roosevelt promoted the interventionist cause via the prophet's twofold role—to warn of impending danger and to call the nation to its highest values. When war came to America in December 1941, he became more of a national pastor, buoying public confidence by means of homilies, humor, and prayer. Once the war's tide turned toward victory, he became more prophetic again, laying out a program of further reform in his State of the Union address of January 1944. The firstfruits came five months later with the GI Bill—a means of bringing hope to thousands by making education affordable for returning members of the armed forces. The New Deal was back as a wartime measure but beckoned toward a broader, more humane democratic future.

The book's third section aims to view the subject whole from two higher vantage points. Chapter 8 provides the book's one concentrated discussion of theology proper by recounting the story of a single evening at the White House on February 19, 1944. That night President and Mrs. Roosevelt hosted a young theologian, Howard A. Johnson, for a private dinner. Johnson happened to be something of an expert on the nineteenth-century Danish philosopher Søren Kierkegaard and helped introduce Kierkegaard's thought to America. The conversation that evening was lively and extensive. Roosevelt prodded Johnson on how to account for such evil as that with which the Nazis had saturated the world, and Johnson answered the president's questions at length out of his knowledge of Kierkegaard. The chapter is a firsthand account told to the author. After recounting Roosevelt's death and the religious resonances of the nation's farewell to him in chapter 9, the book concludes by comparing Roosevelt with two of his predecessors, Abraham Lincoln and Herbert Hoover, to illuminate more clearly FDR's particular profile of character, style, and faith. All three presidents were reformers in their own way and used the language of Christian faith to promote their efforts; yet the three differed markedly on the religious as well as the political substance of their efforts.

In leading the United States through two great crises, Franklin Roosevelt stands in the top echelon of American presidents. His success was not a historical inevitability; in fact, on the economic front the opposite outcome has usually prevailed. More than a decade ago, in the last throes of the George W. Bush administration, Benjamin M. Friedman, a professor of political economy at Harvard, challenged historians to explain this puzzle. America's turn in the 1930s "toward a greater measure of what Roosevelt called 'social justice' stands in sharp contrast to the nation's response to other episodes of economic stagnation, both before and after the New Deal," Friedman notes. "Just why remains unclear."[6] This book contends that FDR himself supplied the answer. He rallied a solid majority of American citizens to a vision of justice and democracy that came right out of Scripture—and his heritage of liberal Protestantism.

PART I

Formation

Chapter One

Son, Vestryman, and Church Politician

O n July 10, 1944, George K. Weston, a resident of Montclair, New Jersey, wrote to the president's press secretary, Stephen Early, about some "foolish remarks" he had recently heard in a sermon. It was an election year; Weston professed himself to be "a staunch Roosevelt supporter," but Montclair was Republican territory. A guest minister had complained from the pulpit that Roosevelt was failing to put "the religious need of the postwar problem to the forefront." Worse still, on the way out of church he alleged to Weston that "Mr. Roosevelt does not contribute a cent to the church in Hyde Park, of which he is a member." Press Secretary Early responded that such rumors habitually arose during an election year. "The President," wrote Early, "does contribute regularly to the support of his church in Hyde Park" and "has been Senior Warden of this church for many years"; further, "much of the business of the church is transacted at his home at meetings where the President presides."[1] The first two remarks were true; the latter was not. In accordance with the canons of the Episcopal Church, the rector chaired all meetings of the vestry, whether they took place in the home of the president of the United States or not. Only once, after the rector joined the armed forces in World War II, did Roosevelt as senior warden chair a meeting.[2]

This episode shows several facets of Franklin Roosevelt's life-long role as an Episcopal layman. First, as president during the worst depression in American history and then during the nation's most far-flung war, he continued his active role in leadership of his parish church. Second, the cut-and-thrust about politicians and religion was not just a phenomenon of election season, nor limited to presidents alone. For all the official rhetoric about "separation of church and state," religion and politics have always intersected in American history—sometimes, as recently, from the Right but just as often from the Left and everywhere in between.[3] FDR would have thus found the New Jersey incident par for the course. He might have added that he had plenty of experience on the other side of the street too, with the church politics in his own denomination. Above all, his curt self-description at that news conference—"I'm a Christian and a Democrat"—indicated how basic religion was to his identity and aspirations, also as a politician. A particular kind of liberal Protestantism shaped his convictions, his values, his ideal of a good society, and the menu of policies designed to make that ideal come true. That worldview was nurtured and stocked by his education at an Episcopal boarding school. Behind that lay the nurture of parents who were faithful churchgoers, mindful of instilling in their son Christian faith and values as they understood them.

Early Nurture

Franklin Roosevelt's paternal line did not begin as Episcopalians, nor was that the heritage of his mother, Sara Delano. As settlers in New Amsterdam in the early 1650s, the Roosevelts had been loyal, leading members in the Dutch Reformed Church. As FDR reported in a history paper he wrote at Harvard, an inscription on a new church that the denomination erected in New York City in 1769 "for the English service" attested that "Mr. Jacobus Roosevelt" had presided at the laying of the cornerstone as "Senior Elder" while construction went forward "under the auspices of . . . Isaac Roosevelt" as deacon.[4] FDR's father, James, was Isaac's great-grandson and was reared in that denomination. Franklin's mother came from a different but no less venerable lineage. Sara's mother, Catherine Robbins Lyman, was a native of Jonathan Edwards's old town of Northampton, Massachusetts, and daughter of a state supreme court justice. Sara's father, Warren Delano Jr., was the scion of an eminent shipping family from near New Bedford, Massachusetts. He became very wealthy very young in the China trade, particularly opium; lost everything in the Panic of 1857; then took his family—Sara included—to Hong Kong to recoup his fortune. The Delano name attested to Huguenot origins (de Lannay, de la Noye), while the Lymans were of old New England stock. Sara's history thus was rooted far back in Puritan New England, although by the time of her childhood the family, like many others of that class, had migrated theologically to Unitarianism.[5]

Sara's kin raised an eyebrow when the widowed and now fifty-two-year-old James proposed in 1880 to marry the stunning young lady only half his age. They raised their other eyebrow at the Episcopal affiliation that James had adopted as a young man. These were not insurmountable objections, however, and Sara joined her new husband in membership at St. James' Episcopal Church in Hyde Park.[6] James had been a vestryman and senior warden in the parish since 1858 and would remain so until his death on December 8, 1900. Franklin was baptized there before he was two months old and was inducted as a child into an "unfailing regularity of Sunday morning church attendance." At a certain age he started offering equally habitual reasons to be excused; father James called them "Sunday headaches." Writes Frank Freidel: "On a cold windy February day when he was ten he [Franklin] fortuitously came down with an almost undetectable ailment, which would have been more impressive had he not laughingly announced its imminence the day before." It was no good; to church he went.[7] If FDR was chronically erratic at Sabbath observance as an adult, he did not neglect his duty as village squire. He was elected to the vestry in 1906, eventually serving as senior warden from 1928 until his death in 1945.

Franklin received his early education from his mother, from his governess, and from the family's substantial collection of books. More on the first two in a moment; first, the books. They served Franklin's fascination with—and began his lifelong passion to protect and conserve—the birds, trees, land, soil, and history of Hyde Park, of Dutchess County, and of the Hudson River valley. Later, the sea, ships, and world geography, physical and social, enthralled him. As for his moral and religious formation, we know that when he fell ill of typhoid in England at age seven, his mother read him "the sentimental and moral children's tales of her youth" in conjunction with Louisa May Alcott's *Little Men*, Daniel Defoe's *Robinson Crusoe*, and Johann David Wyss's *Swiss Family Robinson*.[8] Like other children of his time, Franklin was treated to the popular chapbooks with their nursery rhymes and the moralistic stories of "Peter Parley" that lent instruction in biography, history, geography, and science. From age eight to age ten he read Jacob Abbott's Rollo Series, which encouraged inquisitiveness about foreign lands while also appealing to a sense of honor and exemplary conduct. Abbott was a reformist Congregational minister and professor of mathematics at Amherst College who had a wide reputation both in America and in Europe. Roosevelt's sense of adventure and love of travel were widened by the patriotic if priggish heroes served up by "Oliver Optic" (William Taylor Adams), while the tales of the more business-oriented Horatio Alger inducted him into the primal rags-to-riches mythology of American culture.

These authors marked a turning point in American primary education and moral formation. To mid-nineteenth-century authorities on child nurture, the old-school practice of "drilling children in denominational theology seemed unduly harsh." Instead, "writers of popular fiction insisted that this literature should instruct the modern reader in religious values just as the Bible did."[9] But this could be a treacherous path, as the rise of Mark Twain demonstrated. Roosevelt certainly read *The Adventures of Tom Sawyer* (1876), for he chose it for the collection of books at Top Cottage, the retreat he built on the Hyde Park estate in the 1930s. In fact, he had met the author in 1887 when accompanying James Roosevelt on a trip through New England. James made a point of paying a call on Samuel Clemens at his home in Hartford, Connecticut. It was a memorable event, even if FDR demonstrably misremembered it.[10] However, Twain's masterpiece, *Huckleberry Finn*, published just two years before that visit, does not appear in any Roosevelt library, possibly because of the harsh reviews that the monitors of proper taste and morals leveled upon the book: "its coarseness of language and questionable morals," they intoned, "its very low grade morality" and "rough, coarse, inelegant expressions" rendered it "trash of the veriest sort."[11]

More formal religious volumes abounded in Franklin's library. He chose *Selections from the Psalms of David in Metre: With Hymns Suited to the Feasts and Fasts of the Church* (1865) for the first cabinet in the "President's Room" at Hyde Park, along with other books of hymns and songs such as *The Union Temperance Song Book* (1843), Anna Barbauld's *Hymns in Prose for Children* (1809), and the Bromsgrove Sunday School's *Anthems, Psalms & Hymns* (1809). These no doubt contributed to Roosevelt's marked love of hymnody. His juvenile books included the King James Bible and the Book of Common Prayer along with *The Shorter Catechism of the Westminster Assembly* (1843), John Stirling's *Cathechismus et Articuli Ecclesiae Anglicanae* (1747), *The Sunday Picture Book* (1875), Theodore Soares's *Heroes of Israel* (1908), and the French *Bible du jeune âge: Histoire de l'Ancien et du Nouveau Testament* (1866). He collected some twenty lives of Christ.[12] A brace of "Christmas Carols," one by Charles Dickens, another by Phillips Brooks, sat next to

John Bunyan's *The Pilgrim's Progress*. Both Bunyan's and Dickens's titles made a profound impression on Roosevelt, as we shall see.

Supplementing the nurture of parents and books was the influence of Jeanne Sandoz, an extraordinary young Swiss woman hired in 1891 to be Franklin's governess and teacher. Like her charge, she keenly enjoyed history, geography, and science. Franklin's powers of concentration, his memory, and his ability to read quickly and retain what he had read made him an apt pupil. Sandoz's teaching also conveyed a strong social concern that grew out of her Christian faith. In January 1933, just prior to his inauguration as president, the former governess reminded him that the "ignorance of the masses, the collective selfishness of nationalists, the violence and cupidity of the masters of money, the spiritual weakness and poverty of the men in power led to the world tragedy of 1914." Then, in words that proved prophetic, she challenged him: "The churches and the men now in power must now put the cause of humanity above everything and must not rest until the spirit of the gospel is diffused throughout the external world—that of business, of national and international politics." He soon replied, "I have often thought that it was you more than anyone else who laid the foundation for my education."[13] Her wish for his global influence came true soon enough. Just as Abraham Lincoln's picture adorned the parlors of miners' homes in Yorkshire in the nineteenth century, so in the 1930s Franklin Roosevelt's photograph was tacked up in the one-room homes of the peasants of Luciana in fascist Italy. Carlo Levi recalled in his autobiographical novel *Christ Stopped at Eboli* that two pictures hung "in almost every house": one of "the black scowling face, with its large, inhuman eyes, of the Madonna of Viggiano," the other "a colored print of the sparkling eyes, behind gleaming glasses, and the hearty grin of President Roosevelt." Levi added, "I never saw other pictures or images than these: not the King nor the Duce, nor even Garibaldi; no famous Italian of any kind, nor any one of the appropriate saints, only Roosevelt and the Madonna of Viggiano never failed to be present."[14]

Sara and James Roosevelt

Still, the strongest influence upon young Franklin came from his parents. They shaped his character, his values, and his sense of life's opportunities and obligations. Mother Sara, especially, instilled in him a sense of destiny. He was born to do great things, she was sure, and he had the talent and gifts to accomplish them. Her vision ran with the age's emphasis upon the personal—in regard to her son and also in regard to social obligations. She did not deny the presence of poverty and need in the world but stuck to her class's conventions about how these problems were to be addressed. People of privilege were to undertake charitable gestures, also by way of setting an example, toward individuals known to them personally. Lady Bountiful, in short. Sara took "baskets of food to the sick, flowers to the hospital, and clothing to the poor." She made dolls at Christmas for children in the hospital (the dolls went on the Christmas trees in the wards, not in children's arms), and followed up with patients who had been discharged from the State Hospital for the Insane at Poughkeepsie. Sara remained loyal for twenty years to one insensate woman, ensuring her well-being and paying her lodging bills long after the woman's eccentricities had increased to the point that the landlord was seeking her removal.[15]

This was quite a bit narrower than the holistic public vision of Sara's New England forebears, whether Puritan or Unitarian. Their models of social ethics certainly included personal charity but went well beyond that. In the colonial era their dream had been to build not just good citizens or sound churches but a "holy commonwealth." After the Revolution and religious disestablishment, they resumed that project via organized voluntary crusades against public evils: drunkenness, abusive prisons, exploitation of women and children, and finally slavery. This was the "benevolent empire" of the Second Great Awakening.[16] Its rhetoric could be imperialistic indeed, and by our standards it was highly moralistic and judgmental. Nor did it finally escape its theoretical center in individual free will. But it changed the landscape of pre–Civil War America, especially in the Northeast and the Midwest, and with the Union's triumph in the Civil War, it could claim to have achieved its noblest end. Sara, having come to consciousness during that war and then spending much of her youth abroad, seems to have lost the reforming passion. Or perhaps she thought her role was to model noblesse oblige from the upper echelons of a nation that had achieved as much collective righteousness as was possible. One part of her heritage that she did pass along was the Delanos' remarkably ambitious, adventurous spirit. Here Franklin proved himself to be most decidedly his mother's son.

Father James Roosevelt was a milder and of course much older parent, majoring in care and encouragement for his son. He bore a complicated heritage as to religion and public life. Historically, the Dutch Reformed had kept their distance from New Englanders' zeal, being more concerned to protect their rights in the polyglot colony that had been seized by the English in 1664. However, James's father (Isaac) had insisted that his son go to Union College in Schenectady, New York, a flagship institution of the revival-and-reform complex. Isaac was a high-strung evangelical himself, much given to anxiety over the state of his soul and that of his son. Union's head, Eliphalet Nott, the longest-serving college president in American history, had a reputation for redeeming boys deemed to be bad, or potentially so. But he also aimed to recruit them into the armies of public righteousness. James Roosevelt was sent to Union after a year at the worldlier New York University and stayed on to graduate under Nott's supervision in July 1847. Even at Union, however, he found a way to rebel by joining a secret student society, much to his father's dismay.[17] Once married, James switched denominations, leaving the Dutch Reformed for the Episcopal Church. Given their roots in the Church of England, a religious establishment incarnate, the Episcopalians had a different but no less ambitious tradition of exerting public sway compared to that of Nott's evangelical empire. With its elite membership, the Episcopal Church always faced temptations to complacency. But in the industrial boom of the Gilded Age, significant numbers of its leadership and laity would mount a social-reform movement of their own.

James was a quiet sympathizer with that movement from the quiet niche along the Hudson River where he had settled down. After graduating from Harvard Law School, he joined the prestigious New York firm of Benjamin Douglas Silliman in 1851. There he met many leading businessmen of the day. He gradually moved away from the law to keep company with the executives of the booming railroad, banking, and coal industries. For a moment, as Kenneth S. Davis writes, "untold riches seemed about to pour into the Roosevelt coffers." But it was not to be; the family fortune was seriously damaged in the Panic of 1873. James was not wiped out, however, nor was he left obsessed with failure. "He simply did not care enough for power, economic or otherwise, to be deeply hurt when it was denied him." James felt no appeal at all in "the hugely expensive ostentation so gratifying to the Vanderbilt ego and to that of his social friends, the Astors."[18] Visitors to Hyde Park today can see the contrast between the Roosevelt and Vanderbilt homes, just a stone's throw apart—the one a country house, the other a grand mansion.

James's other ambitions were modest as well. He refused requests to run for Congress or the state legislature. In 1887 he resolutely resisted the offer from his friend, President Grover Cleveland, that he serve as ambassador (preferably to Holland) or in some other public post.[19] The totally opposite attitude that Franklin would show almost suggests overcompensation. James was intent on taking care of his estate as befit a country gentleman, together with the local duties that entailed: serving on the State Board of Charities and with the overseers of the Hudson River State Hospital, and working for the local public school and St. James' Church which "he served . . . with constant zeal." James's father had instructed his son that "the welfare and happiness of nations and individuals depends on the strict observance of the laws of morality and justice—of true religion—not of forms—but of the spirit and affections."[20] In James's case, "the spirit and affections" of religion inclined him toward the early Social Gospel; in Franklin's, they induced a passion to see a more mature Social Gospel implemented in law. Discerning the difference between the mere forms of religion and its true substance thus carried consistently across three generations.

Modern Labor and Its Discontents

James Roosevelt's sense of obligation went beyond the local. He made a point of seeing firsthand the living conditions in the slums of major cities on both sides of the Atlantic. When he and Sara sailed for Europe on their wedding journey, they combined the pleasures of travel with attention to social conditions in other lands.[21] In one important speech, James publicly recounted his observations of Shepherd's Court, St. Giles, and Dudley Street in London, where he had taken the trouble to meticulously measure the sizes of tenement-house rooms with his cane. That speech, undated, was delivered before the "Ladies and Gentlemen of the St. James Guild," probably in the late 1880s or early '90s. Composed in a large hand on seven-by-nine-inch pieces of paper, the manuscript is forty-eight pages long and likely took well over an hour to deliver. On its back, in Sara Delano Roosevelt's hand, is "Written by my husband." Its subject was "Work," and it showed a traditional country gentleman trying to come to terms with the industrial society that had exploded across America and Europe in the wake of the Civil War.[22]

James's talk first of all emphasized duty as a motivation for work. Everyone was individually responsible for his or her success or failure in life. It went on to rehearse the Protestant work ethic, the necessity of "patient labor and application," of "accuracy, method, punctuality, honesty, truthfulness and economy." Then, too, "integrity of word and deed is the very corner stone of all business transactions." To this recital James added a dollop of Anglo-Saxon ethnocentrism, thanking God that truthfulness "is preeminent among the English-speaking race, and one cause (not the least) that this race is today the most widespread and powerful in the world." But the speaker found much to lament as well. The cult of display was "the prevailing sin among all classes of people. . . . You see it everywhere, in public buildings, in your churches, in the streets, on the backs of your wives and children, display in dress, in furniture, in equipage, in entertainments, in marriage—display in funerals." Being of good repute was all well and good, "but the curse of modern society is a respectable sham."

Those with modest incomes could have heard a traditional admonition as well, had they been among the "Ladies and Gentlemen" in attendance. Poverty and hard luck, James averred, were due not to an uneven playing field, or to a distressed environment, or to lack of education, but to deficiency of volition: "it is not the want of *opportunity* but the want of *will* that stands in the way of economy." The results of prodigality were disastrous. "Improvidence," he said, "is chiefly cruelty to women and children; a father spends his surplus means in drink, leaving his wife and children destitute, hungry and to starve. Can any form of cruelty surpass this?" By contrast, striving for improvement gave individuals dignity; "forethought and self-denial is [*sic*] the true basis of manly character." Oddly enough, Jesus's prodigious, and profligate, miracle of feeding the five thousand provided the moral for this tale of calculation and control: the "true spirit of economy [was] . . . expressed by our Divine Master in the words, 'Gather up the fragments that remain, so that nothing be lost'" (John 6:12). James also passed along the usual counsel about women's place in the system: "The very spirit of home depends upon the influence of a good woman exercising her influence upon its members, and especially on the children growing up within it." To bring comfort to the home, "the presence of a well ordered, industrious woman is indispensable."

But then the speaker abruptly changed course. "I wish I could at this point close my lecture and that there was no other picture of worth to present to you this evening. . . . But alas, there is another picture"—indeed, "a picture of want, of misery and death." James brought his audience along on one phase of his honeymoon tour:

> Go with me to the tenement houses of New York, of London or Paris, many of them containing more people than this whole village; in one room you will often find six, ten, aye, fifteen in a family. . . . Or go with me to a cellar in St. Giles, London; there are dozens of them. . . . [Such places] possess no windows and the only way in which light and ventilation can be conveyed to the wretched inhabitants below is through a hole in the pavement. . . . [In them dwell] hideously dirty children—a man writing by the flame of a tallow candle, a woman lying ill [on] a bed, all in this pestiferous and dingy den.

This picture is not overdrawn.

Yet, "there is even a worse picture than this; a day comes when there is no work, nothing laid by, nothing saved, and standing in the corner is a terrible skeleton. Starvation. Are there three more fearful words in the English language than 'I am starving'?" He went on to describe how a gentleman, perhaps he himself, was accosted in the street by a child "with these pitiful words, 'I have had nothing to eat for two days.'" The man went with the child to "what she called her home." There he found the mother, father, and other children in a bare room from which furniture and even extra clothing had long since gone to the pawnbrokers for food; he saw "every member of that family dying of hunger." This, continued Roosevelt, "is not an isolated case: every day men, women, and even little children die from starvation in our great cities."

James then bounced off the expectations his audience had heard confirmed in the first part of his lecture. These suffering people, he insisted, "are willing to work, they seek work—sometimes they obtain it for a short period—and when it is gone, then comes the pinch: food must be obtained. Many are too proud to beg, and lie down to die." Things were different, and worst of all, for women. Men could go to the "boundless plains of the West," but "young working women . . . depend upon the needle for their very existence . . . [they] slave and work early to late for only a paltry sum. When their day of want comes,

God help them!" He retold the story of a young woman who spent her last dollar to go to New York to find employment, found none, and threw herself off the Brooklyn ferry. The lecture ended with James's recitation of the famous poem by the Englishman Thomas Hood, "The Song of the Shirt" (1843): "Work, Work, Work / Till the brain begins to swim. / Work, Work, Work, / Till the eyes are heavy and dim! / Seam and gusset, and seam, / Till over the buttons I fall asleep / And sew them on in a dream! // Stitch, stitch, stitch, / In poverty, hunger, and dirt, / Sewing at once with a double thread / A shroud as well as a shirt."

And James Roosevelt's solution? It remained local. "Here is work," he punned on his title, for "every man, woman, and child in this audience tonight." Whether they were rich or not, everyone had an assignment; everyone could help. Young Franklin knew a bit whereof his father spoke, knew that "for years there had been ten [indigent] families in Hyde Park, that the town had always taken care of them."[23] Such was the time-honored norm for small-town and rural America, but now Father James was sensing that a new order, a staggering new challenge beyond old recipes, was at hand. He didn't know quite what to do. Forty years later, his son would make a wholesale attempt. It would entail major challenges to and changes within the American political system.

James had been reared in a reforming Whig atmosphere fueled by his father Isaac's evangelical Protestantism. The Whig Party coalition sought a stronger central government to promote both economic and moral progress as they envisioned them: improved infrastructure, accelerated industrialization, stronger banks, and more business opportunity on the one hand; temperance, public education, and (for the more radical) women's rights and antislavery on the other.[24] When their party died in 1853, James Roosevelt followed most of his Whig comrades into the new Republican Party, which nominated Abraham Lincoln for president in 1860. But in the long run, New York country gentry like the Roosevelts had a lower degree of loyalty to the GOP than did many, and when the party gave up on Reconstruction and reform in the 1870s, James found himself gravitating to the Democrats. In the election of 1880, he contributed to the campaign of the Democrat Winfield S. Hancock rather than that of Republican James A. Garfield. Four years later his friend Grover Cleveland brought Democrats out of their twenty-four-year wandering in the wilderness and into the White House.[25] The Hyde Park Roosevelts diverged from the Oyster

Bay clan of Theodore on this point, but not in their commitment to reform and community well-being. They would always remain part of the minority in Dutchess County. Franklin would find a way to make them a majority in the nation.

Political details remained for the future. For now, Franklin's home imbued him with a permanent guiding disposition. Writing of him and of his friend, neighbor, and future secretary of the treasury Henry Morgenthau, John Morton Blum explains: "Both were the sons of wealthy fathers, both were comfortable, both enjoyed a degree of easy elegance, yet neither cared for the toys and games of the adult rich. . . . Both, in the best sense of the word, were gentlemen, considerate, civilized, decent men who avoided displays of wealth or emotion. . . . Theirs was a kind of patrician instinct for public service and social welfare. . . . Neither was a radical, neither an intellectual, but both had a respect for intellectuals and an open-minded zest for new ideas."[26]

Parish Politics

For James and for his son, service began at home, with St. James' Church. In 1906, FDR and his childhood friend Edmund P. Rogers were elected to its vestry, joining James Roosevelt Roosevelt (Franklin's elder half brother), Frederick W. Vanderbilt, Gerald Morgan, and others.[27] It was a board notable for its elitism and for its permanence: FDR would remain a vestryman for 39 years, Rogers for 47, Vanderbilt for 33, Morgan for 22. There were no regulations in the canons of the national church, or of the diocese, or in New York state law to prohibit indefinite reelection.[28] The group was close-knit as well as self-perpetuating. Those of his friends who remained on the vestry after 1933 continued to address letters to their senior warden as "Dear Franklin." A few— by no means all—supported Roosevelt politically. "I make no secret," Gerald Morgan wrote him in August 1940, "that I am only too happy to have the chance of voting for you again next November. You just about saved my life three years ago by giving me something to do, and I shall never forget your kindness at that time and ever since." Two weeks later Morgan wrote again, saying that he was giving a thousand dollars to the Democratic National Committee. "This is absolutely not a hint for future favors. It is simply and solely the only way I can show my gratitude to the best of friends for the past."[29]

We can jump ahead in the chronology of FDR's life to trace his record of service to St. James'. When in 1911 it was time to appoint a new rector for the parish, Roosevelt solicited his Harvard friend and classmate Walter Russell Bowie, who had become an ordained Episcopal clergyman. Roosevelt had the year before won a seat in the New York State Senate, and he had democratization on his mind for the church as well. "We want just such a man as you are," he wrote Bowie. The previous rector had not been "very effective in building up the church," having been "inclined to trust too much to the support of three or four rich families in the vicinity." Consequently, "there is a great field for a young and energetic man" to build up "a real congregation, not only in the immediate vicinity but in the back parts of the county." Though it be small, St. James' would be no "sinecure," he challenged Bowie; rather, the parish "as a matter of fact calls for much work and opens up a field of great usefulness."[30]

While Bowie turned down the offer, St. James' had good fortune in its subsequent choices. The rector for 1912–1926 was Edward Pearsons Newton, a rugged Alaska missionary priest who served with notable success in bringing in new members from the vicinity. After Newton, Alban Richey Jr. (1926–1928), an Annapolis graduate, served; he left St. James' to become headmaster of the Holderness School in New Hampshire, but not before making "an excellent start . . . in interesting the villagers and children in the Church."[31] By now Roosevelt was governor of New York, but as senior warden of the parish he took an active part in the process of selecting Richey's successor. He and his Groton School classmate Edmund Rogers, president of the Fulton Trust Company in New York City, reached out to Endicott Peabody, headmaster of their school, for advice.[32] As a result, in 1929 the parish elected Frank R. Wilson of Cornwall, New York. He stayed for fourteen years, until he enlisted as a navy chaplain in early 1943.

In making this appointment, Franklin and his fellows had to overcome his mother's traditionalist tastes. That April, Edmund Rogers wrote FDR—then recovering from polio in Warm Springs, Georgia—that he had informed Sara and the other first ladies of the parish that "the village members felt very strongly that Frank Wilson . . . would be the type of man they would like to have as rector." It was important to continue the work of bringing in villagers "rather than [choosing] a man who would fit into the social life of the more prosperous residents living along the river." At first Sara and company agreed: "we must

work for the villagers, sacrificing our personal feelings in the matter."
Then she had second thoughts. "I think she feels that we should try to
get a Rector & wife with more social qualities than possibly Mr. and
Mrs. Wilson have," Rogers wrote Franklin. He himself remained enthusiastic, however: "Yesterday Mr. Richey and Mr. Wilson changed
places and we thoroughly enjoyed the service and sermon conducted
by the latter." Wilson's style was "simple, and his sermon was interesting, instructive, and left one with something to think about . . . his
sincerity appealed to all members of the parish who were present."[33]

Sara eventually came around and learned to appreciate Wilson.
Four years later, when her son was about to leave for Washington to
be sworn in as president, she wrote this to Frank Wilson: "I thought
your service & address for my son were perfect. I went to church feeling *unnerved*, & I left quite comforted. . . . I enclose a small gift for the
trip to Washington & am so happy that you and your wife are going.
I hope you have your cards, etc. to go to the White House tea." For
their part, the presidential couple and the Wilsons became friends.
The latter visited the White House often for anniversary services of
the first inaugural of March 4, 1933.[34] While the president and the
rector were never on a first-name basis, their friendship was notable.
For over a decade and a half, each unstintingly supported the other. In
November 1930, when political opponents of the governor suggested
to Wilson that he should get rid of his senior warden because he was a
member of the Ku Klux Klan, FDR wrote back, "tell them from me that
I expect to remain Senior Warden of St. James' Hyde Park, Dutchess
County, N.Y. until the vestry throws me out but the cause will not be
a matter of creed, though it might be a failure to attend to my duties
properly."[35] Amid the welter of Supreme Court vetoes of the New Deal's
most important pillars in 1935 and 1936, Wilson wrote Roosevelt: "We
are right behind you. Talking about a New Deal, some of these fellows
don't know a good hand when they see it and that's why they don't
know how to play the game. More power to you and keep a 'lip upper
stiff,' as Andy says."[36]

Frank Wilson deserves more than a passing word, for he reveals
the kind of minister FDR admired. Though born, reared, and educated
entirely in New York State (Columbia University and General Theological Seminary), Wilson was not provincial. Between 1908 and 1911 he
visited some of his mother's family in Germany and learned to speak
the language. He worked a while in the railroad yards and saw com-

bat in France during World War I. At Hyde Park (his third parish) he became the town policeman, drove the fire truck, umpired the town's baseball team's games, was president of the Lions Club, visited parish members, and preached—also necessarily apolitical sermons. He and his wife, Florence May Wilson, raised their three sons in the rectory.[37]

The President as Senior Warden

From the White House, FDR used the minister to keep abreast of local affairs at Hyde Park. Both men believed that the church had a mission beyond the confines of St. James'. Together they contrived to establish a mission station via "Sunday School out at Chapel Corners."[38] They also sought to come to the aid of sister churches. When St. Gabriel's Church in Hollis celebrated its fiftieth anniversary, Roosevelt wrote its rector of the "deep interest" that St. James' people had in St. Gabriel's because "the Stoutenburgh family, who had so large a part in the establishment of the parish fifty years ago, have always maintained an active interest in our Hyde Park church. . . . And it was characteristic of their zeal for the Church, to whose teaching they always bore faithful witness, that they took a leading part in the founding of St. Gabriel's. Their memory is held in grateful remembrance in both churches."[39] In a letter marked "Private and Confidential," Roosevelt wrote Wilson in 1940 about the "serious financial problem" at St. Margaret's Church, Staatsburg. Wealthy families were leaving the area and "will not be succeeded by a new generation that will help to keep the parish going." Should there be a merger with St. James'? "The Bishop is wholly opposed to [such] . . . but unfortunately it is sometimes necessary to look facts in the face."[40]

The two men cooperated seamlessly during the president's planning for a visit to St. James' by King George VI and Queen Elizabeth in June 1939. FDR wrote a long letter to Wilson regarding the church service they would all attend on Sunday, June 11. Since the British were visitors, Roosevelt thought, they should all be seated "up near the front." The king, queen, Sara Delano, Eleanor, and he would "sit in the first straight pew on the left. Your family would sit in the front pew on the right." The president suggested that "parishioners should have first chance" at the remaining sixty seats. Wilson was to give out the requisite tickets at his own discretion. But that was not all. Roosevelt estimated that several thousand people would be outside the church hoping to see the royal couple after the service. Troopers would be needed to rope off sufficient areas for them and keep the highway open. At the conclusion of the service, Roosevelt suggested, the presidential party would "step across the gravel to the edge of the grass and be photographed facing the highway" so that everybody "can see the King and Queen while we are all being photographed." In his seventh paragraph—they were all numbered—he asked Wilson, "Let me know what you think of the above."[41]

In May 1942 the Episcopal Churchman Award was given to the president for his role in "the promotion of goodwill and better understanding among all people." Since during wartime Roosevelt was kept from public appearances as much as possible, he asked Wilson to take his place in accepting the award at a Waldorf-Astoria Hotel gala. Wilson did so, emphasizing how Roosevelt had been "nurtured by his distinguished parents in that atmosphere which reflects the efforts for which you pay him tribute. Obviously he can pursue no other course without violating the precepts of his training." With skillful understatement Wilson told the awards committee: "It is manifest that your associates have agreed by their action that he has not been disobedient to his parents' influence." He then went broader and deeper, speaking of the two phases to which history is always prone. The first "is spiritual; afterwards comes the task of translating the spirit into the form of matter." Our prayers will be "completely answered," he averred, if the people of the nation "will rise up and fight spiritually as bravely and as fearlessly for their cause as they are now fighting with material weapons in their hands." Responding to the advance copy that Wilson had sent him for approval, FDR wrote, "That is a mighty nice little speech of yours and I wish I could be present to hear it."[42]

When the rector of St. James' sought to join the navy as a chaplain, Roosevelt supported him. The president's letter of recommendation to the Chaplain's School in Norfolk, Virginia, described Wilson as "a gentleman of fine spiritual qualities, devoted and faithful in all pastoral relationships . . . [who] has also been a leader in every good work for the well-being of our Hyde Park community. . . . Tactful, courteous, resourceful, wise in counsel, and full of human sympathy." The letter was signed "Franklin D. Roosevelt, Senior Warden, St. James' Church, Hyde Park, N.Y."[43] Upon being accepted and sworn in, Wilson wrote him a note of appreciation: "As for the memorable thirteen and a half years past[,] it would be more than you can take time to read if I were to express to you all the gracious kindnesses and opportunities given us by yourself and Mrs. Roosevelt. Perhaps you will let me say some of these things to you some future day." In early February 1943, just back from meeting Winston Churchill in North Africa, FDR wrote Wilson that he was going to call a vestry meeting at Hyde Park: "As Senior Warden I am going to decline to accept your resignation—and your family has got to stay just where they are [in the rectory]. I am sure we can work things out even if I have to read the service myself on occasional visits!" The president concluded, "You have been grand in everything you have done. All of your parishioners are happy for you and proud of you." The letter was signed "Affectionately your Commander-in-Chief, Franklin D. Roosevelt."[44] It was a closing perhaps unmatched in the history of presidential letter-writing.

The parishioners of St. James' Church did not hesitate to bother their senior warden in the White House about any number of matters: from hiring a new sexton when the thirty-year incumbent had a heart attack, to putting a commemorative brass plate on the wall of the church (approved), to overhauling the organ (he did not think it was needed), to purchasing fire insurance and bonds (approved), to handling the parish's budget deficit. Annual requests for contributions to the "Bazaar and Strawberry Festival," the children's Christmas party, and the "annual clam chowder supper of the Parish Guild" arrived regularly at the White House. Questions about church property, lightning rods, stone walls, and the buildings and trees were matters to which he asked his secretaries, Missy LeHand and Grace Tully, to respond with brief comments. Often he himself replied at length. In the spring of 1943, when Lulu Rogers Taylor of the Parish Guild wrote the president that a new carpet was needed in the chapel, he replied with his blessing: "I spoke to Mrs. Roosevelt about this and she thinks that there are a number of carpets in our house which ought to do for the purpose, at least for a while. . . . I suggest that the Guild should not proceed with the purchase until we have a chance to look. Mrs. Roosevelt and I will do this as soon as we are there for a Sunday."[45] Instead of being burdens, such concerns and responses very likely returned Roosevelt to his sustaining spiritual center at Hyde Park.

Not that the job came without difficulties. When the treasurer of the parish, Arthur S. Halpin, failed to benefit the parish in a local bond issue, Roosevelt sent a memorandum—always a sign of irritation—to his old friend and fellow vestryman Gerald Morgan: "This makes me good and mad. In view of the fact that it was Arthur Halpin himself who was selling these school bonds on behalf of the school trustees, and having my approval the day after he wrote for it, he could very easily have had the purchasing brokerage house set aside $10,000 of them and got your consent and Eddie's [Edmund P. Rogers] by telephone. If Halpin had acted fast he could have got the brokerage house to waive their commission, which probably amounted to about 2% on each bond." Roosevelt asked Morgan if he would "put it up to Eddie [the Wall Street banker] and ask him as a matter of pride and affection in the church, if he would undertake to invest some of our church funds." Otherwise, "it means that we all have to chip in this Spring to make good on the deficit."[46]

Then too there was the continuing problem of scheduling vestry meetings. It was a matter of importance that the senior warden, as the chief lay officer of the church, be present at all sessions. Ordinarily these took place monthly. For St. James' they occurred infrequently, two or at most three times a year. There were gaps of eight, nine, and eleven months, and in 1940 Roosevelt attended only one, a follow-up meeting. Who, though, would vote against reappointing the president of the United States to be senior warden? Attorney Halpin may well have considered such a course in his capacity as church treasurer. In 1936 he wrote peremptorily to the president, "Will you please return [powers of attorney] . . . at the earliest possible date?" Nearly a month later FDR finally responded. Even friend Gerald Wilson had to resort to pleading for a vestry meeting: "No one has been paid since April 15." At best, arrangements remained makeshift and inconstant.[47]

Episcopal Affairs

Roosevelt's church involvement was not reserved for St. James', Hyde Park. In 1914 he was appointed to the board of trustees of the Cathedral of St. John the Divine in New York City, part of the Episcopal Church's strategic campaign to build great edifices as testimony to the faith— and to its own cultural leadership. Roman Catholics had consecrated their imposing St. Patrick's Cathedral in midtown Manhattan twenty-five years before, but the construction of St. John's had lagged. That did not change during Roosevelt's first ten years on the board, owing to World War I and the postwar economic slump. But tacking with the 1920s' boom and boosterism, New York's inimitable bishop William T. Manning asked Roosevelt in 1924 to become national chairman for a fund-raising campaign designed to bring the immense project to rapid completion. No doubt this was because FDR was a former vice presidential candidate and prominent New Yorker with access to important people in the financial world. Roosevelt declined the offer but did deliver the keynote address at a 1925 mass meeting at Madison Square Garden opening the public phase of the campaign. He did well but was not a miracle worker; the project went forward but never has been completed.[48]

Did Roosevelt have any particular interest in or knowledge of cathedrals? Writing from the vantage point of 1939, a fellow trustee, the Reverend William H. Owen, remembered FDR's contribution as minimal. "I have no recollection of Mr. Roosevelt's ever having taken any appreciable part in our debates," he recalled. While Roosevelt appeared to be a "gentleman of great charm . . . I always wondered whether he was a man of brains and mental force." Perhaps Owen's concluding anti-Roosevelt jokes bespoke a political bias behind his recollections.[49] But cathedrals were an abiding interest of the future president. In the summer of 1905, during their wedding trip to Europe, Eleanor and Franklin, like any number of American tourists, visited many of them. He was particularly taken with St. Mark's in Venice, as Eleanor reported to her mother-in-law: "Wednesday morning we again went to St. Mark's for another look at the church which is really lovely though the repairs going on inside rather mars [sic] the effect of the whole. Franklin says he is disappointed in it but it is the only church which he wanted to see twice." Subsequently they viewed churches and cathedrals in Milan, Augsburg, Ulm, St. Blasien, and Strasbourg. In Paris they went to St. Chapelle, Notre Dame, and St. Etienne, although the nightlife in the city proved at least equally interesting. A late dinner and a "prolonged bat" with friends that evening, wrote Eleanor, got them back to the Imperial Hotel at 1:30 a.m.[50]

Owing to his polio, Roosevelt was unable to get to every meeting of the St. John's building committee, but he did offer Manning advice about the problem of long-term versus short-term giving, which he believed was bedeviling the project. On the whole, he thought, wealthy people leave their "church or the Cathedral out of their wills by pure inadvertence." So approaching such people "in the proper way" would not likely hurt their willingness to contribute to the building fund in the near term.[51] Years later, on March 8, 1936, FDR wrote his cousin Daisy Suckley that he wished she could have been with him at the National Cathedral in Washington, DC, for a special service. "I'm so glad they are building it a little piece at a time—it ought to take a full century—I have always wished that Manning had not been in such a hurry with St. John's."[52] He learned that also from Saint Lawrence Cathedral in Rotterdam, Netherlands, a building of special interest to him, since his ancestor Hendrik van Rosenvelt was buried there. Saint Lawrence had taken over a century, from 1449 to 1552, to complete; converted into a Protestant church with the Dutch uprising against Spain only twenty years later, it still made an impressive statement against the skyline of what would become Europe's largest port.[53]

The building of St. John the Divine included many subtexts, most of which Roosevelt could endorse but two that he could not.[54] The Episcopal cathedrals arising these years on the American cityscape were part of a general movement to prove that the new industrial city could be as distinguished for culture as for commerce. The cathedrals' design, usually English Gothic, was meant to elevate the standards of American architecture, which ranged from the prosaic to the gauche to the ugly. The cathedrals would be monuments of beauty and spiritual ideals amid the boisterous materialism of the Industrial Age. Further, they would attest to the reigning Episcopal mind-set that beauty itself, along with ethical ideals like honor, service, and charity, had theological import— in fact, were Christianity translated into public language, uplifting the general culture. All of this Roosevelt believed. He liked most of all the democratic intention behind these buildings. Mighty and magnificent though they were, their vast space and free access meant to welcome and refresh the working classes that were otherwise crowded and jostled by the exigencies of life. As early as 1869, Bishop William Croswell Doane of the Diocese of Albany gave classic expression to this impulse in demanding that cathedrals abolish traditional pew rents and provide for the body as well as the soul: "I have no ambition *to play* at a cathedral (or at anything else) which is utter unreality unless the seats are free. . . . God helping me, if I live long enough the Diocese of Albany will have the *reality* of a cathedral, with all that it involves of work and worship, in frequent services, in schools and houses of mercy of every kind."[55]

But the new cathedrals also spelled an increase in the bishops' authority.[56] They provided administrative space for the centralized control of all activities in the diocese, a step meant to create the "efficiencies" so dear to the business corporations of the day; these set the pace for other domains of American life as well, not to mention providing the lead donors for the cathedral building campaigns. Building a cathedral meant shifting the focus in church affairs from the periphery to the center and making Episcopal churches genuinely episcopal instead of functionally congregationalist in polity. The move hardly escaped Roosevelt's notice—or censure. To him the parish church was more important than the diocese. Roosevelt also would have disagreed strongly with the unchurching of other Christians that came along with the high-church principles that lay behind the cathedral complex. Manning put it plainly: "A priest ordained by a Bishop in direct succession to the Apostles, is indispensably necessary for the celebration of the Holy Communion." Since they lacked that succession, Protestant churches are but "of men's own making." Nor should Episcopalians have anything to do with federations of Protestants or "enter into United Protestant work in Mission fields or elsewhere."[57] Roosevelt, by contrast, cherished just that ecumenicity, from Hyde Park to the international scene.

Not that Manning was averse to political wheeling and dealing. He continued to cultivate the powerful for the benefit of his church and his cathedral. He supported Prohibition and in 1929 sent the president a sermon he had preached on the subject at St. John the Divine. On October 29, 1929, he wrote Herbert Hoover, inviting the president to speak that November on the Sunday nearest Armistice Day at "a service of prayer and thanksgiving for the present movement toward world peace." Given the stock market crash of that very day, however, President Hoover was otherwise occupied. Manning made similarly unsuccessful requests of Roosevelt. In February 1937 he wrote at length regarding an interfaith conference at the cathedral to be attended by Protestant, Catholic, and Jewish conferees "in order to stir in the hearts and consciences of all religious communions a sense of moral responsibility for the abolition of these [New York's] slums." This time the bishop sought only a letter of encouragement.[58]

On the same royal visit to which FDR paid close attention on behalf of St. James' Church, the bishop hoped for some diocesan action. Might the royal couple stop at St. John the Divine on their way through the city from the World's Fair to Hyde Park? Replying for the president, Edwin M. "Pa" Watson advised that there would only be time for a stop of "about ten minutes at Columbia University where the King and Queen will view the original Charter of King's College, the predecessor of Columbia."[59] In September 1941, the bishop tried again, this time apropos of a celebration marking the opening of "the entire length of our great Cathedral revealing its unequaled vista of more than one-tenth of a mile from the West Doors to the High Altar." Manning judged that the event would be "of the highest importance not only to our own Church but in the Religious Life of our Country." While others were trying to "tear down and destroy all that Christian civilization stands for," New York Episcopalians would initiate a "whole week with Services of Special Intercession relating to the World Situation at this time." The event "offers a unique occasion for you to speak to the Country from the Cathedral with the building of which you were so closely associated and of which you are still a Trustee." At the end of the letter, Manning suggested that the president speak on "the night of Sunday, December 7th, the final day of the observance."[60] The president did not accept, and he would have been otherwise occupied even if he had.

Manning did play better on other occasions. Although he was personally opposed to a third term for Roosevelt in 1940, he refused to connive at political games behind the ecclesiastical screen. In 1932 he had helped raise over a million dollars through one of his own diocesan committees to address the crying needs of the Depression. Overhead costs of the campaign were less than 1 percent and were paid for by the committee itself. Still, they found that the money "thus far raised has been pitifully inadequate." In the last three months of 1932, the City Mission Society had to turn away no fewer than 1,800 referrals from Episcopal churches alone, and new applications were coming in "at the rate of 250 per week."[61] In his address to the convention of the New York diocese in May 1933, the bishop entreated clergy and laity alike to rise to the occasion: "The need is immediate. The responsibility upon us is a sacred one. I beg you each one to do your part and to bring this appeal home with all your power to the people of your parish."[62] Bequeathed an estate on the Hudson, Manning donated it to become a relief and training center for unemployed young men and boys. When in July 1933 labor leaders in the city approached him about giving the unemployed part-time work on the cathedral, he agreed. Shortly after the diocesan convention, he wrote to Roosevelt: "I hope you are not feeling the strain too much. Your task is a terrific one, but you have accomplished marvels already, for which we all rejoice. God's blessing and guidance be with you."[63] It was one of his finer hours.

Eastchester

Throughout his life, Roosevelt believed that Christian faith and democracy were inseparable. He was equally sure that the Episcopal Church had contributed positively to the cause of religious liberty in America. The latter, as Mark Twain remarked on other occasions, was a "bit of a stretcher." Nowhere was this more apparent than in the case of St. Paul's Church, Eastchester (now Mount Vernon), New York, where none other than Sara Delano Roosevelt served as the honorary chairwoman of the "Historic Saint Paul's Restoration Fund for the one hundred fiftieth anniversary of the ratification of the Bill of Rights." Sara spoke with pride of "the part played by this ancient church in the establishment of our basic freedoms," adding that in "these days [it was 1941], when they are challenged in so many parts of the world, it is our duty not only to defend them, but to cherish them and preserve such shrines of freedom as is St. Paul's." A letter requesting donations went to Elinor Morgenthau, who was Jewish, but that was no hindrance.[64] Shrines to freedom deserved support from all sources, especially those that would benefit most from overcoming prejudice. Mrs. Morgenthau sent twenty-five dollars.

The village green at Eastchester had indeed hosted significant events that eventually contributed to the Bill of Rights, but St. Paul's had not. Quite the contrary. Over the decades of the eighteenth century, a tug of war took place between members of the Church of England and affiliates of the "Dissenting" churches in Eastchester. Far from proclaiming religious rights, the Church of England tried to force members of dissenting communions—who constituted the overwhelming majority of New York residents—to return to or submit to Anglican authority. That entailed seizing the church founded at the site of St. Paul's in 1665 from Congregationalists and Presbyterians and securing it for the purposes of the Church of England. And so it remained, down to the Revolution.[65]

A more propitious site for celebrants of religious freedom and ultimately the Bill of Rights was the village green. Somewhere in its vicinity, Anne Hutchinson had been killed by hostile Indians in 1643.

On July 14, 1931, then-governor Franklin D. Roosevelt gave a talk there in which he invoked his "great, great, great, great-grandmother, Anne Hutchinson." As her flight from intolerance had cost Anne her life, it was his hope that the site "will be recognized as a symbol in America in all the years to come . . . to those of all faiths and creeds—something that will lead us to be better Americans."[66] The "site" to which the governor was alluding was not the green, however, but St. Paul's Church, whose 265th anniversary the occasion was celebrating. The hope remained, however, and eventually became father to the claim. Ten years later, as the world was descending into war, FDR wrote W. Harold Weigle, St. Paul's rector, that the founding of the church in 1665 emphasized the importance that the early pioneers placed on "the everlasting reality of religion." He went on to aver: "The world never was more in need of the plain teachings of the Sermon on the Mount than it is today. I trust that the solemn Thanksgiving service you are planning to hold in commemoration of the founding of the parish will inspire all who participate to stand steadfast in their witness to the faith which is their richest heritage."[67]

Conclusion

Franklin Roosevelt was launched from the cradle on a religious trajectory. As a child and youth, he was brought up in the church. He knew and ever treasured its hymns, liturgy, Scripture, and prayers. Through his father, his Swiss governess, and later his wife, Eleanor, the Social Gospel and its causes in the Progressive Era became his. He would bring them into the New Deal in different garb. Nor did he forget the more traditional charity of his mother. These strands would be woven together at Groton School under the work and example of its redoubtable headmaster and most muscular Christian, the Reverend Endicott Peabody.

Chapter Two

Endicott Peabody, Spiritual Father

Tin basins, black soapstone sinks, and cold showers. Long rows of doorless cubicles, six feet by ten, with little furniture. Daily chapel and compulsory athletics; stiff collars and patent-leather shoes in the evening. The "shouted commands of dormitory prefects" enforcing a "strict and unyielding hierarchy based on seniority" upon a "hundred or so brawling boys." So go the usual Dickensian descriptions of life at Groton School. Looming over it all was Endicott Peabody, "his anger more formidable, his love deeper than that of anyone they would ever know." "Nails and notebook, boy," the rector demanded at the beginning of Sacred Studies class, whereupon, cleanliness being in the general vicinity of godliness, "the pupil must show his fingernails were clean and his notebook ready to receive jottings from the rector's wisdom." Grades from this and from all courses were posted for all the world to see. Such was the school at whose doorstep Franklin Roosevelt was deposited on September 15, 1896. He was fourteen.[1]

Four years later he would leave for Harvard—his body filled out, his mind better stocked, and his soul stamped by the inimitable founder, head, and guide of one of America's premier prep schools. Endicott Peabody's influence on Roosevelt was deep and lasting. He officiated at Franklin and Eleanor's wedding and quickly reached out to the couple when Franklin contracted polio in 1921. He presided at the worship service held on the eve of FDR's inauguration as president in 1933. The two stayed in regular touch by mail and occasional visits over the course of FDR's presidency. Peabody was Roosevelt's lifelong pastor. He functioned as his spiritual father—indeed, as a second father outright. When Franklin left home for Groton, Peabody was a vigorous thirty-nine years old. James Roosevelt was sixty-eight, old enough to be Franklin's grandfather and nearing the bottom of a long decline in health. He would die during Franklin's first semester at Harvard. By then, Mother Sara had moved to Cambridge to be close to her boy, but Peabody remained sufficiently close by in Groton to receive Franklin's regular visits to his old school. There the student could renew the lessons in manliness, character, and social Christianity he had received under the man aptly known as Master. "As long as I live," Roosevelt told the *New York Times* in his first term as president, "the influence of Dr. and Mrs. Peabody means and will mean more to me than that of any other people next to my mother and father."[2]

New England and Old

As both his Christian and his family names indicate, Endicott Peabody was among the bluest of New England bluebloods. The family fortune had been made, as had the Delanos', in the East Asian trade of the early nineteenth century—again, including opium. Endicott was a lineal descendant of John Endecott, the first and often repeat governor of Massachusetts Bay Colony who was known for his ferocity toward the Pequot Indians, the Quakers, and the Anglican Church. Ironically, Endicott Peabody served his whole career as a clergyman in that church's American cousin and devoted his life to raising the influence of the Episcopal Church in national life.[3] His brief was to make that happen first of all through church boarding schools designed to shape the rising American elite of the Industrial Age into responsible public servants. They were to be stout in character, committed to ordered liberty in politics and Christian ideals in religion. They were to find and follow the narrow path between the callow aristocracy of new money (or old) and the corruptions attendant upon mass democracy.

In these aspirations Peabody was a true and proper son of the Puritans. For heir and ancestors alike, the Christian faith was to be deeply personal, fed by private devotions and regular introspection. But it was also to command public space according to the standards of divine righteousness. The old Puritan leadership had been as elitist as Peabody's Episcopalians, but the best ideals of both aimed at turning leaders into genuine servants of the common good. Wealth and power were not for personal aggrandizement; they entailed obligations, and the sons of privilege would be judged by their exercise of that responsibility— judged by their countrymen, by posterity, and by a righteous God. Peabody's mission was to make Groton School an incubator of such leaders.[4]

It was a mission outreach of the church. As he declaimed at the 1900 dedication of Groton's new chapel, a service Franklin Roosevelt attended, the new edifice stood for "the essential idea of the school, the marrow and pith of her life, the soul of all her being." Groton was a church school, "not simply a School to which is attached a system of religion after the manner of the Episcopal Church."[5]

Peabody learned his vocation from personal experience in English boarding schools. In 1871 his father, who worked for J. S. Morgan & Company, was posted to the firm's London office. The fourteen-year-old "Cottie" was enrolled at Cheltenham, one of the newer nineteenth-century "public" (i.e., private) schools founded to serve one branch or another of Britain's rising professional classes. Cheltenham's niche was future officers and administrators in the empire's foreign service.[6] As distinct from the old elite "Nine" schools (Eton, Harrow, etc.) geared toward the traditional aristocracy, Cheltenham attracted a prosperous middle class that wanted their sons to be turned into "gentlemen." It mixed classical studies with some science and world languages (including Hindustani and Sanskrit) tailored to military and diplomatic careers. It maintained evangelical Anglican practices and prohibitions—the first including preaching and family prayers, the latter including horse racing, dancing, theater, alcohol, and tobacco—and honored the Anglican heritage of social reform exemplified by William Wilberforce's crusade against slavery. Peabody directly adopted Cheltenham's idea of the school being an extension of the birth family as well as its emphasis upon corporate worship in the school chapel.[7] He also followed its move from strict evangelical doctrine to a more tolerant "broad church" reading of Christian theology. All in all, Peabody's "five years at Cheltenham initiated a lifelong appreciation for godliness and good learning, muscular Christianity, gentlemanly service, and Broad Churchmanship."[8]

Peabody was also deeply impressed by the Anglican cleric and social reformer Charles Kingsley. As Regius Professor of Modern History at Cambridge, where Peabody went to study law, Kingsley fired the imagination of the young American with his passion and activism for social justice.[9] Kingsley had joined in the Chartist demonstrations of 1848 with their demands for secret ballots, parliamentary redistricting, and universal suffrage; he went on to write the famous Chartist novel *Alton Locke* (1850).[10] Further, having learned "from first-hand experience the terrible conditions of the agricultural and the industrial labourer," he became a Christian socialist advocating not just political but economic reforms, like labor's right to organize.[11] Peabody went away convinced that Kingsley lived up to the admonition of the prophet Micah (6:8): "'He hath showed thee, O man, what is good and what doth the Lord require of thee, but to do justly and to love mercy, and to walk humbly with thy God.' This was the foundation of Kingsley's own life," Peabody declared, "and I wished to make it mine."[12]

Muscular Christianity as Social Christianity

Peabody returned to the United States in 1881 to prepare for the ministry at the Episcopal Theological School in Cambridge, but after just one semester he was whirled away to the drastically different world of Tombstone, Arizona.[13] The place was notorious for (if not the exact site of) the battle of the O.K. Corral that had occurred three months before his arrival. Surrounding the town was a no-man's-land of unreconciled Apaches and cattle rustlers. Mining interests (Republican) and cattle interests (Democratic) clashed in blazing gunfights, breeding corruption and murderous vendettas. Into this setting strode a strapping, physically hard-as-nails twenty-four-year-old who had already proved himself by starting a mission church in Boston's tough South End.[14] He allied himself with the more settled elements in town and preached the virtues of patriotism, good citizenship, and loyalty to a higher order. He raised enough money in his six months in Tombstone to replace the church that had burned down the previous year. He proved an able boxer who took on any challenger and never lost a bout.[15] He ventured out to get to know the miners, teamsters, saloon keepers, and gamblers in town. He broke with Cheltenham rules to drink beer and attend the races. He even took his fund-raising campaign to the poker tables in the saloons. He told the gamblers that he would keep on preaching against their custom but asked for contributions nonetheless. He got them, and the church got built.

Peabody thus breached class lines as effectively as his Groton protégé Franklin Roosevelt would over a long, successful political career. Some of his political agenda carried over too. A decade after Tombstone, during the depression of 1893, Peabody voiced sympathy for the demands of rural populists. More broadly, he promoted a liberal agenda drawn from "groups like the Greenbackers, labor unionists, Social Gospelers, unreconstructed abolitionists, and feminists."[16] He was a member of the Massachusetts Child Labor Committee and the Society for the Prevention of Cruelty to Children. He wanted his students to ally religion with republican liberty rather than with mindless reaction. Promoting justice was also prudent, he thought, in restraining the tendency of democracies to decline into self-interest, license, and mob violence. The genial toughness and serious religious purpose that won him friends and respect in Tombstone Peabody passed along to the boys in his school.

If Charles Kingsley was his British model, Peabody's American hero was Phillips Brooks, rector of Trinity Church, Boston, then bishop of Massachusetts. A larger-than-life preacher, Brooks was instrumental in introducing the American public to the liberal theology that accompanied the Social Gospel. "To Brooks more than to anyone else," writes Frank Ashburn, "Peabody looked for guidance and inspiration."[17] Brooks wrote the Groton School hymn and its graduates' prayer, chaired its board of trustees, and was the only individual to have had a building on the school's grounds named after him. To Roosevelt, Peabody passed along Brooks's optimism, broad churchmanship, and image of America as a "great household land." Particularly the latter, the concept of the nation as a caring community, sank deep into Franklin Roosevelt's thinking, clearly connected at once to the gospel and to social justice. In his Labor Day address for 1938, FDR declared that it was becoming clearer every day that "the one great lesson of history—the lesson taught by the Master of Galilee—[is] that the only road to a happier and better civilization is the road to unity— the road called the 'Highway of Fellowship.'"[18] FDR would drive that rhetorical highway regularly during his presidency.

Liberal Protestant theologians of the previous generation had sought to reconcile Christianity with new discoveries in natural science—Darwinism especially—and with the historically contextualizing "higher criticism" of the Bible. Brooks and Edward A. Washburn, the philosopher-theologian of the liberal movement in the Episcopal Church, answered such challenges by "point[ing] to the historical Christ and to his moral excellence as evidence of the supernatural origin of Christianity."[19] The challenge for the next generation was to translate Christ's commandment of love into terms relevant to a world shaped by the industrial economy. The Social Gospel was that translation.[20] To love one's neighbor now meant to socialize sacrifice, to move from a competitive to a cooperative economy, to practice selflessness rather than to pursue self-interest. It meant diminishing class distinctions and acknowledging all people as children of God. It meant broadening charity from a one-to-one gift into a system-wide practice embodied in law and supervised by official authorities, be they corporate or state. For all its criticisms of greed and extortion, factories and trusts, the Social Gospel meant to be "good news." It envisioned a happy, harmonious future for all as class conflict ebbed away, as materialistic drives made way for personal, spiritual fulfillment—and as the bounty of the industrial system produced a materially ample life for all. Many preachers of the Social Gospel were not averse to promising and celebrating what would later be known as a consumer society. Franklin Roosevelt would echo that theme as president when he pushed for greater "purchasing power" as an antidote to economic lethargy. Like him, the Social Gospel, for all its critique of the industrial capitalist system, was premised on progress and bathed in lively hope for the American future.[21]

A similar mix of motifs and motives characterized the Progressive movement that was the Social Gospel's political corollary.[22] Roosevelt encountered it both at Groton and in his president-cousin, Theodore Roosevelt. Progressivism sought to bring the raw industrial machine of the Gilded Age under public control, to remove its hardest edges and stabilize its wild oscillations. "Control" involved governmental regulation but also the moral censure of "the people"—as it turned out, white middle-class Protestant people who could be aghast at the outrages wrought by the system but also worried about the possibility that it might blow up and cost them their comfortable place within that system. At the same time that they sounded such themes of order and control, however, Progressives yearned for growth, freedom, and vibrant new experiences. Finally, while attentive to issues of class and gender equality, white Progressives north and south were less discerning—and too often retrograde—on matters of race. The heyday of Progressive reform, 1895–1920, marked the nadir of African Americans' post–Civil War fortunes. Franklin Roosevelt's New Deal upgrade of the Progressive agenda only began to redress this weakness; a fuller measure awaited the still later progressive passions of the civil rights movement and the Great Society initiatives of Lyndon Johnson. For now, the creative tension between personal revitalization, systematic regulation, and Protestant moralism drove the movement's success; their contradictions spelled its demise in the 1920s.

The Headmaster

Peabody injected Progressive strains into the curriculum and co-curricular activities at Groton School and inspired many boys to live by them, not least by his powerful personal presence. To the boys—his boys—he was *paterfamilias*, the personification of God the Father "who just walked back and forth in the cool of the day."[23] He could be scary. To be summoned "to the Rector's study by a note from a grim-visaged study hall prefect" led one boy, the son of future secretary of state Dean Acheson, to imagine dismissal and a dreary train journey back home. C. Douglas Dillon, a future secretary of the treasury, semester after semester read on his report card, "Good but could do better, E.P." The same notation, "Good but could do better, E.P.," constituted his final evaluation.[24] The future governor of New York, Averell Harriman, sarcastically suggested that Peabody "would be an awful bully if he weren't such a terrible Christian." To a guilt-ridden Francis Biddle, FDR's future attorney general, it seemed as if the "rector preached directly at us when he talked about impurity," that is, masturbation.[25] Even a president of the United States was not exempt from Peabody's rules. Once, when Theodore Roosevelt wanted a son to get an exemption to visit the White House for a special occasion, Peabody refused. Roosevelt was furious and said so. The rector was adamant. Still, the two remained friends.

But Peabody could also show pastoral sensitivity. Once, during the presidential campaign of 1932, when future Harvard dean and White House adviser McGeorge Bundy said his "good night" to the rector and Mrs. Peabody, as all the boys did, the headmaster noticed that his coat was covered with Hoover buttons. Candidate Roosevelt was due to visit the school the next day. Peabody took Bundy aside, complimented him on his "clear expression" of preference, and suggested that everyone at the school had the obligation to greet Governor Roosevelt politely. "He then went on to say," recorded Bundy over fifty years later, "that it might be possible to attend to manners without abandoning conviction if, for one day, I would be willing to wear my buttons on the underside of my lapel." Bundy quickly agreed. "I would, of course, have obeyed an order, but this way I was allowed to bargain equally with a man who was obviously more powerful and important than either candidate."[26] Peabody also made room for those who did not conform, who were not the captains of teams or fine-tuned Latin scholars, who were "poles asunder from the Groton boy he approved." One of these, Ellery Sedgwick, found himself as a student at marked difference with Peabody in "point of view"; yet the rector "rescued me from complete unbelief in myself and gave me a degree of self-confidence which through all changes and chances I have never quite lost."[27]

The positive and negative of Peabody met at one spot: the unbending integrity that thrust him up "as a rock, seemingly unchangeable amid a turbulent sea of change." Whether Groton boys "wrecked themselves against him or clung to him as a refuge . . . they could count on him to be always there, exactly there, an eternal feature solid and incorruptible in a generally fluid and dissolving temporal scene."[28]

A major function of prep school turned out to be the networking that helped sew together a future governing class. Peabody brought reformers into that mix. His close friendships with Jacob A. Riis and Theodore Roosevelt provide a case in point. The Danish immigrant newspaperman-photographer Riis's widely read book *How the Other Half Lives* (1890) was the *Uncle Tom's Cabin* of the Progressive Era.[29] It exposed for all to see who had not seen or refused to see the shocking conditions in the packed tenements of New York City. Riis laid bare the whole of it: "the opium dens, abandoned children who lived under the wharves, Mulberry Bend which 'reeked with incest and murder' . . . commercialized vice of all kinds in the Tenderloin, stripteases in concert halls . . . painted male prostitutes at American Mabille, and legions of ill-fed families whose dream of opportunity in a new land had proven to be a mirage." Riis took Roosevelt as city police commissioner on escorted tours of the scene.[30] TR and Peabody were already close friends. Roosevelt had visited his friend Peabody in Salem in 1879 when the future president was courting Peabody's cousin, Alice Lee. A year later Peabody was an usher at their wedding, and four years after that, when, on the same day, both Alice and Theodore's mother died, the one in childbirth, the other of Bright's disease, Peabody rushed to the scene to comfort his friend. He even invited Theodore to come and teach at Groton.[31] The two men shared belief in manly exertion, progressive social ideals, and service to the community. In 1912, TR's son Quentin, then a student at Groton, wrote home that the rector would support him as president along with the rest of the Bull Moose (National Progressive Party) ticket.[32]

Peabody's friendship with Riis, the former peddler, farm laborer, carpenter, photographer, and now lion of the grand lecture tour, demonstrates how Progressive ties could cross the class divide. Riis's third book, *The Making of an American*, singled out Groton's rector for particular praise: Peabody was one of a small group "who taught me why in this world personal conduct and personal character count ever for most."[33] The rector had Riis regularly visit Groton to speak to the boys. In January 1900, Franklin Roosevelt wrote his parents that Riis had regaled the Missionary Society with "stories of his experiences with 'Teddy' on the police force in N.Y." Riis followed that the next night with "a most interesting lecture on the poor in New York . . . there was great enthusiasm over him."[34] The correspondence between Peabody and Riis, which covered nearly a quarter-century, maintained a striking degree of familiarity. Riis called the rector "Reverend Abbott," for "I can't think of any other or greater rank to bestow upon you this minute." Later it was "Brother Peabody" and "Dear Old Friend," signed "Affectionately." Upon Riis's death in 1914, Peabody conducted the funeral service for this "cherished friend."[35]

Peabody shared with Riis a certain hierarchy of ethnic groups that, typically of the time, put people of northwestern European derivation at the top, with other Europeans falling somewhere below. Africans placed at the bottom. Still, New England had an abolitionist heritage, and in Franklin's second year at Groton, the rector introduced his charges to African American attorney Thomas C. Walker. The son of an enslaved woman, Walker enrolled in the Hampton Institute in Virginia, where he was a pupil of Booker T. Washington. Walker then studied law with a white attorney and was admitted to the bar in 1886.[36] Roosevelt was impressed. Walker "told us what good Hampton is doing among negroes," he wrote his parents. "He has argued before the Court of Appeals at Washington, and is very prominent in his own state."[37] The boys—FDR among them—raised the then-respectable sum of $125 for the Hampton Institute.

Progressive Economics

Peabody would show a similar development on economic issues—simultaneously with his former student, as it happened. In the years 1910–1919 he became interested in the National Consumers' League (NCL) founded by the indefatigable Florence Kelley. Kelley made the NCL into a leading promoter of labor legislation for the protection of women and children. Its various city chapters "white-listed" local shops and factories that provided proper wages, working environments, food, and safety precautions for their workers. It was hoped that consumers would buy from approved companies only. The NCL attracted any number of young reformers, particularly women like Eleanor Roosevelt, Maud Nathan, and Molly Dewson; like Jane Addams and Ellen Gates Starr in Chicago; and, in New York, Frances Perkins, the young factory inspector and street-corner exhorter.[38] Some of them would become very influential in Roosevelt's political career.

Peabody took it upon himself to burn the NCL brand into the hides of the clergy. He delivered a major address in Boston to that effect in 1897, when fifteen-year-old Franklin Roosevelt was beginning his second year at Groton School.[39] The fault for much of the damage spread by the new industrial system lay with "the trusts whose souls are not their own," the rector began. They "injure the community," from laborers to consumers to small business, by their lack of humane concern. The problem partly lay in the academy in that the established "scientific" political economy with its "old mechanical theories" fixated on producers' costs ignored the costs extracted from the lives of workers. But this meant that the responsibility for laborers' well-being now lay with the buying public: "the producing man is essentially the servant of the consuming man[,] and the final direction of industry lies with the consumer." If consumers "purchase things produced below the point at which life can be supported[,] they are themselves oppressing the poor and needy." Hence the system of "white lists" would work to ameliorate the "barbarous conditions" of industrial America.

The steps that Peabody suggested to bring about improvement were the Progressive standard and the antecedent of the New Deal: extra pay for overtime work (which was not then given), a ban on child labor in factories, the abolition "forever" of sweatshops, the enforcement of laws mandating seating for workers on the job and for sanitary lunchrooms and restrooms on breaks. On the macro level, Peabody commended NCL support for "Trades Unions, Union Labels, the eight-hour day, and many kindred subjects." But there was a personal ethical component vital to the mix as well. Peabody dwelt on "humane and considerate behavior toward employees." He called up to view that "class of people who never appear before the Public—the vast horde of men and women herded together in tenements and hovels of the lowest quarters of the cities." He reminded the clergymen of the "hundreds and thousands of human beings working in our cities under circumstances which take away all possibility of joy or even decent living." A cry had gone up: "O God, that bread should be so dear, / And flesh and blood so cheap." Pastors needed to make that cry heard by their parishioners.

Peabody was passing along the vivid reports compiled by his (and Groton's) friend the Reverend William S. Rainsford. Rainsford was rector of St. George's Church at Stuyvesant Square in New York City, a Christian socialist—and the pastor of J. P. Morgan. Rainsford's Christmas letter of 1896 told of "Lilly B.," who worked at Macy's. "For 10 days before Xmas she worked until 10.30 P.M. every weeknight, and from 9 in the morning till 5 on Sunday. No food was provided while the young girl endured this strain. She gets $4.00 a week as regular wages. When she got home Christmas Eve she fainted from exhaustion." After giving other examples from his friend, Peabody concluded: "Such work as this simply destroys their youth and prepares them for a faulty and decrepit womanhood." As a result of their association, Rainsford advised Peabody on founding a camp for boys from the slums, first on Squam Lake and then on Newfound Lake, both in New Hampshire.[40] Young Roosevelt, like other Groton boys then and later, served there as a counselor.

Peabody not only spoke about the social ills besetting urban America; he brought his boys into contact with the poor. He arranged with Riis for Groton boys to see social conditions in New York firsthand. Already in the late 1880s, the school's Missionary Society involved both faculty and students in social outreach. Teachers and boys alike were elected by the membership. From the outset the society was influenced by Frederick B. Allen, the tireless publicist for the destitute and founder of the immensely successful Episcopal City Mission in Boston. Under its aegis were a variety of organizations: a convalescent home, a Sailors' Home, and laundries; a Girls' Friendly Society, which taught trades and homemaking; a prison visitation program and a rescue mission for transients and alcoholics that provided fresh clothes, food, counseling, and work.[41] Allen himself spoke to the Groton boys about the City Mission's work, telling them "first of the laundries which have been lately started to which many poor girls come to learn to wash and mend their clothes." He went on to speak of the public playrooms for children, of summer picnics, and a day "either in the country or at the seashore" during which "two thousand four hundred children were . . . enabled to get one day of fresh air during the summer." His repeat visits made Frederick Allen something of a fixture at the school.[42]

Sometimes the ills of the new order hit very close to home indeed. That happened during the Panic of 1893, which triggered a severe economic depression. J. P. Morgan, a Groton trustee, had become a titan of finance by facilitating foreign investment in American industry. On this occasion he used a rebound off those capital flows to make a killing. The panic began when many European creditors suddenly dumped their American securities on the market, causing a steady raid on the gold reserves of the treasury. President Grover Cleveland turned to Morgan and August Belmont to buy government bonds to staunch the flow. Demanding high interest rates and harsh terms, the Morgan-Belmont syndicate ended up pocketing seven million dollars profit from the deal. American agrarians west of the Allegheny Mountains were furious. Cleveland seemed to have knuckled under to "selfish financiers [who] had waited till the government was at their mercy, and then had seized it by the throat."[43] No doubt recalling his own experience in the West, Peabody wrote his closest friend and the Episcopal bishop of Arizona, Julius W. Atwood, that he disliked the deal. Nothing could foment more dissatisfaction in the West, he judged; moreover, the maneuver "does not seem to me altogether above suspicion. I can't quite understand a man like Mr. Morgan making money out of the country's need." Groton trustee or no, the "fewer such men we have in this country the better say I."[44]

The Preacher of Righteousness

But Peabody had a foot in yet another camp; his progressive Social Gospel views came along with more traditional moral concerns. He worried about the loss of the sanctity of the Sabbath. The year before his address to the clergy of Boston on behalf of the Consumers' League, he spoke on "the Sunday problem." Taken at a dead run, the paper briefly viewed the history of the Lord's Day from New Testament times to New England, ending breathlessly with Methodism in the eighteenth century. Peabody tried to cram in evidence from every age in church history to demonstrate a consensus about the importance of observing the fourth commandment. His prescriptions sought to avoid the extremes of "minute Pharisaic enactments . . . and narrow conformity" on the one hand and "the utter disregard of the Lord's Day such as en-visioned by the Book of Sports" on the other.[45] To prohibit running or a walk "in his garden or elsewhere, except reverently to and from meet-ing, was unthinkable." But he also recognized that in "England and the United States of America there is a laxity" regarding Sunday worship. The substitution of golf, bicycling, baseball, and particularly theater, "which come[s] in under the guise of sacred concerts," cannot "fail to arouse anxious thought." His solution was to offer "more activity & more democracy & more spontaneous heart to heart talk with people. Our church is too rigid, too self-conscious, too dreadfully respectable and dignified & we do not get the people to come to Church or instruct them when we get them there." If Sunday ought to be a day for families in their homes as well as in their churches, for those people for whom it was the one day in the week for relaxation, the "open public library, & museum & place of entertainment" might serve as a functional equiv-alent. Traditional mores needed to take serious account of the needs of the laboring poor.[46]

Peabody made sure that the very ablest guest speakers occupied the Groton chapel too. Of course, what is said in the pulpit is one thing, and what boys actually hear is quite another. But for those with ears to lis-ten there were memorable sermons. Ellery Sedgwick recalled the "vast, benevolent bulk" of Phillips Brooks and his "torrential eloquence."[47] Another of Roosevelt's younger contemporaries vividly recalled Henry S. Nash, the homely, humorous professor of New Testament at the Episcopal Theological School where Peabody had studied: "I heard him preach once when I was a boy at Groton," declared John Richards, and "I still remember that as one of the great sermons I have heard."[48] The rector took his own part in the pulpit with utmost seriousness. He alternated between making traditional affirmations and awakening a critical sense about religion. In one of his most noteworthy sermons, preached in the fall term of Roosevelt's senior year, he performed both exercises on the—by then—hoary old theme of Darwinism.[49]

On the one hand, speaking out of an overconfident tradition and comfortable class position, Peabody underestimated the challenge that Darwin's form of evolutionary biology posed to the Christian faith. More likely, he adopted one of the purpose-filled alternatives to Dar-winian theory strictly speaking and smuggled it in under the great sci-entist's name as it was popularly understood. Episcopal bishop William Lawrence, who, after Brooks, was chairman of the board of trustees of Groton School, had led the way on this front by coming to a certain separation of science and religion.[50] Peabody repeated it: "Render unto Darwin the things that are Darwin's and unto God the things that are God's." He then turned Darwin's work into a parable about character, specifically the virtue of perseverance. Darwin, like Saint Paul, reached forth for those things that were before, Peabody intoned on his text of Philippians 3:13–14; the scientist pressed forward intensely and effectively toward his great end. The boys should do likewise, both for the kingdom of God and for worthy professional goals. As for the perhaps troubling substance of Darwin's teaching, Peabody found in it a lesson of moral formation instead. Darwin shows that what a man would be he grows to be. And so the rector enlisted the great scientist in his (Peabody's) persistent criticism of overindulgence in food, drink, fine apparel, and so forth.

But Peabody then turned the tables and asked hard, critical questions of religion—particularly of the complacent external piety that too many American Christians practiced, even while complaining of Darwinism. Why was it, he asked, that Saint Paul pressed forward and reached "for the prize of the high calling of God in Christ Jesus"? Not for the apostle were the mere "wearing of certain garments" or the "pronouncing of particular Shibboleths," Peabody reminded his listeners. Likewise, Jesus chided those who tried to pass via outward conformity; they were like "whited sepulchres that without were fair but within were full of all manner of uncleanness" (Matt. 23:27). Many critics of Darwin mounted elaborate scholarly defenses of traditional theology. But was faith a matter of intellectual assent only, based on adherence to "the veracity of historical statements"? Such "may be genuinely received by a man & yet not influence his conduct," the rector warned. Similar was a "warm feeling" toward an institution or a person. "Do you feel deep love for Christ? But feeling is a fickle thing. If a man's religion depends on emotion, then he must be continually wavering between ecstasy & despair." Is then Christianity a life? To be sure, the motivation for faith is often explained that way. "And yet, yet if it were life"—that is, consistency in conduct and behavior—"how many of us have failed? How little could Saint Paul claim it when he cried, 'The good that I would, I do not, & the evil that I would not, that I do.'"

If faith, then, is ultimately based neither on legalisms nor on intellectual assent nor on emotional response nor on steady conduct, in

46

what *did* it consist? Peabody drove home his point with words dear to his Puritan forebears' hearts: "God has chosen us for Himself, as He has chosen nations and individuals to whom He has given much." This "election" was not a free pass, he hastened to add. Just the opposite: it involved a call to responsibility, to action, and to work. True faith was the affirmative response to that call. That is why the boys should press forward with Saint Paul to claim "'the prize of the high calling of God in Christ Jesus.'" Or, as Jesus himself admonished, "Seek ye first the kingdom of God and His righteousness." In short, rich, privileged kids had better get moving. On the one hand, that entailed the usual observance of clean living, truthfulness, a sense of honor, and reverence. On the other hand, it mandated concern for "the thousands of poor & sick men who live near you . . . [and who] are overwhelmed by the flood of misery which sweeps them hopelessly on." Amid the students' increasing strength, happiness, abundance, and knowledge as sons of Groton, God was calling them to the one great work "which Christ came into the world to reveal: the building up of the Kingdom of God."

The rector gave the Puritan-style "improvement" (application) of the Scripture flat out: "men who look after themselves alone are stupid." The person who "sits in his club & ridicules everyone who is trying to relieve the needs of the poor" or tells you "he will not go into politics because . . . politics are so corrupt" will not hesitate to stoop to bribery or espouse tax laws that will benefit himself alone. Peabody knew his audience: "If polo & golf & yachting and all the different amusements of an idle man were sufficient to satisfy an immortal soul, then would the idler, [the] loafer be the happiest of men." But that was the road of damnation, and boring besides. Divine election meant "self-sacrifice and heroism." Christianity, if it meant anything, meant "brotherhood . . . the purifying & uplifting of public life so that government shall be carried on by men who are honest in private & in public . . . who are working for the interests of their city & state or nation & not for their own mean profit."

In another sermon that eerily presaged Franklin Roosevelt's own career, Peabody asked his audience to imagine two individuals in a crisis when "a call comes" that offers "a chance for unselfish leadership."[51] One of them lets his sympathies narrow down to his immediate circle; "the other has constantly taken into account a larger and larger set of people, his community, his state, his country." With that broader vision "he is ready for action." Snobbery in America is "a grotesque thing," Peabody declared. The greatest danger to the republic lay "in the rise of classes who do not understand and cannot sympathize." The danger was that "Money segregates, and taste segregates, and any privilege that man has segregates, if the man lets it." Instead, we must take our privileges "and use them for the good of the whole, to broaden our sympathies instead of narrowing them."[52] Yet in the end the rector remained hopeful. On the last Sunday of Roosevelt's last year at Groton, June 24, 1900, Peabody welcomed the seniors to a new generation in American life. Instead of their predecessors' subservience to "positivism in philosophy, utilitarianism in morals & naturalism in art & poetry," youth today, Peabody averred, "is attracted by the ideal, the dreams of social fraternity, of self-renunciation, of devotion to the little, the miserable, the oppressed, devotion like the heroism of Christian care."[53] It was as much an injunction as a description, but beneath the technical terms, Roosevelt got the message.

Two Women Passionate for the Oppressed

Two women who would be highly influential in Roosevelt's life personified the new type of young people Peabody was hoping for. It is worth following their track for a moment to discern the connections between their religion and social commitments as these would work into Roosevelt's political career. The closest influence would be that of Eleanor Roosevelt. In 1900, as Franklin was graduating from Groton, Eleanor was in the middle of her four years at Allenswood Academy in Wimbledon, England. Designed to be a girls' "finishing school," Allenswood at the hand of its headmistress, Marie Souvestre, had brought Eleanor to life, learning, and self-confidence after a girlhood of fear, grief, loss, and terrible feelings of inadequacy. The role of religion in this rebirth had been ironic, for Ms. Souvestre was an outspoken freethinker who challenged Eleanor over the necessity of traditional faith for doing good works. The teenager's response was not to discard religion, however, but to find her own true footing within it, a deep vein of religious feeling that quickened her acute moral sense and sustained her lifelong passion on behalf of the needy and disregarded.[54]

She began to serve immediately upon her return to New York, working at the Rivington Street settlement house on Manhattan's Lower East Side. Modeled on Hull House, begun by Jane Addams in

Chicago a dozen years before, Rivington pulled Eleanor beyond the holiday charities she had learned as a child to come to grips with the causes of and possible cures for the systemic poverty and exploitation she witnessed all about her. She threw herself into the work, to the neglect of the social whirl expected of an elite debutante such as herself. She joined research and lobbying efforts meant to goad city government to redress wrongs and neglect. She broadened her scope by joining the New York chapter of the National Consumers' League, helping to conduct the investigations that determined whether stores qualified for the "white label."[55] All the while she "attended church faithfully" along with weekly Bible classes led by a Barnard graduate and Bible scholar, Janet McCook, with whom she carried on regular discussions of religion.[56]

After marrying Franklin in 1905, Eleanor was soon absorbed in child rearing, including shepherding the young ones to church as Franklin went off golfing on Sunday mornings. But her zeal for broader service was rekindled during World War I, when she volunteered to work on—and soon was helping to administer—knitting projects at the Navy Department and serving soldiers and sailors at the Red Cross canteen. After the war was over, she worked long hours to improve care for wounded veterans at St. Elizabeth's Hospital in Washington, DC.[57] The achievement of women's suffrage led her to become involved with the League of Women Voters (LWV) to track legislation of particular interest to women, in which connection she developed lasting ties with women lawyers and labor organizers. By the time Franklin was elected governor of New York in 1928, Eleanor was a chief conduit to him of policies researched and designed by the LWV and the militant Women's Trade Union League to promote labor causes and larger social-policy reforms that would eventually show up in the New Deal.[58]

All these activities, notes Eleanor's close friend and biographer, Joseph P. Lash, were "strongly . . . grounded in religious conviction." Eleanor "was the most faithful of churchgoers, the most sincere of communicants, for whom prayer was not a matter of rote but a daily influence in her life . . . a kind of continuing exchange with God, a way of cleansing the heart and steadying the will." She habitually clipped out prayers from various sources and carried them around in her purse. One such enjoined her to "think seldom of your enemies, often of your friends and every day of Christ." According to Lash, she circled the phrase about Christ. These prayers functioned "to recall her to her

Christian vocation," concludes Lash. "As completely as she could, she wanted to live according to Christ's teachings," for "fundamentally," beneath all her politics, journalism, feminism, and advocacy, "she was a woman with a deep sense of spiritual mission."[59]

A religious passion was just as animating for one of the most important labor activists whom Eleanor brought to Franklin's attention: Frances Perkins.[60] Perkins was born (on Beacon Hill, no less) in 1880 to a venerable New England family but was reared in a modest small-business household in Worcester, Massachusetts. She absorbed the reigning doctrine of the family's Congregational church but rebelled when it came to economics, identifying instead with the laborers' cause. Crucial in this conversion was the same testimony of Jacob Riis that Roosevelt was hearing at Groton. College for Perkins meant Mt. Holyoke, where the fires of social Christianity were burning strong. In 1902, her senior year, she met Florence Kelley of the National Consumers' League and determined to turn her passion for the poor into a career in social work.[61] Frances moved to New York City, then to Chicago and a close-up view of the work at Hull House; from that she settled upon labor issues as her true calling. She moved to Philadelphia for graduate studies at the Wharton School, then in 1909 to Columbia in New York City. Soon she was running the NCL's New York office, pushing educational and lobbying campaigns to outlaw child labor and promote labor unions. She joined the women's suffrage movement in the process. All these strands came together in one galvanizing moment when she witnessed the 1911 Triangle Shirtwaist fire, in which 146 workers, mostly young immigrant women, were incinerated in a factory notorious for its bad working conditions.[62]

Frances threw herself into the campaign to redress this horror with investigation, agitation, and legislation. That meant confronting the Tammany Hall powers in the city's Democratic Party. She built an alliance with Robert Wagner and Al Smith, two labor- and reform-minded rising stars in the organization, and won a seat on state investigating committees that would see into law no fewer than two dozen bills regulating factory conditions and terms of employment. During Smith's governorship of New York across much of the 1920s, Perkins turned the state's previously moribund Industrial Commission into a powerful agency on behalf of factory safety and workman's compensation. When Roosevelt became governor in 1929, he promoted her in that capacity and forged the relationship that flourished to the very end of his presidency. Perkins became the Labor Department's first female, and longest-serving, secretary; from her desk came key pieces of New Deal legislation: the Civilian Conservation Corps as an emergency recovery act, and the Social Security and the Fair Labor Practices bills of enduring social legislation.[63]

Perkins's long crusade for justice was ultimately grounded in and fueled by religion. Her "life-changing" steps in Chicago included not just Hull House and a commitment to labor but also a move from her native Congregationalism into high-church Episcopal practice.[64] As often happens along that trail, the beauty of the Anglo-Catholic liturgy seems to have been the first attraction. But its regular weekly renewal, its act of connecting the individual believer today to the vast "cloud of witnesses" from across the whole range of Christian history—and likewise to a richer array of social ethics than those of the moment—proved vital not just to maintaining Perkins's personal well-being but also to directing and sustaining her work across the years. As she looked back upon her long career, she concluded that advocates for the poor who were moved simply by humanitarian concerns tended to get "discouraged and quit the struggle." The ones who kept at it over the long run from the Progressive Era through the New Deal "were those who had most directly experienced the mass misery of the poor in the country's great industrial cities and those who had a religious basis for their work."[65]

From the start of her time in Washington, Perkins made a habit of going not only to the Anglo-Catholic St. James Episcopal Church but also on overnight retreats to the All Saints Convent of Episcopal nuns at Catonsville, Maryland. She participated in its round of daily prayers, relished its long hours for silent reflection, and spent a good deal of time in personal prayer in its chapel. In the two hours excepted from the rule of silence, she liked to discuss the principles of social legislation with the house's reverend mother. Sharing a common faith with Roosevelt made theirs more than a positive working relationship; they had a trusted personal bond. As we will see numerous times in the pages to follow, some of the keenest insights into FDR's character and motivations came from Perkins's eye.[66]

The President's Pastor

These redoubtable women lay in Roosevelt's future. Endicott Peabody loomed now. As a headmaster in an age of titans, he pushed his agenda. He rejected laissez-faire individualism in economics even though his school was built upon and supported by the fruits of just such operations. In its own way, the cooperative ethos that he sought was not unknown to such men as J. P. Morgan. Trustee Morgan supported both Groton School and his own socialist rector, William S. Rainsford, as well as his giant international bank. Nor did Peabody diminish the importance of individual responsibility and initiative in his church's teaching. He combined them with Social Gospel Christianity.[67] He had no interest in educational psychology, and the melancholy spirit portrayed in the writings of Harold Frederic and Henry Adams was foreign to him.[68] In his dislike of the overrefined and the overdressed, he was closer to William James than to his younger brother, Henry. Peabody believed along with William that "if there is to be anything inherently valuable in living, it must be a living of a certain sort, in which one both serves a moral ideal and believes it."[69] He did not shiver on the shores of faith; he confidently walked the beach and marked the view. In all this, Franklin Roosevelt was his faithful spiritual son.

The correspondence between the two continued across their lifetimes. As Kurt A. Klingbeil has written, Peabody's "letters to FDR are filled with words of encouragement and moral and spiritual advice which the President seemed to appreciate. . . . 'God bless you, my dear Franklin, and give you wisdom and strength.'" Theirs was "a pastoral relationship."[70] In 1913, when FDR was appointed assistant secretary of the navy, Peabody wrote him: "Your friends at Groton—and they are numerous—are delighted over your appointment to High Office. It is a great triumph of Honesty and Loyalty over the lower powers which are trying to best the Country." Concurrently, Roosevelt's classmate and Harvard roommate, Lathrop Brown, had been elected to Congress from New York's First District as a Democrat. Peabody added, "With you and Jake Brown among our rulers we are feeling very influential."[71]

The subject of religion was never far from the surface in these letters. The rector participated in the inauguration day services at St. John's Church in Washington, DC, in 1933, as well as in the later, wartime anniversary commemorations thereof in the White House. Peabody knew how important those services were to Roosevelt. In 1935 the administration took the unprecedented step of sending out a letter to over 120,000 clergy asking for counsel and advice on the government's new social security and public works programs. Thousands replied, Peabody among them.[72] After his customary salutation "My dear Franklin," the rector continued: "I want to assure you of my lasting conviction that you have one supreme purpose in mind, the guidance of this country in such a way that all its citizens who are minded to do honest work shall have a chance to secure a living free from anxiety and with an opportunity for the development of which they are capable." Peabody thought that Roosevelt's inquiry had "made a deep impression upon the minds of people all through the country[,] and many were strengthened in their faith by your example." In a time of "unsteady faith," how fortunate to have "a spiritual leader at the head of the nation [who] brings fresh power to the individual and to the cause of Christ and His Church."[73]

The encouraging words continued in the years when FDR's attention had to turn to foreign affairs. After the famous "Quarantine" speech in Chicago on October 5, 1937, the rector wired: "Grand Stop I rejoice in your splendid great effort to bring peace to this distraught world Stop our love to you all. Endicott Peabody."[74] Roosevelt replied that he deemed the quarantine policy "more Christian, as well as more practical than the previous suggestion that the world should go to war" with Germany or Japan.[75] After war abroad began anyway, another "My dear Franklin" letter expressed gratitude for the "privilege of journeying along with you in friendship[,] rejoicing that you have tried faithfully to carry out the high ideals that God has set before you."[76] Replying to "Dear Mr. Peabody" a few days later, the president thanked him for his "guiding hand" and "inspiring example": "Nor am I unmindful of all that your counsel and friendship have meant as we have journeyed along together through so many years. For all that you have been and are to me[,] I owe a debt of gratitude which I love to acknowledge."[77]

Peabody found the president's address to Congress the day after Pearl Harbor to be "magnificent"; it would "do more than anything else could have done to steady us all and give us confidence in final victory." The rector was thankful that Roosevelt had "been given the power to lead us at this time," as he was for "the moral and spiritual ideals for which you have so consistently aimed during these last nine years."[78] Perhaps the highest praise the headmaster gave to his former pupil was contained in the 1935 response to the letter to the clergy. "I have thought," wrote Peabody, remembering his own ordination to the priesthood, "that the guiding principle of a man's life should be the motive which Jesus revealed as his fundamental purpose: 'For their sakes, I sanctify myself that they also may be sanctified through the truth'" (John 17:19). Then, turning to the president with a virtual laying-on-of-hands, Peabody concluded, "I most heartily congratulate you that you have such an opportunity to carry out this great purpose in your own life with a view to inspiring a mighty company of your fellow-countrymen."[79]

Conclusion

An even more remarkable benediction came at the very end of Peabody's life. On November 17, 1944, the old headmaster headed out to drive an old family friend to the train station in nearby Ayer, Massachusetts. She was Mary Louise Ackland, and she had been helping care for Peabody's wife, Fanny, after surgery. She was now headed home to Canada. His eighty-seven years had taken a toll on Peabody. Kneeling for family prayers was a bit of a chore, and sometimes memory failed him. On that day, Ackland noticed, Peabody was momentarily confused as to how to start the car but quickly recovered and laughed about his initial fumbling. He "was happy and confident, and every inch a man in control of the situation." But at a slight bend in the road, the car slowly swerved off the track. To Ackland's warning "there was no answer." She noticed a "strange expression on his face," took the wheel, steered the vehicle to the side of the road, and turned off the engine. Then "with very heavy breathing his head fell back and his whole body slumped."[80]

Passersby stopped to help, but to no avail. Wartime travel difficulties made it imperative that Ms. Ackland continue her return journey to Ottawa. She did so reluctantly, but she took time the next day to write down the incident in detail for Peabody's daughter. Her account is most valuable to history for its reference to Franklin Roosevelt. "For no particular reason and somewhat to my surprise," Ackland remembered, Peabody said just before his stroke: "You know there's no doubt but that Roosevelt is a very religious man." They turned out to be his dying words.

The next day the president wired Mrs. Peabody: "I am, of course, deeply distressed and the news has come as a real shock. Eleanor sends her love with mine. The whole tone of things is going to be a bit different from now on, for I have leaned on the Rector in all these years far more than most people know. You will understand this. We are thinking of you. My love and sympathy to all the children. Franklin D. Roosevelt."[81]

Chapter Three

Groton and Harvard—Race, Religion, and Leadership

Franklin Roosevelt was born near the top of American society. At school and college, he was inducted into the ways and means of staying there. The experience was not altogether pleasant, but he learned to adapt and at least get along with his peers. He also began to fathom the momentous changes the nation was undergoing in leaving behind the Gilded Age and moving into the Progressive Era. Endicott Peabody meant Groton School to be a place where rising leaders might learn to channel that change to "sound" and "healthy" ends by way of a socially engaged Christianity. So formed, Roosevelt went on to Harvard, where he got advanced lessons in activism—and career making. During those years, it helped that he had a kinsman in the White House. His biographers agree that Franklin Roosevelt left Harvard with a lot to learn about himself and the world. Here we focus on what he had already learned to date.

School Days: Happy and Unhappy

Despite its demanding regimen, Groton was not all cold baths and root canals. The new arrival was bundled along to tea in "Mrs. Peabody's Parlor," where the rector's wife dispensed comfort for the homesick and card games or hymn sings for the rest. Her beauty and her concern for "my boys" were at once evident. The school provided ample opportunities for developing talents and having fun. There was a dramatic society, a choir and a yearly choir festival in Boston, a glee club, and debating societies, junior and senior, all of which Franklin joined early and enthusiastically. (He demurred at the orchestra.) The rector often read stories to the boys in his study, as did dormitory masters to the younger ones at bedtime each night. Each December the rector's father read Dickens's *A Christmas Carol* to the entire school in three sittings. The students were not only on the literary receiving end; they were given the responsibility of editing —and typesetting—the institution's major publication, the *Grotonian*. For the Christmas service the boys themselves decorated the chapel. Besides compulsory athletics (football, baseball, and crew), they were free to play golf and lawn tennis, canoe on the Nashua River, and go sledding, skating, and skiing in the winter. Often with faculty members they played a fast English handball game called fives. In many of these activities, including team sports, Peabody himself participated.[1] In the spring there were hikes and picnics: "Today," Franklin wrote his parents in his senior year, we went "on a picnic with Mr. & Mrs. Peabody about five miles off to a high hill where there was a most glorious view. We all enjoyed it immensely, & had a roaring good time."[2] That autumn Roosevelt enthusiastically related to his parents that he and some of his friends had revived the school's Natural History Society. They had the help of famed zoologist and anthropologist Edward S. Morse, director of the Peabody Museum in Salem and curator of the Boston Museum of Fine Arts.[3] Franklin had brought this interest with him to Groton and maintained it for the rest of his life.

Yet he was not particularly happy at school. Unused to competition, regimentation, and living in close quarters with other boys, he was constantly on his guard. He had entered his class a year late, after other boys had already formed friendships. Tall, conspicuous, and slightly superior in manner, he invited a degree of roasting. For home consumption, writes Geoffrey C. Ward, he put on a brave face and developed a "pattern of concealing his genuine feelings while seeming faithfully to be revealing all."[4] The habit would stand him—and the nation—in good stead in future crises. But at Groton it cost him, no doubt contributing to painful memories of the school. In 1942, FDR confided to his cousin and confidante, Daisy Suckley, that he had been "unhappy in school, for his bringing-up, with his parents, travelling, etc. made him old for his age, and he found other boys so young and immature and ignorant that he supposed he showed his opinion of them, & they in turn didn't like him."[5] In fact, it was Franklin who often appeared immature to others. He was self-absorbed and found it difficult not to win the acclaim he had grown to expect.[6] Wanting to be liked and admired, he remembered old hurts and "failures." Suckley noted how much he needed the reassurance of close friends. After his 1943 State of the Union speech, she wrote in her diary: "He inquired almost like a small boy: 'Did you think that the speech was all right? Did you like it?' I reassured him!!!"[7]

Peabody meant Groton to be an ideal Christian community. There was to be no "fagging" as in the English schools, where younger boys were expected to do menial tasks for older students. Nor would he allow corporal punishment. But if Groton was officially ruled by "overwhelmingly good—sanely good" persuasion and example, it had a grim underside. As the rector, the faculty, and even many parents knew (the latter in advance of enrolling their boys there), Groton upperclassmen inflicted harsh and brutal hazing upon younger students who were deemed to lack "good form." Anyone who failed to show proper school spirit or was fresh or funny-looking or otherwise not a "good fit" was subjected to "boot-boxing" or "pumping." The first saw the hapless offender muscled by members of the football team into a small crate that was sealed and then kicked and pounded with a terrifying violence. "Pumping" was the waterboarding of its time. First offenders got ten seconds of near-drowning, with repeat doses if they failed to apologize for their putative offense.[8] The younger boys had heard of this bullying even before they arrived at school. Franklin expressed relief to his parents and his aunt, Annie Lyman Delano, that in his first few days "I have not been put in the boot-box yet," whereas one unfortunate "has been boot-boxed once and threatened to be pumped several times."[9] Though he never suffered those cruelties, Franklin did face a milder hazing. During first term he was "trapped in a corner of the corridor and ordered to . . . dance." A gang slapped hockey sticks at his ankles to make him step high and fast. Inventive under stress, Franklin toe-danced and spun around, faking high spirits "as if he were part of the fun instead of its object." In other words, Franklin did what the upperclassmen demanded "with such good grace that the class soon let him go."[10] The life skills of evasion and adaptability came very early.

There are other dimensions to Roosevelt's painful memories of his years at Groton. He learned to confront adversity and not retreat from the rough-and-tumble of adolescence. He played contact sports, however unsuccessfully, and relished visits to Oyster Bay, where he romped with TR and "his tireless brood."[11] Contemporary impressions of Roosevelt given by others at the school, both masters and boys, indicate that he did in fact achieve a measure of respect. Those who later remembered him as a misfit could well have been speaking out of political motives; surely a Democratic president did not "fit" with Groton.

Roosevelt's grades over his four years at school were respectable but not brilliant.[12] He was strong at French, German, algebra, geometry, history, and sacred studies, consistently weaker at English literature, English composition, and physics. He ended up graduating ninth out of twenty.[13] The rector's end-of-year comments over the years were probably the most revealing: "Very good," Peabody said of Franklin's first year. "He strikes me as an intelligent and faithful scholar, and a good boy." The next years were "Very fair" and "Very good; he is developing most satisfactorily." At graduation Peabody reflected, "He has been a thoroughly faithful scholar and a most satisfactory member of the school throughout his course. I part with Franklin with reluctance."[14]

Over time, Roosevelt came to feel freer and surer of himself, occasionally breaking the rules of comportment.[15] Class cohesion disallowed making friends with members of other grades; Franklin ignored the etiquette and consistently looked out for his young cousin, Warren Delano Robbins. At the same time, he seems to have thought a good deal about the success and position he should have. This trait, along with a tendency toward self-absorption and a need to exaggerate, has received deserved attention from his biographers. Yet a different picture emerges from his school-aged letters to his parents. Here was a boy who meant to be thoroughly engaged, steady, not up one minute and down the next. The voice was not muffled, nor the colors faded. Like most teenagers, young Franklin worried about physical prowess, status, and popularity.

He also had troubles with his health. In late April 1898, scarlet fever broke out at Groton School, and most of the boys went home. Franklin was one of thirty-five to remain, and he came down with the disease. Since in extreme cases it can lead to heart and kidney complications, mastoiditis, deafness, delirium, and even death, his parents hurried back from Europe and took him home to Hyde Park.[16] His scarlet fever turned out to be mild, but other illnesses came in turn. In 1912 it was typhoid fever, again a dangerous disease with its potential for (fatal) peritonitis.[17] Throughout his life he was subject to sinus infections. Young Franklin put up with these stoically—a good sign, considering worse was to come. One of the culprits might have been his isolation as a boy at Hyde Park; more regular contact with other children might have helped build his immunities. Yet Roosevelt, then and later, did not strike observers as particularly sickly. To Grace Tully, one of his secretaries who observed him daily in later life, he was, except for the results of infantile paralysis, "robust in body and vigorous in mind. Through the seventeen years preceding his death he had no serious illness."[18]

Cultivating Manliness

Beyond body and brain, what did Groton do for Roosevelt's soul? What were its ethos and worldview? Why, specifically, the bullying that had him dancing in the corridor in his first term, laughing and pretending to like it? Peabody's goal of self-government involved self-discipline and accepting responsibility, but it also entailed the mutual policing of "proper form." The rector identified righteousness with Christian faith, virtue with democracy, and nobility with concern for the poor and disadvantaged. But these values, he insisted, needed to be invigorated with martial manliness so that the nation's future leaders would be tough enough to take up and endure the fray. Here Groton took full part in the cult that celebrated the military heroes, both medieval and modern, of the Anglo-Saxon "race."[19] Alongside plaster busts of heroes such as Homer and Caesar, Columbus, Washington, and Grant, Peabody placed in Groton's main schoolroom a replica of that bard of noble knighthood, Sir Walter Scott.[20] The school's songbook contained many martial entries, such as "The British Grenadiers," "Scotland's Burning," "Marching through Georgia," "Dixie," and "The Battle Hymn of the Republic."[21] For a more pious variety of hero, Peabody imported missionaries who were to "arouse tremendous enthusiasm in a boy's heart. Many an instance might be quoted," he claimed, "of a desire to die a martyr's death in Africa on the part of a boy whose people have no higher aim for him than social prominence or financial success in Wall Street."[22] Franklin's letters home indicate he remained immune to this particular lure, and Peabody's effort to connect martyrdom with the habits of "self-reliance and regularity" might simply have "later prove[d] useful in a business career."[23] But his intention, in season and out, was to harness wild young horses to the ends of disciplined vitality.

The fears and demands of the time gave Peabody's version of the Social Gospel some startling connections with the movement that, rightly or wrongly, is taken to be its opposite, social Darwinism.[24] At the very time that Anglo-Saxons were discovering, from Jacob Riis and others, how immigrants and the underclass lived, they adopted tribal rites of their own, not least to reassure themselves that, as the "fittest," they deserved to command everyone else.[25] During the 1890s alone, a dozen or more societies such as the Daughters of the American Revolution, the Sons of the American Revolution, the First Families of Virginia, and the St. Nicholas Society of New York organized under the nostalgic guise of bringing back the "sweet fancies of the past." In the process they were inculcating in their own young people an identity to preserve and defend.[26] Ritual reenactments of the "founders" served to remind one and all whose country the United States really was, just as stories of the noble achievements of the fathers were to steel the descendants in the values that would keep the nation deservedly theirs.

Beyond ethnicity, culture-formers like Peabody yearned to dispel the industrial class conflict that, by the mid-1890s, the moment of Roosevelt's matriculation at Groton, had been regularly roiling the national scene for twenty years. Peabody's Social Gospel measures proposed to do justice; his call to vigorous manhood was designed to keep order. Just as he had charmed the cowboys and stood up to the threats of the Arizona gunman, so now his wards would learn to toughen and maintain themselves individually and corporately with courage and rectitude. If "curious veins of casual hostility and sociable sadism" lay in Groton's initiation rites, the result was worth the price.[27] Along with Peabody, Theodore Roosevelt of "the strenuous life" and J. P. Morgan's Social Gospel pastor William S. Rainsford were simultaneously reformers and celebrants of ruggedness and combat. The few must win the struggle for survival, the reformers believed, not only for their own sakes but also for the benefit of the less fortunate. Ultimately the elite bore the white man's burden. The new sport of American football provided the favored training ground. It was debuted and perfected in the Ivy League, and when the deaths and maiming exacted there proved too scandalous, Theodore Roosevelt convened a meeting at the White House to sort out a more tolerable set of rules. Both at Groton and at Harvard the undersized Franklin went out for the team. If the crusades of imperialism, progressivism, and social Darwinism had, in retrospect, conflicting goals, they came together at the time as crusades meant to "banish gloom and anxiety in favor of an optimistic, adventurous engagement in social change." Together, concludes historian Christopher Lasch, they effected "the moral and intellectual rehabilitation of the ruling class."[28]

The Specter of Race

The racial dimension of "Anglo-Saxonism" raises the question of how our current understanding of that term—mostly in terms of "black" and "white"—figured in Roosevelt's own life and formation. First of all, "whiteness" was a status that many recent immigrants from Europe had not yet attained. They were instead cast racially "in a series of subcategorical white groupings—Celt, Slav, Hebrew, Iberic, Mediterranean, and so on," all beneath "a supreme Anglo-Saxondom."[29] Second, the dawning era might have been "progressive" for Northern whites, but it spelled the nadir of African Americans' post–Civil War fortunes. The 1896 presidential election witnessed a decisive change in northern Republican opinion about regional loyalties, at the expense of black people. William Jennings Bryan's southern and western populists were deemed to be "agitators," dangerous "disunionists," a "mob." White Southerners were no longer rebels and traitors but victims of radical agitators, just as they had been in 1860. The "bloody shirt" went into the closet, and white harmony, North and South, was called up against radical farmers and striking immigrant laborers.[30] Not accidentally, 1896 saw the Supreme Court hand down its decision in *Plessy v. Ferguson*, giving legal sanction to the system of segregation known as Jim Crow.

As Franklin Roosevelt matriculated at Groton that very year, it is no surprise that he echoed common racial epithets. Thus he wrote home that Groton "played a little micky team from the village."[31] Later he ventured an anti-Semitic pun in noting the triumphal homecoming of Admiral George Dewey ("Jewey") from his triumph in the Spanish-American War. What is more remarkable is how rarely Roosevelt indulged verbal racism. Paternalistic it might have been, but a positive and significant impression came from his dealings with Mrs. Freeman, the widow of a black Civil War drummer boy, who lived alone near Groton. In January 1899, together with his classmate Warren Motley, Franklin was appointed by the school's Missionary Society to care for her. Franklin wrote home that the two of them visited her a couple of times a week "to see that she has coal, water, etc., feed her hens if they need it, and in case of a snow-storm we are to dig her out, & put things ship-shape. It will be very pleasant as she is a dear old thing, and it will be a good occupation."[32] The ultimate proof lay in the pudding. Four decades later, in his spectacular reelection triumph of 1936, Roosevelt racked up huge majorities (70 to 80 percent) among Northern urban ethnic voters.[33] His presidency also marked the decisive turn of African Americans from the party of Lincoln to the Democratic column. In 1938 he wrote a remarkable memo to Attorney General Francis Biddle insisting that, as "the guardian of the Constitution," Biddle should test in the courts the "unreasonable restrictions" on blacks imposed by Southern states' poll taxes.[34]

The Dawn of Political Consciousness

How much of his times registered on young Roosevelt while he was still a schoolboy? His letters give no indication that he thought specifically about labor relations, much less the plight of black Americans. Yet they contain plenty of evidence that by the end of the decade his interest in politics and world affairs was growing. Franklin's parents regularly sent him the frothy *Illustrated London News* and the weekly news journal the *Great Round World*. He delighted as well in *Survey Graphic* and *Scientific American*, to which he continually referred in his letters home. By his senior year he was asking for the *New York Herald* and *Tribune* as well.[35] When Social Gospeler William Rainsford came to Groton in the fall of 1897 and talked about the recent purge of New York City's reform administration, Roosevelt pricked up his ears. "It was extremely interesting," he wrote home; Rainsford "talked in pretty strong language against the [Thomas C.] Platt & Tammany machines & especially against the *former*."[36] No doubt the speech repeated thoughts that Rainsford had expressed earlier in a critical speech to Democrats at the Cooper Union in which he told his unwilling listeners that the Platt machine was corrupt and that the income from streetcars be redirected to reduce rents and taxes.

In January 1898, when Roosevelt was not yet sixteen, he participated in a Debating Society contest over the annexation of the Hawaiian Islands, the bill for which was pending in the Senate. Roosevelt, assigned the negative side, argued that there was no more reason to annex Hawaii than Nicaragua.[37] By terms of "the Monroe Doctrine we are not only supposed to keep foreign powers from these countries but not govern them [ourselves] or own them," and he cited in support the work of putative imperialist Alfred Thayer Mahan: *The Influence of Sea Power upon History* (1890). If the navy needs a mid-Pacific coaling station, "Pearl Harbor, a port in one of the islands [already] belongs to the United States. All that is needed is a little inexpensive dredging and we shall have a coaling-station without annexation." If another is needed, "why not fit up one of the Aleutian Islands in the North[?]" We should either leave Hawaii alone or else found a republic "in which all Hawaiians shall be represented." The inhabitants of the Hawaiian Islands were not ignorant people, so why did the United States "shrink from submitting the treaty to a general vote of the inhabitants"? Because, he averred, "they would vote against it to a man." Islanders should not be annexed without their consent. In words that were prophetic of his later stance on the post–World War II era, he asked, "Why take away the nationality of a free people?" More broadly, why "should we soil our hands with colonies"? America should not meddle in the lives of peoples so different from us and who are so far away. Years later, Roosevelt as president would combine the Wilsonian idea of self-determination with Admiral Mahan's proposition that "by looking after its own self-interest, a great power can keep an unstable world in balance."[38]

A year later, in 1899, the South African War broke out, with the Boer and Orange Free State armies initially defeating the British. Now a warlike seventeen-year-old Franklin wrote exultantly to his parents, "Hurrah for the Boers! I entirely sympathize with them."[39] His parents, who were pro-British, thought otherwise and told him so. But he stuck to his guns and took up that side in a January 1900 debate at school. "I think you misunderstand my position in regard to the Boers," he wrote home; "the Boers have the side of right . . . [and] for the past ten years they have been *forced* into this war."[40] He conceded that now that full-scale war was under way, "it will be best from a humanitarian point of view for the British to win speedily and civilization will be hurried on, but I feel that the same result would surely have been obtained without war." Roosevelt's anti-imperialism extended to the Philippine Islands. The same month that the schoolboys were arguing about the Boer War, they took up the question of Philippine independence. Franklin and two friends argued for the proposition that the United States promise the Filipinos independence, although it should be done once "they are in a fit condition to receive it."[41] In sum, whatever his racial attitudes toward the domestic scene, his writing and comments as a schoolboy give early indications of Roosevelt's anticolonialism and belief in the self-determination of peoples.

Religion at Groton

The evidence concerning Christianity and the church is equally marked. Much more then than now, the school chapel and its activities were central to the life of Groton. Franklin joined the choir and thereafter frequently commented in letters home on the enjoyment he gained from it. His pleasure in singing hymns lasted for the rest of his life.[42] Groton provided some of the best visiting preachers in the church, and young Roosevelt frequently took note of them in his letters home. In May the school joined with Lawrence Academy and the Groton townspeople in four ecumenical services. After the first one Franklin attended in 1897, he reported: "We sang several hymns and a Mr. [Charles Henry] Brent of St. Stephen's Church, Boston gave us a splendid address, 'How to Pray,' from the theatre-stage. It was sort of a prayer-meeting and the house was full."[43] In June of the same year he remarked with equal enthusiasm on the preaching of William S. Rainsford; Leighton Parks of Emmanuel Church, Boston; and Social Gospeler Philo W. Sprague of Charlestown, Massachusetts, all of whom ranged from "splendid" to "good" to "very good."[44] On February 5, 1899, he was entertained by the Anglo-Catholic bishop of Vermont, Arthur C. A. Hall, who "preached a good sermon in the chapel this morning. He is a jolly old man and told us some good stories at Mr. G[ardner]'s this afternoon."[45] In May 1900 he was impressed with a "good sermon from Dean [Le Baron Russell] Briggs of Harvard." At one point during Lent in 1899, he complained humorously to his parents, "We are having a service every day this week, so I have thought of moving all my belongings to the chapel & living there for good."[46]

At the end of the previous year (1898), he was elected to the Missionary Society. On December 4 he wrote his parents: "We had my first meeting tonight, and a splendid talk by a Mr. [William J.] Batt, chaplain of the Mass. Reformatory at Concord. It was very interesting[,] all about the fine things they do for the prisoners."[47] Until the late 1890s, most of the Groton Missionary Society's efforts involved boys teaching Sunday school in local churches, raising money, holding church services, and acting as counselors at the school's summer camp for poor boys at Squam Lake. They would follow up by visiting the boys in Boston "to get to know them better . . . [and] to be able to start them in work."[48] Out of this concern grew the tradition that Groton graduates attending Harvard College would be expected to spend time on a regular basis at the Sir Galahad Club in South Boston.[49] Due to a lack of organists in the Groton area, Franklin had volunteered his services. "I have almost forgotten how to play the piano, but have been practicing on the small organ in the school-room and can play four hymns fairly decently." Once, when there were only seventeen people of farm families from the neighborhood at the service, "I drummed the organ for all it was worth & drowned out the singers, but I got on fairly well for the first time and only got off the time once in the four hymns. It was hard as I had to pump, play, and use the swells [change volume] all at the same time."[50]

His most striking involvement with the church at Groton, however, was with St. Andrew's in the town of Ayer. This was a church run for railroad workers and their families by the school's Missionary Society. Peabody himself served as rector of the parish for forty-two years, though the actual services were conducted by Groton's faculty and students, and then by a regular vicar.[51] At St. Andrew's, Franklin became very much involved with the children of the parish and in teaching Sunday school. In the fall of 1899, he announced to his parents that "our Sunday School was a howling success," to which he added the less-than-impressive qualifier, "12 children from 6 to 20 years old." He also enjoyed the association with the faculty who oversaw St. Andrew's. He got to know Clifford S. Griswold, a graduate of the Episcopal Theological School, whose physics class was "a study of beauty and thought" as well as a case study in the complementarity of religion and science. With Griswold he went to Boston to buy Christmas presents for the children.[52] At the Jordan Marsh store they walked the floor "for *two mortal hours*!!! We bought everything, toys, games, cards, books, etc. till I could hardly stand up." In January "there was a heavy crust over everything, so Mr. Griswold and I put on our skates and *skated* on the crust, 'cross' country over barbed wire fences to Groton and from there more than a mile beyond to visit the family of a member of our Sunday-School . . . it was glorious fun."[53] Such experiences in the world of adolescents played a significant part in shaping attitudes.

Central to Roosevelt's involvement with the church at Groton was the Reverend Sherrard Billings. Billings was second in command of the school. He was short, black-bearded, masculine, athletic, and popular with the boys.[54] Despite his occasionally martinet-like style, students came to him with their troubles and concerns. Billings taught Latin, led the choir, oversaw both the Missionary Society and the Debating Society, and was a good, sensitive preacher. He insisted that the boys learn citizenship, become effective public speakers, and have knowledge of world affairs. Franklin was thrown together with him in many of these activities, and the two became good friends.[55] At graduation, Roosevelt was surprised to receive the Latin Prize, since his grade in that subject in his final semester was only a B.[56] No doubt Billings's hand was in the bestowal. When FDR married in 1905, Billings wrote with obvious affection: "It has been a dream of mine for some years that you would be a man widely useful to your country and a sympathetic wife will be a great help to you on the road to realizing my dream and I am thankful and glad."[57] After FDR's nomination for president in 1932, Billings wrote how much he liked the Democratic platform and his acceptance speech. Roosevelt replied to "Mr. B" that he was "very much touched by your writing me" but had to remind his enthusiastic supporter, "Of course, I am not in the White House [yet]."[58]

How much of a role did religion at Groton School play in shaping young Roosevelt? Was it simply part of the furniture, or did it have a significant impact on his emerging character? The answer is both. To begin with, he did not question or doubt what he heard and experienced in worship at the school. If occasionally there was too much chapel, it was part of the givens of life, the order of things, its services as regular as the planets in their courses. Boys might listen and learn, or tune out, or without any fuss occupy some middle ground of feeling and aesthetic appreciation. Certainly Christianity as the inherited wisdom of the elders became a fixed element in Franklin's character. At times that tradition wore his patience, but as the end of his schooling approached, he was "feeling very blue" about leaving. His thoughts turned to the old chapel, where he had spent so much time. "They expect to be in the new cathedral the first Sunday next autumn," he mused about the new chapel under construction.[59] But he would miss the simpler building, and he never forgot the hymns. Given his interest in the navy, it is not surprising that its official hymn, "Eternal Father, Strong to Save," was a great favorite.

And then there were the strong personalities that touched his life—some permanently, others temporarily. The three founders of Groton—Peabody, Billings, and the classicist William Amory Gardner—were, like Riis and Rainsford, men of integrity who spoke with authority and on point. They possessed spiritual toughness. The ever-available Gardner taught that all subjects at Groton were sacred; they offered "plenty of chances for an alert master to instill a good deal of ethics, ay, of religion into everything taught in his class."[60] Gardner made it a rule that "boys were welcome at all times to bring forth their moral and spiritual perplexities to masters." Christianity held the truth about every person's relation to God and God's relation to the world. That faith led Gardner and the others to demand that young people gain insight into the lives of others and develop sympathy for different types of people, especially those less fortunate. Roosevelt's roster at Groton was full of Christian reformers, above all Endicott Peabody himself. In 1944, FDR's cousin Daisy Suckley wrote in her diary about the influence of the rector on Roosevelt. She found Peabody to be "a *lovely* person" and "felt his spirituality." With some surprise and delight, she noted that he "calls the P[resident] 'my boy,' and I noticed a look of real & deep happiness in the P's face, when talking to him, which he rarely has. It is a look which shows a state of mind completely devoid of anything but affection & trust & respect & a mutual understanding."[61] Peabody and the others had led him to enlarge his already active imagination, to absorb the varied human experiences that lay around him, and to respond to them with sympathy, respect, and a commitment to fair play.

Harvard

In the fall of 1900, Roosevelt moved on to Harvard College. It was a promotion from the austere regimen of Groton, but on a deeper level it was virtually a seamless change. The college recognized that Groton boys had already fulfilled the courses usually required of freshmen, so Franklin could now study whatever he wanted.[62] He lived in palatial quarters off-campus on Mt. Auburn Street in Westmorly Court, part of the "Gold Coast," and visited and dined with family friends along "Tory Row" (Brattle Street). He went to society dances in Boston's Back Bay and on Beacon Hill.[63] Girls were now in the picture, particularly his Hyde Park neighbor Mary Newbold, with whom he had grown up and who was destined to become an emancipator of American women, a nationally prominent tennis player, and one of the first women to fly an airplane. At age six, FDR had taken Mary for a drive in his pony cart; now he took her to the Harvard-Yale game. The other girls with whom Roosevelt seems to have been smitten were all from prominent Massachusetts families with long pedigrees. His fifth cousin, Eleanor, had already come up in a letter to his mother from Groton in 1898 as someone who "would go well and help to fill out chinks" at a Christmas house party.[64]

But for the rest, Groton was still all around. His friends were Groton alumni; they ate by themselves at a reserved table; there was an annual dinner of the Groton Club of Harvard; and on an ordinary evening, "the fun began" with classmates from Groton and other private schools at Sanborn's, the local billiard parlor. Sanborn's was on Massachusetts Avenue, which separated the Gold Coast elite from the larger group of high school graduates who came from more ordinary backgrounds and lived in Harvard Yard. Their segregation worried Endicott Peabody, who rightly judged that Harvard was "one of the least democratic institutions in the country."[65] In the meantime, the old school tie still bound Franklin to his alma mater. His trips back to Groton on weekends were a regular feature of his college life.[66]

That life was frenetic. "Any chronicle of Roosevelt at Harvard," writes Frank Freidel, "must inevitably bear outward resemblance to *Stover at Yale* with its hero ever striving onward and upward from one extracurricular triumph to another."[67] Roosevelt played freshman football—again unsuccessfully. In early 1901 he went out for crew with slightly more success and was again elected captain—of the third shell. The next year he stroked the second boat of the Newell Boat Club.[68] He was elected secretary of the Freshmen Glee Club, joined the Harvard Social Service Society, and gained a niche on the staff of the *Harvard Crimson* newspaper. He was also involved in the college's Memorial Society and in its Political Club. In late October 1900, he took part in a huge eight-mile torch-light parade of Harvard and MIT students on behalf of cousin Theodore for vice president. Two years later, with TR in the White House, Franklin wrote to his mother that he was "just back from a Dinner of the Mass. Republican Club, of 1000 people, at which Sec. [Leslie M.] Shaw of the Treasury and Senator [Henry Cabot] Lodge made most interesting addresses."[69]

At Harvard, Roosevelt wanted power and popularity, and the unlimited opportunities that the college afforded were the first step to getting it. The choice he made among them was telling: not club life or sports or studies but the college newspaper. From having been one among sixty-eight students who initially tried out for the *Crimson*, he ultimately became its president, and in that capacity spent an extra year at the college. Running the *Harvard Crimson* was no joke. In an article entitled "Roosevelt at Harvard" that the *New York Times* ran in July 1920, at the start of FDR's vice presidential run, Eustace Hale Ball, a classmate, wrote that the *Crimson* was "the most 'professional' college journal in any American university." With "its own linotypes and high-power presses, with its book publications, with its complete and successful business organization, from a competitively chosen staff of reporters, circulation men and advertising solicitors to its own corps of newsboys, the *Crimson* is unique."[70]

Beneath what Geoffrey Ward aptly calls the "glossy, gregarious exterior," the *Crimson* enabled Roosevelt to start broadening his views and circle of acquaintances. Over the years he was loyal to contemporaries such as Walter Russell Bowie, his coeditor, who was neither a Brahmin nor in the crowd at Sanborn's. Bowie's mother took in boarders in their home in Richmond, Virginia, and he himself had been a scholarship student at the Hill School.[71] Still, as Roosevelt's friend Tom Beal put it, "I think it doubtful whether you would consider his association with others in college as democratic and widespread." Robert W. Ruhl, a crusading journalist in Oregon, was downright hostile: "I was a Crimson editor when FDR was on the board, but saw little of him, and that little I did not much like. He impressed me as a bumptious, cocky, conceited chap with a great name but nothing much else." Ruhl also asked some of Roosevelt's contemporaries on the *Crimson* what they had thought of him, "and they said Franklin had a lot on the ball, and the nerve of a brass baboon."[72]

By 1903 Franklin was coeditor of the *Crimson* and handing out advice to incoming freshmen. His counsel was self-revealing. The freshman should "keep constantly before him" the responsibility "to be always active." The alert man would soon discover that the "opportunities are almost unlimited." Athletics, "a dozen kind—and athletic managements, literary work on the University publications," present themselves along with "philanthropic and religious work, and the many other interests that are bound to exist." The freshman should choose an activity and "go into it with all his energy." "Every man should have a wholesome horror of that happy-go-lucky state of doing nothing but enough classroom work to keep off probation." Clearly missing from the advice was a call for sustained intellectual engagement with academics. For Roosevelt it was "not so much brilliance as effort that is appreciated here—determination to accomplish something."[73]

Throughout his college years Roosevelt accepted the hierarchy and elitism of Harvard's undergraduate clubs "that he came eventually to deplore." He refused, as editor of the *Crimson*, to accede to pleas not to publish the names of students elected to elite coteries.[74] These were limited to the high-toned few, approximately 15 percent of the undergraduate body, winnowed from the masses by a multiyear selection process. Roosevelt entered the contest himself, his eyes on the peak of all peaks, the Porcellian Club, where his father and cousin Theodore had belonged. Yet FDR was blackballed, perhaps because of a scandal involving the marriage of his half nephew, Tadd, to a New York prostitute. Roosevelt confessed that his failure to make Porcellian was "the greatest disappointment he ever had."[75] Eleanor Roosevelt thought that it developed in him greater humility and concern for the underprivileged, but also contributed to his feelings of inferiority.[76] If so, it did not stop him. Moving on from the episode, says biographer Geoffrey Ward, Roosevelt "would never again exclusively rely on position and congeniality to get ahead, would no longer depend on others to notice him; instead he would do his energetic best to carve out a constituency of his own."[77] Moving forward also called on his native ability to snap back from "disappointments," as he later would from catastrophes both personal and national.

Religion at Harvard

At Harvard, Roosevelt, along with his roommate Lathrop Brown and their friends, attended local churches such as Trinity Church in Copley Square and Emmanuel Church on Newbury Street, where Groton trustee Leighton Parks was rector. Roosevelt went twice, once to an afternoon service and at another time to hear Peabody preach; on a trip to New York he visited Calvary Church, and of course Sunday chapel was a regular feature of his frequent visits to Groton. True to his obligation as a member of Groton's Missionary Society, Franklin in his freshman year went to work with the church's boys' clubs in the slums of Boston. In November 1900, he wrote his parents, "On Monday I went into the boys' Club, and helped amuse them for two hours in the evening. It is one of the poorest quarters in Boston and it is the head church mission of that part." At the boys' club affiliated with St. Andrew's mission church on Chambers Street in the old West End, he hung out with the youth, "teaching, helping out with entertainments, [and] participating in sports." The next moment in his letters he was dining with friends of his family: "My dress suit looked like a dream and was much admired."[78]

Sophomore year, Roosevelt turned his attention to Harvard's Social Service Committee (SSC). During this time it comprised over one-sixth of undergraduate students, yet—the Progressive Era with its Social Gospel being in full swing—was only one of five such organizations, the others being formed along denominational lines. All were under the umbrella of the Phillips Brooks House Association. The SSC was devoted to sending out volunteers two by two to assist at, or even run, eleven local church clubs for boys. Harvard students made friends with the boys, organized country excursions, and provided "Entertainment Troops" for them. Beyond that, the SSC collected and distributed clothing for the Seamen's Friend Society, for Boston's hospitals, for the city's famed Associated Charities, as well as for the Tuskegee Institute in Alabama and Thomas C. Walker's Hampton Institute in Virginia. SSC men who understood foreign languages gave English instruction to Portuguese, Italian, and Russian immigrants. Roosevelt raised money for the organization and was elected treasurer in 1902. Besides this thick roster of activities, SSC members heard from visiting progressive leaders such as the Episcopalian Robert A. Woods and Jacob Riis. These planted seeds of the future president's sympathies and policies; forty years later he would remember his volunteer work in a radio address about children in a democracy.[79]

Freed from required freshmen courses, Roosevelt took advantage of Harvard's elective system to load up on history, government, and economics. He took a three-course sequence surveying European history from the Roman Empire to the present, plus specialty courses on Tudor-Stuart England and German history from the Reformation to the close of the Thirty Years' War. There were quality scholars on the podium: Archibald Coolidge, whose *The United States as a World Power* (1908) argued that America could no longer remain aloof from world affairs; Edward Channing, whose *The United States of America, 1765–1865* (1896) deflated popular myths tricked out as historical fact with professional aplomb; and, most notably, visiting professor Frederick Jackson Turner, who offered a course entitled "The Development of the West." Roosevelt also armed himself for future years with the history of international law and the Federal Reserve System given by Charles Sumner Hamlin.[80] His writing and oratory benefited from a phalanx of luminaries, above all the legendary composition professor Charles Townsend Copeland—affectionately known as "Copey" to thousands of Harvard graduates, not least to FDR, who came to be counted among his many friends. Copey was renowned for being able to "fill a lecture hall to overflowing with university students of every degree of sophistication, just to hear him read." His selections ranged across British and American literature, and especially the Bible. "Copey read so imaginatively, he was so vivid himself, that students had the enjoyable feeling of seeing luminously what they had before been wholly unaware of, or had felt but vaguely."[81]

In all this, however, Roosevelt did not give back as much as he received. His report card for freshman year offered an unrelieved company of Cs.[82] At the end of sophomore year, May 1902, he failed a final examination in economics, took a make-up test, passed it, and became a friend of the teacher. This was the brilliant assistant professor Abram Piatt Andrew, who went on to become a congressman from Massachusetts and then assistant secretary of the treasury in the Taft administration. Roosevelt talked with him at length, took horseback rides with him, and visited Andrew at his home in Gloucester. Given his critical dealings with the treasury in future years, we may hope that Franklin paid better attention to such personal tutelage than he did in class.

Questions Literary and Religious

In the meantime, FDR continued to collect books. He became the librarian of two campus organizations and served on the library committee of the Harvard Union, which was open to everyone. In that connection he regularly frequented bookstores, also for personal acquisitions. Two writers of particular religious relevance appear in this number: the nineteenth-century French literary critic Charles Augustin Sainte-Beuve, who promoted the cause of liberal Catholic reformers from the highest circles of French intellectual culture, and the eighteenth-century German dramatist Gotthold Ephraim Lessing, who was destined to have an immense influence on the history of theology in both Germany and England. We know that Roosevelt read them both because he marked up the volumes in his possession.[83] While he never recorded any specifics about the influence of these two, they had a close affinity to the liberal theological tradition in which he was raised.

Roosevelt's copy of *Selected Essays from Sainte-Beuve* is signed "Franklin D. Roosevelt/Westmorely 27"; he probably read the volume for his course on modern French literature. Along the way, FDR became acquainted with such nineteenth-century eminences as Hugo, Balzac, and Chateaubriand, all of whom allied themselves with the renowned priest and writer Felicite Lamennais. Haunted by the violence and failure of the French Revolution, Lamennais was anguished by the prospect of an unending oscillation between despotism and anarchy. "The only solution was separation of Church and state and a union of the cause of Catholicism and liberty," his biographer Peter Stearns puts it; "society needed both religion and liberty." Lamennais believed that democracy's source lay in the Gospels. This was an electrifying combination. Even before she met him, George Sand called Lamennais "Christ's only apostle on earth." The leading lights of the day published in Lamennais's periodical *L'Avenir* (The Future) under its motto, God and Liberty. Sainte-Beuve even became a Catholic, temporarily, under Lamennais's influence. The lure was not the church in itself but "the Church as an agent of social renewal" in the cause of the liberation of humankind.[84] This would be a cause dear to the future president's own heart at the head of a party that attracted most of the country's Roman Catholics, whether liberal in their theology or not. FDR at least had a model of linking Christianity and democracy in their own religious lexicon.

Lessing's *Werke* came Roosevelt's way from his aunt, Annie Delano Hitch, Sara Roosevelt's older sister and a great family favorite. We do not know if Hitch read German, but we know that Roosevelt did and that he read Lessing's *Werke* somewhere in his modern European history sequence. He found much to like in the German, but not all. Lessing's was a classic life of the eighteenth-century Enlightenment. The son of a Lutheran minister, he became cool toward creeds during his theological studies at the University of Leipzig in the late 1740s. In fact, Christianity and the teachings of Christ came to seem to be two different things to him. The real gospel had existed long before the Bible: "The religion is not true because the Evangelists and Apostles taught it, but they taught it because it is true."[85] Thus, the real marrow of Christianity lay in humane values, universal brotherhood, and a basic moral code that had been overlaid with the "accretions" of theology.

Lessing's most famous play, *Nathan der Weise* (1779), laid out these themes in a parable of religious toleration and humanity's continuous "progress" toward a purer, more universal ethical code finally untethered from any specific faith tradition. Roosevelt certainly took to heart the emphasis on toleration, on development, and on interfaith cooperation. Neither for Lessing nor for Roosevelt did toleration mean indifference; it meant embracing humanity in whatever national or religious uniform it wore. The lesson would come back memorably in his famous denunciation of religious intolerance in a 1928 campaign speech on behalf of Alfred E. Smith, the first Roman Catholic to contend for the White House.[86] But the grounds of Lessing's values did not convince Roosevelt. The German dramatist substituted a philosophy of history for the central person of history, Jesus Christ, as he was described in the Bible. By proposing a "thousand thousand" years of evolution in spiritual progress, Lessing substituted for Christianity or any other actual historical religion a different framework in which thereafter these were to be understood.[87] Roosevelt did accept from Lessing's intriguing work, and from the more general liberal theological tradition of which it was a grandfather, the ideals of cosmopolitanism, toleration, and divine immanence in history. FDR understood that immanence as Providence. But by his confidence in prayer, his biblical rhetoric, and his reliance on certain scriptural texts, he remained within the "storied world" of Christianity.

Conclusion

During Roosevelt's educational years and especially at Harvard, his independence of mind increased. The boy who had stalked and mounted his own birds, maintained his stamp collection, and wrangled an extra German class out of the authorities at school constantly expanded his horizons. Choosing his own college courses, exercising responsibility for his clubs by collecting books, managing the *Crimson* and composing editorials for the betterment, as he believed, of his peers gave him purpose, satisfaction, and an outlet for his ambition. He did not work for high grades and did not receive them. His reading does not seem to have been determinative of his beliefs; Sainte-Beuve, Lessing, and others contributed to the liberal, literary atmosphere around him and so to his general mind-set but not to his core convictions. He was not an intellectual and took what he wanted from his reading. More important to him was choosing his own college courses, stroking a crew, collecting books for his club, and above all serving as editor of the *Crimson*. These broadened his contacts, with people and the world, and prepared him for the political life he would lead thereafter.

PART II

Faith

Chapter Four

Hope—Polio and the Great Depression

Franklin Roosevelt felt the lure of politics already at Harvard, but its attraction burgeoned after his graduation in 1904. So he set out to emulate the career of his kinsman Theodore Roosevelt. He married within the family, to his fifth cousin Eleanor, and at their wedding on March 17, 1905, President Theodore gave the bride away. Franklin pursued—not very hard—a law degree at Columbia and a practice on Wall Street, but his real passion was for politics. Aided by his mother's money, he campaigned for the New York State Senate in 1910 and, surprisingly, won. He immediately helped lead a mini-insurgency that shook up the powers in Albany. Another Progressive Roosevelt had launched his career.

Some observers at the time, and historians later, dismissed these early moves as attention-seeking shenanigans aimed at no agenda beyond self-promotion. Certainly, Roosevelt knew that politics was not a sport for innocents and showed a lot of bald-faced ego at this stage of his career. But he also maintained the values of the Christian faith that he had gathered from his family and his nurture at Groton School, and he received a continuing education in the progressive application of these values from his wife, Eleanor, and her circle, including Frances Perkins.

Admittedly, FDR could frustrate these idealists with his political maneuverings. He was in the grip of facts, not of theory. He knew all too well that in politics "facts" could change, and the unexpected could suddenly emerge to capsize anticipations. But even if he subscribed to no complete political philosophy, he consistently steered his course by fixed flags on the horizon of the future. The chief of those markers were faith, hope, and charity, the triumvirate that Saint Paul laid out at the conclusion of the famous thirteenth chapter of his first letter to the Corinthians. It was Roosevelt's favorite text from Scripture. At every inauguration—as governor of New York State in 1929 and 1931, and then as president in 1933, 1937, 1941, and 1945—he took the oath of office with the Bible opened to that passage.[1] The book upon which he placed his hand was a family Bible that had been printed in Holland in 1686 and that contained the record of eight generations of the Roosevelt family.[2] In the King James translation that Roosevelt knew best, the chapter reads:

> 1 Though I speak with the tongues of men and of angels, and have not charity, I am become as sounding brass, or a tinkling cymbal. 2 And though I have the gift of prophecy, and understand all mysteries, and all knowledge; and though I have all faith, so that I could remove mountains, and have not charity, I am nothing. 3 And though I bestow all my goods to feed the poor, and though I give my body to be burned, and have not charity, it profiteth me nothing. 4 Charity suffereth long, and is kind; charity envieth not; charity vaunteth not itself, is not puffed up, 5 doth not behave itself unseemly, seeketh not her own, is not easily provoked, thinketh no evil; 6 rejoiceth not in iniquity, but rejoiceth in the truth; 7 beareth all things, believeth all things, hopeth all things, endureth all things. 8 Charity never faileth; but whether there be prophecies, they shall fail; whether there be tongues, they shall cease; whether there be knowledge, it shall vanish away. 9 For we know in part, and we prophesy in part. 10 But when that which is perfect is come, then that which is in part shall be done away. 11 When I was a child, I spake as a child, I understood as a child, I thought as a child: but when I became a man, I put away childish things. 12 For now we see through a glass, darkly; but then face to face: now I know in part; but then shall I know even as I am known. 13 And now abideth faith, hope, charity, these three; but the greatest of these is charity.

Faith, hope, and charity promised a more inclusive community where greater fairness, opportunity, and equality could be realized. They marked out the trail Roosevelt meant to follow. Along that trail there would be delays and detours and bushwhacking; such obstacles were to be expected in the saber-toothed country of American politics. But Roosevelt believed his principles belonged to a providential order. He had learned that he had a part to play in that order and possessed the freedom and responsibility to play it. Progress was not inevitable, but ultimately God was on the side of those who worked in that direction. Work it was; collective and future-oriented it had to be. Roosevelt sounded that note, fittingly, in a 1936 speech at Liberty Island marking the fiftieth anniversary of the Statue of Liberty. Thinking of the hopes of the millions of immigrants who had passed that icon, Roosevelt intoned, "we are all bound together by hope of a common future."[3] As in the individual's life, so in the communal life of the people, each generation had to start where the previous one left off and strive to correct past mistakes. They had to learn to "walk" all over again. After 1921, so too did Franklin Roosevelt.

Hope amid Suffering

Christian theologians note that, of Paul's list of virtues, charity alone endures for eternity; yet, hope and faith are essential along the earthly way. Hope figures as the motor dynamic of faith out of which we can live by love. John Calvin, the godfather of early American theology, wrote, "faith believes God to be true, hope awaits the time when his truth shall be manifested; faith believes that he is our Father, hope anticipates that he will ever show himself to be a Father toward us . . . hope nourishes and sustains faith." Calvin went so far as to say that when hope is taken away, "however eloquently or elegantly we discourse concerning faith, we are convicted of having none."[4] We take up Roosevelt's religious career under the sign of hope, then, because in his fortieth year, just one year after his run for the vice presidency, Roosevelt's promising career and personal faith were cast into deep darkness for long months while hope languished.

Roosevelt apparently contracted poliomyelitis or infantile paralysis while visiting a Boy Scout camp in August 1921. On the twentieth of the month he arrived, overextended and run-down, at the family's summer home at Campobello, an island off the coast of Maine in the Bay of Fundy. Instead of resting, he kept up a feverish pace of activity that included a swim in the chilling waters of the bay. That night he experienced such intense pain that he could not bear the "feel of his pajamas or even the rustle of a breeze." Massaging his limbs only aggravated the illness and his pain. By week's end he had lost all movement below the waist. Through the sympathies of Endicott Peabody and the timely intervention of Roosevelt's able and distinguished uncle, Frederic A. Delano, the family secured the services of Dr. Robert W. Lovett, chairman of the Harvard Medical School's Infantile Paralysis Commission and author of the classic *The Treatment of Infantile Paralysis*. He examined the patient on August 25 and stopped the massage that Eleanor and others had been administering; it "will prolong hyperesthesia [abnormal sensitivity] and tenderness." More ominously Lovett added, "There is likely to be mental depression." One polio victim remembered crying out, "I can't find my body."[5]

In the days that followed, as the paralysis ebbed, the brutal and terrifying pain increased. That Roosevelt could bear. The greater agony came in days of hopelessness and fear of being marooned in a backwater. The depression that Dr. Lovett predicted indeed descended. The vigorous activist who had always been a man of projects now could not even sit up in bed, much less walk to the bathroom. Richard Thayer Goldberg, a psychologist specializing in the rehabilitation of the handicapped, gave an acute analysis of FDR's case. An "enormously ambitious politician" now faced the prospect of political powerlessness. Equally discouraging, "social acceptance of the disabled was minimal" at the time. The full impact of what had happened to him was devastating. Short of death itself, he faced the specter of chronic disability and mere survival.[6]

Roosevelt may have thought his illness was divine retribution for sins committed, not least his affair with Lucy Mercer. Eleanor had discovered it at the end of his trip to inspect World War I battle sites, and after harrowing discussions with her and his mother, Franklin had promised to mend his ways. Still, the Roosevelt marriage was never the same again, and his guilt over having betrayed Eleanor was slow to fade. Now, in addition, he had come down with a *child's* disease and "felt humiliated by his regression to a child-like dependence on others for his daily needs." When Endicott Peabody said to Eleanor that she "must have had a very anxious time," he could hardly have known about her round of changing catheters, administering enemas, and catching bits of fitful sleep on a sofa in the sick room. In the end, remarks Goldberg, Eleanor's strength of character pulled them both through. She who had a "deep need to be wanted, saved him from political oblivion." They would depend on each other for the rest of their lives.[7] Uncle Frederic A. Delano wrote with "fatherly advice": "I feel the utmost confidence that you will emerge a better and stronger man." The convalescence "will give you time for reflection and that alone is worth a good deal." While we need not "exclude the supernatural power of our Heavenly Father," Delano continued, he found "more truth than poetry in the saying, 'God helps those who help themselves.'" Delano, a formidable and neglected figure, would repeat his assistance to FDR later on in becoming "the father of New Deal planning" in 1933 and in his strong advocacy on behalf of GIs returning from World War II.[8]

Years later, in January 1944, when Roosevelt addressed the National Foundation for Infantile Paralysis, he intimated that his own struggle with the crippling disease was similar to warfare: "And just as in war," he said, "there is that subtle weapon that, more than anything else, spells victory or defeat. That weapon is morale—the morale of people who know that they are fighting 'the good fight'—that they are keeping the faith—the only faith through which civilization [or the individual] can survive—the faith that man must live to help and not destroy his fellowmen."[9] He fought the good fight on a large scale at Warm Springs, Georgia, both for himself and for others who suffered from polio and whom he inspired at his chosen place of regeneration. But he also reached out personally. When a friend and neighbor in Hyde Park, Gerald Morgan, was diagnosed in the early 1930s with cancer, he confided in Roosevelt not only about the disease but also about the "spiritual crisis" that ensued. FDR, relates Morgan's son, "inspired my father" with hope, so that "he 'got religion.'"[10]

Did Roosevelt, like Saint Paul after being blinded on the Damascus road, go "away into Arabia" for further struggle and soul-searching, "the young prince retreating into the wilderness to find salvation"? FDR had read about Paul in James Stalker's vivid biography. At Groton and elsewhere, his generation was taught to set to work on the lessons at hand, to complete the task, to hike the trail and not complain of thirst. Sara and James Roosevelt were positive, hands-on parents in this regard. "Their methods of discipline encouraged independence, initiative, mastery, and self-reliance—traits that would help him overcome the crisis of disability in middle life." He must now learn to live with withered legs, to regain mastery over life, and not to bemoan his fate. During the mid-1920s, Roosevelt not only worked to stem the tide of his own dejection but also helped others do likewise. He became kind-hearted, more patient with others and himself, less impulsive and more interactive with a wider range of social groups. Though confined to his home, through Eleanor he met women in the trade union movement. Driving his own car with hand instruments, he visited poor dirt farmers in Georgia and learned, as any politician must, to eat his butter-dipped catfish from tin plates. At Warm Springs he came to know all sorts and ages of men, women, and young people. He hired physiotherapists and local high-school boys who pushed the wheel-chairs. The other patients helped restore his innate hopefulness and good cheer. Among those around him he created a democratic spirit, considerateness, a common determination to recover, and, above all, assurance. He became as much an expert in rehabilitation as anyone else in those days.[11]

For pupil and teacher alike, the trick was to face the disease head-on, to keep experimenting with techniques to rebuild strength, and above all to not lose confidence. "Dr. Roosevelt's" active role in both helping patients at Warm Springs and founding the National Foundation for Infantile Paralysis was a significant step forward. He also started thinking about adequately funding medical care for peo-ple suffering from diseases other than polio. He made Warm Springs attractive with good food, parties, theatricals, and bridge and poker games as well as with innovative therapy. Since polio struck teenag-ers, he made it possible for young people to continue "to exercise the skills, traits, and habits . . . [of] interpersonal contact before the illness." Above all they needed to recover a sense of physical and mental self-worth, a challenge made even more difficult by having contracted the disease at a crucial stage in life. In addition to the "push boys," Roo-sevelt obtained from a nearby women's college eight girls majoring in physical science. "In a very tangible sense," writes Gallagher, "the presence of these young men and women interacting with patients helped keep Warm Springs a lively place. There was flirting, falling in love, sexual hanky-panky—and much gossip about it all."[12] Life, it was agreed, must be as nearly normal as possible.

During his 1932 campaign for president, Roosevelt delivered a re-vealing address at the Oglethorpe University commencement. In it he transposed onto a national canvas the restorative experimentation he had so sedulously pursued at Warm Springs. Into a draft speech writ-ten by Ernest K. Lindley of the *New York Herald Tribune*, FDR inserted his own words: "This country needs, and unless I mistake its temper, the country demands *bold persistent experimentation*. If it fails, admit it frankly and try another. But above all try something." Marc Shell sug-gests that the lessons Roosevelt learned in the rehabilitation of his own body and of the minds and bodies of the others at Warm Springs were what led him to attack the paralysis of the body politic. "So 'bold persistent experimentation' became the rallying cry for the New Deal."[13]

Religion and Sympathy

Throughout his own illness, declared Frances Perkins, Roosevelt "had a great strengthening of religious faith. He believed that Divine Providence had intervened to save him from total paralysis, despair, and death. His understanding of the spiritual laws of faith and of the association of man's feeble powers with God's great power must have come at this time." His was a theory of revelation compounded of pain, crisis, and exertion. "Struggling on his braces and crutches down to the end of the driveway at Hyde Park, FDR came to meet the local citizens—the mailman, the delivery boys, neighboring tenants. He met them not as lord of the manor passing in his limousine, but as a human being, visibly struggling with his problems as his neighbors struggled with theirs."[14] Through humiliation and loss he grew in stature. Between 1921 and 1924, Perkins was "instantly struck by his growth." She wrote, "The man emerged completely warmhearted, with humility of spirit and with a deeper philosophy. Having been led to the depths of trouble, he understood the problems of people in trouble."[15] According to Perkins, Roosevelt underwent "humiliating episodes of being physically helped. In these he showed courage. . . . I began to see what the great teachers of religion meant when they said humility is the greatest of virtues and that if you can't learn it, God will teach it to you by humiliation. Only so can a man be really great, and it was in these accommodations to necessity that Franklin Roosevelt began to approach the stature of humility and inner integrity which made him truly great."[16]

Others were equally struck by the alteration. He had grown to such a degree "that old friends who knew him as the debonair assistant secretary of the Navy hardly recognized him." In Akron, Ohio, Eleanor Roosevelt was asked, "Do you think your husband's illness has affected your husband's mentality?" It was a hostile question, betraying the kind of insinuations of mental damage often used by his enemies. Showing no emotion, she replied evenly, "I am glad the question was asked. The answer is Yes. Anyone who has gone through great suffering is bound to have a greater sympathy and understanding of the problems of mankind." Reports Joseph Lash, "The audience rose and gave her an ovation."[17]

Some who saw Roosevelt frequently during his illness were not as aware of change as others. Thus his son Elliott denied that there was any shift or deviation in his father resulting from his illness.[18] Whatever the case, henceforth Roosevelt would prove to be cool in crises and increasingly disciplined and confident in the business of governing. Still, like anyone else, he knew doubt. He confided such privately to his son James, as the young man helped his father to bed on election night 1932. Hoover had conceded, yet the victorious Roosevelt was afraid. Writes Frank Freidel, "as James kissed him goodnight, he revealed himself as he seldom did even within his family. Previously he had never admitted to more than a single worry, a paraplegic's fear of fire, but that night he confessed he was afraid of something else."

"Afraid of what, Pa?" James asked.

"I'm just afraid I may not have the strength to do this job. After you leave me tonight, Jimmy, I am going to pray. I am going to pray that God will help me, that he will give me the strength and the guidance to do this job and to do it right. I hope you will pray for me too, Jimmy."[19] Then the compass swung around: hope and confidence reasserted themselves. He had kept in mind his own advice as editor of the *Harvard Crimson* when he had gratuitously urged the incoming student to "keep constantly before him the responsibility to be always active."

But polio did not make a saint out of FDR. If it increased his sympathy for the poor, he could be ruthless when it came to dealing with other politicians, as he demonstrated when he ran against Wendell Willkie during the election of 1940.[20] FDR loved the political battle. He dramatically rekindled his career with the "Happy Warrior" speech nominating Alfred E. Smith for the presidency at the Democratic Convention of 1924. Although he meant the title for Smith, the crowd seemed to award it to Roosevelt himself. The *New York Times* reported, "The most popular man in the convention was Franklin D. Roosevelt. Whenever word passed around the floor that Mr. Roosevelt was about to take his seat in the New York delegation, a hush fell over the [Madison Square] Garden. On his appearance each time there was a spontaneous burst of applause."[21] From then on, his political fortune resumed its ascent. Under increasing pressure to help Smith win the presidency in 1928, Roosevelt, at first reluctantly, ran for governor of New York. Testing his faith, he took what Kenneth S. Davis calls "the blind existential leap, in his belief that this was God's intention."[22] Now he had to convince the electorate that his illness had neither destroyed his ability to govern nor cut down his chances of winning.

On October 22, Roosevelt gave a speech at Rochester in which he addressed his own illness head-on. This turned out to be most uncharacteristic; he would mention it in public only once again, near the end of his life, on March 1, 1945, when he reported to Congress on the Yalta Conference with Stalin and Churchill. He begged their pardon for speaking from his chair: "It makes it a lot easier for me not to have to carry about ten pounds of steel around on the bottom of my legs," he explained.[23] In 1928, however, it was the question of fitness, not physical discomfort, that required him to address the subject. Candidate Roosevelt admitted that polio interfered with self-reliance and prevented "useful activities," but it would not prevent him from being an effective governor. By "personal good fortune I had been able to get the very best kind of care," he continued, so that "from the physical point of view I am quite capable of going to Albany and staying there two years." He impishly added that he "could not vouch for the mental side of it."[24]

In the Rochester speech, Roosevelt placed his own disability in a larger context: the plight of crippled children and adults. There were, he declared, over one hundred thousand people in the state of New York who suffer from "infantile paralysis, tuberculosis, occupational and other accidents . . . who are seriously crippled, most of them so seriously that they are unable to live normal and useful lives." Proper treatment would make a good investment: "money spent on them by the State will come back many times through their increased productiveness." Exaggerating, he claimed that he had "seen thousands of examples of crippled adults and children, who by proper care have been restored to normal life." In his mind he compared the rehabilitation center at Warm Springs, Georgia, with the lack of therapeutics in the state of New York, where few could "afford to pay the heavy cost of obtaining proper private treatment." The most significant statement of the address dealt with the larger humanitarian issue. With children particularly in mind, Roosevelt declared, "We must come to a better realization that this care is as much a part of the duties of the local and State Governments as it is for those Governments to provide funds for the development of a child's education."[25] This was the politics of hope for those whose lives had been besieged by adverse circumstances. If the scope of his promise failed to embrace everyone equally—for instance, African Americans—the purpose remained unchanged: hope for a better future for everyone.

At Christmastime 1932, after his election to the presidency, Frances Perkins wrote FDR in a directly religious vein out of her experience as state industrial commissioner, and in view of the road awaiting him: "I incline to prayer when I think of all that the humble and lowly and hurt of this land are expecting of you. . . . Joy in the humble homes and the laughter of courage, hope and happiness on the lips of working millions . . . you dear friend are perhaps the tool for this lowly purpose."[26]

The Rhetoric of Hope

Nowhere was this inspiriting more evident than in the first inaugural address of March 4, 1933, and in the first "fireside chat" eight days later. Observers immediately remarked on the sudden change of atmosphere that swept the country with these two addresses. Roosevelt "blew hope into the deflated body of the country like a boy blowing up a balloon." It would be "difficult to exaggerate the extent of the change in national mood which took place during Franklin Roosevelt's first thirty-six hours in the White House." Roosevelt's "words carried a promise more immediate and vital than they [the American public] had known before—a promise the more breathtaking because it transcended their earlier hopes." Overnight, it was "strikingly evident" that he had restored faith and hope to the nation. The forthrightness and self-assurance of the inaugural address elicited nearly 500,000 letters and thereafter "an average of 5,000 to 8,000 a week during his long term in office." An aghast, mesmerized public at last found its voice. Again and again they thanked the president "for dispelling their fears, stiffening their courage, and rekindling their hope."[27]

The first inaugural is divided between roughly one-third "ethics," as FDR called the restoration of the values he sought, and two-thirds "action." He began by assuring Americans: "This great nation will endure as it has endured, will revive and will prosper."[28] This sentence was followed by the speech's most famous line: "the only thing we have to fear is fear itself—nameless, unreasoning, unjustified terror which paralyzes needed efforts to convert retreat into advance." The new president knew a lot about paralyzing terror, nameless, unreasoning, sudden, and unjustified fear. He too had passed through "arduous days" and had found ways to convert retreat into advance. "Having emerged from near death" himself, observed Richard Goldberg, "nothing on earth would ever seem as dangerous" to Roosevelt again.[29]

His own paralysis was a metaphor for what happened to the nation in the 1920s and 1930s. There was no ignoring the difficulties, said the new president: public morale and market values shrunken, taxes raised, the ability to pay fallen, government income curtailed, the means of exchange frozen, farmers' markets lost, family savings gone, a host unemployed while others toiled for little return—all while "plenty is at our doorstep." What this material plight demanded first, the new president boldly declared in religious vocabulary, was a cleansing of "the high seats of the temple of our civilization." That is, monetary profit had to be replaced as the lodestar on America's horizon with better, more noble social values—with "the thrill of creative effort, the joy of achievement," the moral stimulation of work done for the good of all, and the sacred trust of high public office. Political position must not be measured by false standards of "pride of place and personal profit." National confidence would thrive, he said, only on honesty, honor, faithful protection, and unselfish performance. Cynics might call this mere candle lighting. Roosevelt did just that—and in a world that had grown dark for too many people.

He was also a candle-maker. After ethics came action. "This Nation calls for action, and action now": to put people to work, to stimulate better use of land and natural resources, to redistribute population, to give farmers better prices for their products, to equip them to purchase the goods of urban industry, and to prevent foreclosures on homes and farms. The present economic paralysis and its unruly progeny, "speculation with other people's money," could be overcome only by local, state, and national governments planning for and supervising transportation, communications, banking, credits, investments, and the currency. "These are the lines of attack," Roosevelt declared. Then came a challenge to citizens themselves: "If I read the temper of our people correctly, we now realize as we have never realized before our interdependence on each other; that we cannot merely take but we must give as well; that if we go forward, we must move as a trained and loyal army willing to sacrifice for the good of a common discipline, because without such discipline no progress is made, no leadership becomes effective." But he did not censure the people. He reassured them. Do not distrust democracy, he advised. They themselves had not failed. In fact, through the democratic process they have "registered a mandate . . . [for] direct, vigorous action. They have asked for discipline and direction under leadership. They have made me the present instrument of their wishes. In the spirit of the gift I take it."

Ronald Isetti has rehearsed the biblical images in FDR's first and second inaugural addresses, showing how the New Deal was "firmly anchored in the moral-religious tradition of earlier reform movements in American history." Out of the prophetic tradition of Scripture, then very much available to Americans, Roosevelt spoke of dark days, of "withered leaves," suggesting the aftermath of a plague of locusts, of people "stricken" by adversity, of high seats, and notably of "money changers" fleeing the temple. He spoke of covenants: in the second inaugural address and elsewhere he called Americans back to the "ancient faith" and couched his appeals in the metaphors and similes of wilderness wanderings, of promised lands, of lights shining in darkness, of sowers of seeds, of Good Samaritans. Opposite them he used images of golden calves, of "savage wolves" prowling around in sheep's clothing, of palaces and "entrenched greed." By such means Roosevelt stiffened courage, restored faith, and rekindled hope. Isetti summarizes it this way: "Explanations for the Great Depression, couched only in economic terms, would not have been satisfying to a people schooled in the Bible and its stories and conditioned, for better or worse, to think of political affairs in terms of the categories of good and evil. Technical talk of the gap between production and consumption, although appropriate, would not have assuaged primordial fears, instilled hope and confidence in the future, or placed the nation in the context of a transcendent mission and purpose."[30]

Invoking labels of good and evil runs a high risk, especially if the speaker uses them to inculcate fear. Roosevelt aimed to build confidence instead. Indeed, his rhetoric on high ceremonial occasions like presidential inaugurations realized his old yen to give sermons, just as the fireside chats, in their intimacy, resembled pastoral counseling sessions. In both cases he showed the rare faculty of communicating himself to masses of people, making his words of hope relevant and believable. The voice itself was reassuring, said his friend and *New York Times* editorial writer Anne O'Hare McCormick; listeners caught his warmth and buoyancy of spirit. He was with them in the work ahead. "He did not pose as a great man. If he posed at all, it was not as somebody on an eminence, but as one who lived comfortably at all levels, a human being to whom nothing human was alien. He did not stoop and he did not climb; he was one of those completely poised persons who felt no need to play up or down to anybody."[31]

Ordinary people "felt—correctly—that he liked them and cared about them," writes Arthur M. Schlesinger Jr. "They saw him primarily in personal terms, not only as strong and effective, but as warm and understanding, carrying an authority to which they were glad to submit and a humanity in which they felt total trust."[32]

In this nexus Roosevelt appealed to a common understanding between speaker and listener of exactly how conditions were in the nation and, equally important, how they ought to be. He knew it was now his responsibility in the great economic crisis to speak with candor, honesty, and decision. To that situation he brought a quality of "long-headedness," writes Jonathan Alter, "a way of peering forward, fixing a point far away on the horizon, then tacking toward it without much worry about the day-to-day choppiness en route." This "focus on the bigger picture would serve him well."[33] Hope was thus anchored in the future, not in nostalgia for the past.[34] And now it could command all the power of office conferred upon Roosevelt by the voters; the American people "have made me the present instrument of their wishes," declared the first inaugural. But this power, the new president made clear, would be legitimate by its accordance with the right and fit ideals that pervaded the national community and constituted its social anchor. Considering the nightmare that the country was living through, FDR's first inaugural played up the rituals of legitimation by which national power was transferred. The scene at the Capitol itself, the presence of the Congress, of the Supreme Court, and of honored guests, all surrounded the occasion with the full range of official authority. The celebratory parade that followed voiced the people's assent.

Roosevelt thus had the authority to act and meant to use it. The question was, How? He pursued a combination of urgency and calm loyalty to constitutional ways. He would enforce the law—and uphold the people's right to change that law. In times of national emergency, such as on March 4, 1933, he spoke of the exercise of "broad Executive power." He would do so again after the outbreak of World War II.[35] This was a delicate balance, requiring high levels of trust that crossed Roosevelt's ability to be politically ruthless and deceptive. But he gained that trust by clearly meaning to expand rights and opportunities, especially to those who did not have them. He resolved to increase advantages for the sake of the "Forgotten Man." The government, including the Constitution and the courts, was the servant, not the master, of the public good, he reminded the people. This Hudson River aristocrat reached back to retrieve earlier norms, traditions, and democratic ways of behaving. For FDR, "government was the moral agent of community; it served society by assuming responsibility for an equitable balance of interests" between liberty and unity.[36]

In the first months of his administration, FDR brought the political process in Washington to new life. In his choice of advisers, cabinet members, and heads of agencies, he cast a wide net. There were liberal Democratic reformers, Republican agrarians, tariff reducers, social workers, fiscal conservatives, and for the time a remarkable number of African American professionals, such as Robert C. Weaver, who was assistant to Clark Foreman at the Interior Department. There were southern and western liberals and a fleet of young attorneys and academics who had been shaken by the economic collapse of the country. The potential of the New Deal excited young people with the possibilities of giving voice to the voiceless. Not since Reconstruction had the nation known and grasped so many initiatives.

Faith and the Philosophers

We can understand Roosevelt's religion better by seeing it in contrast to the doubts about religion—especially the political usefulness of religion—cast by progressive philosophers of his era. Most intellectuals of his time found the idea of any providential order baseless at best and dangerous at worst. Stuart Hampshire spoke for the first category. To him, the effective forces of history seemed to be compounded of technology, communications, and centralized political organization that had no inherent logic beyond further aggrandizement of power. Certainly, any "hope of continuing improvement" in society or morality "is now largely without evidence," declared Hampshire. Just as certainly, any such hope that might have survived could have nothing to do with divine government. Yet Hampshire noted a common, enduring regret over the "draining of moral significance from ceremonies, rituals, manners and observances which imaginatively express moral attitudes and prohibitions." Those who jettison the faith and hope that created the rituals often retain the idea that humanity has a "unique" worth, and they seek some *"rational* basis for acting *as if* human life has a value, quite beyond the value of any other natural things."[37]

The argument that providential thinking is dangerous has been best voiced by political philosopher Isaiah Berlin. His liveliest fear was of the great tyrants of his time—Hitler, Stalin, et al.—who, "infatuated with darkness, the night, the unconscious, [and] the hidden powers which reign equally within the individual soul and in external nature," proposed grand schemes of deliverance that wound up sacrificing people to the Moloch of totalitarian control. Berlin distrusted visionaries of all types, whether optimists or pessimists, Christians or Enlightenment rationalists, nineteenth-century Romantics or neo-medieval dogmatists. Fairly or unfairly, writes Alasdair MacIntyre, he insisted that the pursuit of any single moral—and consequently social—ordering that attempts to enforce "the hegemony of one set of goods over all others is bound to turn into a straitjacket and very probably a totalitarian straitjacket for the human condition." Plato's elite sages, Christian prophets, seventeenth-century metaphysicians, eighteenth-century empiricists, and nineteenth-century purveyors of progress, whether toward a transcendent goal (Hegel) or a rational society (Marx), all shared the common error of believing that the establishment of certain knowledge in the external world could be applied to politics and other domains of human behavior. The modern era's "vast new realms of scientific knowledge based on mathematical techniques" simply poured the old "dogmatic nonsense" of traditional metaphysics and theology into the new wineskins of supposedly irrefutable laws, uniformities, and expectations of a perfectly harmonious social system.[38]

Berlin didn't buy any of it. Yet he admired men and women who should have "known better" but kept calling on the morally and spiritually significant: Winston Churchill, Chaim Weizmann, Anna Akhmatova, and Franklin D. Roosevelt, whom he depicted in one of his great biographical essays.[39] The precondition of a decent, "moral" society was for Berlin, as it was for FDR, the acceptance of social and political confusion. At best, said Berlin, we can hope to minimize collisions "by promoting and preserving an uneasy equilibrium, which is constantly threatened and in constant need of repair."[40] Roosevelt would have agreed, but he held on to a divine providence that carried him much further. Political, spiritual, and intellectual discord could be overcome, he believed. Hopeful but not starry-eyed, he glimpsed on the horizon a heart of grace that, however dimly perceived, was there for all to see. For Berlin, such thinking was a magic lantern show, an illusion that had time and again proved destructive of humane community. Better to have a modest and sustained emphasis on human rights and constitutional ways of organizing society, reducing political tensions and making room for self-expression. That is why he admired the American president. While Berlin decidedly did not advocate any kind of political or ethical orthodoxy for modern society, Roosevelt found in "orthodoxy" a revelation of kindness for the poor, the uneducated, the dispossessed, and those who had lost hope. When he began his first inaugural in 1933 with the sentence "This is a day of national consecration," he did two things. He preserved the moral significance of ritual and ceremonies, and at the same time he drew people together for common purpose.

At the end of his essay "From Hope and Fear Set Free," Berlin suggested that while we may say that knowledge is good, to say that it is generally identical with freedom is questionable. The inevitable conjunction of knowledge and freedom was for him a notion "rooted in the optimistic view . . . that all good things must be compatible and that therefore freedom, order, knowledge, happiness, and a closed future must be at least compatible, and perhaps entail one another in a systematic fashion."[41] But if FDR was set free from fear, he was not "set free" from hope. He assumed a providential order that ultimately guided world events. He believed that people in positions of authority must apply themselves and be in touch with that guidance, that through faith one could "fight the good fight."[42] Roosevelt concluded that God had reached down into *his* hopelessness. Thus there was nothing left to fear, as he famously said in the first inaugural address, "but fear itself." Moral progress and the unique worth of humankind were verities. He believed that all "good things" were and *must be* compatible, and that if knowledge and freedom were not coterminous, they certainly assisted each other.

While for Roosevelt there were certain "laws" that governed politics, they were not of the supposedly modern scientific type that promised a harmonious social system. He was too good a politician to believe that they did or could. For Roosevelt, the laws of political "physics" remained permanently in place: they were the traditions of the land, the Constitution, the prerogatives of Congress and of the judiciary, the governments of the states, the power of the presidency itself, *and* the current political realities of the day. As in sports, so in politics these principles had their counterpart in the inevitability of "error in all its lurking multiplicity." The politician had better know the niceties, rules, and deceptions of the game. By knowledge, luck, skill, and daring, Roosevelt more often than not beat the odds in the political ballpark.[43] His enjoyment at winning was palpable. He committed errors when he ignored or tried to change the laws of political physics—trying to purge his party or stack the Supreme Court. Yet he maintained his faith and confidence in democracy.

End Times and Political Ends

What Christian visions of hope were open to Franklin Roosevelt? At one extreme in his day was apocalyptic, "end-times" religion; at the other extreme was utopianism. During the first half of the nineteenth century, the end-times option existed in Roosevelt's own Episcopal Church, closely connected with views of the afterlife that were fixated on heaven and hell.[44] But the growing awareness of historical development and Darwinian evolution after the Civil War made apocalyptic warnings about divine judgment seem an embarrassment. The defenders of orthodoxy turned their attention instead to the debate over the historical veracity of the Genesis creation stories in an attempt to preserve human dignity from the race's purported descent from the apes. Meanwhile, technological and economic progress made the promise of utopianism seem more plausible, especially among so well-placed and prosperous a group as Episcopalians. Yet their own Social Gospel prophets pointed out the suffering and discord attending that progress, which made social perfection a distant dream.

Within these bounds, what did FDR actually believe? First, Thomas H. Greer points out that with Adolf Hitler in mind, FDR rejected the notion of "fate." In the closing days of the 1936 campaign, he declared, "Men are not prisoners of fate, but only prisoners of their own minds. They have within themselves the power to become free at any moment." How, asks Greer, does this openness to possibilities in the future square with his reference to the "mysterious cycle of human events"? In this way: Roosevelt "*did* believe in a divine destiny, but he could not accept the thought that Hitler's New Order was part of God's plan. In other words, there could be no fate, no 'wave of the future' outside of God's testament."[45] In addition, Roosevelt shared the "millennialist dimension of Social Christianity's ideology," which maintained that it was in the nature of Christianity "to cherish the hope that the process of God's creative work is not ended, its potency not exhausted in the present visible system of things."[46] Humanity had its own responsibility and role to play in that process.

Second, FDR's eschatology fit with the larger Progressive and populist movements of the early twentieth century. Social Christians were not successful in bringing working people, the rural poor, and the urban masses themselves into their churches. They had their greatest effect only later through the influence of Social Gospelers such as Frances Perkins and Harry Hopkins, along with Roosevelt himself. Even then, capitalism endured, and forces opposing Roosevelt were unconvinced. As Paul Boyer has pointed out, among apocalyptic biblicists, "responses to the New Deal ranged from skepticism to outright hostility."[47] FDR's view of God's future for humankind was expressed in terms of social progress. In his final inaugural address, on January 20, 1945, Roosevelt recalled the words that his "old schoolmaster, Dr. Peabody," had uttered "in days that seemed to us then more secure and untroubled": "Things in life will not always run smoothly. Sometimes we will be rising toward the heights—then all will seem to reverse itself and start downward. The great fact to remember is that the trend of civilization itself is forever upward; that the line drawn through the middle of the peaks and the valleys of the centuries always has an upward trend."[48]

How that curve was to be ascended mattered to Roosevelt just as much as where it was headed. Here he provides an instructive contrast to one of the most popular utopian novels ever published in America, *Looking Backward, 2000–1887* (1887), by the reforming journalist Edward Bellamy.[49] Five different editions of the book appear in the Roosevelt library, and from the Progressive point of view there was much to like in it. Bellamy envisioned Boston in the year 2000 as a society in which the collective reorganization of wealth and industry has eradicated slums, crime, warfare, most diseases, and—wonder of wonders—advertising. Improved ethics and better social intelligence among the formerly victimized middle class have overcome an evil system based on competition. Every citizen is taken care of from the cradle to the grave. This state of affairs was not to be achieved by social action, protests, strikes, or party politics, Bellamy assured his readers, but by the quiet evolution of "common sense." Where that quality came from he left unanswered; the details of the transition were conveniently ignored. More ominous were the public rituals of mass conformity and power by which the community celebrated its solidarity. The other center of gravity was the private home. Notably, people no longer *go* to church; instead, services are piped into Back Bay lounges where worshipers sit in virtual congregations, in isolation from any group larger than a few friends. Despite having Christian overtones, Bellamy's society, as its critics pointed out, was in fact totalitarian. By contrast, Roosevelt consistently emphasized community throughout his career, the gathering of people into interdependence via families, churches, workplaces, political assemblies, and communal rituals. He envisioned a complex reformed society, not a monochromatic perfection that would in fact amount to an Isaiah Berlin nightmare.

Another volume in the Hyde Park library testified to one more side of Roosevelt's progressive faith. This was *For God and the People: Prayers of the Social Gospel Awakening*, published in 1910 by Walter Rauschenbusch, the foremost theologian of the movement.[50] Myra H. Avery, a reformer and old family friend, gave Roosevelt the book in 1931, knowing his love of published prayers. His thank-you note said "those lovely books of yours . . . gave me the greatest possible pleasure."[51] Indeed, Rauschenbusch's prayers rose high above the commonplace. They held forth a "vision of a righteous and brotherly social life" accompanied by the "triumphant chords of social hope." As James Livingston notes, Rauschenbusch did not espouse a perfect society but "*progress toward* Christianizing men and institutions."[52] In lyrical terms, *For God and the People* commended human solidarity in which individuals "are one with our fellow-men in all our needs." It set forth "the hope of seeing a divine social order established on earth," not simply waiting in heaven; the development of that order "would be the highest proof of God's saving power."[53] Rauschenbusch's "Prayer for the Cooperative Commonwealth" made a direct political appeal to the establishment of democracy at the American founding. It remained for the Founders' descendants to complete their work so that "both government and industry shall be of the people, by the people, and for the people." On that "oncoming great day of God . . . all men shall stand side by side in equal worth and real freedom."[54]

Like Endicott Peabody, Rauschenbusch decried the "luxuries that debilitate," the "accumulations of property that can never be used," and "the terrible powers of organized covetousness and institutional oppression" that had piled up during the Gilded Age. So would Roosevelt say in the aftermath of the Roaring Twenties. In his message to Congress on tax revision on June 19, 1935, FDR warned, "Great accumulations of wealth cannot be justified on the basis of personal and family security." Rather, they "amount to the perpetuation of great and undesirable concentration of control in a relatively few individuals over the employment and welfare of many." In his book of prayers, Rauschenbusch sought men and women who would bear "a striking resemblance to Jesus of Galilee," most of all in turning away from the reigning individualist-covetous type of society. The more that happened, "the more just and humane its [society's] organization becomes." Roosevelt directly echoed the sentiment at a Labor Day rally in 1938 when he explained his aim of attaining, not just for the elite but for "the rest of America—the overwhelming majority of America—a humane and modern standard of living." "Clearer every day is the one great lesson of history—the lesson taught by the Master of Galilee," FDR declared, "that the only road to peace and the only road to a happier and better civilization is the road to unity—the road called the 'Highway of Fellowship.'"[55]

The Works of Righteousness

In accord with what appeared to him to be God's testament in Jesus Christ, with confidence in the potential in all humanity, and with the conviction that progress demanded boldness on the new administration's part, Roosevelt in his inaugural address of 1933 promised "direct, vigorous action." The Social Gospel ideas of Perkins, Harry Hopkins, Henry Wallace, Eleanor Roosevelt, and their associates were about to be tested, and the question was whether they would be ground to dust or become the agent of promised change. The policies and programs implemented by the New Deal have been detailed and evaluated a hundred times. The quick tour of its highlights that follows aims not to join that list but to demonstrate how FDR put wheels on his rhetoric of hope. For these programs did impart hope to the sad, sorrowing, and anxious on the political landscape of 1933. In that, they were for Roosevelt the works of righteousness that amounted to Jesus's test of "true religion." They testified to Roosevelt's notion of progress, even of divine providence.

On March 21, 1933, the new president sent a message to Congress outlining his proposal for a Civilian Conservation Corps (CCC). It was his personal idea, and it became one of the most popular New Deal programs. It put to work three million young men aged fifteen to twenty-five for a dollar a day plus food, clothing, and lodging. Eighty camps provided by the army and hundreds of others outside of military jurisdiction gave these youth expertise, discipline, and self-esteem. "Most of them had never held full time jobs. Most of them had dropped out of school," writes their historian. "Few had any idea of a future for themselves. Many freely acknowledged that they were headed for criminal activity. They had little sense of their own abilities, much less confidence in them. The CCC gave them purposeful lives." Instead of aimlessly riding the rails, they began to believe in themselves and in the future of their country. This being a *civilian* corps, its officers could not rely on military discipline but had "to lead by persuasion and example, separating the true leaders from the martinets." Though regulations forbade it, many school buildings went up nonetheless, aided by community members who scrounged up materials and mobilized after-hours labor. By June 1937, "thirty-five hundred young men had learned to read, over one thousand had earned high school diplomas, and thirty-nine emerged with college degrees." The boys gained weight and strength through their work. Their paychecks sustained their families and helped local retailers. Americans across the country told Roosevelt, "Please, please don't close our camp. Send us another one." In the end there were nearly 2,500 in all.[56]

There were thousands of testimonials to the program's success. On top of them stands this sample of its accomplishments: 46,854 bridges; 8,065 wells and pump houses; 5,000 miles of water supply lines; 27,191 miles of fences; 4,622 fish-rearing ponds; 3,116 fire lookout-towers; 800 state parks; 46 model recreation areas with cabins, dining halls, baseball diamonds, and newly dug lakes giving access to city dwellers. In addition, three billion trees were planted and 3,462 beaches were improved. The CCC boys also worked at flood control, firefighting, and the restoration of places that had suffered hurricane and tornado damage. They built Virginia's Skyline Drive, the Blue Ridge Parkway in North Carolina, Birch Creek Camp in Montana, and the superbly acoustical Red Rocks outdoor concert theater in Denver, Colorado—to name just a few. They restored Revolutionary, Civil War, and Spanish colonial heritage memorials. "La Purisma Mission near Lompoc, California, was lovingly rebuilt brick by brick using original adobe construction. Members of the company, 'a bunch of Brooklyn toughs,' cried when they left it."[57] The experience amounted to the building blocks of human hope.

Accompanying the CCC proposal was a call to create a Federal Emergency Relief Administration (FERA) and a Public Works Administration (PWA). The former was under the supervision of Harry L. Hopkins, the latter under Interior Secretary Harold L. Ickes. Both men, often as not on bad terms personally, would stay with Roosevelt from the first day of his administrations to the last and would even go on for a time to serve Roosevelt's successor. When things went against him, Hopkins took his knocks without a murmur. He had successfully run the relief effort in the state of New York while Roosevelt was governor and so had FERA make direct grants for relief to state governors. As administrator, Hopkins moved with great speed. Inside the first year FERA had disbursed $1.5 billion and aided seventeen million people, all "with a staff of 121 persons and a monthly payroll of $22,000."[58]

Harold Ickes, by contrast, moved slowly and methodically. He was a Republican who had turned Bull Moose Progressive in support of Theodore Roosevelt in 1912. A workaholic, courageous and incorruptible, "Honest Harold" was always in the process of resigning from the administration over real and imagined slights. Roosevelt was forever charming his secretary back into the fold. PWA was the heavy lifter of New Deal organizations, hiring not the CCC's younger men but older workers for mammoth-scale projects: streets and highways, electric power projects, airports, dams, levees, canals, sewage systems, ships for the navy, and attractive housing projects in a dozen cities. Ickes maintained high standards of planning, design (often the finest Art Deco), and construction. PWA housing projects were a godsend to the poor; clean, safe, and solidly built, over a third of them were for African Americans. Ickes and Roosevelt proved to be cold-eyed judges of the worth of projects submitted to the administration. The withholding of funds in the face of violations left PWA "remarkably free of corruption."[59]

No accomplishment was more significant than the creation of the Tennessee Valley Authority (TVA). The TVA was the spectacular reforming move on FDR's part, the expansion of a single dam into a massive experiment in regional planning and improvement. The project directly benefited millions of lives across seven states, wiping out malaria, restoring the soil, implementing flood control, planting two hundred million trees, creating hundreds of thousands of acres of parks and recreation grounds, and generating power for homes and factories of industries old and new. A decade later, historian Henry Steele Commager wrote that the "success of the TVA was such a triumph as even its original proponents had scarcely dared to anticipate."[60] The hope it brought to hitherto hardscrabble folk proved contagious.

Still, as Sarah T. Phillips has shown, Roosevelt's desire to decentralize TVA administration "appeased the valley's agricultural establishment." TVA "never attempted to reach the 'bottom third'—the poorest farmers, the tenants, or the landless" who lacked the lobbying influence of the larger and better-organized Farm Bureau Federation.[61] Secretary of Agriculture Henry Wallace toured the South in 1936 and returned "shaken, horrified by what he had seen." City people, he subsequently wrote in the *New York Times Magazine*, "should be thoroughly ashamed" of the fact that a third of the farmers in the country lived "under conditions . . . much worse than the peasantry of Europe."[62] This was the country recorded in Erskine Caldwell's *Tobacco Road* (1932). Roosevelt did not own a copy of the novel, nor do we know if he ever read it, but he knew the country from his rides out of Warm Springs in the 1920s. Later he acquired Caldwell's documentary book, *You Have Seen Their Faces*, a striking volume put together in 1937 by the author and his wife, the great photographer Margaret Bourke-White.[63] FDR had seen their faces, too.

The poor were better served in the Rural Electrification Administration (REA), begun in 1935 in conjunction with the TVA. The REA set up nonprofit cooperatives to build power lines where none had before existed. At the time, only 11 percent of America's farms had electricity (in Mississippi, less than 1 percent), and so they missed out on the great leap in productivity, not to mention convenience, that electrification had brought to the cities in the 1920s. Now country people could have a share not just in refrigeration but in renewed hope.[64] It came against the entrenched opposition of the rich and powerful. Morris L. Cooke, the REA's first director, quickly realized that the most efficient course was not to operate as a relief agency but to issue low-interest loans for the construction of new power lines into electricity-starved rural areas. Utility companies already operating in these areas could rapidly extend their lines and seemed likely recipients for the loans. But their executives turned a deaf ear, and when Cooke shifted to the creation of nonprofit rural electric cooperatives that would receive the loans instead, the established companies "employed every device and dirty trick they could think of" to keep the cooperatives out and the rates high. They were outmatched, "overwhelmed for almost the first time . . . in all their long history of arrogant, exploitive chicanery."[65]

Finally, there was what George McJimsey calls "the New Deal's symbol of hope for the unemployed," the Works Progress Administration (WPA). It too came under the direction of Harry Hopkins, who in the bitterly cold winter of 1933–1934 had managed the WPA's precursor, the popular Civil Works Administration (CWA). From November through March, CWA put 4.25 million people to work in blue-collar jobs of constructing roads, sewers, and public buildings, and white-collar jobs such as editing, translating, creating public art, and producing archives. These workers did not get a humiliating handout; they got cash for their work at the prevailing minimum wage. Checks were dispensed by the Veterans Administration, the only organization with a national reach. Within its first two weeks of operation, the efficient Hopkins had seen pay envelopes go out to eight hundred thousand workers.[66]

The WPA came into being a year later. The nation's continuing economic crisis dispelled any question of balanced budgets or "individualism" versus government involvement. The president sought to go beyond the unrestorative dole and, by means of an appropriation of $4.8 billion, to put the 18 million unemployed back to work. This was the opening wedge of the New Deal's lasting legacy. Socially, FDR wanted security; economically, regulation; and physically, planned development. As historian David Kennedy put it, "Roosevelt now sought not simply recovery but a new framework for American life, something 'totally other' than what had gone before." Overall, he determined to impart to "ordinary Americans at least some measure of the kind of predictability to their lives that was the birthright of the Roosevelts and the class of patrician squires to which they belonged."[67] The WPA would implement a broad program of regional planning by which the Hudson Valley squire, with his country idealism, sought to return people to the land. Upgraded rural communities would add industrial components to attract people from overcrowded cities. Electric power would improve rural homes and farms; dams would control floods; restorative forestry and scientific crop rotation would stop soil erosion. Other projects would reclaim blighted areas both in the countryside and in the nation's urban slums. Over the next seven years, the WPA employed 8.5 million people (20 percent of the labor force). Three million signed on in the first year, 90 percent of them off the relief rolls. Unlike the CCC, the WPA did not train workers but made use of the skills they already possessed.

Project approval rested with the Works Allotment Division, chaired by the ever-suspicious Harold Ickes alongside the "spendthrift" (in Ickes's view) Harry Hopkins, who as administrator wanted to decentralize oversight of the actual operations. Local people were to provide the projects and supervise the work, and speed was of the essence. Hopkins also provided employment for people in the arts, theater, music, and writing. The Federal Writers' Project built pride in the various states and territories through the publication of the American Guide Series. These fifty-five fat volumes were, as Hopkins put it, designed "primarily to give useful employment to needy writers and research workers." Recognizing that the nation possessed a wealth of knowledge about local histories, ethnic groups, industry, farms, folklore, education, religion, architecture, the arts, roads, and cities, the project "sought to create a comprehensive portrait of America." Never before had the country undertaken such an enterprise. "The result," Hopkins wrote in an explanatory page, "is a collective work to which all the writers and research workers contributed according to their talents." The end product gave the writers pride in what they had accomplished; it also gave readers pride in what they learned about their communities and states.[68]

Historians have been divided in their evaluation of this undertaking. "In the end the WPA proved itself a dynamic force," reads a positive assessment. "Roosevelt's leadership plus the imagination and drive of Hopkins and his staff revolutionized the national government's role in aiding the unemployed." They provided "an unprecedented approach to an economic crisis of unprecedented proportions." Yet even in its heyday, the same historian says on the same page, the WPA "was little more than a palliative, reaching barely one third of the unemployed. Its contribution to economic recovery was negligible." The program's "improvised nature, squabbles and compromises with organized labor, congressional restrictions, uncertain funding, and external patronage pressures encouraged inefficiencies and invited public skepticism."[69] Congress made the WPA responsible for its conduct to the president; thereby it promised to provide ammunition to Roosevelt's now-vocal enemies. They did not disappoint. Most of the time, accusations centered on workers seen leaning on their shovels.

In retrospect, the initial cooperation that Roosevelt sought between conflicting interests during the Depression proved elusive. The profit motive, American competitiveness, and "rugged individualism" worked against his hopes of drawing together the larger social groups and interests in the nation once the immediate crisis of early 1933 had passed. Roosevelt wanted "fair" competition, "reasonable" prices, "living" wages, and voluntary cooperation; above all, he sought what was "democratic." Instead, he ran up against the particular interests of major blocs: farmers, labor unions, small businesses, consumers, and the owners and operators of major industries. Beyond everyone's recognition of the need for action, the interests of these groups of citizens hardly coincided. Farmers were generally opposed to labor unions, to government spending, and to relief in general. Big business complained of government regulation by the National Recovery Administration (NRA) initiated in 1933 to expand the economy and to control production, fix prices, and oversee working conditions by means of voluntary codes. Small businesses complained that the NRA in fact promoted monopolies. Farm policy within the administration was divided between those who wanted to restrict production to drive up prices and those who wanted high tariffs to protect domestic pricing along with export subsidies to help "dump" surplus agricultural products abroad at a low price. Community builders wished to integrate town and country by "developing a shared awareness of the region's peculiar needs." They came up against rural suspicion of urban culture. At the same time, the countervailing forces of mechanized and chemically dependent agriculture were transforming family farms into business enterprises. At base, self-reliance conflicted with the need for greater efficiency in a modern democracy.[70]

Then, too, the president's own mind was at first divided. On the one hand, there was his personal audacity (using over two-thirds of his own fortune, he had purchased Warm Springs for $200,000 in 1926).[71] On the other hand stood his Dutch thrift. In 1932 he campaigned on the platform of a balanced budget, and even in the busiest years of New Deal legislation he chafed against the prospect of government waste and welfare dependency. Fatefully, in April 1937 he informed Congress that he would cut back on all public works programs in an effort to restore "business confidence." The results were disastrous. When in

1938 he renewed his call for deficit spending, Secretary of the Treasury Henry Morgenthau objected. In the light of their long personal friendship, it was a painful moment when the president slammed his hand down on the table and demanded the change. The confrontation left Morgenthau "almost physically ill," but he finally went along.[72]

Yet Roosevelt lived up to the promise of his second inaugural address of January 20, 1937. He wanted the abundance of America to be "translated into a spreading volume of human comforts hitherto unknown." He wanted the "lowest standard of living . . . raised far above the level of mere subsistence." He wanted people to have their chance, and with it a richer life in every sense of the term. He wanted the restoration of hope through difficulty. He had experienced that personally. He inspired others to the same possibility, and did his best to make it plausible.[73]

Chapter Five

Charity—the Cooperative Commonwealth

Franklin Roosevelt's three Christian principles were faith, hope, and charity. Hope served as his leading theme from his fall to polio in 1921 through the first phase of the New Deal. Then charity took over, defining the ideal structure for reform that Roosevelt hoped to implement. Faith would emerge more prominently in the grim years leading into World War II, 1938–1942. But hope was never left behind. It provided the enduring inspiration for Roosevelt and the leadership he sought to lend. He would need it, for in designing a new deal for the American people, Roosevelt was expanding upon the conventional understanding of Christian love and expanding his own "idea of social welfare into the concept of *social justice*."[1] He knew his Bible—and his Greek. His job was to draw the connection between that knowledge and the American scene he faced at the beginning of his presidency, and to convey the resulting mandate convincingly to Congress and the electorate.

Traditionally charity—*charis*—stood for the grace or loving-kindness of God toward humanity. Christians find this quality preeminently in the life and teaching of Jesus Christ, particularly in his death and resurrection, charity's highest manifestation. "Greater love has no one than this," said Jesus, "to lay down one's life for one's friends" (John 15:13). At the heart of God's grace is love—in the Greek, *agapē*—of which *charis* was the expression; modern versions of the New Testament substitute the word "love" for the King James's "charity." It holds both priority and primacy in the lexicon of Christian virtues. Paul himself, in his famous discourse on the subject, declared love to be greater than either faith or hope. For Paul, love as *agapē* had a specific meaning that is generally not understood today. Ordinary friendship, affection for children, and erotic relationships had their own words in the Greek; *agapē* was distinguished by self-giving, by seeking not its own welfare but that of others, enemies as well as friends. Such love was generous, uncalculating, and benevolent, and on the Christian understanding, rooted in the undeserved graciousness of God. The briefest, most elegant description of *agapē* is found in 1 Corinthians 13:4–8: "Love is patient and kind; love is not jealous or boastful; it is not arrogant or rude. Love does not insist on its own way; it is not irritable or resentful; it does not rejoice at wrong, but rejoices in the right. Love bears all things, believes all things, hopes all things, endures all things. Love never ends" (RSV).

Paul sought to extend this graciousness to human relations among and between Christians. *Agapē*, whether translated as "love" (which William Tyndale used in his primal English translation of the New Testament, 1525) or as "charity" (from *caritas* in the early fifth-century Latin Vulgate of Jerome), entails far more than the almsgiving it had come to mean in Roosevelt's youth, even though the term's connection with "charitable institutions" is obvious. It involves fundamental, all-encompassing attitudes and dispositions. And it hardly comported with the prevailing assumptions and practices of American politics as Roosevelt encountered them. His great task was to convey the religious ideal through the political system. It would take all his energy, drive, and imagination.

Love as a Social Ethic

Throughout his formative years, Roosevelt was familiar enough with the concept of charity from reading his Bible and attending church services. Every year, on the last Sunday before Ash Wednesday and the beginning of Lent, whether at St. James' Church, Hyde Park, or in the Groton School chapel, the passage from 1 Corinthians 13 was read aloud as the first lesson from the Bible for the day's worship. Outside the sanctuary, however, "charity" had come to signify a lesser thing: the annual giving of Thanksgiving and Christmas Day baskets of food to the poor. It was associated with the noblesse oblige of the wealthy. While such donations might mean the difference between hunger and holiday for many, some preachers and commentaries of the time tried to recover the term's broader, more complex meaning.[2] Charity was to be discerned on three fronts, they said: in God's love toward humanity; in human love toward God; and in self-giving love toward others. This third meaning involved a wider fellow-feeling and a greater liberality than Christmas baskets of food.

Such "fellow feeling" was key to Roosevelt's New Deal goals and proposal. But these new departures rested in his thinking on old American verities. His first inaugural address invoked "the simple rules of human conduct [that] we always go back to" and "the clear consciousness of seeking old and precious moral values."[3] Abraham Lincoln's "with malice toward none, with charity for all" illustrates the meaning perfectly, but Roosevelt went further and rooted charity, as Lincoln did not, in the "lofty teachings of the Master." He quoted with approval Thomas Jefferson's assessment of Jesus, who, the sage of Monticello remarked, "pushed His scrutinies into the heart of man; erected His tribunal in the region of His thoughts, and purified the waters at the fountainhead."[4] Even if Jefferson the rationalist did not affirm the divinity of Christ, Jesus functioned for him, according to Hans Frei, as "a point of crucial integration between the contents of his imagination and the moral life of the everyday world."[5] Roosevelt disagreed with Jefferson's premise but fully shared his application.

Jefferson, of course, had subjected the Bible to draconian editing, literally cutting out of the text anything that conflicted with his standards of reason. That included Saint Paul's epistles. His example, if not his method, was followed exponentially over the next 150 years. None of this appeared to bother FDR. Once, when Eleanor "expressed cynical disbelief" about the Spiritualists' contention that they could carry on conversations with the dead, he replied, "I think it is unwise to say you do not believe in anything when you can't prove that it is either true or untrue. There is so much in the world which is always new in the way of discoveries that it is wiser to say that there may be spiritual things which we are simply unable now to fathom. Therefore I am interested [in] and have respect for whatever people believe, even if I cannot understand their belief or share their expectations."[6]

Nor were his insights into the word "charity" remarkable. They had been around for a long time, perhaps most notably in the American context in the founding document of the Puritan colony of Massachusetts Bay. Its first governor, John Winthrop, entitled his address "A Model of Christian Charity." Americans remember it today for its concluding promise (actually, just as much a warning in Winthrop's mind) that the colony would be a "city on a hill." Roosevelt never invoked that phrase. Instead, he made the principal theme of Winthrop's speech—that the colonists prioritize their neighbors' well-being, that they sacrifice their "superfluities" (luxuries) for others' "necessities"— the core principle of the New Deal.

Biblical commentators and expositors of Roosevelt's day were well aware of the meaning of charity as *agapē*. Episcopal clergy read such sources in preparing sermons; so did schoolmasters such as Endicott Peabody in getting ready to teach his students. F. W. Farrar, an English popularizer of Paul's epistles, noted that sixteenth-century English reformers such as Matthew Tyndale, Thomas Cranmer, and the translators of the ever-popular Geneva Bible had used the term "love" for *agapē* in the 1 Corinthians passage, and so applauded the "great gain" made when the Revised Standard Version "restored to this passage the word 'love'" instead of the King James Version's "charity."[7] Other commentators agreed with Farrar. H. L. Gouge taught that *agapē* "is the love that leads us to sacrifice ourselves to others, as contrasted with the love that desires to appropriate to ourselves things or persons outside us."[8] Gouge and similar preachers were beginning to tie love to social concern and not just to individual piety. They needed to.

Earlier nineteenth-century commentators had tended to equate charity with piety and personal righteousness, waxing sentimental in the process. They often quoted bad poetry. They promised that "faith will become ever more intense, hope ever brighter, and love, the sustainer of both, ever more deep and energizing." The result would be an internal flame inextinguishable "even to the last sigh" of death. Despite the crossfire of Jesus's own life as narrated in the Gospels, many late nineteenth-century expositors saw love for God as "the *passive* principle" that predominates in faith and in hope.[9] Farrar and others thus disagreed by casting love toward God as a dynamic principle. Jesus, they averred, was a figure not simply for private contemplation but for public replication. *Agapē* led to action. It was not an aloof "noble pride" but "an aggressive form of goodness." In a more communal and less private faith, "love sends us out after our fellows" in concern for their welfare, said Thomas Edwards.[10] Moreover, it binds its participants in mutual recognition as members one of another. Farrar looked with a jaundiced eye at sectarian zealots who forgot this lesson. "The Protestant damns the Catholic," chided this Anglican clergyman, while his own "Church sneers at Dissent, and Dissent at the Church, and all agree in consigning pagans and heathen of every grade to nethermost perdition."[11]

Franklin Roosevelt was in Farrar's camp. He thought primarily in terms of community-centered Christianity and service to others rather than in terms of either personal or denominational piety. In extemporaneous remarks at the Hyde Park Methodist Church in September 1933, he advised "that in our religious worship we should work together instead of flying off on different tangents and different angles, pulling apart instead of pulling together as a unified whole." He noted approvingly that there had been "a splendid change" and that ministers from different churches were meeting with each other "to help solve community problems together."[12] Such attitudes permeated the liberal theological and Social Gospel atmosphere to which the young Roosevelt was exposed. They would lead him to assert in a radio address in February 1936 that against the threat of unbelief, "you and I must reach across the lines between our creeds, clasp hands, and make common cause." He lamented the eternal trick of the demagogue, who espouses "doctrines that set group against group, faith against faith, race against race, class against class, fanning the fires of hatred in men too despondent, too desperate to think for themselves."[13] It was toxic for church and state.

It was toxic for the world too. In his first State of the Union address after the outbreak of World War II, Roosevelt repudiated those who used "rabble-rousing slogans on which dictators could ride to power."[14] Five days later, at a Jackson Day Dinner, he noted that the devil "can quote past statesmen as readily as he can quote Scripture, in order to prove his purpose."[15] Instead, Roosevelt consistently sought to restore the simplest meanings of basic texts. In extemporaneous remarks to Protestant ministers in 1938, he summarized the goals of his administration with a primal appeal: "We call what we have been doing 'human security' and 'social justice.' In the last analysis all of those terms can be described by one word; and that is 'Christianity.'"[16] The Christianity, to be sure, of the liberal "Protestant establishment" in which he had been born and reared. Until the mid-1960s, it thought of itself as representing the aspirations not only of the people in its pews but of the nation itself. The evangelicals, fundamentalists, holiness churches, and Pentecostals who would try to seize custody of the culture in the last third of the century were not yet in the establishment's sights.

Love as Political Goal

The controlling assumption of the New Deal, to Roosevelt's mind, was that *agapē*'s "kindly touch of human sympathy" and the efforts of private charities and social-services agencies must now be supplemented by the action of government at all levels—national, state, and local—to overcome the effects of mass unemployment.[17] He took justice a step beyond the Progressive Era's voluntary organizations for awakening conscience. By the end of his presidency, he was calling for a new bill of rights that would be implemented by the government itself. Justice demanded that the nation as a whole discharge the fresh obligations to which its citizens were now declared to be entitled.

Next to 1 Corinthians 13, FDR loved Jesus's Sermon on the Mount as recorded in Matthew 5–7. In January 1938, amid growing doubt and uncertainty abroad, he wrote to Methodist bishop Ernest Lynn Waldorf of the "need to return to religion . . . as exemplified in the Sermon on the Mount."[18] His domestic legislation sought to implement the call to justice laid out in one of the Beatitudes early in the sermon: "Blessed are they which are persecuted for righteousness' sake: for theirs is the kingdom of heaven" (Matt. 5:10 KJV).[19] On this verse, philosopher Nicholas Wolterstorff argues that the "word translated as 'righteousness' is in the Greek original *'dikaiosune,'*" which would better be translated as "justice." It is astonishing, Wolterstorff observes, that "translators were not struck by the oddity of someone being persecuted because he is righteous. My own reading of human affairs is that righteous people are either admired or ignored, not persecuted; people who pursue justice are the ones who get in trouble." In our day, "righteousness" has come to connote more a trait of personal character, often suggestive of *self*-righteousness, Wolterstorff observes; it did in Roosevelt's day, too. Justice, by contrast, "refers to an interpersonal situation; it is present when persons are related to each other in a certain way . . . the concept of the virtue of justice presupposes the concept of those social relationships that are just."[20] Roosevelt aimed at just that sort of justice.

He outlined that aim most boldly, and with direct reference to 1 Corinthians 13, in his speech accepting renomination for the presidency on June 27, 1936, at Franklin Field in Philadelphia. It proved to be one of the most memorable events in his presidency, a speech that echoed long after he himself had passed from the scene. Some one hundred thousand people heard it live, and millions more listened in by radio. The convention organizers had built up a sense of anticipation perhaps unmatched in American political history. A sixty-piece military band played patriotic music as people gathered in their seats in the stadium. The Philadelphia Symphony Orchestra under Leopold Stokowski lent a touch of class. Metropolitan Opera star Lily Pons sang (quite incongruously, as it turned out) Sir Henry Bishop's "Lo, Here the Gentle Lark." Journalist Raymond Clapper noted the atmosphere: "Something had happened to that audience. It had been lifted, not to a cheap political emotional pitch, but to something finer. It was ready for Roosevelt."[21]

But a near calamity almost cut the occasion short. Just before 10 p.m., Roosevelt's limousine circled the stadium and stopped at the speaker's stand. The president was helped out of the car, stood erect, and began his troublesome and awkward way to the lectern. As usual, he "walked" on the arm of his son James as the orchestra played "Hail to the Chief." The applause was thunderous. Roosevelt tried to shake hands with well-wishers as he moved along to the podium. Suddenly he was jostled, lost his ever-precarious balance, and fell. The Secret Service chief, Mike Reilly, managed to get his shoulder under the president's body before it hit the ground, but the pages of the speech scattered everywhere. Immediately Roosevelt was surrounded by his entourage, and they went to work: the brace on his leg that had come undone was snapped back into place, his clothes brushed off, his tie straightened. Obviously shaken, the president murmured, "And keep your feet off those damned sheets." Later he confessed, "It was the most frightful five minutes of my life."[22] The white-bearded poet Edwin Markham, whose hand FDR had tried to reach, was sobbing; the president stopped, smiled, and pressed the old man's arm reassuringly. At the lectern, as the applause roared up at him, FDR got his pages in order. He was about to summon the nation to "a war for the survival of democracy."[23]

The speech began with his thanks to all Americans who "have sustained me in my task" over his first term in office. People had rallied together to "achieve recovery and destroy abuses." Above all, "my friends, we have won against the most dangerous of our foes. We have conquered fear." But then, as he turned to the prospects of a second term, his tone shifted to fighting words. The "war for the survival of democracy" would be a war on "the economic royalists" who had abducted the nation for their own gain. It became unmistakably clear, as

Cass R. Sunstein points out, that the president was "seeking change of the most fundamental kind." Roosevelt declared 1936 a year equal in importance to 1776. Political tyranny had been wiped out in Philadelphia in July 1776, he reminded the gathering, but since then "a new challenge had arisen in the form of economic powers that 'sought to regiment the people, their labor, and their property.'" America had fallen under a "new industrial dictatorship" with "an almost complete control over other people's money, other people's labor—other people's lives." Like the British in 1776, the "royalists" of the twentieth century wrapped themselves in the flag and the Constitution. Yet it was not the Declaration of Independence's laws of nature and of nature's God that had erected this oppressive order, Roosevelt thundered; rather, it had been built by the current laws of the land. He meant to change those laws.

In that effort he would reawaken the country to the Founders' self-evident truths and inalienable rights, but to these propositions he added another: "Today we stand committed to the proposition that freedom is no half-and-half affair. If the average citizen is guaranteed equal opportunity in the polling place, he must have equal opportunity in the market place." That citizen has a right to an "opportunity to make a living—a living decent according to the standard of the time, a living which gives man not only enough to live by, but something to live for." Government must protect and extend that right: "Government in a modern civilization has certain inescapable obligations to its citizens, among which are protection of the family and the home, the establishment of a democracy of opportunity, and aid to those overtaken by disaster."

Having dealt with his opponents and his essential agenda, Roosevelt pivoted once more, now to his favorite line from Saint Paul. "We do not see faith, hope and charity as unattainable ideals," he declared, "but we use them as stout supports of a Nation fighting the fight for freedom in a modern civilization." For unlikely as it might seem, "it has been brought home to us that the only effective guide for the safety of this most worldly of worlds, the greatest guide of all, is moral principle." He turned the Pauline triad into grounds for political action:

Faith—in the soundness of democracy in the midst of dictatorships.

Hope—renewed because we know so well the progress we have made.

Charity—in the true spirit of that grand old word. For "charity" literally translated from the original means love, the love that understands, that does not merely share the wealth of the giver, but in true sympathy and wisdom helps men to help themselves.

Answering the high and rising tide of criticisms about "soulless big government," Roosevelt lined out a high ideal of his own: "We seek not merely to make Government a mechanical implement, but to give it the vibrant personal character that is the very embodiment of human charity." It would be something of a secular church, with goals of redemption and the venerable civic virtue of courage: "We are poor indeed if this Nation cannot afford to lift from every recess of American life the dread fear of the unemployed that they are not needed in the world. We cannot afford to accumulate a deficit in the books of human fortitude."

There followed his memorable peroration, sounding the theological virtue of love: "Governments can err, Presidents do make mistakes, but the immortal Dante tells us that divine justice weighs the sins of the cold-blooded and the sins of the warm-hearted in different scales. Better the occasional faults of a Government that lives in a spirit of charity than the consistent omissions of a Government frozen in the ice of its own indifference."

He concluded on the unmistakable note of a collective religious calling: "There is a mysterious cycle in human events. To some generations much is given. Of other generations much is expected. This generation of Americans has a rendezvous with destiny." That destiny started at home, where "in the place of the palace of privilege we seek to build a temple out of faith and hope and charity." But it embraced the whole world. In many lands people had lost their freedom or grown "too weary" to carry on the fight to preserve it. To that Roosevelt declared: "I believe in my heart that only our success can stir their ancient hope. They begin to know that here in America we are waging a great and successful war. It is not alone a war against want and destitution and economic demoralization. It is more than that; it is a war for the survival of democracy. We are fighting to save a great and precious form of government for ourselves and for the world."

There Roosevelt ended, to thunderous applause. As the presidential car was leaving the field, the band struck up the Democratic marching song, "Happy Days Are Here Again."[24] "I think [the address] was the greatest political speech I have ever heard," wrote Secretary of the Interior Harold L. Ickes. "It was really a strong and moving statement of the fundamental principles underlying our politics today, and he put the issues so clearly and so strongly that I do not know how anyone can fail to understand them." Two days later Ickes added that the president's address had "created a profound impression in the country."[25]

Translating Love into Policy

FDR would return to his three principles from Paul both privately and publicly on later occasions. For the immediate task he had to translate the call of charity into proposals for domestic policy. He had to do so in the face of shrill and ceaseless protests that, on the one hand, he was subverting the Constitution and that, on the other, his bald use of power violated the true spirit of religion. He answered in a way that his longtime critic but eventual ally Reinhold Niebuhr, the nation's foremost theological ethicist, finally commended. Power and evil were not the same thing, and in no society, especially a modern industrial one, would the use of power be suspended. Power had to be deployed toward the ends of justice, which in this world is the best fulfillment of the law of love possible for collective matters.

What specific values and policies sprang from his noble ideal of charity? The answer started to emerge already in the early 1930s when, as governor of New York, Roosevelt sought to enhance security, peace, education, recreation, and a chance to succeed in life for as many as possible. On these priorities he was consistent. Near the start of his second term as president, he listed his objectives concretely: decent hours and wages; a chance for "adequate recreation, better housing, sounder health"; reasonable business profits with protection against unfair competition and with fair prices for consumers; "planning and use of natural resources for the benefit of average men and women"; and finally, security against the hardships of old age, unexpected unemployment, criminality, and war. His vision required, first of all, "a decent floor for those at the bottom," and second, security and safety for American laborers on farms and in factories.[26] Individuals had a right to proper working conditions, unemployment insurance, and medical help against accidents on the job. At the same time, it was essential to strengthen social ties, community involvement, reciprocity among groups of friends, and larger friendships across boundaries of division.

Historians David M. Kennedy and Jonathan Alter agree that the key word in all this program was "security": "I place the security of the men, women, and children of the Nation first," Roosevelt declared. In the early days of the New Deal, he had to bend every effort toward recovery from economic paralysis and relief for the unemployed. But by 1935, says Kennedy, instead of these alone or "a later generation's social and political holy grail" of "perpetual economic growth," Roosevelt sought "a new framework for American life, something 'totally other' than what had gone before." He wanted "the steadying hand of 'that organized control we call government' to sustain balance and equity and orderliness throughout American society." Roosevelt's was a Progressive Era "dream of wringing order out of chaos, seeking mastery rather than accepting drift, imparting to ordinary Americans at least some measure . . . of predictability." Safeguarding people remained his preeminent goal. "You and I agree that security is our greatest need," he said in a fireside chat on April 14, 1938. "Therefore, I am determined to do all in my power to help you attain that security."[27] This would require special measures for the people who start life at the bottom, who become "trapped" there and never make it upward. "We are going to make a country," he remarked to Frances Perkins, "in which no one is left out."[28]

He traced the evolution of his own thinking on these matters in a speech to the Young Democratic Clubs of America in 1935. In the first decade of the present century, he recalled, the mood in America was one of exultation and achievement under the spell of "rugged individualism." Leaders assumed that this was guaranteed to bring fullness to all the people eventually "and that the grim specter of insecurity and want among the great masses would never haunt this land of plenty as it had visited other portions of the world." He and others of the privileged class had accepted uncritically their elders' talk of the "perfection of America." "I did not know then," the president continued (not altogether truthfully, for he knew better from Peabody, Riis, Perkins, Eleanor Roosevelt, and his own observations), "of the lack of opportunity, the lack of education, the lack of many of the essential needs of our people who lived not alone in the slums of the great cities and in the forgotten corners of rural America but even under the very noses of those who had advantages and the powers of Government of those days."

But since those illusory days, Roosevelt declared, cruel suffering, stark necessity, and grave economic distress had taught Americans that no social class can "safeguard its own security" independent of the general community. The "dream of the golden ladder—each individual for himself"—has been replaced by cooperation.

He commended the young Americans before him for placing emphasis on "sufficiency of life, rather than on a plethora of riches." They were aptly looking for basic safety for themselves and their families. They wanted a communal effort. To realize those hopes, the economic structure of the country must be saved from "confusion, destruction and paralysis." Through employees' awareness of the inner workings of corporations, through collective bargaining, and by means of "adequate public protection of the rights of the investing public," the rising generation's objectives could be achieved. In 1911, Roosevelt remembered, he had worked in the New York state legislature for sanitation, for industrial protection, "for preventing child labor, and night work for women," for factory inspection, and for workmen's compensation. Those in the Progressive movement, he recalled, were opposed by many of the same people who, in 1935, "are crying aloud about the socialism involved in social security legislation, in bank deposit insurance, in farm credit, in the saving of homes, in the protection of investors and the regulation of public utilities."[29]

In his concern for security, Roosevelt was not always consistent. In the early days of his first administration he had threatened to veto the Glass-Steagall Bill that gave the newly established Federal Deposit Insurance Corporation power to guarantee bank deposits up to $2,500; in 1933, over 95 percent of all individual accounts were under that amount. When it became clear that congressional approval was overwhelming, he acquiesced.[30] On the other hand, the concern for security led to the creation of two of the most significant bills of the New Deal era. The first established the Home Owner's Loan Corporation (HOLC) to protect small homeowners from foreclosure. Only recently recognized by Jean Edward Smith as a "lifesaver for millions of Americans" and the initiator of a housing boom that continued until 2007, the HOLC had by 1936 made more than one million loans totaling $3.1 billion. The services of this lesser New Deal agency "struck so close to home that parents passed on to their children the story of how Franklin Roosevelt saved the very house they lived in."[31]

The second bill, "the most important single piece of social legislation in all American history," was fittingly entitled the Social Security
Act of 1935.[32] Roosevelt's words signing the act into law were simple;
it would "give some measure of protection to the average citizen and
to his family against the loss of a job and against a poverty-ridden old
age." Still, the law was but the "cornerstone of a structure which is . . .
by no means complete." Security required prosperity, and prosperity
required some redistribution of income. From day one Roosevelt en-
deavored to increase the purchasing power of the impoverished. As
the new president stated in his first inaugural address, not only did
the country have a "host of unemployed citizens," but also "an equally
great number toil with little return." He proclaimed the same theme
two months later before the Chamber of Commerce.[33] The "greatest
primary task is," he said, putting "people to work . . . and making income balance outgo." It was a theme he would return to again and
again.[34] On April 14, 1938, in the wake of the cruel recession of the
previous year, he said in his "Fireside Chat on Economic Conditions"
that "the first duty of government is to protect the economic welfare
of all people," especially when "the products of their hands . . . ex-
ceed the purchasing power of their pocketbooks."[35] He meant to build
from the bottom up, to protect the "little fellow," to increase his buying power, to maintain a decent wage scale, to put humanity first and
profits second.[36]

Toward the Common Good

It was not just the poorest who could be helped. In the same speech to
the Chamber of Commerce, Roosevelt pleaded for the welfare of the
whole: "It is ultimately of little avail to any of you to be temporarily
prosperous while others are permanently depressed. I ask that your
welfare merge into the welfare of the whole, that you view recovery in
terms of the Nation rather than in terms of a particular industry, that
you have the vision to lay aside special and selfish interests, to think of
and act for a well-rounded national recovery."[37]

Economic security "is not to be achieved by aiming for restriction
of national income . . . but by aiming for more abundant and more
widely distributed national income."[38] To achieve that, he added pro-
tections for collective bargaining and for the rights of investors and

depositors. He sought cooperation among business, the professions, labor, and government. Instead of minimum wages and maximum hours, the second should be reduced and the first increased. No more than his critics did he relish the demeaning dole for the unemployed. It was far better to put people to work, to give them value and usefulness in their own eyes and in the eyes of others. That in turn meant cooperation and subvention on a scale never before undertaken in America. It was not a matter of getting government "off the backs of people" but of government standing at their elbows with a helping hand. When someone argued that labor unions might get too powerful, Roosevelt replied, "Too powerful for what?"[39]

Roosevelt's intention was not to eradicate capitalism. On the contrary, like his cousin Theodore, Franklin knew that capitalism had to be saved from capitalists. In a rousing campaign speech at the New York Democratic State Convention on September 29, 1936, he argued that "liberalism becomes the protection of the far-sighted conservative." That is, the "true conservative seeks to protect the system of private property and free enterprise by correcting such injustices and inequalities as arise from it."[40] Cooperation meant a new attitude and policy locally, nationally, and internationally, that of the good neighbor.

The business community would not buy it. In the summer of 1934, Roosevelt organized a Committee on Economic Security to pursue three main ends: old-age security, unemployment compensation, and health insurance. Roosevelt was forced to drop the latter already in 1935. As Kenneth S. Davis remarks, the politically powerful and "implacably hostile" American Medical Association "could be counted on ever after to oppose, powerfully, any legislative proposal which might conceivably affect, reduce in the slightest, the private-entrepreneurial nature of American health care delivery."[41] In Peter Arno's unforgettable cartoon, such was the gaggle of wealthy, cheerfully vacuous, East Side New Yorkers in their Panama hats and evening dress who solicited friends with "Come along. We're going to the Trans-Lux to hiss Roosevelt."[42]

Income redistribution also entailed tax reform. On June 19, 1935, in a message to Congress on the subject, he laid out his principle: "The transmission from generation to generation of vast fortunes by will, inheritance or gift is not consistent with the ideals of the American people."[43] It could not be justified on the basis of family security, nor was creative enterprise "stimulated by vast inheritances." It blessed neither the bequeathers nor the receivers. His critics saw this as the greatest threat to individual liberty. At an important press conference with the Society of Newspaper Editors on April 21, 1938, he was challenged for claiming that capital gains taxes should be governed by principle and that those who had more money should be taxed at a higher percentage rate:

Q. What you refer to as principle is not principle in a moral sense; it is just a theory on one sort of taxation.

The President: Well, I don't know. I think it goes a little deeper than that.

Q. Is it a moral principle?

The President: I do think so.

Q. That is what is meant by principle[?]

The President: I think that it is a moral principle. In other words, I think that a man with an income, whether it is from capital gains, or stock, or bonds, or a newspaper, who is making a million dollars a year—and we know a good many people in this country who are doing it . . . I think he ought to pay a larger percentage of his income to the Government than the man who is making a salary as managing editor of $10,000 a year.[44]

Roosevelt had already declared in an address at Roanoke Island, North Carolina, on April 18, 1937, that "the Nation, by an overwhelming majority supports my opposition to the vesting of power in the hands of any class, numerous but select."[45] Indeed, in the stunning election victory of 1936 it had done just that, and in his second inaugural address the next January Roosevelt fixed his sights on subordinating private power and special interests to public need and the common good.[46] Individualism, either rugged or bedded down in dividends, was to be replaced with the value of cooperation. In his annual message to Congress on January 3, 1938, he warned that "speculative income should not be favored over earned income. . . . Abuses by individuals or corporations designed to escape tax-paying by various methods of doing business, corporate or otherwise . . . must not be restored." He deplored the "unfair competition which drives smaller producers out of business locally, regionally, or even on a national scale; intimidation of local or state government to prevent laws for the protection of labor by threatening to move elsewhere; the shifting of actual production from one locality or region to another in pursuit of the cheapest wage scale."[47]

Philosophical Questions

Roosevelt's intended redesign of the nation's "house" involved, as John Gunther wrote in 1950, the most formidable single problem of the century: properly conceptualizing "the interrelation between liberty and security. Liberty of thought, liberty of movement and expression, liberty of political mechanisms and procedures." These freedoms Roosevelt set beside "security against want, security against revolution, security against aggression both foreign and domestic—these were the two irreconcilables he sought to reconcile." His entire twelve years in office, wrote Gunther, are explained by his premise of an accord between the two goods.[48] Gunther thought Roosevelt succeeded at reconciling them, but others disagreed. More broadly, the issue involves fundamental questions in political philosophy—the classic balance between the good of the one and the good of the many. It also involves our own, more recently emphasized question of pluralism—justice for the many parts within the whole.

Utilitarians answered the first question with their doctrine that conduct is morally good if it promotes the greatest happiness of the greatest number. FDR's emphasis on the good of the whole might be taken to comport with, or to have been directly shaped by, that doctrine. Certainly he and just about everyone else were influenced by the likes of Jeremy Bentham, John Stuart Mill, and Henry Sidgwick. Bentham's *Introduction to the Principles and Morals of Legislation* held an important place in his study at Hyde Park. Roosevelt even believed the "principle of the greater good for the greater number" to be the "cornerstone of democratic government."[49]

But on a central count, FDR either consciously or unconsciously separated himself from the utilitarians, especially from Jeremy Bentham. In his "science of legislation," Bentham laid it down that "the general rule" for increasing the national wealth "is that nothing ought to be done or attempted by government. The motto, or watchword of government on these occasions, ought to be—*Be Quiet.*" Government interference was needless, indeed pernicious, said the Englishman; conduct in the open market would bring about its own rewards and punishments to the maximum good of the maximum number of the individual actors in question.[50] Roosevelt thought otherwise for reasons that Henry Sturt cites: "He [Bentham] never faced the question of how a man is to be induced to act morally in cases where these sanctions [of penalties and rewards] could be evaded or did not exist."[51]

Beyond the question of utilitarianism has arisen more recently the question of pluralism. John Rawls's *A Theory of Justice* sets the issue best in defining "justice as fairness" in which every individual, not merely the greatest number, is to be protected. "*Each* member of society," writes Rawls, "is thought to have an inviolability founded on justice or, as some say on natural right, which even the welfare of everyone else cannot override. Justice denies that the loss of freedom for some is made right by a greater good shared by others." If it is true that "the plurality of distinct persons with separate systems of ends is an essential feature of human societies," Rawls continues, "we should not expect the principles of social choice to be utilitarian." But it also might make it difficult to warrant FDR's appeals to the common good. Is pluralism a recipe for individualism? Rawls thinks not, so long as we distinguish between the love of humanity and the sense of justice: "the former is manifest by the greater intensity and pervasiveness of this desire and in a readiness to fulfill all the natural duties in addition to that of justice, and even to go beyond their requirements."[52]

This is what Roosevelt meant when he interpreted charity as "social-mindedness." But the question of pluralism pops up again in light of the specifically Christian roots of Roosevelt's concept of charity. His own answer to the question was not to put aside his personal beliefs but to seek their application in a body of legislation bearing common assent. He believed that in a liberal democratic country, politicians could, when deciding social issues, translate their own theological understandings and perspectives into law while trying at the same time to discover shared premises and common ways of agreement. Was that a peculiarity of his time or social context? Was American pluralism less divisive in the 1930s? Or did the religious character of the nation in Roosevelt's day just *seem* less pluralistic than now? It seemed possible in the 1930s and '40s to think of Catholic, Protestant, and Jew as somehow the only faiths in the nation worth thinking about. Indeed, FDR *stretched* the canvas of the acceptable by adding the Jewish element of the triad; he was the first president to speak of a "Judeo-Christian tradition."[53]

Whether it was fair or not, Roosevelt could indeed count on a common heritage in which all three faiths participated and out of which he could speak simply and frankly. Shared premises and common ways of agreement appeared to be self-evident and readily available to everyone. In a campaign address in 1932, he could state that the "ideal of social justice of which I have spoken—an ideal that years ago might have been thought advanced—is now accepted by the moral leadership of all the great religious groups in the country."[54] Later, with the advent of World War II, his viewpoint widened to include other religions. In a speech on preparedness in 1941, he asserted that Hitler meant "to abolish all existing religions—Catholic, Protestant, Mohamedan [*sic*], Hindu, Buddhist, and Jewish alike."[55] In addition, his own beliefs were broad enough that he could speak out of them even when dealing with specific matters, as we shall see in the next chapter. Above all, he did not use his personal religion as a tool to convince voters of his own piety; he used it to throw light on common needs and to underwrite common purposes.

This was a matter of personal, intimate concern for him. In September 1933, FDR made some informal remarks at the Methodist church in Hyde Park in which he revealed his intimate knowledge of the religious history of Dutchess County. The speech captured both the unity and the diversity he had learned there and is worth quoting at some length. Roosevelt recounted that he had worked with the Methodist minister to compile the early records of the church and of the others in Hyde Park township. Quaker preachers were the first to arrive at the "Krum Elbow Precinct" in prerevolutionary days, said the president. It was not until after the Revolution that the community decided that they ought to have a meeting house to suit all their various loyalties, and so in 1789 there was organized the Stoutensburg Religious Society, an association of men and women who wanted a place in which to worship. As a result, they put up the first church. It was a tiny structure, seating fewer than fifty people, Roosevelt went on, but by resolution it was open to every good and recommended preacher and to every Christian society.

Roosevelt was heartened that Baptists, Methodists, the Dutch Reformed, Presbyterians, and Episcopalians had joined forces, "and for a number of years, in fact for a whole generation, this entire community worshipped in this house of the Religious Society."[56]

Such a concert of interests FDR sought in and from all quarters in the nation. This was the model of that reformation of American life he determined to undertake. For the infinitesimal Religious Society of 1798, with its five sets of Protestant worshipers, he would substitute farmers, laborers, professionals, and businesspeople, all woven into a national society, a unity of neighbors and citizens from coast to coast. He took that aspiration a step further in 1940 to include the nations of the world. The rising threats in the world were making a mockery of such unity. Dictators were riding "rabble-rousing slogans" to power, and once there, were "saddl[ing] their tyrannies on whole nations and on their weaker neighbors." "This is the danger," he concluded, "to which we in America must begin to be alert."[57]

A Community of Localities

Roosevelt could claim some success in achieving a concert of interests from the support he received from a considerable number of top American executives: William Woodin of the American Car and Foundry Company (who became secretary of the treasury in 1933); Averell Harriman and Carl Gray of the Union Pacific Railroad; Thomas Watson of IBM; Daniel Willard of the Baltimore and Ohio; Walter Teagle of Standard Oil; Myron Taylor of US Steel; Gerard Swope of General Electric; Otto Richter of AT&T; Ernest Draper of Hills Brothers; James Forrestal of Dillon, Read (later, the last secretary of the navy and first secretary of defense); Marion Folsom of Eastman Kodak; and others.[58] "Some of the most practical, hard-headed and ambitious men I know," he said in 1933, "have been so buffeted by circumstances these last few years that they realize that they must all get down on their knees together in a new humbleness of spirit—out of which grows united and effective action."[59] A few years later he could claim that in the difficult climb out of the depths of the Depression, "the spirit of charity showed itself unselfishly and generously."[60] While there was some evidence for his words, they were also a combination of advocacy and wishful thinking. The results were ambiguous: in the early days of the New Deal, cooperation between the different interests in agriculture and in industry ran up against the "ideology of competitiveness . . . [which] was so strongly ingrained that it could defeat any effort against it."[61]

New Deal government got the reputation for being remote, centralized, and just "too big." If so, it was ironically against Roosevelt's wishes, for he ceaselessly underscored the importance of state, county, and village initiatives. Even more, the spirit of charity required face-to-face knowledge; people needed to know their neighbors to recognize them as neighbors. Roosevelt himself was constantly reaching out to remind local communities of their importance and promise. At Vassar College on August 26, 1933, he spoke extemporaneously on the "Golden Rule in government." In a "national sense," he maintained, the faceless "many" are really our neighbors, "the people of the United States as a whole," and so "to our national life" there should be at a minimum the extension of "the old principle of the local community, the principle that no man, woman or child, has the right to do things that hurt his neighbor."[62] Nor should any be singled out for special privilege at the expense of others. If the "science of politics, indeed, may be said to be in large part the science of the adjustment of conflicting group interests," then gathering a wide exposure of opinion and wisdom was of the essence. As he said at the Jackson Day Dinner of January 8, 1940, the White House—and surely he himself—had operated by "buil[ding] up a vast mosaic of the state of the union from thousands of bits of information—from one man or woman, this thought; from another, data on some event, a scrap here perhaps and a scrap there; from every Congressional district in the Union; from rich and poor; from enthusiast and complainant; from liberal and conservative; from Republican and Democrat."[63]

The lockstep of totalitarian states and the oligarchy of the rich and successful were weaker for ignoring that wisdom. But conversely, Roosevelt reminded his listeners, "the individual citizen contributes most to the good of the largest group only when he or she thinks in terms of the largest group." Only with such a dual wide perspective "can democracy and the republican form of government permanently succeed."[64] He likewise enjoined the 1933 graduating class at the Naval Academy. Officers should be men of broad culture and understanding, said the commander in chief: "I ask you to avoid an exclusive relationship to your own clan—to your clan of the Navy or to some other special Government service or to the clan of your profession in civil life.

Remember to cultivate the friendships of people, not alone of your own class or profession, but the average run of folks, the same folks you would have known and liked and affiliated with had you not been chosen to enter and graduate from a highly specialized institution of higher education."[65]

The president certainly was as good as his word. As much as his physical condition permitted, he kept close to ordinary people in their daily lives. He loved to travel and to meet and talk with as many as possible, and he trusted their capacities and intelligence. He learned their ways, their needs, their hopes, and their language. Cooperation with Congress was another phase of local consultation; understanding the particular talents and quirks of legislators was vital for navigating the road to the general welfare. These familiarities opened the door to a crucial part of effective leadership. "Roosevelt considered that it was his duty to sense and carry out the popular will," remarks Thomas H. Greer; "at the same time he sought to guide that will according to his lights . . . ; his greatest single task [was] that of *teacher*."[66] In an important campaign speech to the Commonwealth Club in San Francisco in September 1932, he declared: "Government includes the art of formulating policy and using the political technique to attain so much of that policy as will receive general support; persuading, leading, sacrificing, teaching always, because the greatest duty of the statesman is to educate."[67]

That education campaign went on through four national election campaigns, more than a dozen annual addresses to Congress, thirty fireside chats, and press conferences without end. At his 211th press conference, on June 7, 1935, he aptly summarized the social objective of his administration:

It remains just what it was, which is to do what any honest Government of any country would do: to try to increase the security and happiness of a larger number of people in all occupations of life and in all parts of the country; to give them more of the good things of life, to give them a greater distribution not only of wealth in the narrow terms, but of wealth in the wider terms; to give them places to go in the summertime—recreation; to give them assurance that they are not going to starve in their old age; to give honest business a chance to go ahead and make a reasonable profit, and to give everyone a chance to earn a living.[68]

In these goals Christian faith played a significant role. Frances Perkins, who spoke to him in a language they shared, that of the household of faith, wrote with her usual acumen about what the mature Roosevelt had learned in his years of public service: "Foremost was the idea that poverty is preventable, that poverty is destructive, wasteful, demoralizing, and that poverty in the midst of potential plenty is morally unacceptable in a Christian and democratic society. One began to see the 'poor' as people, with hopes, fears, virtues, and vices, as fellow citizens who were part of the fabric of American life instead of as a depressed class who would always be with us."[69]

Conclusion

In the background of Roosevelt's thinking lay the cumulative influence of Scripture and the principles of American democracy. In his case their roots were to be found in the Christian Social Gospel, in Progressivist exposés of the back alleys of corruption, and in those individuals who helped shape his mind and spirit. This rested up against two other important elements in the emerging political and social liberalism of the 1930s, for which Roosevelt along with others was responsible. One was the belief, derived from the turn-of-the-century German study of the social sciences, that the state was an initiating creative power acting for the benefit of its citizens. The other was in many respects its antithesis: belief in the prior significance of the free individual. Populism was a particularly American phenomenon in that it regarded people, not the state, as the locus of virtue. FDR had faith in the American people. He did "not embrace church dogma—the doctrine of original sin and consequent depraved nature of man," writes Thomas H. Greer, "but accepted as a premise the essential goodness of most human beings."[70] Sin for him was the destruction of community and fellowship by self-love exhibited in the denial of security for all by the greed of some. FDR tried to resolve the contradiction between these two values in his "Cooperative Security" speech at Marietta, Georgia, on June 8, 1938. He urged his audience, "let us never forget that government is *ourselves* and not an alien power over us."[71]

Neither the idea of the state nor populism, however, turned out to control American liberalism; both were drawn into it piecemeal as parts of a pragmatic, relativistic leadership. The idea that the state had some sort of mysterious existence independent of ordinary people or that the voice of the majority of citizens was the voice of righteousness finally violated a skeptical American temperament. Besides, the then-regnant understanding of pluralism with respect to problems "assumed that social relationships were or could be harmonious, but because such relationships were always changing, harmony required constant adjustment and decisions." In the mind-set of leaders in the 1930s and '40s, pluralism required "widespread sharing of decision making and saw leadership as facilitating rather than directive."[72] It had to be respectful of liberty of thought, of movement and expression, and of political mechanisms and procedures. Thus it fit well with Roosevelt's concept both of democracy and of Christian charity.

Those two principles, Christian charity and democracy, were the sources off which Roosevelt drew, the markers by which he would steer. He did not live up to them consistently, but he thought them the most promising guidelines for the country and, as he later came to hope, for the other nations of the world. Charity, properly understood, involved fellow feeling and the simple rules of human conduct: justice for the poor, sufficiency for all. Beside liberty he then set security and the other specific values that buttressed it. Together these would bring about a renewed, more harmonious society with equal rights for all, not one reduced to utilitarianism or only the rights of the many, nor oligarchy and the privilege of the strong. He rejected rule by proclamation as practiced in the burgeoning dictatorships of his time. He meant to be a teacher who persuaded others of the necessity of harmonizing different interests in the spirit of charity.

Chapter Six

Faith—"Yes, a *Very Simple* Christian"

The hardest years of Franklin Roosevelt's presidency came in his second term. His overwhelming victory in 1936 made him overbold in pushing his agenda and punishing his opponents. He tried to circumvent the Supreme Court's veto of key New Deal measures by proposing to "pack" that bench with new and more friendly appointees. The move immediately backfired. In the congressional primary elections of 1938—absent the savvy of Louis Howe, his chief political adviser, who had died two years earlier—FDR intervened directly to try to oust Democratic conservatives who had slowed down reform. His efforts failed in every case, leaving him with more powerful enemies in his own party and a larger Republican opposition in both the House and the Senate.[1] In between these two missteps he sent the economy, which had been steadily recovering, back into recession by trying to balance the budget. This was an old campaign pledge from 1932 and warmed his "thrifty Dutchman['s] heart," but it set off waves of selling on Wall Street that made October 1937 look like a replay of October 1929.[2] When the contraction continued the following spring with precipitous falls in farm prices, the president was forced to ask for a special appropriation to revive the economy.

Meanwhile, on the international scene, the tide of an expansionist fascism was clearly rising. Germany had seized the Rhineland in 1936, the firstfruits of its rapid rearmament in violation of the Versailles Treaty. Fascist forces under General Francisco Franco were waging civil war to overthrow the republican government of Spain. Japan, which had occupied Manchuria already in 1931, invaded the heartland of China itself in 1937. Roosevelt tried to rally the American people to face this menace, but support was tepid and opposition fierce. He was accused of plotting to be a dictator. Simultaneously, charismatic figures were rising at home who—in Roosevelt's mind—truly did harbor such aspirations.

At this nadir of his presidency, Roosevelt's convictions about democracy faced their sternest test. He had to rally on the other pole of his faith, Christianity, to help meet the challenge. Faith itself, the third article of Saint Paul's triad, became the watchword of the era.

Religion and Democratic Civilization

Frances Perkins once told Mrs. Roosevelt, "You know Franklin is really a very simple Christian." There was silence for a moment, and then "with a quizzical lift of her eyebrows," the first lady replied, "Yes, a *very simple* Christian."[3] Elsewhere Eleanor Roosevelt expanded on her remark more generously:

> I always felt my husband's religion had something to do with his confidence in himself. . . . It was a very simple religion. He believed in God and in His guidance. He felt that human beings were given tasks to perform and with those tasks went the ability and strength to put them through. He could pray for help and guidance and have faith in his own judgment as a result. The church services he always insisted on holding on Inauguration Day, anniversaries, and whenever a great crisis impended, were the expression of his religious faith. I think this must not be lost sight of in judging his acceptance of responsibility and his belief in his ability to meet whatever crisis had to be met.[4]

For Christians, faith is an inner conviction, a solemn pledge on the part of people singly or together. It begins with *God's* faithfulness (Rom. 3:3–4) and the gift that goes with it—the human response of trust in him (Mark 11:22–26; Rom. 1:16; 3:22). As one of the Christian virtues, faith involves an ongoing conversation between God and the person who calls upon him. In the classic definition of Hebrews 11:1, faith is the "assurance of things hoped for, the conviction of things not seen." The Christian faith is grounded in the certainty that God has made himself known in the historic person of Jesus of Nazareth, who was born in a manger, had no place to lay his head, and died on a cross. Faith is not *imago*, daydreaming, but a clarifying perspective that comes from outside the self as attested to by many. It comes, as might seem odd, with reminders of human frailty and a sense of humor (Matt. 7:15; Luke 6:41). It accomplishes three things. First, it brings an awareness that God transcends all human limitations and insufficiencies. Second, it gives the recipient what Germans call *Sachlichkeit*, a sober sense of the reality of things. Third, it produces community.

The relationship between this faith and what is conventionally called "the Christian faith" is more complex than it at first appears. Faith in the latter sense is "the body of Christian dogma" that, as John Rawls states, should more accurately be labeled "belief." Belief involves *assent* to propositions; faith calls for *consent* of one person to another. "People of faith are in community with God," Rawls continues.[5] It was in that spirit of consent and community that Roosevelt spoke to the nation of the importance of faith at a crucial moment in American history, when the way ahead was unclear.

That moment was his State of the Union address on January 4, 1939.[6] Never before had any chief executive argued so strongly for the principle and urgency of faith. Nor was this Roosevelt's custom; he spoke of faith only with intimate friends, and even then infrequently. His bold speech on this occasion must be understood against the background of events in Europe and East Asia. "In reporting on the state of the nation," he began, "I have felt it necessary on previous occasions to advise the Congress of disturbance abroad and of the need of putting our own house in order in the face of storm signals from across the seas." Alas, there was now "need for further warning." Since 1931 "world events of thunderous import have moved with lightning speed.... All about us rage undeclared wars—military and economic.... All about us grow more deadly armaments—military and economic." Against the rising menace, Roosevelt told the assembly, "three institutions" remained "indispensable to Americans, now as always."

> The first is religion. It is the source of the other two—democracy and international good faith. Religion, by teaching man his relationship to God, gives the individual a sense of his own dignity and teaches him to respect himself by respecting his neighbors. Democracy, the practice of self-government, is a covenant among free men to respect the rights and liberties of their fellows. International good faith, a sister of democracy, springs from the will of civilized nations of men to respect the rights and liberties of other nations of men.

"In a modern civilization," Roosevelt continued, "all three—religion, democracy, and international good faith—complement and support each other." Religion was the wellspring of the other two, their touchstone and guarantor: "Where freedom of religion has been attacked, the attack has come from sources opposed to democracy. Where democracy has been overthrown, the spirit of free worship has disappeared." Finally, "where religion and democracy have vanished, good faith and reason in international affairs have given way to strident ambition and brute force." Hence, any "ordering of society which relegates religion, democracy, and good faith among nations to the background can find no place within it for the ideals of the Prince of Peace." The United States, he insisted, "rejects such an ordering, and retains its ancient faith."

All this was preface to Roosevelt's policy proposals to bolster American defenses. These naturally began at home, but home now expanded to include the entire Western Hemisphere. He strained to invoke a history of good faith and harmony of purpose in hemispheric relations "under a common ideal of democratic government, a rich diversity of resources and of people." Living together "in mutual respect and peace," the nations of North and South America stood aligned against the "new philosophies of force." But the Americas stood ready as well to "take counsel with all other nations of the world to end . . . aggression." The world had grown so small that "no nation can be safe in its will to peace so long as any other powerful nation refuses to settle its grievances at the council table." In words that anticipated Pearl Harbor two years later, Roosevelt suggested that "effective timing of defense and the distant points from which attacks may be launched are completely different from what they were twenty years ago." The new range and speed of offensive action mean that "survival cannot be guaranteed by arming after the attack begins." But Roosevelt underscored the spiritual resources that lay beneath and beyond all such material measures, "the tenets of faith and humanity on which their churches, their government, and their very civilization are founded. The defense of religion, of democracy, and of good faith among nations is all the same fight. To save one we must now make up our minds to save all."

In the State of the Union address, religion and "ancient faith" were one and the same. FDR used them interchangeably. Perhaps he learned in Latin class that *religio* meant to tie, to bind back, to restore traditional ways, and so, in invoking religion, he was recalling his countrymen and countrywomen to their heritage. Two months later, in a speech delivered for the 150th anniversary of Congress, he reiterated that freedom of religion was not only essential to the "rights of mankind" but also one of the "origins of representative government." Conversely, where democracy was snuffed out, where it was curtailed, there, too, the right to worship God in one's own way was circumscribed or abrogated. He invoked Jesus's story of the Good Samaritan to issue a challenge: "Shall we by our passiveness, by our silence, by assuming the attitude of the Levite who pulled his skirts together and passed by on the other side, lend encouragement to those who today persecute religion or deny it?"[7]

World Events

Behind the urgency in Roosevelt's mind lay an ominous crescendo in international events. In March 1938 Hitler invaded Austria, Franco's armies in Spain were about to cut the country in half, and the Loyalists were close to collapse. By the end of the year, the Spanish people faced starvation. On September 29, Britain and France struck their infamous deal with Hitler at Munich, capitulating to his demand for the annexation of Sudetenland from Czechoslovakia. In Parliament Winston Churchill denounced this as the "first foretaste of the bitter cup which will be proffered to us year by year." Roosevelt was equally stunned. He told the cabinet that British prime minister Neville Chamberlain and his French counterpart, Édouard Daladier, would now (mixing his biblical metaphors) "wash the blood from their Judas Iscariot hands." With cables pouring across his desk from London, Paris, and Prague reporting "events that outraged logic, morality, and every principle of civilized intercourse between sovereign states," FDR felt "ever more acutely his helplessness in the face of onrushing catastrophe."[8]

Then, on November 10, 1938, came *Kristallnacht*, the Night of Shattered Glass, in Germany. Two weeks earlier, ten thousand Polish Jews who had long lived in Germany were suddenly deprived of all possessions except the clothes on their backs, given ten Reichmarks (four US dollars), and herded on to waiting trucks and trains to be deported to Poland. When the son of one of the evicted attacked the German embassy in Paris in response, Nazi propaganda minister Joseph Goebbels executed swift and brutal revenge. Twenty thousand Jews were arrested; scores were murdered on the spot, and the rest sent to concentration camps. Nearly two hundred synagogues were burned, and homes and shops owned by Jews were looted and destroyed. Hermann Goering's office blamed the Jews themselves for the destruction and subsequently decreed that they pay for repairs to the damaged property. The *New York Times* reported from Berlin that the "wave of destruction, looting, and incendiarism [was] unparalleled in Germany since the Thirty Years' War, and in Europe generally since the Bolshevist revolution."[9]

In that light, the failure of an international conference for relief of Jewish refugees held at Evian-les-Bains the previous July seemed all the more egregious. Inspired by Roosevelt, the gathering had little support in America.[10] Emergency Jewish immigration into the United States was opposed by 72 percent of the population. The Veterans of Foreign Wars, the Daughters of the American Revolution, the American Coalition of Patriotic Societies, members of Congress, not a few Catholic newspapers, as well as anti-Semitic Protestants denounced it. The events of *Kristallnacht* reversed the mood temporarily. Many anti-Semites, such as Henry Ford, fell silent, even if some, like Ambassador Joseph Kennedy and the fire-eating "radio priest" Father Charles E. Coughlin, soon returned to action. Jack L. Warner of Warner Brothers studio in Hollywood commended Charlie Chaplin for his (Chaplin's) forthcoming satire on Adolf Hitler, *The Great Dictator* (1940). Chaplin's movie helped solidify anti-Nazi feeling by showing Hitler and his followers to be not only evil but also sick. During filming, Warner wrote Chaplin that he and his wife "had a very lovely visit with the President last Friday and during our conversation the President brought up your picture *The Dictator*. He said he hoped you would not put it aside and would make it . . . if the President of our country is interested in your making the picture it certainly has merit."[11] In fact, alone among world leaders, Roosevelt made a public statement about *Kristallnacht*: he "could scarcely believe that such things could occur in a twentieth-century civilization."[12] In the meantime, he recalled Ambassador Hugh Wilson from Berlin for consultation; Wilson never returned to Germany, nor was he replaced.

Still, American opinion on immigration, Jewish or otherwise, did not change. Opposition to a liberalized entry policy for Jews actually rose significantly during the winter of 1938–1939, after *Kristallnacht*, to reach 77 percent.[13] Nativism, anti-Semitism, and fears of swollen unemployment rolls took their toll. The Federal Bureau of Investigation and the visa section of the State Department, under the anti-Semitic assistant secretary Breckenridge Long, dug in their collective heels against admitting Jewish refugees.[14] The American Jewish community itself was divided. When *Fortune* magazine polled Americans in mid-1939 about opening the doors to European refugees, 85 percent of Protestants, 84 percent of Catholics, and an astonishing 25.8 percent of Jews answered no.[15] Even the Jews in FDR's administration, including those in the White House, were not of one mind. All in all, Robert Rosen concludes, "Roosevelt, like the American Jewish leadership, undoubtedly felt that he had done the best he could with the tools he had been given," yet he "never fully understood or knew Hitler's insane, half-secret war or the Holocaust the way we do now."[16]

Personal anxieties added to the troubles of the year. In September 1938 son James Roosevelt underwent a major operation at the Mayo Clinic while cousin and favorite confidante Daisy Suckley suffered from a lingering illness. With the news of German demands for the Sudetenland, FDR lamented to Daisy that the world "is full of dynamite." Both James and Daisy recovered, but Roosevelt remained depressed, his faith shaken. He wrote Daisy wistfully about better personal days to come: "Somehow, some way—And it's good to live a bit in the future. . . . Things are worse abroad & while of course a war does not mean us in it, it does change so many things—hate—all our 'economics'—industry, agriculture, etc. . . . Did you hear Hitler today? His shrieks, his histrionics and the effect on the huge audience—They did not applaud—they made noises like animals."[17]

Roosevelt as Dictator?

Fears of fascism permeated American society in the 1930s, not only concerning foreign affairs but also about developments at home. The accusations were pointed at Roosevelt, but they also clung to some rising stars on the American scene. Amid charges that he wanted to become a dictator, Roosevelt's attempt to reorganize the agencies of the executive branch went down in the House, by seven votes. The allegations of his supposed totalitarian leanings were particularly strong from his enemies on the right. One historian of the Far Right finds its "nucleus" in the 1930s among ordinary citizens, self-described "'100%'

Americans, active since the 1910s," who "found in the Roosevelt admin-istration proof that their fears had been justified all along." Unlike alli-ances among religious conservatives in the 1980s and 1990s, however, in the 1930s there was "no necessary connection between conservative theology and the far right." Ordinary Christian fundamentalists were "largely oblivious to politics" and more concerned with building their own seminaries, missionary societies, and publishing houses. In fact, "a majority of devout fundamentalists, because they were poor, southern, or both, voted for Roosevelt." To be sure, some of the shriller among them, like the anti-Semitic Gerald B. Winrod, cried out against admin-istration policies that expanded federal authority. Winrod feared that the "bank holiday [of March 1933] exposed Americans to the dictatorial lash that already afflicted Fascist Italy and Nazi Germany." Likewise, he said the Civilian Conservation Corps was preparing young men "to take up arms overnight," while the National Industrial Recovery Act "placed the whole nation 'under military discipline.'"[18] For Winrod, the "coils of dictatorship" were tightening in America. That did not keep him, in the end, from becoming pro-Nazi.

Politicians and business leaders also spread the alarm. The power-ful Jouett Shouse, a former congressman and, after that, assistant sec-retary of the treasury under Woodrow Wilson, chaired the executive committee of the Democratic National Committee and helped reshape the party in the 1920s. Because of Shouse's close ties with former New York governor and 1928 presidential candidate Alfred E. Smith (who hankered to run again in 1932), Roosevelt maneuvered Shouse out of the party chairmanship. Shouse responded by founding and serving as the only president of the American Liberty League. Among its no-table members were Smith; the Democratic presidential nominee of 1924, John W. Davis; Nathan Miller, chief counsel for United States Steel; and Republican congressman James W. Wadsworth of New York. Historian Justus D. Doenecke writes that the Liberty League's advisory council "involved magnates from General Motors, Montgomery Ward, Sun Oil, General Foods, International Shoe, and Consolidated Gas."[19] Shouse and those around him alleged that the New Deal was a "sin-ister conspiracy to subvert the Constitution, destroy democracy, and implant a dictatorship by expanding federal authority."[20] The League published many alarmist pamphlets, including *The Way Dictatorships Start* and *Will It Be Ave Caesar?* But it never attracted more than 36,000 members out of a nation of 130,000,000.[21]

The more powerful National Association of Manufacturers (NAM), with a membership of 109,000 in 307 affiliated trade groups, also took aim at the New Deal. Its roster of leading companies was impressive: Chase National Bank, Goodyear Tire and Rubber, General Electric, IBM, Alcoa, and others. General Motors and E. I. DuPont reached millions with their advertising on behalf of NAM; it spent $800,000 on its anti–New Deal program in 1937.[22] Henning W. Prentis Jr., president of the Armstrong Cork Company of Pittsburgh, the manufacturer of one-half of the linoleum sold in the United States and an educator of note, became its leading spokesman. Against the descending "economic dictatorship in the New Deal," he helped popularize the rapidly rising term "free enterprise." Against FDR's three principles of religion, democracy, and international good faith, Prentis offered his own "tripod of human freedom": "representative democracy," "civil and religious liberties," and "the institution of private enterprise." Mimicking Roosevelt's approach, Prentis intoned: "Throughout the ages these institutions have gone hand in hand; they are inseparable. When one goes all go."[23]

The frequent charge that Franklin Roosevelt sought absolute power invites a more detailed comparison between him and Adolf Hitler. Historian John Garraty notes the striking outward parallels between the two. Both came to power in early 1933 and died in the spring of 1945. Both wielded "enormous psychological influence" over their citizens by their striking oratory, Hitler's hypnotic, Roosevelt's assuring. Both sought to overcome poverty and increase prosperity; both clearly identified the sources of their nations' ills; and both emphasized the "suffering of the times rather than attempting to disguise or minimize it." Both sought to exert executive control over vast bureaucracies. Both pursued narrowly nationalistic economic policies. Both idealized "rural life and the virtues of agricultural existence" and so sought to decentralize industry and entice workers to go back to the land. Both sought strong measures to bring about a national unity in which public interests overrode private affluence. Both embodied the ideal of national progress, of training, loyalty, and willingness to sacrifice for the larger good. Both sought change by renewing their countries' spirit and turning defeat into victory. Finally, both "also agreed that the crisis called for personal leadership more forceful than that needed in normal times."[24]

Below such similarities, which Roosevelt's enemies enjoyed pointing out, lay more crucial, and fundamental, contrasts in ends and means, purpose and method. Hitler wanted to avenge national humiliation under the Versailles Treaty. To accomplish that he increasingly ruled by fiat, exercising force from above over the minds and bodies of everyone. Leni Riefenstahl's *The Triumph of the Will* perfectly captured this spirit and style. In contrast, Pare Lorentz's *The Plow That Broke the Plains* (1936) and *The River* (1938), and the still photographs of Dorothea Lange, Walker Evans, Margaret Bourke-White, and Gordon Parks took a calmer, more documentary approach. Riefenstahl showed forth national power; the Americans revealed an impoverished humanity that still managed to retain its dignity.

Hitler's assumptions about authority gave little consideration to justice or empathy. His was a "power based on fear, power seeking domination, power always edging toward violence." Faith was to be in him alone.[25] Likewise, he moved to radically simplify society, abolishing trade unions, stripping universities and churches of their independence, and scuttling the German federal system. The army's new oath pledged "unconditional obedience to Adolf Hitler, the *Führer* of the German Reich and people, Supreme Commander of the Armed Forces."[26] By contrast, Roosevelt's was a rhetoric of temperateness and humane considerations, and his tenure saw thriving, expanding pluralism in American social structure and political operations, sometimes frustrating his ideals. Americans entering military service or civilian office pledged loyalty to the Constitution of the United States.[27] Faith was to be put in citizens elected to fill the offices it enjoined.

In the process of building community, the right for FDR was prior to the good. Hitler sought to rehabilitate the dignity of the German people by any means, right or wrong, and in a zero-sum game at the expense of other "races." For Roosevelt, the goal was not to inflate one good at the expense of others but to increase respect for all people equally. Egotism, the desire to dominate and exploit others, was to him the root of sin. The totalitarian dictators, Roosevelt told Bishop Henry St. George Tucker, were "strangers alike to the love of God and of man; they know no Christian impulse—neither mercy, justice, or compassion."[28] Then there was the difference between the two leaders in the treatment of opponents. To a reporter's question in 1933 about the death penalty, FDR replied: "I would like to see capital punishment abolished throughout this country. . . . Having to pass on the question of the death penalty . . . is the most disagreeable function that a Governor or the President has to perform."[29] By contrast, in the first week of July 1934, Hitler murdered those he suspected of disloyalty to him, including a former chancellor and his wife. Since the body of one enemy was found hacked to pieces, July 4 was aptly called "the Night of the Long Knives."[30]

Domestic Dictators

Roosevelt, too, worried about the danger of dictatorship in the United States. Dictatorship threatened the second, democratic, pole of his religion. The country's long tradition of political demagoguery had, in his eyes, come to a dangerous new pitch in the flamboyant senator from Louisiana, Huey Long. The "Kingfish," as he was called, had hoped to spearhead Roosevelt's presidential campaign in 1932 by traveling the country in a special train equipped with loudspeakers to give scores of speeches every day filled with "homespun humor, biblical quotes, and promises to redistribute the wealth"—and not incidentally to promote himself. Roosevelt had wisely turned down the offer. Long campaigned on his own anyway, attracting large, enthusiastic crowds of Depression-weary midwestern and southern farmers. Roosevelt worried "that if the Depression was not curtailed soon, the American people, much like those in Germany and Italy, would lose patience with the democratic process and turn to radical leaders like Huey." For his part, Long complained about Roosevelt's evasiveness: "When I talk to him he says, 'Fine, Fine, Fine!,'" he complained after visiting Warm Springs. "But Joe Robinson [Senator Joseph Robinson of Arkansas] goes to see him the next day and again he says, 'Fine, Fine, Fine!' Maybe he says 'Fine' to everybody." The vituperative Long wore loud clothes, entertained packed Senate galleries, abused the filibuster, and insulted fellow senators. "A mob is coming to hang the other ninety-five of you scoundrels," he declared on the Senate floor, "and I'm deciding whether to stick here with you or go out and lead them." During a dinner at Hyde Park in 1932, as she listened to Long dominate conversation at the other end of the table, Sara Roosevelt asked in a loud whisper, "Who is that dreadful man?" Roosevelt told Rexford Tugwell, "It's all very well to laugh over Huey but actually he is one of the two most dangerous men in the country. We shall have to do something about him."[31]

Long had gone to Washington as a senator in 1930 convinced "that his destiny would lead him to the presidency." However rude or vulgar, the Kingfish could be quick thinking, cool, and decisive in the political fray. His knowledge of parish politics in Louisiana was encyclopedic. William E. Leuchtenburg concludes: "Long's Louisiana served as a model for the kind of despotism the New Dealers feared the country might experience if they did not succeed, for in that state Huey had come a considerable way toward creating a personal dictatorship."[32] By 1935, he had succeeded in pushing Roosevelt and the New Deal further to the left. In early 1935 some Democratic Party leaders feared that before the nominating convention in 1936, Long would take advantage of the business community's growing hatred of Roosevelt and pit his strength against the president in the primaries. Republican money was even finding its way into Long's Share Our Wealth Clubs, even though their purpose was to effect a thorough redistribution of wealth by confiscating fortunes of over $8 million and guaranteeing a basic income to all Americans.

As a result, "Long's national reputation grew at an astounding rate through the spring and summer of 1935. . . . [He] seemed to many to be on the verge of creating a genuine new force in American politics, one whose ultimate power nobody could yet predict."[33] Paranoia about homegrown fascism now gripped the Left as well as the Right. During the early summer of 1935, novelist Sinclair Lewis, influenced by his anti-Nazi wife, the journalist Dorothy Thompson, wrote *It Can't Happen Here*, a novel about the rise to power of an American dictator. The next year Lewis turned the book into a play. Produced by the Federal Theatre of the WPA, it opened simultaneously in 1936 in eighteen cities across America and eventually was watched by five hundred thousand people. Besides the English-language productions, there were Spanish and Yiddish versions, and an African American cast performed it in Seattle.[34]

As it turned out, Long was assassinated on September 8, 1935, before Lewis's play went into production. But there remained FDR's second "most dangerous man in America," this one in the military, General Douglas MacArthur. MacArthur was aristocratic, handsome, and charming, the son of an army general, physically fearless and much decorated for his frontline service in World War I. As superintendent of West Point after the war, he undertook needed reforms of the curriculum and of the treatment of cadets. In 1930 Hoover appointed him chief of staff of the army, whereupon he set about reorganizing the army's nine corps, tried to stop base closings during the Depression, and built up the Air Corps. The result was that when another war came, "the U.S. army would achieve a battle-winning integration of planes, tanks, trucks, artillery and infantry in attack or defense that no other force in the world could even approximate, only envy." During World War II, MacArthur's desire to recapture the Philippine Islands rather than invade Taiwan was vindicated. Later in the Korean War, his strategy of the Inchon landing of September 15, 1950, was a work of military genius. As supreme commander for the Allied Powers in Japan after the surrender of September 2, 1945, he governed the defeated nation with prudence and tact. Some of that wisdom was given to him by the Japanese foreign minister, Mamoru Shigemitsu, who convinced MacArthur to work through a Japanese government and not rule by edict. MacArthur also retained the emperor Hirohito and treated him with dignity and respect.[35]

But there was another side to Douglas MacArthur that aroused FDR's suspicions. Throughout his career, he showed himself to be self-important, aloof, and often unwilling to take advice. "He talks," said Roosevelt, "in a voice that might come from the oracle's cave."[36] Often wearing a kimono over his uniform, MacArthur delighted in posturing before a full-length mirror in his office. Never one to consider the needs of subordinates, he surrounded himself with flatterers whom he then drove relentlessly. When General George C. Marshall visited him in the Far East in December 1943 and MacArthur referred to "my staff," Marshall replied, "You don't have a staff, General. You have a court." For MacArthur, history was the sum of the biographies of great men, among whom he placed himself. When the National Father's Day Committee named him "Number One Father for 1942," he replied that he hoped his young son would remember him when he was gone by repeating the simple prayer, "Our Father, who art in Heaven." It was, remarks Eric Larrabee, "a lapse in the sense of the appropriate that staggers the imagination."[37] Finally, on April 10, 1952, President Harry S. Truman fired him for insubordination.

MacArthur's worst but most revealing moments occurred in the summer of 1932 when, disregarding President Hoover's order, he led American soldiers to attack the "Bonus Army" of veterans of World War I. These bedraggled, penniless, and even starving men marched on Washington to demand their promised bonus for service in the war. In full uniform, with eight rows of ribbons bestrewn "from clavicle to navel," MacArthur ordered General George S. Patton's cavalry to cross the Anacostia River at night and drive the hapless marchers from their "Hooverville." MacArthur was convinced that the Bonus Army was communist-inspired, and likewise that he was the man of destiny, the "savior of the nation's capital from anarchy." As Roosevelt remarked to Rexford Tugwell, "You saw that picture in the *Times* of him after the troops had chased all those vets out with tear gas and burned their shelters. Did you ever see anyone more self-satisfied? There's a potential Mussolini for you. Right here at home."[38] True to form, MacArthur became the darling of the right wing. Herbert Hoover urged him to run for president in 1948 and 1952, even though the general never harbored that aim or aspiration. That did not stop Wall Street financiers and Midwest Republican newspapers, led by Robert McCormick's *Chicago Tribune*, from supporting him.[39]

Roosevelt massaged the general's ego, kept him on as chief of staff until 1935, and saw that he got the Congressional Medal of Honor during World War II. But he also let MacArthur know who was in command. In 1935, Roosevelt let him go to the Philippines; he would not return to the continental United States until 1951. Eric Larrabee sees the general as the idol that Roosevelt was only too happy to have his—Roosevelt's—enemies worship. "This resonant figurehead" was in fact "a politically hopeless cause, and the more of Roosevelt's opponents who could be persuaded to join it, the safer the President would become."[40] In the end, FDR achieved enough success with the New Deal, with his rallying rhetoric, and by redirecting attention to threats abroad to stave off dictatorial threats at home.

Civil Religion or Biblical?

To what extent did Roosevelt's defense of democracy contribute to what is called civil religion?[41] As his 1939 State of the Union message demonstrates, he was not shy in appealing to a transcendent religious reality that he held to be the source of both democracy and international trustworthiness. His appeals to equality, justice, and human rights had a devotional, religious quality. Recognizing that Americans placed a high valuation on religion itself, he sought in his first inaugural to employ the simplest biblical metaphors as a means of reaching his audience and integrating a diverse society. But all this is better defined as *public* religion, not *civil* religion of the classic type.

Roosevelt steadfastly avoided indiscriminate nationalism and a cult of patriotism that made the nation the object of reverence. Such terms as "New Israel," "Promised Land," and "Chosen People" are absent from his vocabulary.

Some historians have criticized Roosevelt for appealing to religion at all. Thus Kenneth S. Davis sharply disagrees with FDR's claim in the 1939 State of the Union address that religion promotes human rights and morality. "History teaches a different lesson," opines Davis. "Religion breeds strife and tyranny far more often than it does peace and freedom. Witness, in our time, the tragic horrors of fused religion and tyranny in Franco's Spain; in the ayatollahs' Iran; and in Mussolini's Italy, Hitler's Germany, and Stalin's Russia in so far as Fascism and Nazism and Communism were religious passions."[42]

This is a perennial criticism, and in Roosevelt's case it has engaged a number of thoughtful interpreters. "Of all the violences and hatreds of humankind," writes federal judge and Catholic ethicist John T. Noonan Jr., "that based on religion has been the most injurious, not because of the intensity of feeling and ferocity of execution that it has engendered—mere political ideologies have done greater damage in these respects—but because of the harm it has done religion itself, mocking its mandates, denying its duties, perverting its purpose. None, I dare declare, is more hateful to God."[43]

To tame the political dangers of religious particularism—that is, conviction of and appeal to a specific faith tradition—two alternatives besides atheism have been offered. The first was broached by French sociologist Émile Durkheim in his *Elementary Forms of Religious Life* (1912). According to Durkheim, religion is the projection of a society's consciousness of itself. That collective belief creates the sacred, and, reciprocally, the sacred creates the society. "Society itself is a religious phenomenon." People at worship, Durkheim argued, do not know what they are really worshiping; they have in view a transcendent being, not the collective solidarity on this earth of which that being is a projected expression.[44] For Durkheim, the transcendent God, to whom believers pray in worship, must be eliminated; yet what amounts to a collective self-worship must be maintained or else society will not survive. For Noonan, by contrast, while religious belief surely carries the freight of human need and desire, it is "a relation not to a thing but to a person." More precisely, "religion is a relation to a Being conceived of as having intelligence and volition. Intelligent, willing human beings respond to an intelligent, willing God. This relationship requires a response to a Person."[45] In Noonan's phrase, it is in the "transcendental traffic" with a person, not just a Durkheimian concept, that the essence of religion lies.

The concept of civil religion fudges the issue. Sociologist Robert N. Bellah presented its case in his influential 1968 essay "Civil Religion in America," although the practice itself long antedates it.[46] Bellah argued that above and beyond all their particular denominations, Americans together observed—and so were bound together as a people by—a civil religion that put a twist on Durkheim. This religion did not deny some (vague) transcendent being entitled "God" but invoked him from nature rather than from the revelation of one (or more) of the specific historical religions like Judaism, Christianity, or Islam. This civil religion had its own sacred scriptures—the Declaration of Independence, the Constitution, the Bill of Rights, and the Gettysburg Address; its own saints, like Washington and Lincoln; its holy days of obligation, like the Fourth of July; and its sacred sites, like Valley Forge, Appomattox, and Normandy. In Noonan's judgment, "Durkheim's thesis [was] made less absolute and adapted to the facts of American practice, even altered to admit the existence of God. The compelling clarity of the original concept" was lost in the process, "but a more useful explanation of the United States" might have come into view.[47]

Whether or not such a civil religion exists, it was not Roosevelt's. The imagery he employed remained overwhelmingly biblical and not national in character.[48] FDR's was a public religion that placed American national life in the context of Scripture. But it was more than that. With FDR specifically in mind, Noonan maintains that while civil religion "plausibly explains some American practices" and events, it also "obscures the place of persons in creating the practices. Nations do not worship, people do. Persons have their own religions not identified with any hypothetical religion of the nation." Individuals exhibit understanding, intention, and interiority; collectives do not. Through their liturgies, people relate to a Being of whose intelligence they wish to avail themselves, whose aid they request, and whose will they seek to obey. Bellah's collectivist reconstruction of civil religion ignores personal piety. As a leading counterexample, Noonan commends Roosevelt's D-Day prayer of June 6, 1944. "Uttered with the urgency of a supreme occasion, it is laced with specific Christian concepts." Drawing off the Episcopal liturgy, Roosevelt did not accommodate his words to convention. Says Noonan: "No impersonal supervision is addressed but the God of the Our Father taught by Jesus," even though to avoid offending Jewish listeners Roosevelt did not mention Jesus by name. Far from being formulaic, the prayer was at once collective and individual. It amounts to a "shining instance of personal convictions placed in a public context."[49]

D-Day and Prayer

As in his address to Congress of January 1939, so in the D-Day prayer of 1944 the president referred to "our religion." The prayer was written at the Charlottesville, Virginia, home of Roosevelt's longtime assistant Major General Edwin M. "Pa" Watson and his wife, Frances. Only a very few close friends were present: daughter Anna Roosevelt and her husband, John Boettiger; the Roman Catholic Watson; FDR's secretary, Grace Tully; and his cousin Margaret Suckley. Before writing the prayer, Boettiger and his father-in-law carefully went over relevant portions of the Book of Common Prayer. We may assume that, true to form, Roosevelt then dictated his thoughts out loud for others to refine.[50] While the wording and subsequent editing were a joint effort, the primary inspiration and final approval were, as usual, entirely Roosevelt's. There is but a single draft of the result. It is revealing to track the corrections made in FDR's hand. In what follows, additions to the draft are bracketed and excised portions are struck through.[51] The general rhythm of the prayer is that of the Book of Common Prayer. The president delivered it on the memorable evening of June 6:

> My Fellow Americans: [Last night, when I spoke with you about the fall of Rome, I knew at that moment that troops of the United States and our Allies were crossing the Channel in another and greater operation. It has come to pass with success thus far.]
>
> And so in this poignant hour I ask you to join me in prayer.
>
> "Almighty God: Our sons, the pride of our nation, this day have set upon a mighty endeavor, a struggle to preserve our Republic, [our religion], and our civilization, and to set free ~~millions of other human beings, now in bondage~~ [a suffering humanity].

"Lead them straight and true; give strength to their arms, stoutness to their hearts, steadfastness to their faith.

"They will need Thy blessings. Their road will be long and hard. The enemy is strong. He may hurl back our forces. Success may not come with rushing speed, but we shall return again and again; and we know that by Thy grace, and by the righteousness of our cause, our sons will triumph.

"They will be sore tried, by night and by day, without rest—till the victory is won. The darkness will be ~~split by the fire of many cannon~~ [rent by noise and flame].[52] ~~Silence will not reign.~~ Men's souls will be shaken with the [terrible] violences of war.

"These are men lately drawn from the ~~avocations~~ [ways of peace].[53] They fight ~~never~~ [not] for the ~~love~~ [lust] of conquest. They fight to end conquest. They fight to liberate. They fight to let justice arise, and tolerance and good will among all ~~our~~ [Thy] people. They yearn but for the end of battle, for their return to the haven of home.

"Some will never return. Embrace these, Father, and receive them, Thy heroic servants, into Thy kingdom.

"And for ~~those of~~ us [at home]—fathers, mothers, [children], wives, sisters and brothers of brave men overseas ~~we~~—whose thoughts and prayers are ever with them—help us, Almighty God, to rededicate ourselves [in renewed faith in Thee] in this hour of ~~greater~~ sacrifice.

"Many people have ~~pleaded with me~~ [urged that I] call the nation into a single day of special prayer. But because the road is long and the ~~need~~ [desire] is great, I ask that our people ~~give thought to the~~ [devote themselves in] continuance of prayer. As we rise [to] each new day, and again when each day is spent, let words of prayer be on our lips, invoking ~~Divine~~ [Thy] help to our efforts.

"Give us strength too—strength in our daily tasks, to redouble the contributions we make in ~~building armaments and supplies for the~~ [the physical and material] support of our armed forces.

"And let our hearts be stout, to wait out the long travail, to bear sorrows that may come, to ~~transfuse~~ [impart] our courage unto our sons wheresoever they may be.

"And, O Lord, give us Faith. Give us Faith in Thee; Faith in our sons; Faith in each other; faith in our united crusade. Let not the keenness of our spirit ever be dulled. Let not the impacts of temporary events, of temporal matters of but fleeting moment—let not these deter us in our unconquerable ~~spirit~~ [purpose].

"With Thy blessing, we shall prevail over the unholy forces of our enemy. Help us to conquer the apostles of greed and racial ~~vanity~~ [arrogance]. Lead us to the ~~preservation of our Republic~~ [saving of our country] and with our sister nations into a world unity that will spell a ~~powerful~~ [sure] peace—a peace invulnerable to the schemings of unworthy men. And a peace that will let all men live [in freedom] ~~according to their own desires~~, reaping the just rewards of their honest toil.

~~'So be it.~~ "[Thy will be done,] Almighty God.

"AMEN."

[Signed] Franklin D. Roosevelt

Along with FDR's significant additions of "our religion," "children," "renewed faith in Thee," and the final ending came his ever-present desire to simplify the text, to make it taut and sharp: "suffering humanity," "rent by noise and flame," "saving of our country," and "in freedom" replace wordy phrases. The prayer ends with the decisive "Thy will be done" from the Lord's Prayer instead of the resigned, almost offhand "So be it." Throughout, FDR chose vigorous words that slanted toward the biblical: he substituted "ways" for "avocations"; "urged" for the theatrical "pleaded with me"; "impart" for the medical-sounding "transfuse"; and the stronger "arrogance" (Prov. 8:13; Isa. 13:11) for the languid "vanity" following the word "racial." He rejected proposals for "a single day of special prayer" and urged daily intercessions for loved ones during the war. The word "faith" is repeated six times.

The D-Day prayer displays the faith of Franklin Roosevelt. As Grace Tully observed, "No words ever came from a soul more deeply moved, from a leader more conscious of the terrific responsibility involved in sending tens of thousands of the best of a nation's young manhood into hazardous battle."[54]

FDR was not reluctant to pray aloud on public occasions. Twice in late 1940 he used the prayer "For Our Country" from the Book of Common Prayer, once in his final radio speech on election eve and again five days later in his Thanksgiving Day Proclamation. Written during the Gilded Age of late nineteenth-century America, the prayer's majestic—and critical—cadences make bold to ask for "honorable industry, sound learning, and pure manners." It entreats God to "save us from violence, discord, and confusion; from pride and arrogance and from every evil way." In the light of the Nazi threat to the Western Hemisphere that year, what followed could hardly have been more relevant: "Defend our liberties and fashion into one united people the multitudes brought hither out of many kindreds and tongues." This was followed by the petition "Endue with the spirit of wisdom those to whom in thy Name we entrust the authority of government." Roosevelt could hardly have avoided thinking, in 1940, of Congress and of himself as Britain and democracy's peril deepened.

The words took on new meaning beyond the ordinary round of elections. The "spirit of wisdom" culminated for his administration in the Lend-Lease Act of March 11, 1941. Such use of church language, together with church involvement by leading politicians, was not at all unusual at the time. Sometime later, Frances Perkins recalled that during Lent that year, prior to the passage of the Lend-Lease Act, she had been in a Bible study group at the Church of the Ascension and St. Agnes in Washington, DC. Among the participants, besides herself, had been Vice President Henry A. Wallace, British ambassador Lord Halifax, and William H. Davis of the War Labor Board.[55] Prayer-book language could fit well with political considerations. On Thanksgiving Day 1940, a prayer for "justice and peace at home" coincided with FDR's promise not to send American boys into war; at the same time came words of national aspiration to "show forth thy praise among the nations of the earth." Finally, in prosperous times, after reminding listeners that the hearts of Americans should be filled with thankfulness, Roosevelt prayed somberly that God, "in the day of trouble[,] [would] suffer not our trust in thee to fail."[56] Consciously or not, many members of Roosevelt's generation wove religious language into their understanding of world affairs. Whether he composed a prayer or read one from his prayer book, Roosevelt was sure-footed and pitch-perfect.

The Roots of Faith

Which religious culture influenced Roosevelt and shaped his character? We should search for this beyond theology, in a more general type of Christian literary work stretching from Augustine's *Confessions* to Dante's *Divine Comedy*, from Shakespeare's *The Tempest* to the seventeenth-century English authors John Donne, George Herbert, John Milton, and John Bunyan to the twentieth century's Dorothy Sayers, William Faulkner, and Ignazio Silone. These all paint a narrative, almost pictorial tradition of Christian faith. They conduct a dialogue between Christianity and the contemporary world that is graphic and arresting, with a meaning that can be either implicit or manifest. In our own time, we have seen Martin Luther King Jr. engage in such a dialogue. As Brad R. Braxton writes, "For King Scripture was a storybook whose value resided . . . in the evocative images, in the persuasive, encouraging anecdotes of the audacious overcoming of opposition, and in its principles about the sacredness of the human person."[57] The same can be said of Franklin Roosevelt's words.

The ultimate strength of the D-Day prayer and the president's recitation of the prayer for the country rests, as Judge Noonan observes, in the compact presentation of "Christian theological themes germane to the crisis at hand" and, above all, with the sincerity of the one who prays them. On those occasions, art, ethics, and faith interact in what George Steiner calls the "grammar of the overwhelming"; the spell of the narrative, the awakening of human freedom "in its particular literary and political settings," commands the listener's attention.[58]

Permeating both Protestant culture in general and FDR's imagination in particular was John Bunyan's metaphoric drama *The Pilgrim's Progress*. Bunyan related the inner, Pauline journey of the faith of an ordinary person who was neither great saint nor great sinner. Christian is a modest pilgrim who follows his Lord at a distance. As in the Gospels themselves, parables replace abstraction and catch us up in their concreteness. In the most desperate circumstances of his journey, Christian is engulfed by darkness; he is alone, and frightened, in an atmosphere "rent by noise and flame," as Roosevelt put it in the D-Day prayer. His path is perilously narrow. On one side is the ditch of false doctrine into which the blind have always led the blind; on the other side is the quagmire of immorality that offers no firm place for a foot because it has no bottom. When amid the gloom the pilgrim seeks to shun the one peril, he is in danger of tipping over into the other. His adversary is no longer Apollyon, the angel of destruction, but only flame, smoke, "hideous noises," and a "company of *Fiends* coming toward him." At the gate of Hell itself, Christian "is forced to put up his Sword and betake himself to another weapon called *All-Prayer*, so he cried in my hearing, *O Lord, I beseech thee deliver my Soul*."[59]

Here Christian's—and Bunyan's—subjective self is objectified in Jesus Christ. "Me thought," wrote Bunyan elsewhere, "it was as if I had seen him born, as if I had seen him grow up, as if I had seen him walk [through] this world, from the cradle to his Cross." Geoffrey Nuttall writes that behind the path of Christian in the book is the path of Christ, the greater pilgrim, and so extraordinarily convincing is Bunyan's *Pilgrim's Progress* "that the reader fortunate enough to have read it or had it read to him in childhood has scenes that stay with him all his life."[60] In his struggle with polio and in wartime, Roosevelt resorted to All-Prayer. He borrowed from the same scene of the confrontation with Apollyon, only this time from the beginning of Christian's progress through the Valley of the Shadow of Death. Here Christian confronts those who would turn back. In like manner, in his second inaugural address, the president asked, "Shall we pause now and turn back on the road that lies ahead?"[61]

Such analysis hardly seems to fit the character of a Hudson River squire, much less that of a professional politician. Yet Roosevelt, naturally and with ease, filled the commonplace with new meaning when he spoke over the radio. His ability to picture the gains and losses of his fellow countrymen and -women, to enter their homes, and to use the language of ordinary life to get his point across is well known. That he derived such ability from the literature he read and from the considerable intellectual stores that he brought to the White House seems a reasonable assumption. It was a part, perhaps a significant part, of a wider world of interest in people and in politics. His intellectual background should not be overstated, but by the same token it should not be ignored. The tradition of Christian literary expression nurtured his faith.

He often resorted to well-worn observations. In addressing the Young Democratic Club of Baltimore on April 12, 1936, he spoke of the "spirit of youth." He hoped his listeners would not underestimate the significance of that spirit. The day before, he reminded them, "Christendom celebrated Easter—the anniversary of the Resurrection of Our Lord who, at the beginning of His ministry was thirty years old and at His death was only thirty-three years. Christianity began with youth and, through the last two-thousand years, the spirit of youth has revitalized it."[62] Later in the year, in the final address of the 1936 presidential campaign, he spoke of the unadorned, homely quality of faith. Referring to the American people as a whole, he opined that "they have thought things through to where the eternal simplicities mean more than the fuzz-buzz of technical talk." Americans, he concluded, "know that the important thing is the spirit in which Government will face problems as they come up and the values it will seek to preserve or to enhance. At bottom these are the things that count."[63]

Gary Scott Smith summarizes the base of Franklin Roosevelt's faith: "While he was not very concerned about the intellectual or devotional aspects of Christianity, he appeared to be genuinely moved by biblical stories, episodes in church history, moral ideals, and occasionally by worship experiences, ranging from singing Methodist hymns to participating in the Episcopal liturgy."[64] That base supported much more besides, Smith would agree. As FDR wrote to Daniel A. Poling on June 15, 1938, "the message of the Nazarene is a vital and compelling force in the lives of millions of men and women." He went on to speak of "this weary world" and could not think of any problem that "would not find ready solution if men and nations would rule their lives according to the plain teaching of the Sermon on the Mount."[65] When Eleanor Roosevelt once pressed him about the truth of Christian doctrine, he replied, "I never really thought much about it. I think it is just as well not to think about things like that too much."[66]

In sum, Roosevelt's faith was clothed with the vestments of family history and tradition: the Rotterdam Cathedral where an ancestor lay buried and the 1686 Dutch Bible on which he took the oath of office seven times. He was steeped in the ancient faith in St. James' Church, where the family worshiped and to which later he gave paternal oversight. His religion grew in the old chapel at Groton School, in the services and preaching of Endicott Peabody and others. Faith was embodied in the hymns he had come to love and learned to play at the mission church in Ayer. Roosevelt hoped that others, however differently they expressed their faith, were rooted in a similarly meaningful heritage.

From such sources he gained a serenity that manifested his faith. Arthur M. Schlesinger Jr. writes, "He himself offered no clues; he was, he used to say, 'the least introspective man in the world.'" But the clues lay everywhere, and Schlesinger got it right: first came toughness, "character, temperament, experience, triumph over catastrophe." As Attorney General Francis Biddle put it, "He had got on top of life. Nothing could touch him." But there was more. His faith, said Rexford Tugwell, was "a source of detached exaltation which could not be touched by the outcome" of any venture he tried. As Eleanor Roosevelt reflected, "He felt guided in great crises by a strength and wisdom higher than his own."[67] Consent to and trust in that Other were not only a private matter but also a public responsibility that involved support for the kind of government at home and abroad that increased human freedom and dignity. In the D-Day prayer, he was able to make his private faith public without turning it into a narrow nationalism or imposing it on people of other convictions.

Chapter Seven

Prophet, Priest, and President— FDR in World War II

The most troublesome period for Roosevelt's foreign policy came between 1939 and 1942. In those years the European democracies fell, Britain and the Soviet Union barely held on against Nazi conquests, and the United States was attacked and her Pacific fleet all but destroyed at Pearl Harbor. Up to that December day in 1941, the United States was involved in an intense war of words at home over what course to take in world affairs. The contending parties, those for intervention abroad and those against it, could both appeal to robust traditions in American history. Both raised pointed fears about the future should the nation not follow their course. In this context, hope for the future and any sense of common purpose were in short supply.

As the earliest and strongest voice of the interventionist camp, Roosevelt finally prevailed in this contest because his prophecies about fascist aggression turned out to be true. Even more, he succeeded, far better than his opponents, at cultivating a sense of hope about what America could be, not just what it should avoid. It was to be a community of solidarity and sacrifice in defense of Christian democracy. From that would come new opportunities for ordinary people and the extension of liberty for all. This became his sustained theme to the American people during the long, difficult years of World War II. We can say that in the prewar period the president acted as a prophet, issuing urgent warnings. Once the war came he turned more pastoral, endeavoring to sustain people in the faith. The firstfruits of that faith were to be an extension of those domestic reforms that had animated his earliest years in office.

Two Prophets

FDR's earliest attempt to rouse the nation against the fascist threat came in his famous "Quarantine Speech" in Chicago on October 5, 1937. It called for the United States to cut off trade with aggressor nations— Germany, Italy, and Japan—because when the precepts of religion were not observed, the most Christian thing to do was to "quarantine" the rule breakers. If aggression continued, it would have to be stopped by force. Roosevelt sounded like a prophet here in both senses of the term: making predictions about the future and recalling the people to their true tradition, even at the cost of sacrifice. He warned of a "reign of terror," of "international lawlessness," of the systematic violation of treaties. There would be more bombing of civilian populations, like the destruction of Guernica in the Spanish civil war the previous April. If the present course continued, all over the world "every precious thing will be in danger . . . all will be lost or wrecked or utterly destroyed." Nor did the nation's historic insulation from global threats matter any- more: "let no one imagine that America will escape, that America may expect mercy, that this Western Hemisphere will not be attacked and that it will continue tranquilly and peacefully to carry on the ethics and the arts of civilization." Roosevelt's speech was warmly received that day in 1937 by the crowd of fifty thousand. But the cheering soon ceased, and in the long run the "Quarantine Speech" proved to be a nonstarter.[1]

He took up the theme again the next year before a Canadian audi- ence at Queens University in Kingston, Ontario: "We in the Americas are no longer a faraway continent to which the eddies of controversies beyond the seas could bring no interest or no harm." The "ocean is not necessarily a barrier—it is a broad highway."[2] On May 10, 1940, the day Germany invaded the Low Countries and France, Roosevelt reminded the Pan-American Scientific Congress meeting in Washington about how science had generated radically expanded powers for good—and for evil. In this context he invoked the resources of religion: "in the New World we live for each other and in the service of Christian faith." However gilded that claim was in fact, he called the assembled scien- tists to turn their efforts to the cause of "moral order" and "human decency."[3]

With some justice his critics accused Roosevelt of trafficking in fear. He retorted that his speech reflected simple realism. He restated this in stark terms in one of the most important speeches he ever gave, a radio address declaring an "unlimited national emergency" on May 27, 1941. It came at the nadir of the struggle in Europe. German forces were driving the British out of Crete, while the *Bismarck*, the world's most heavily armed battleship, ranged the Atlantic after having sent its British equivalent, the *Hood*, to the bottom in ten minutes with one shell, killing all but three of fourteen hundred hands aboard. The German navy was sinking merchant ships more than twice as fast as Britain and the United States could produce them.[4] Hitler's invasion of the Soviet Union, which eventually represented the Allies' salvation, was still nearly a month away. For the moment, the war was frighteningly concentrated, narrow.

The president's speech rehearsed the events in the year since the fall of France in May 1940. "Our whole program of aid for the democracies has been based on hard-headed concern for our own security." That aim having failed, a grim picture lay in store for the Western Hemisphere were Hitler to defeat England. German forces would quickly hop over the Atlantic, subjugate Latin America as they had the Balkans, and begin to strangle America and Canada. "No, I am not speculating about all this," said the president. "I merely repeat what is already in the Nazi book of world conquest."[5] Keeping in mind the "lightning speed of modern warfare," the United States could not wait until the enemy landed on its shores; it had, now, urgently, to defend the North Atlantic supply line to Britain and render "every possible assistance to Britain" as well. Those who claim "we are disunited and cannot act" speak from timidity and in the vain hope of preserving "peace at any price. . . . To them I say this: never in the history of the world has a Nation lost its democracy by a successful struggle to defend its democracy." Yes, he acknowledged, there were "sincere, patriotic men and women whose real passion for peace has shut their eyes to the ugly reality of international banditry." But by now they had to be "embarrassed" at how their language mirrored the propaganda of democracy's totalitarian enemies abroad and of groups at home who are "devoted to bigotry and racial and religious intolerance." Such "sinister" tones aimed "to confuse and divide our people and to destroy public confidence in our Government." Their words constituted "the advanced guard of physical attack."[6]

A diametrically opposite call had been sounded just one month before in New York City by a great American hero, Colonel Charles A.

Lindbergh. Lindbergh was fourteen years past his pioneering trans-atlantic flight as the "Lone Eagle," the epitome of American dar-ing and aspiration. But now he was anything but optimistic. It was "idealistic" interventionists like Roosevelt that showed a "disdain of reality," he charged. The grim course of recent history taught a different lesson. The Nazi juggernaut was unstoppable on the con-tinent of Europe. Every nation that sided with England had fought "against hopeless odds" and gone down to defeat, taking "countless thousands of young men to death." America was "no better prepared today than France" had been at her hour of doom. Even if the United States raised a large enough army, it would be out of the question to land and maintain it on a hostile coast. Its one-ocean navy faced a two-ocean challenge, and its ill-equipped air force was no match for Germany's.[7] He ought to know; Lindbergh had inspected the Luft-waffe three times at the behest of its head, Field Marshal Hermann Goering. He had come away convinced—and had so reported to the State Department, the French air ministry, and the British govern-ment—that German arms were unconquerable. In short, Lindbergh too trafficked in fearful prophecies: fear of too strong an enemy, fear that "war between Germany on one side and Britain and France on the other would destroy Western civilization and open up the flood-gates for the spread of Soviet power and communism in Europe."[8] Instead, and he repeated the phrase three times, it was urgent to cultivate and maintain "an independent American destiny" untram-meled by the rest of the world.

In fact, the balance of armed power was already turning in the Allies' favor; time was on America's side. But these developments were not yet evident, even to the most sanguine.[9] Lindbergh therefore had an audience for his pleas that America stay out of the war. To "take a course to which more than eighty percent of our citizens are opposed" would destroy democracy, he said. It was the interventionists who were giving "comfort to an enemy" by sowing divisions of opinion at home over the issue of a "foreign war." America should concentrate on its historic policy of defending the hemisphere. Let us "turn our eyes and our faith back to our own country before it is too late" and develop our own civilization, free of global entanglements.[10] With all that, however, Lindbergh had his own preferences for how the war abroad should turn out. On July 1, less than two weeks after Germany invaded the Soviet Union, Lindbergh sneered before an audience in

San Francisco how the same "idealists who have been shouting against the horrors of Nazi Germany are now ready to welcome Soviet Russia as an ally." He "would a hundred times rather see my country ally herself with England or even with Germany with all her faults, than with the cruelty, the godlessness, and the barbarism that exist in the Soviet Russia."[11]

Two American Traditions

The advice to stay at home was by no means new in America; it was long-standing and deep-seated. Had not George Washington in his farewell address warned against foreign entanglements? Early in the nineteenth century, Americans turned inward under the influence of the Louisiana Purchase, the Monroe Doctrine, and Secretary of State John Quincy Adams's continental vision of a nation spanning from the Atlantic to the Pacific. At midcentury the Civil War determined once and for all that the new republic would remain a single political entity. Stable constitutional arrangements and the successful integration of thousands of immigrants as laborers under a business oligarchy increased both patriotism and confidence in American exceptionalism. Ignoring Indians and African Americans, the white majority believed that America had escaped on its own shores Europe's endless repressions and squabbles. If World War I involved the country in foreign disputes, this proved to be a temporary departure; on March 19, 1920, the Senate voted not to join the League of Nations. From then until the Neutrality Act of 1935, isolationism attracted many thoughtful men and women. In a Roper poll taken shortly after war in Europe began in September 1939, three out of eight Americans wanted the United States to "take no sides and stay out of the war entirely, but offer to sell to anyone on a cash-and-carry basis." Three out of ten wanted nothing to do with either side; they did not even endorse trading with the belligerents. Barely one American in fifty felt that the United States should enter the war at once on the side of England and France. Europe, a majority concluded, was the same old sausage sizzling in its own juice.[12]

But there were countervailing forces. Americans had always been a seafaring people too. New England's sea captains, the Delanos not least among them, went fishing, whaling, and trading, especially with

Europe and East Asia. After the Civil War, Philadelphia and Newport News, Virginia, improved shipbuilding with steam technology, while New York City, with its 770 miles of waterfront, became the center for rail connections, waterborne commerce, and finance. In the Spanish-American War the United States acquired its first overseas colonies, and in 1905 its first truly international president, Theodore Roosevelt, arbitrated a peace conference to settle the Russo-Japanese War. A bloc of American maritime and admiralty lawyers led the way in designing a uniform global law of the sea.[13] With his high ideals for self-determination, President Woodrow Wilson fought World War I to universalize Theodore Roosevelt's peacemaking activity. That he was not successful, Franklin Roosevelt, Wilson's assistant secretary of the navy, thought a tragedy.

These contradictory strains in American history showed through in the swirl of American public opinion between the outbreak of war in Europe in September 1939 and the Japanese attack on Pearl Harbor in December 1941. While fully 84 percent of the public declared themselves to be pro-Allies across this period, in November 1940, 88 percent wanted to stay out of the fighting. That figure dropped, but only to 79 percent, by the time of Roosevelt's "Unlimited National Emergency" speech in May 1941. After the Lend-Lease bill passed the Congress overwhelmingly that March, "70 percent felt that the President either had gone too far or was now doing enough to help Britain." The isolationists took heart from the fact that almost 40 percent of Americans were against helping Britain if such aid risked America entering the conflict. Yet, by May 1941 two-thirds "believed that it was more important to help Britain than to keep out of the war, while five-sixths assumed that the United States would eventually enter the conflict."[14] Apparently Roosevelt's effort to educate the American people was succeeding. But that success came against a broad, complex, and sometimes surprising body of opposition.

For one thing, both sides on the question mobilized a remarkable range of talent and leadership across the fields of business, labor, journalism, education, and religion.

Leading Noninterventionists

Business

Richard Bissell (Yale University; Department of Commerce, 1942)
Merwin K. Hart (Utica Mutual Insurance; state government)
Jay Hormel (Hormel & Company; meatpacking)
James D. Mooney (General Motors, Overseas)
Eddie Rickenbacker (Eastern Airlines; World War I flying ace)
Lessing Rosenwald (Sears, Roebuck and Company)
Edward Ryerson (Inland Steel; Chicago philanthropist)
Robert E. Wood (chairman, America First Committee)
Robert R. Young (Chesapeake & Ohio Railroad)

Labor

William R. Hutcheson (United Brotherhood of Carpenters)
John L. Lewis (United Mine Workers, Congress of Industrial
    Organizations)
Kathryn Lewis (United Mine Workers)

Newspaper publishers and journalists

John T. Flynn (city editor, *New York Globe*)
William Randolph Hearst (seven dailies, including the *San
    Francisco Examiner* and the *New York Morning Journal*, five
    magazines, and two news services)
Roy Larson (general manager, *Time* magazine)
Colonel Robert R. McCormick (*Chicago Tribune)*
Oswald Garrison Villard (*New York Evening Post*, the *Nation*)

Education and academia

Harry Elmer Barnes (historian, Columbia University)
Charles A. Beard (dean of Progressive historians, Columbia
    University)
Edwin M. Borchard (Yale University)
Robert Calhoun (religious historian, Yale University)
Edward S. Corwin (constitutional law and jurisprudence, Prince-
    ton University)

Robert Hutchins (president, University of Chicago)
Philip C. Jessup (Columbia University)
Clay Judson (Chicago Council on Foreign Relations)
John Howland Lathrop (War Resisters' League; professor of
    international law; Unitarian minister)
Felix Morley (president, Haverford College)
Alan Valentine (president, University of Rochester)

Religion

Catholic World (Paulist)
William H. Chamberlin (*Christian Science Monitor*)
Commonweal
Lawrence Dennis (*Weekly Foreign Letter*, African American)
John Haynes Holmes (native fascist, Unitarian minister, editor of
    the bimonthly *Unity*)
Stanton B. Leeds (*Social Justice*)
Charles Clayton Morrison (*Christian Century*)
A. J. Muste (executive secretary, Fellowship of Reconciliation/
    FOR).
Porter E. Sargent (educator and publisher)
John Nevin Sayre (FOR; Episcopal Pacifist Fellowship; editor, *The
    World Tomorrow*)
Francis X. Talbot (*America*; Jesuit)

Cultural commentators

E. E. Cummings (modernist poet)
Walt Disney (Hollywood director)
Lillian Gish (Hollywood actress)
Sinclair Lewis (Nobel laureate novelist)
Alice Roosevelt Longworth (Washington, DC, socialite, daughter
    of President Theodore Roosevelt)
Frank Lloyd Wright (foremost American architect)

Leading Interventionists

Business

Charles G. Dawes (Chicago City Bank and Trust; Vice President of
    the United States, 1925–1929)

Thomas W. Lamont (J. P. Morgan and Company)

Frank Vanderlip (National City Bank)

J. S. Wanamaker (American Cotton Association; South Carolina Bankers Association)

Labor

Lewis Corey and Murray Gross (International Ladies' Garment Workers' Union)

George Counts, Benjamin Davidson, James Loeb (American Federation of Teachers)

David Dubinsky and Sidney Hillman (American Labor Party)

A. Philip Randolph (Brotherhood of Sleeping Car Porters)

Newspapaer publishers and journalists

Hamilton Fish Armstrong (*Foreign Affairs*; president, Council on Foreign Relations)

Ulric Bell (city editor, *Louisville Courier Journal*)

Robert Bendiner and Freda Kirchway (*The Nation*)

Claire Boothe (*Vanity Fair*)

Kenneth Crawford (*PM*)

Russell W. Davenport (*Fortune*)

Eileen Hughes (*Atlantic Monthly*)

Colonel Frank Knox (publisher, *Chicago Daily News*; secretary of the navy, 1940–1944)

Henry G. Leach (*Forum*)

Dwight Macdonald (*Partisan Review*)

Helen Hill Miller (*London Economist*)

New York Herald Tribune columnists Joseph Alsop (FDR's cousin), Robert Kintner, Walter Lippmann, Walter Millis, and Eric Sevareid (Paris)

James Reston (London correspondent, *New York Times*)

Chester Rowell (*Fresno Republican*)

Laurence Stallings (literary editor, *New York Sun*; editor, *American Mercury*)

Arthur Hays Sulzberger (*New York Times* and *Chattanooga Times*)

William Allen White (*Emporia Gazette*)

Education and academia

Frank Aydelotte (Swarthmore College; director of the Institute for Advanced Study at Princeton)

Stringfellow Barr (St. John's College)

Lyman L. Bryson (Columbia Teachers' College; director of education, CBS)

John Childs (Columbia Teachers' College)

James Bryant Conant (Harvard University)

William A. Eddy (Hobart and William Smith Colleges)

Samuel Bradshaw Fay (twentieth-century German history, Harvard University)

Frank Graham (University of North Carolina)

Edward P. Hubble (lawyer and astronomer, Mt. Wilson Observatory, Pasadena, California)

Frank Kingdon (Dana College)

Max Lerner (Sarah Lawrence; Williams; Brandeis University; the *Nation* and the *New Republic*)

Samuel Eliot Morison (America colonial history, Harvard University)

Mary E. Woolley (Mt. Holyoke College)

Religion

John C. Bennett (Congregationalist, theologian at Union Theological Seminary)

Sherwood Eddy (YMCA)

Francis J. McConnell (Methodist bishop)

John R. Mott (Methodist layman; leading advocate of global missions and ecumenism)

Cardinal George Mundelein (archbishop of Chicago; founder of Associated Catholic Charities)

Reinhold Niebuhr (professor of social ethics, Union Theological Seminary)

Henry Sloane Coffin (Presbyterian, president of Union Theological Seminary)

Ralph W. Sockman (Christ Church, Methodist, New York City; professor of homiletics, Union Theological Seminary)

Robert E. Speer (Presbyterian, global missions and ecumenism)

Henry P. Van Dusen (Presbyterian, professor at Union Theological Seminary)

Cultural commentators

Margaret Culkin Banning (novelist and Roman Catholic advocate of women's rights)

Dorothy Canfield Fisher (American Youth Commission; Montessori educator; novelist of women and the family)

Waldo Frank (Communist mystic novelist)

Lewis Mumford (author of *Men Must Act*, 1939)

Lyman Beecher Stowe (preacher, lecturer, and editor on the staff of Doubleday Doran)

Dorothy Thompson (International News Service and the *Philadelphia Public Ledger*)

Alexander Woollcott (drama critic and leader of the Algonquin Round Table wits)

In addition, both sides were bipartisan. Interventionism called forth some Republican congressmen and newspaper editors who had consistently opposed Roosevelt on the New Deal. The party's presidential candidate in 1940, Wendell Willkie; Kansas publisher William Allen White; and prominent attorneys Lewis Douglas, Frederick R. Coudert, and Grenville Clark all took leadership positions in pro-intervention lobbies.[16] At the same time, the anti-interventionists included some prominent Democrats, like Senators Burton K. Wheeler and David I. Walsh and national committeewoman Janet Fairbank; progressive Republicans like the La Follette brothers of Wisconsin and Senator Gerald P. Nye of North Dakota; and important voices further to the left, including the perennial Socialist nominee for president, Norman Thomas; "America's #1 pacifist" (so designated by *Time* magazine) A. J. Muste; and Muste's colleague in the Fellowship of Reconciliation, John Nevin Sayre. Black America's leading radical, W. E. B. Du Bois, had choice words for those who were thundering about the aggressions of Germany, Japan, and (after the Nazi-Soviet Pact) the USSR: "England has been seizing land all over the earth for centuries with and without a shadow of rightful claim: India, South Africa, Uganda, Egypt, Nigeria, not to mention Ireland. The United States seized [part of] Mexico from a weak and helpless nation in order to bolster slavery; and incidentally when Italy took Abyssinia she was enabled to do it by means of the oil and supplies which America furnished. . . . This is the sort of world that has grown suddenly righteous in defense of Finland."[17]

Eventually, anti-interventionist sentiment coalesced around the America First Committee (AFC), which had been organized in September 1940 by some students at Yale Law School: R. Douglas Stuart Jr., scion of the Quaker Oats fortune; future Yale president Kingman Brewster; future Peace Corps director R. Sargent Shriver; future Supreme Court justice Potter Stewart; and future president of the United States Gerald R. Ford. They promptly enlisted Herbert Hoover and his ambassador to Japan, William R. Castle, in the cause, and those two in turn rounded up an extraordinary variety of others: historian Charles A. Beard; famed architect Frank Lloyd Wright; John Foster Dulles, who a long decade later would become secretary of state; Hollywood eminence Walt Disney; Hugh Johnson, the volatile head of FDR's National Recovery Administration; Nobel Prize–winning novelist Sinclair Lewis; the serially outspoken daughter of Theodore Roosevelt, Alice Roosevelt Longworth; and the tirelessly crusading reform journalist Oswald Garrison Villard, editor of the *New York Evening Post*, owner of the *Nation*, and a grandson of William Lloyd Garrison.

Fatefully, the Yale organizers of AFC invited Charles Lindbergh to speak to them. Eventually he came to represent anti-interventionism for much of the public. In October 1940, some 3,000 students turned out to cheer Lindbergh at Yale's Woolsey Hall, and the national speaking tour that followed brought out increasingly larger crowds the longer it lasted. By spring 1941, his addresses in Chicago, New York, and Minneapolis each brought 10,000 into the house; on May 3, 15,000 in St. Louis; on May 23, 25,000 at Madison Square Garden; in June, 80,000 both in Philadelphia and at the Hollywood Bowl. Often cries of "our next president" could be heard in the stands.[18] This left the AFC hostage to Lindbergh's views and mistakes. The worst occurred in September 1941 at an address at Des Moines, Iowa. To his standard speech Lindbergh added a new note of urgency, even hysteria, making allegations against "subterfuge and propaganda," "war agitators," and "dictatorial procedures on the part of the president and his appointees." These parties were plotting, said Lindbergh, "first, to prepare the United States for foreign war under the guise of American defense; second, to involve us in war, step by step, without our realization; third, to create a series of incidents which would force us into actual conflict." All the while, he added, the propaganda machine would churn on with its "smear campaign" against those who opposed intervention.[19]

He named three groups as the worst offenders: the British, the Roosevelt administration, and the Jews. Behind them "are a number of capitalists, Anglophiles, and intellectuals . . . [and] Communistic groups." The reference to the Jews triggered an uproar. "Their greatest danger to this country lies in their large ownership and influence in our motion pictures, our press, our radio and our government," Lindbergh charged. Certainly "we cannot blame them for looking out for what they believe to be their own interests, but we also must look out for ours." His subsequent protestations that he admired "the Jewish race" came too late, and the fallout in the AFC's ranks was immediate. Norman Thomas bewailed the great harm Lindbergh's speech had caused and demanded that he be jettisoned: "Whatever may be true of the future, at present when we need some figure around whom to rally our forces in Washington, and the country, Lindbergh isn't the man and there is no one else in his place." John Flynn, leader of the New York branch of the AFC, found "it incredible . . . that Col. Lindbergh without consulting anyone literally committed the America First movement to an open attack on the Jews." When the New York papers got in touch with him, Flynn despaired, "I cannot for the life of me think of anything to say." AFC chairman Robert E. Wood considered disbanding the organization entirely. But its founder, Douglas Stuart, along with Herbert Hoover, Alfred M. Landon, and Father Coughlin, was all for holding the course.[20]

Varieties of Anti-Interventionism

Lindbergh's Des Moines speech has served to obscure the variety and salience of arguments in the anti-intervention coalition. It had three distinct points of view: outright pacifism, an older isolationism, and a noninterventionist internationalism. The three were neither identical nor interchangeable. Pacifists such as Muste and Sayre of the Fellowship of Reconciliation (FOR), the prolific novelist Kathleen Norris, and Quakers such as Milton Mayer of the Associated Press were against intervention on religious grounds, but they were not isolationists. They opposed all wars and killings wherever they might occur, but as the presence of leading Quakers such as Burns Chalmers in war zones attests, they were neither aloof in mind nor cloistered from bodily harm and danger. Pacifists did not join the AFC; "America first" had a noxious ring in their ears.

Stay-at-home isolationists, on the other hand—Lindbergh, Colonel McCormick, the two Progressive La Follettes of Wisconsin, and Senators Arthur Vandenberg, Gerald P. Nye, Robert A. Taft, and Charles W. Tobey—were not pacifists. Neither was FDR's ambassador to Great Britain, Joseph P. Kennedy, who seconded Lindbergh's judgment about the superiority of Germany's Luftwaffe. He was not just for "appeasement one hundred percent," said Kennedy. "I'm for it one thousand percent."[21] But isolationists parted ways with noninterventionists over the matter of aid to Britain. The latter favored it "within legal bounds."[22] In sum, pacifists acted out of their religious convictions and moral revulsion at violence, killing, and war. Isolationists reached back to traditional American policy and antiforeign outlook. Noninterventionists concentrated on strategy and tactics, essaying a policy of prudence.

All three groups were shaped by the disillusionment Americans experienced after World War I. In the 1920s and '30s pacifism was tightly linked to hopes for social change and greater justice in a nonviolent world. Thus Reinhold Niebuhr of Union Theological Seminary in New York City—who began, like FDR himself, as a disciple of Woodrow Wilson's idealism—thought as late as the presidential campaign of 1936 that the Roosevelt administration was "positively sinister in its navalism" and regarded FDR as a "conniving charlatan."[23] Many noninterventionists were devoted to promoting civil liberties and constitutional rights in a more equitable society. Two feminist pacifists, Tracy Mygatt and Frances Witherspoon, and their Bureau of Legal Advice, laid the foundation for the American Civil Liberties Union. Over all these and more lingered the influence of contemporary antiwar writers like John Dos Passos, Ernest Hemingway, and Erich Maria Remarque, whose *All Quiet on the Western Front* (1929) showed the senseless horror of war and the hollowness of much of its cheap talk about patriotism, duty, and valor.

The American religious community also played a vocal role on both sides of the issue. In 1938, after contact with the anti-Nazi German theologian Dietrich Bonhoeffer and British jurist Stafford Cripps, Reinhold Niebuhr changed his mind about Roosevelt and aid to the Allies. Two years later, he broke his long-standing friendship with *Christian Century* editor Charles Clayton Morrison over a review of his, Niebuhr's, *Christianity and Power Politics*. Morrison deemed the book a "flat repudiation of idealism" and accused it of "abandoning the world to unregenerate devices." Niebuhr was furious—and unforgiving.[24] Such polemics cut through many of the nation's largest church groups, including Roman Catholics, Methodists, and Presbyterians.

It polarized Roosevelt's own Episcopal Church too. In 1939, approximately half of its clergy stated that they did not propose to sanction any future war. In a February 1940 poll of Chicago's Episcopal clergy, only eight out of twenty-six agreed that the United States should declare war on Germany and send troops in case the Allied cause grew parlous. The president listened to church leaders he respected. This was especially true of his Harvard friend the Reverend Walter Russell Bowie: "He was the sort of person Roosevelt worried about," wrote Rexford Tugwell. "If such people did not approve of him, he was very uneasy—and fairly often they let him know how they felt."[25] Pacifist bishop W. Appleton Lawrence of western Massachusetts joined with John Nevin Sayre in forming the Episcopal Pacifist Fellowship (EPC) on November 11, 1939, Armistice Day. The EPC took an absolutist position and asked all Episcopal clergy to sign a pledge refusing to participate in or give moral support to any war. Roosevelt's denomination also had notable interventionists, however: prominent clergy such as Howard Chandler Robbins and Bishop Will Scarlett of Missouri espoused cooperative security. So did Virginia layman Francis Pickens Miller, secretary of the World Student Christian Federation and an organizer of the YMCA.

The commanding bishop of the Diocese of Southern Ohio, Henry W. Hobson, took on the AFC directly. On October 21, 1941, he addressed a hard-hitting letter to AFC chairman Robert E. Wood, demanding that Wood live up to his promise that he and other America Firsters would report for duty should a shooting war with Germany begin. It already has, Hobson barked. "The Nazi rattlesnakes in the Atlantic are uncoiled" in the German attack on Allied shipping. Perhaps, Hobson granted, the America First movement began with "an honest illusion" that the nation could "ignore the world-wide struggle for freedom," but that "mirage has faded." Its spokesmen such as Lindbergh have become "dealers in the Nazi technique of terror." In fact, "America First has become the first fascist party in this nation's history . . . [infiltrated by] the paid agents of Hitler imported here to disrupt, disunite and mislead most Americans." It was time for Wood "to disband your organ of Nazi terror and hate."[26]

The AFC countered that *it* was the nation's prime voice against totalitarianism. Its New York City head, John T. Flynn, worried about wealthy and powerful persons "snooping about" along with the Roosevelt administration to plot dictatorial control of the nation. Intervention "will be a nice, respectable movement," he wrote, "dominated by fascist ideas but never calling itself fascist." Clay Judson believed that a war "to crush Germany, and its aftermath, would destroy democracy and individual freedom." Making matters worse was the startling success of the German invasion of the USSR in the summer and fall of 1941. In a letter to Robert M. Hutchins at the end of October, Douglas Stuart declared that "it would seem Russia is all through." Not that that was any great loss. Wood, Lindbergh, Hoover, and Congressman Hamilton Fish all argued with some justice that Stalin was no better than Hitler. But Judson underscored how the "*total* war" manifested on the eastern front meant that "the destruction of property would be equaled by the destruction of human life." Reflecting the views of Ambassador John Cudahy in Dublin, William R. Castle concluded that "the chances for England to survive" had become "almost nil." All the more reason to make America "a citadel of democracy which cannot be overthrown." That meant building up the nation's military strength at home and supporting a negotiated peace between Germany and Britain. Rejecting that option and prolonging the war, Stuart wrote Hutchins, had appalling moral implications. "Do you believe in buying time with other nations' blood? . . . If you believe that the war can be won by blockading the continent of Europe, do you think . . . that the cause of democracy can be advanced by the slow starvation of the women and children of France, Belgium, Holland, Denmark, Norway—and finally the people of Germany itself? . . . In what respect do you disagree with the teaching of Christ, 'Blessed are the peacemakers'?"[27]

Mixed with assessments of wars abroad was a welter of fears about the home front. Cutting the production of peacetime goods would, despite increased military spending, produce unemployment, the isolationists charged. Relief rolls would mysteriously rise at the same time that increasing factory production created housing shortages in the cities. Rearmament in 1941 had brought Detroit lucrative military contracts for planes, tanks, and trucks. But automobile manufacturers, fixated on peacetime profits, had already boosted their goals for the output of civilian goods by 20 percent over 1940. Suspicion that this "dictatorial" president meant to make over America hardly abated when price-control legislation was introduced into Congress. Writes Richard Parker, "Republicans never tired of fearing FDR's covert designs as war neared, and the idea of price controls over free-market capitalism stirred the deepest of those fears."[28] Bitter strikes such as the one against Ford in April caused leading isolationist senator Burton K. Wheeler and his politically active wife, Lulu, to take alarm. As Roosevelt urged military preparedness, the specter of revolution rose before the Wheelers' eyes.

In granting "any and all powers necessary to expedite the defense program" without limit, isolationists warned, "Congress will be little more than a Reichstag rubber stamp." If Lindbergh and others feared communism more than Nazism, Chester R. Bowles, an ardent New Dealer, major advertising executive, and collaborator of Eleanor Roosevelt's, worried that the president's foreign policy would give rise to fascism at home. Barring a few Nazis "kicking around in the back streets," he thought, most are "pretty well concentrated 3,500 miles away." In the meantime, businessmen "who are now in Washington working for the O.P.M." (Office of Personnel Management) were gaining "immense knowledge of our industrial facilities" and, he feared, "will tend sharply towards Fascism" after war production ended. Bowles concluded, "A civil war at that point is by no means impossible, although it is probably unlikely."[29] Whatever the case, democracy would be the loser. From March 1933 onward, many Americans feared that too much power was being put into one man's hands. Mistrust of communism and mistrust of fascism worked on each other. The more they did, the more theirs was the language of despair.

Just that marked the AFC's chief limitation, judges its best historian, Justus D. Doenecke. The AFC's "broadcasts, petitions, telegrams, and rallies were all reactive. As an emergency action group, the AFC lacked the time and resources to offer a comprehensive alternative to Roosevelt's program." Even though many of its members had been against the New Deal to begin with, "the AFC never supplemented foreign policy with any domestic program" and "offered no real vision of America's place in a postwar world."[30] The noninterventionists' legacy, "like that of the interventionists they so bitterly fought, contains prophetic elements as well as foolish ones," particularly a "healthy suspicion of executive power."[31] Perhaps the movement even contributed to the president's skill in directing the nation toward the place it needed to go. He had to avoid the conspiratorial hysteria they exhibited about Jews and communists and devious British plots to draw America into the war. From the start, Roosevelt reversed their extraordinary inability to admit the barbarity of Hitler and his Nazi acolytes. Most of all, he surmounted the noninterventionists' greatest shortcoming, their gloom and lack of hope for the future. Prophets, no matter how gloomy the prospects they decry, always include a vision of hope and inspiration. Lindbergh and the AFC lacked that; Roosevelt did not. Once his prophecies came true, he would have to maintain the vision in the face of the direst circumstances.

The War Comes Home

On the morning of December 7, 1941, the US Pacific fleet was virtually wiped out by a Japanese surprise attack on Pearl Harbor. The damage to the air force was extensive as well, and the casualties horrifying. Roosevelt was shocked at the news and stricken by an immediate awareness of his own part in the debacle. His beloved navy had been shamed, and he himself had failed to anticipate possible Japanese designs. As his speechwriter Robert E. Sherwood later put it, "all possible explanations and recitals of extenuating circumstances cannot wipe out the responsibility of all concerned, including the Commander in Chief, for the appalling unreadiness" exhibited that day.[32]

As the stunning news spread that afternoon, Frances Perkins witnessed the president sitting, quiet and concentrated, in command of himself amid the bewilderment and confusion of those around him. "His voice, as he told Naval aides what to reply to dispatches, was low. He wasn't wasting any energy." The "jittery conduct of some of the most eminent of our government officials was downright disgraceful," wrote Sherwood, but the "atmosphere inside the White House was very different. . . . Here one felt was the United States of America" at its best.[33] At 8:40 p.m., the cabinet secretaries filed into Roosevelt's study. "This is the most serious meeting of the Cabinet that has taken place since 1861," he opened. Then he reviewed the losses at Pearl Harbor and read aloud a draft of the speech he intended to give to Congress and to the nation the next day. After the cabinet came the leaders of Congress. "They sat in dead silence," writes James MacGregor Burns, "as the President went over the long story of negotiations with Japan." FDR then somberly reviewed the attack and casualties of the day, offering no comfort. The navy in Hawaii, he said, "was supposed to be on the alert." Senator Tom Connally of Texas blurted out, "They were all asleep! Where were our patrols?" The president said he did not know. Someone finally allowed, "Well, Mr. President, this nation has got a job ahead of it and what we have got to do is roll up our sleeves and win the war." Roosevelt seized on the remark, and the atmosphere changed. Outside the White House that evening, people gathered at times five deep along the iron fence, peering at the lights, "incredulous, anxious, waiting for some sign; . . . [a few] could be heard singing, 'God bless America.'"[34] For his part, Frances Perkins noted, Roosevelt now submerged his own plans and hopes "in the large and desperate duties of saving the country."[35]

The next day, December 8, waves of applause greeted the president as he entered the House of Representatives chamber on Capitol Hill. His address was short and unadorned. Except for the penultimate sentence, every word was his. That sentence, "largely suggested" by Harry Hopkins, read, "With confidence in our armed forces—with the unbounded determination of our people—we will gain the inevitable triumph—so help us God." It was short, admirable, and formidable. Sherwood concludes, "I do not think there was another occasion in his life when he was so completely representative of the whole people."[36] Thereafter they did not doubt his tenacity of purpose nor, because of him, their own ability to respond. As Roosevelt had brought hope and resolve to his countrymen and -women in 1933, he did so again in 1941.

At the beginning of 1942, writes H. W. Brands, FDR became the "most powerful man in American history. He headed a government stronger and more unified for war than any American government before it. He led a nation with greater capacity for war than any other nation in world history. He stood as first among equals in the most formidable wartime alliance ever gathered."[37] And Roosevelt, always conveying a spirit of goodwill, kept his head amid a welter of details, kept his eye on important objectives, and kept the whole machine moving in the direction of victory and peace. Cheerful and strong, he showed an unfaltering "capacity to inspire those who had to do tough, confused, practically impossible jobs."[38] In short, he exchanged his role as a prophet for that of a priest.

He exemplified the new role in a radio address on his sixtieth birthday, toward the end of January 1942. Circumstances abroad had not improved at all. The Japanese offensive in the Pacific was rapidly progressing, and while the Russian winter and Red Army had halted the Nazi advance on the eastern front for the moment, the ultimate outcome of that contest was anyone's guess. Nonetheless, the day was given over as usual to raising dimes and dollars for the victims of polio. In his remarks that night, FDR related his mixed emotions. "In the midst of world tragedy—in the midst of sorrow, suffering, destruction, and death—it is natural for most of us to say even on a birthday or a feast day: 'Isn't the word "happy" a bit out of place just now?'" He had thought so that morning, but those who poured out their donations to combat polio had changed his mind. "I want to say—very simply— thank you." Americans had evidenced a "great reassurance that comes from the deep knowledge that most of this world is still ruled by the spirit of Faith, and Hope, and Charity." With them stood "those Nations which still hold to the old ideals of Christianity and democracy." The donations of the day carried on a tradition of service to humanity in general and to "the cause of little children" in particular. Such service rose above the "torpedoes or guns or bombs" of war to honor the perennial, truly valuable things.[39]

By now the Roosevelts had a large personal stake in the war. All four of their sons were in uniform. Eleanor "grieved for the young men who were going off to war," wrote her confidant Joseph Lash, "for she knew what the last war 'did to people's souls,' and she dreaded it for this generation." A few days before Christmas, Lash talked with a despondent Eleanor, who "mentioned having had a hard day and then burst into tears." The presidential couple had bid farewell to their sons Elliott and James, the latter headed for Hawaii. Of course they had to go, Eleanor told Lash, "but it was hard; if only by the law of averages, not all her boys would return. She wept again."[40] The other two sons, Franklin Jr. and John, would enlist as well. All went overseas, and all four received decorations for valor in combat. When, nonetheless, a Republican congressman publicly attacked the sons' war records and implied that they were being mollycoddled, Eleanor found FDR "literally white and shaking with anger." Shortly thereafter Elliott wrote, "Pops, sometimes I hope that one of us gets killed so that maybe they will stop picking on the rest of the family."[41] Death indeed struck the inner circle of the White House, but at Harry Hopkins, who lost his son Stephen in February 1944 in the Marshall Islands.

In his new role Roosevelt tried to encourage a careful balance in popular opinion. At a press conference on May 22, 1942, he cautioned against the sharp ups and downs to which the news made people prone. "It is going to be a long war, and there is no reason for being over optimistic one week and over pessimistic the next week." He thought the press could "help very much on that."[42] Even more it needed to discourage the temptation "to resort to mass reprisals" against the enemy. Those would reveal civilization to indeed be a veneer and the endurance of principles an open question. Roosevelt promised sure punishment of the Nazi ringleaders who were "responsible for the organized murder of thousands of innocent persons and the commission of atrocities which have violated every tenet of the Christian faith."[43] But otherwise, mass reprisals and vengeance were not the way in which civilized people carried themselves. That policy would not by any means be easy. Americans came from a culture that valued the individual, but people in uniform came to realize that they were expendable. GIs did not think in terms of high principles, and civilians were susceptible to panic and suspicion. Just those drove the worst domestic failure of Roosevelt's wartime administration, the mass incarceration of Japanese Americans. There FDR fell far short of his own counsel.

Pastors are finally shepherds—leading, guiding, cautioning, encouraging, protecting, and comforting. As such Roosevelt frequently resorted to humor, and at peak moments to public prayer. Through it all he sought to build a sense of community and start to make good on promises of shared reward for shared sacrifice.

Humor

The good shepherd knows how to use humor to alternately disarm, quiet, or inspire his flock. Roosevelt resorted to it frequently, even to the point of appearing flippant to very serious people. Solemn utilitarians like Herbert Hoover and certified wise men like Walter Lippmann, John Maynard Keynes, and George Kennan came away from conversations with him with the impression that "he was at heart not a serious man, but a trivial hollow one."[44] Often enough FDR talked in an agreeable rattle to put off a visitor he did not want to hear. Yet humor for him was also a gateway to trust and ultimately to faith itself. His easy informality, his lack of personal luxuries, the "worn old prayer book at his bedside" that Perkins noted, went with his quickness in spotting fuss and self-importance in others.[45] He displayed a contradictory character that one authority on the subject associates with the clown—a combination "of solemnity and fun, of gravity and hilarity, of danger and absurdity, of wisdom and idiocy, and of the sacred and the profane."[46]

On this score Roosevelt seems to have absorbed a good Christian tradition. Commenting on the role of medieval clowns, Joseph W. Bastien notes that their antics "were not intended to desecrate the sacred but dispel some of the rigidity and pomposity of church-goers. The laughter of fools was praise to a God who disdained pride among his people."[47] It was a truth well understood by Francis of Assisi. The Bible itself is divine comedy in turning the world upside down. Pharaoh, Ahab, and Herod strut and fret their hour upon the stage and then are heard no more. The Bible repeatedly levels warnings "about putting too much faith and trust in human strength, wisdom, and achievement," says commentator Conrad Hyers. Evil is "the inevitable result of pride, arrogance, and boastfulness. 'Pride goes before destruction, and a haughty spirit before a fall' (Prov. 16:18)."[48] Meanwhile, those who understand the limitations of power and admit their own tendency to err gravely can adapt to the ever-changing demands of life and learn to laugh at themselves.

In this connection Erich Auerbach's comparison of biblical figures with heroes of classical antiquity is telling. People in "the Old Testament are so much more fully developed, so much more fraught with their own biographical past, so much more distinct as individuals, than are Homeric heroes," says Auerbach. With Priam, Hector, Achilles, and Odysseus, everything is in the foreground, everything is brought to light, everything explained; "never is there a form left fragmentary or half illuminated, never a lacuna, never a gap, never a glimpse of unplumbed depth," nothing like the heavy silence at the approaching sacrifice of Isaac in Genesis 22 that overwhelms the reader with suspense and catches her up in its urgency. In the Bible David's crime against Uriah the Hittite and his adultery with Bathsheba do not entertain us; they implicate us. "You are the man!" Nathan the prophet shouts in the royal face, and in ours (2 Sam. 12:5–9).[49] Yet, while duly punished, David is not cast off. He remains king; sees Solomon, his son by Bathsheba, named to his throne; and is even drolly comforted in his old age by the comely virgin Abishag. We might hope for something similar.

With his ear for the Bible, his love of biography, history, genealogy, and above all, his interest in all sorts and conditions of humankind, Roosevelt not only understood his own limitations but could also admit them and laugh at himself. At a critical moment, January 6,

1942, one month after the destruction at Pearl Harbor, he held what became known as the "Budget Seminar." Resting on his desk before him were reams of detail on such matters as the fiscal calendar in wartime, curtailed civilian steel production, conversion of factories, and civilian bureaus in the war effort. This is, he said, "the biggest Budget in the history of any Nation, any time." In mock comfort Press Secretary Early gestured to the newsmen in the front row: "Look at these financial experts, sir." Reporter: "We are already groggy." The president: "A very small group. I'm glad to welcome the financial editors of the country! (*Laughter*)." Second reporter: "We will be after this." The president: "Of course, very few newspapermen know the difference between a dime and a dollar anyway. But then, on the other hand, very few Presidents do. So we are even." He then went on to confess his own inadequacy: "By the way, I have always felt uncertain as to whether to write a Message to Congress, or a speech, on New Year's. I always get mixed up—and you do, and the public does—between the fiscal year and the calendar year. I don't think the public understands the difference. You don't all understand the difference half the time. I make mistakes."[50]

FDR persistently turned to humor in his press conferences before and during the war. In February 1941 he sent W. Averell Harriman to London as "defense expeditor" of Lend-Lease. One newspaper reporter asked an organization-chart question: "Mr. President, what is Mr. Harriman's relation to our Embassy over there? Does he represent you directly?" The President: "I don't know and I don't care." The reporter persisted: "Mr. President, how does he report?" Roosevelt once again: "I don't know and I don't care. . . . I suppose he will report to the proper authorities." Such humorous, throwaway lines turned people from the irrelevant to the consequential. When a few months later Harry Hopkins was sent to visit Winston Churchill as the president's personal envoy, some news commentators found sinister import in the appointment. At a press conference, a reporter asked, "Mr. President, will Mr. Hopkins be a dollar-a-year man?"—that is, one who served the country in wartime without other remuneration. The president: "No, he will not." Reporter: "Will he be an Administrative Assistant, then, sir?" The president: "No, I don't know what he will be, but it won't be a dollar-a-year man." Reporter, persisting: "Will he get paid?" The president: "Yes, sure. He's a Democrat! What a foolish question." "Loud laughter" ensued.[51]

But he knew when not to answer questions and did not make mistakes when national or Allied security was involved. With German armies sweeping across the Soviet Union in July 1942, anxiety about the fate of that nation was acute. At his next press conference on July 9, a reporter asked a seemingly innocent question: "Mr. President, what can we do to relieve some of this German pressure on Russia?" Startled, FDR replied: "I wouldn't tell you if I—I wouldn't say if I could. I won't tell you. Obviously the question shouldn't be asked or answered." When another reporter asked about supplying the Soviet Union, "Mr. President, now that they [the Russians] have got this rubber, what are they going to do with it?" The president: "Use it. (*Laughter*)."[52]

He was also quick to recognize those who showed imagination and independence even to the point of great risk. Major General George S. Patton Jr., who was a pioneer in shifting from cavalry to tanks, visited the White House a few weeks before the American expedition started for the invasion of North Africa on November 8, 1942. "I asked him whether he had his old cavalry saddle to mount on the turret of a tank, and if he went into action on the side with his saber drawn. Patton is a joy." Nearly a year later, Patton sent the map he had used in the Sicilian campaign as a gift to the president. FDR replied with thanks, and a joke. "You are doing a grand job in the advance" in Italy. It has been suggested "that after the war I should make you Marquis of Mt. Etna. Don't fall into the crater."[53] Patton's character kept him right at the edge, and when he slapped a hospitalized soldier whom he thought cowardly, he fell into another sort of crater and was relieved of command. He was restored only after D-Day and then proved to be the greatest American field commander of the war. Roosevelt used humor in his relationship with Patton both to tweak his rank and to show respect for his ability and dignity. Instead of breeding contempt, Roosevelt's informality served to lighten the general's load of care and also brought the general into his circle of friends.

Finally, Roosevelt used humor as a deadly, effective weapon against his political enemies. The most famous skewering came in an address to the Teamsters Union in Detroit during the 1944 reelection campaign. He spoke up for his "little dog, Fala," with mock indignation that delighted the millions listening on the radio and left his critics cowering before the collective ridicule.

These Republican leaders have not been content with attacks on me, or my wife, or my sons. No, not content with that, they now include my little dog, Fala. Well, of course I don't resent attacks, my family doesn't resent attacks, but Fala does resent them. You know, Fala is Scotch, and being a Scottie, as soon as he learned that the Republican fiction writers in Congress and out had concocted a story that I had left him behind on the Aleutian Islands and had sent a destroyer back to find him—at a cost to the taxpayer of two or three, or eight or twenty million dollars—his Scotch soul was furious. He has not been the same dog since. I am accustomed to hearing malicious falsehoods about myself—such as that old, worm-eaten chestnut that I have represented myself as indispensable. But I think I have a right to resent, to object to libelous statements about my dog.[54]

Community

For FDR a stronger sense of community was a high priority in the war effort, both as a means and as an end. He did not regard America as sacred, but he did see it suffused with a precious spiritual quality. It was something of a congregation that he could address in an intimate, pastoral way. His excellence as a communicator lay just here, in an uncanny ability to reach ordinary people in their particular circumstances. On normal occasions he sounded homey and avuncular. On election eve 1940, he spoke to the American people "from the quiet of my home in Hyde Park," where he was surrounded by his family, as they were by theirs. After his listeners have "eaten their supper in peace, they will be able to sleep in their homes tonight in peace." Tomorrow they would go to the polling place, discuss the nation, the weather, "and the prospect for their favorite football team. . . . And I suppose there will be a few warm arguments." But each American would remember that "this vote I am casting is the exercise of my highest privilege and my most solemn duty to my country."[55] Americans would also remember that many around the world had lost that privilege, and that their duty was to stand in for them, voting also on their behalf.

He could sound like Jimmy Stewart in a Frank Capra movie (or perhaps Capra imitated Roosevelt). At a press conference in October 1942, he celebrated the "perfectly grand spirit" with which local farming communities had risen to the challenge of bringing in the harvest with so many hands gone off to war: "the banker, and the editor of the paper, and the drugstore fellow, and the garage man, and the children, they all give up what they are doing and go into the fields for three or four days, and—by gosh!—get the crops in." He went on to praise the ten million people who had volunteered for civilian defense work.[56] His State of the Union message for 1942 riffed on the long lists of Whitman's *Song of Myself*, with praise for the "owners, managers, and supervisors," as well as "the draftsmen and the engineers" and ordinary "workers—men and women—in factories and arsenals and shipyards and mines and mills and forests—and railroads and on highways." Praise also went "to farmers who have faced an unprecedented task of feeding not only a great Nation but a great part of the world."[57] His fireside chat opening another war bond campaign in 1943 praised the citizens of a Mississippi River town for joining together in a desperate effort to raise the levees during a flood; once again, "business men, workers, farmers, doctors, preachers—people of all races" lent a hand. So also in the war bond drive at hand, his listeners were raising the American levees against totalitarianism, "filling the bags and placing them against the flood."[58]

Roosevelt also spoke directly to those in the military. He praised their newspapers for being open to "your own ideas, and the humor and the freedom to express them." He reminded them of their personal stake in the conflict, "your homes, your families, your free churches, the thousand and one simple, homely little virtues which Americans fought to establish."[59] He sent a memo to the secretaries of War and Navy about the special needs of those serving in the tropics, in remote and neglected islands outside combat zones, on cramped submarines, on "smaller ships like Navy tugs and patrol vessels in distant parts." He got specific: "I think it is just as necessary, this coming winter, to move people out of Attu or Kiska to Alaska for four or five weeks—say one third of the garrison at a time"—as to relieve personnel on "Christmas, Palmyra, Johnston, or even Fiji or New Caledonia or Espiritu Santo, if they have been there over a year." Finally, it might be good to have two crews for every plane in both the army and the navy "for the sake of the officers and men themselves and also for the sake of greater efficiency."[60]

When he went to the Hawaiian Islands in summer 1944 to confer with the Pacific command, he had himself wheeled through the naval hospital outside Honolulu. In the amputee wards he talked to "as many of the boys as he could at their bedsides from his wheel chair." His purpose "was to give them courage and hope for the future by letting them see that he, too, could not walk any better than they—that he too had to be wheeled around—this President of the United States."[61] Unknown except to son James, just before leaving San Diego for the conference, he had suffered an alarming gallbladder attack that left him white and prostrate on the floor.[62]

He showed a pastoral touch at grim moments as well. That was required especially during the Battle of the Bulge, the week before Christmas 1944. It was the greatest single American engagement of World War II and had casualty lists to match. While it proved a disaster for the German high command, the initial surprise of the attack and the advance of German troops hovered over the president's usual Christmas Eve message to the soldiers.[63] It was "not easy to say 'Merry Christmas' . . . in this time of destructive war," with American troops spread around from "the bitter cold of the front lines in Europe . . . [to] the heat of the jungles and swamps of Burma and the Pacific islands." Their thoughts, he was sure, "turn to us here at home around our Christmas trees, surrounded by our children and grandchildren and their Christmas stockings and gifts—just as our thoughts go out to them, tonight and every night in their distant places." He would "make their day of home-coming as early as possible," even though "we cannot say when our victory will come." Meanwhile, he asked the nation to join him in prayer for the protection of "our gallant men and women in the uniforms of the United Nations," and beseeched God to "receive into his infinite grace those who make the supreme sacrifice." They died "in the cause of righteousness," toward that new day when "the spirit of Christmas" would be realized in a "peace on earth in which all the Nations of the earth will join together for all time."[64]

Another New Deal

It was not enough to talk about sacrifice; some concrete rewards were needed as well. FDR offered a bold down-payment with the GI Bill that he signed into law on June 22, 1944. It included "enhanced unemployment and pension benefits, significant help in finding new jobs, generous economic assistance for all levels of education and low-interest loans for buying homes, farms, and businesses." To Roosevelt's mind, it gave "emphatic notice to the men and women in our armed forces that the American people do not intend to let them down."[65] He re-

membered the Bonus Army debacle of 1932 but also the public's uneas-
iness over crass cash payments for public service. So he had the bill put
the "focus on opportunity" instead, on giving "a hand-up instead of a
hand-out."[66] Remarkably, Roosevelt's uncle, Frederic Delano, as head
of the Post-War Manpower Conference, had devised such a provision
already in the early 1940s as part of a plan to promote economic growth
and national progress.[67]

It was estimated at first that perhaps 7 percent of returning ser-
vicemen and women—between one-half and one million individuals—would avail themselves of these opportunities.[68] In fact, roughly
50 percent did, 7.8 million. The national college graduating class of
1950 more than doubled that of 1940. James T. Patterson concludes that
the GI Bill helped "millions of Americans . . . acquire skills and technical training, to move ahead in life, and therefore return in income taxes
the money advanced to them by the government. It was the most significant development in the modern history of American education."[69]
These opportunities turned out to be skewed by race and gender, however, as might have been expected from a bill authored by John Rankin,
a racist and anti-Semitic congressman from Mississippi. Local officials
got to administer the aid, and many bankers and college-admissions
officers denied it to religious and ethnic minorities, African Americans
above all.[70] Still, the block was not uniform, and the path of upward
mobility was opened wider, or for the first time, for everyone from
Catholics and Jews at Ivy League universities, to Latino and East Asians
in job and housing markets, to cadres of African Americans who would
provide crucial leadership in the civil rights movement.

The GI Bill was also the firstfruits of a larger agenda that the president had announced in his 1944 State of the Union address. He meant
to restart the New Deal as partial repayment to the nation for the sac-
rifices it made during the war. His promise of broader opportunities
and economic advance played well with liberals and the general public
alike. He spoke out of genuine conviction, historian John Morton Blum
suggests, "but also, as was his way, for the record of history perhaps,
and immediately for the mustering of the left flank of his party."[71]
Throughout the war years he spoke repeatedly of the road ahead. His
new package of reforms sought to pave that road, or at least provide
future generations with a blueprint.[72]

The 1944 State of the Union address outlined Roosevelt's campaign platform for that election year.[73] It was also a peak moment in

American social and constitutional history. In that address Roosevelt proposed nothing short of a second Bill of Rights. At the beginning of the republic, he declared, "certain inalienable *political* rights" were assured citizens, "among them free speech, free press, free worship, trial by jury, freedom from unreasonable searches and seizures." Now it was time for, "so to speak, a second Bill of Rights under which a new basis of security and prosperity can be established for all—regardless of station, race, or creed." Roosevelt enumerated eight of these:

> The *right* to a useful and remunerative job in the industries or shops or farms or mines of the Nation;

> The *right* to earn enough to provide adequate food and clothing and recreation;

> The *right* of every farmer to raise and sell his products at a return which will give him and his family a decent living;

> The *right* of every businessman large and small to trade in an atmosphere of freedom from unfair competition and domination by monopolies at home or abroad;

> The *right* of every family to a decent home;

> The *right* to adequate medical care and the opportunity to achieve and enjoy good health;

> The *right* to adequate protection from the economic fears of old age, sickness, accident, and unemployment;

> The *right* to a good education.

The core theme of the New Deal reappeared: "All of these rights spell security. And after this war is won we must be prepared to move forward, in the implementation of these rights, to new goals of human happiness and well-being." For establishing such security was the most important step in establishing "America's own rightful place in the world," and that was the most important step in securing world peace. FDR was most concerned with avoiding the disasters, foreign and domestic, that had occurred after the end of the First World War. Once again, all the platitudes about sacrifice had to be matched by deeds; they "impose upon us all a sacred obligation to see to it that out of this war we and our children will gain something better than mere survival."

International Community

Roosevelt had already broadened his concern for community to the global scene. Once he confided to Frances Perkins that after "this damn war is over" he wanted to go to the Middle East and start a TVA: the "reason the Near East is so explosive is because the people are so poor. They haven't enough to eat. They haven't enough possible occupations. They need a food supply, and they need to raise it themselves." Water, he had found out, was fifty feet down; people could irrigate at night by means of Worthington pumps.[74] The State of the Union address in January 1942 lifted the sights much higher. If "our enemies are guided by brutal cynicism, by unholy contempt for the human race," the Allies "are inspired by a faith that goes back through the years to the first chapter of the Book of Genesis: 'God created man in His own image.' We on our side are striving to be true to that divine heritage."[75] Nearly seventy years later, such remarks sound self-serving. At the time, his words braced the arm and nerved the will of people the world over, and simultaneously educated Americans to their new global responsibilities.

To those subjugated by totalitarian forces abroad, he communicated a resolute heart of grace. As Sherwood puts it: "Roosevelt's was the voice of liberation, the reassurance of the dignity of man. His buoyancy, his courage, his confidence, renewed hope in those who feared that they had lost it."[76] To steer clear of the vagueness of Wilsonian idealism and to head off any subsequent isolationism at the end of hostilities, Roosevelt sought consistently to build a sense of community among the Allies and to influence the wartime generation. He wanted a *United* Nations, not a *League* of Nations. Throughout the war he spoke of the "gospel of brotherhood," of "community spirit," of "the injunction to love thy neighbor as thyself"; "the whole world is one neighborhood," he declared, and "we have learned to be citizens of the world."[77]

At other times he sounded Manichaean, dividing the world into starkly opposed moral sides. At the end of his "National Emergency" speech in May 1941, he described the issue as being one "between human slavery and human freedom—between pagan brutality and the Christian ideal. We choose human freedom—which is the Christian ideal."[78] A year earlier, in accepting the nomination for a third term, he spoke of "religion against godlessness; the ideal of justice against the practice of force; moral decency versus the firing squad; courage to speak out and to act versus the false lullaby of appeasement."[79] He was not far off the mark with respect to the character of the Nazis, and the United States did indeed save Western civilization from the armed horror of totalitarianism. But he was speaking less out of a smug view of American exceptionalism than of a new vision of transnationalism in which the country was one part of the global community. It was no simple task to cast America's place in that new order. As president, he had to make patriotic statements celebrating American greatness, and his very optimism betrayed excessive confidence in the ability of his nation to set the pace and the program for a peaceful world order. However good his intentions, there was a certain arrogance about those Worthington pumps. There was as well something naïve about his notion that Jews could simply be given a state of their own in the Middle East.[80]

Nevertheless, Roosevelt was the heir of the newer transnational outlook of American self-understanding. In May 1941 he told Norman Thomas that "99% of us Americans . . . are not very different from other people in the world."[81] He had an early exposure to that view at Harvard College's history department, preeminently from Archibald Coolidge but also from the iconoclastic Edward Channing and the Eurocentrist Silas MacVane. If FDR listened attentively to Frederick Jackson Turner himself, in History 10-B, the year (1903) the famous historian was on leave from the University of Wisconsin, he could have detected "the inevitability of trans-nationalization" in Turner's description of the settlement and occupation of the American continent.[82] Later, as John Milton Cooper points out, Roosevelt accepted President Wilson's call for national self-determination. FDR's Four Freedoms of January 1941 "unmistakably recalled the Fourteen Points" of his predecessor. But did this "generosity" toward the poorer many imply that to some degree the mightier few—or at least America—would follow a foreign policy that truly fostered not only self-determination but also self-realization?

Alas, no. The new anti-isolationist "transnationalism" fed instead into the imperial presidency. This, writes Cooper, "has been Franklin Roosevelt's chief legacy to his presidential successors."[83] Whether the fault was his or simply the result of the expansion of American power is debatable. Certainly his own strictures against France and Britain resuming their empires in the postwar world would leave some doubt.

Prayer

The expectation that the pastor lead in public prayer put Roosevelt in a bind.[84] His own prayer book was well worn from personal use, but he especially disliked being stared at in church while he said his prayers. His speeches frequently alluded to the prayer "For Our Country" from the Book of Common Prayer, and his D-Day prayer we have already scrutinized. Still we may be skeptical. Didn't the culture demand that on public occasions every president of the United States doff his cap to the Divine Emeritus? During times of crisis, didn't prayer become a political means of gaining support for high-stakes policy? Was there not a yawning gap between political intention and inner conviction?

Historians cannot finally fathom their subjects' authenticity of heart, but we can learn something about Roosevelt by looking at his public petitions on more ordinary moments than the D-Day occasion. On Christmas Eve 1941, just seventeen days after Pearl Harbor, the president issued a "Message to the Nation" appointing New Year's Day 1942 as a national day of prayer, "of asking forgiveness for our shortcomings of the past, of consecration to the tasks of the present, of asking God's help in the days to come." In the dawning struggle, he said, the American people needed divine guidance to remain "humble in spirit, but strong in the conviction of the right; steadfast to endure sacrifice, and brave to achieve a victory of liberty and peace. Our strongest weapon in this war," he concluded, "is that conviction of the dignity and brotherhood of man which Christmas Day signifies—more than any other day or any other symbol. Against enemies who preach the principles of hate and practice them, we set our faith in human love and in God's care for us and all men everywhere."[85] This was nothing Roosevelt had not said before and was something he would repeat again and again in the months to come. It was a fair measure of his own faith and of the conviction that he hoped was common to the nation.

Roosevelt also conducted public prayers on the anniversary of his inauguration. On the original occasion, March 4, 1933, he arranged for a service at St. John's Church, Lafayette Square, conducted by Endicott Peabody and including family, close friends, and his new cabinet. It was unprecedented in presidential history.[86] The tenth-year anniversary, January 20, 1943, was observed in the East Room of the White House, owing to wartime safety precautions. TVA director David E. Lilienthal was in attendance and was deeply impressed by what he witnessed: "I sat on the end of a large arc in which the chairs had been placed so that I was quite near the President, who sat of course directly in front of the pulpit. He takes these services with great intensity; I couldn't help observing his intensity and the unusual set grim look on his face."[87] Roosevelt had reason for a steely countenance. Eight million tons of shipping had been lost in the Atlantic in 1942, the difficult conquest of Italy was still five months off, and the cross-channel invasion of northern Europe was over a year away. When the Navy Hymn was sung for the recessional, recorded Lilienthal, the president's "voice rose clear above all the 'mumblers' around me. I was struck hard as I heard him sing out 'Oh hear us when we cry to Thee, for those in peril on the sea!'" At the moment, Lilienthal was not thinking of the convoys, patrols, and the people in them for whom the president was responsible but of Roosevelt's four sons, all of whom were in uniform and at sea. Particularly "there flashed through my mind the picture of John, the youngest, the long, lanky 18-year old . . . with whom I had breakfast on the South Portico years ago." Now, at twenty-seven, a navy lieutenant, Lilienthal imagined, he must have been in the minds of his father and mother as the president's "baritone sounded the words of the prayer, 'for those in peril on the sea.'"

Roosevelt could also have been remembering the service of morning prayer he had held with Winston Churchill aboard the battleship *Prince of Wales* in Placentia Bay off Newfoundland on August 10, 1941. The occasion was the negotiation of the Atlantic Charter, by which the two leaders pledged mutual assistance short of war and a common commitment to principles of freedom for the postwar world. That result had been disappointing to Churchill, who wanted more, but the Sunday morning service sealed a deeper bond between the two leaders. Some four thousand sailors from the two navies joined in singing "O God, Our Help in Ages Past" and then "Onward, Christian Soldiers," which left Churchill in tears. The Royal Navy chaplain read from

Joshua 1: "Be strong and of good courage; be not afraid, neither be thou dismayed: for the LORD thy God is with thee whithersoever thou goest." The service concluded with the same US Navy Hymn, "Eternal Father, Strong to Save."[88] Roosevelt sailed away declaring the service to have been the "keynote" of the entire meeting. To date he had been a prophet to his people; that weekend sealed the trajectory that would by year's end call on him to be a priest. The song, the prayer, and the faith remained the same, and would continue so until the very end. At the president's funeral service in that same White House East Room, the opening hymn was "Eternal Father, Strong to Save."[89]

PART III

Interpretation

Chapter Eight

"Who Is Kierkegaard?"

On the cold winter evening of February 19, 1944, the assistant minister at St. John's Episcopal Church walked across Lafayette Square to the White House to have dinner with President and Mrs. Roosevelt. He was Howard A. Johnson, twenty-nine years old. Though his uniform was clerical, not military, he served his country and his president well that night. Throughout, Johnson did most of the talking. Roosevelt listened more than he held forth, asked questions, took notes, and kept the young curate late. As Frances Perkins subsequently wrote of that evening, "He [Roosevelt] spoke of it a number of times, so that one may assume it was an important intellectual experience for him."[1]

The subject of conversation was the evil of Nazism and its relation to the Christian doctrine of original sin. Johnson spoke of both in his animated way and in the process introduced Roosevelt to the thought of the nineteenth-century Danish philosopher Søren Kierkegaard. Here was a new resource for understanding what had long troubled Roosevelt as a puzzle, a "mystery of iniquity," as Paul's second epistle to the Thessalonians put it. Kierkegaard helped explain the evil that Nazism had unleashed upon the world, while also harboring warnings against some potential dangers in the Allies' war against it.

The President's Dinner Theologian

Howard Johnson was a bright and promising theologian, sophisticated in conversation, cheerful, even witty, in manner. Born in Atlantic, Iowa, in 1915, he graduated from UCLA in 1936 with a major in political science. He spent the next three years at the Episcopal Theological Seminary in Virginia, from which he graduated with highest honors. In the course of his studies, however, he experienced religious doubt and was ready to abandon both the ministry and his faith. Then, on his own, he discovered Søren Kierkegaard's *Philosophical Fragments*. From this treatise and others by the same author, Johnson found "the point of view which enabled anything that I was being taught in the seminary to fall into place and make eminent good sense."[2] Having grown up in what Kierkegaard derided as the sterile observances of "Christendom," Johnson now discovered a "living" Christianity that reanimated his faith. *Philosophical Fragments* brought him to the vital center of the New Testament and set him on a course to expand the president's theological horizon on a February evening in 1944.

In 1940 Johnson was ordained to the ministry of the Episcopal Church. Before entering parish ministry, however, he decided to pursue further graduate studies, this time in philosophy at Princeton University. There he was befriended by Walter Lowrie and his wife, who, childless, took him in and treated him like a son. Lowrie was a leading Episcopal liturgical scholar who had served as rector of St. Paul's-Within-the-Walls in Rome, where he had written on early Christian art. But his strong and lasting influence came from introducing both Kierkegaard and Karl Barth to the American scene in the 1930s. Lowrie taught himself Danish—astonishingly, and fairly accurately—as he worked along on his translation of Kierkegaard, and Johnson collaborated in that enterprise. While their early and eulogistic view of Kierkegaard as revitalizer of the faith has since been surpassed in subtlety and complexity, in their day they broke new ground.[3] Lowrie and Johnson were largely responsible for the enthusiasm that marked Kierkegaard's initial reception in America. Yet continued study at Princeton did not seem fitting to Johnson once the country was at war. Enlistment as a chaplain was one option, but he and others felt he would be of more help at a strategic location in the nation's capital. That turned out to be St. John's Church, directly opposite the White House. He was installed there in 1943 as a regular parish priest with added emphasis on teaching and preaching. He also taught a course in Kierkegaard at the Virginia Theological Seminary across the Potomac River.[4]

On January 16, 1944, at Johnson's invitation, Eleanor Roosevelt spoke at the parish's supper club. In keeping with the president's epochal State of the Union address delivered less than a week earlier, Eleanor spoke of the tasks that lay ahead for the future of the nation. She, like the president, clearly had in mind reviving the New Deal at home and projecting it abroad as well. The next day Johnson sent Mrs. Roosevelt a note of thanks, remarking that her address had left an "extremely sobering" effect. "I cannot hold back the wish," he concluded, "that I might be able to render you some service" in return.[5] The first lady replied that she thought Johnson could indeed be of "great help during the war period and to those who are concerned about the future." She added an invitation: "Perhaps you would like to come and talk with me sometime."[6] A few weeks later the curate followed up by calling Mrs. Roosevelt's social secretary; an invitation to dinner arrived in the mail the next day. Not knowing what sort of affair this might be, Johnson consulted an associate justice of the Supreme Court who was a member of St. John's. He was assured that the formatting and color of the invitation card indicated a small, informal occasion.

Promptly at 7:15 that Saturday evening, Johnson crossed from the church to the entrance of the White House, showed his invitation to the guards, and was waved in. At the doors on the north portico he was greeted by the head usher: "Good evening, Mr. Johnson, the President is expecting you." To a relatively unknown assistant minister, the salutation was wondrous, the opportunity astonishing, and the setting intimidating. As Johnson wrote Lowrie a month later, the "experience of having dinner in the White House" was "Cinderella-like."[7] When he was escorted to the family quarters upstairs and found Roosevelt alone in the Oval Study, his confidence wavered. The atmosphere was simple and cordial, however, and one of the president's infamous martinis quickly put Johnson at ease.

Not unmindful of his pastoral responsibility and of the burdens carried by his wartime president, Johnson at once asked after Roosevelt's health and well-being. FDR replied that he was able to sleep soundly at night and was helped to do so by reading detective stories; currently Dorothy Sayers was a favorite. After some further conversation about Sayers's *The Nine Tailors* and *Gaudy Night*, Johnson, now "in an evangelistic mood," threw out: "You know of course, Mr. President, that Dorothy Sayers is even more important for her theological writings."[8] As Frances Perkins added with understated humor in her own account of the evening: "The President had never heard of her theological writings."[9] (Secretary Perkins, who was theologically knowledgeable, had.) Nonetheless, the ever-curious Roosevelt asked Johnson for detail. In the course of their conversation, Roosevelt observed that he had long been troubled by the problem of evil, particularly with respect to the Nazis. Here, Kierkegaard would become of help. But first there was more Sayers.

Some twenty minutes into the conversation, Mrs. Roosevelt arrived, full of apologies for being late. She had with her a young soldier, Pfc. James C. Agey, who was an aspiring biographer.[10] So it was that the four of them sat down to dinner in the West Hall. The conversation about Dorothy Sayers's theological point of view resumed. Three days after the dinner, Johnson sent Mrs. Roosevelt one of Sayers's pamphlets, *The Greatest Drama Ever Staged*. It "is short, profound, witty and apropos of our conversation Saturday night," he wrote. Although "the pious" had deemed it "offensive, flippant, irreverent" for not observing the comfortable stereotypes of religious propriety, "there are many of us who thank you *de profundis* for helping to break the [same] stereotype."[11] Two days later in her column, "My Day," Eleanor Roosevelt spoke of Sayers's pamphlet: "It is startling but it jolts our complacency and that may be good for us."[12]

Eleanor would find a lot to like in Sayers's career. Sayers was among the first women to receive graduate degrees from Oxford University (1920). She began her career in an advertising agency and ended it as a medieval scholar, having become an essayist, novelist, and playwright along the way. She is best known today for her immensely successful Lord Peter Wimsey detective mysteries, especially as adapted for the *Masterpiece Theatre* television series. Not just a popular writer, Sayers joined the ranks of England's remarkably creative theological dramatists of the 1930s and '40s—T. S. Eliot, Christopher Fry, and Charles Williams—who all aspired to blend ancient tradition with modern idiom.[13] While all of them had a certain razzmatazz, none gained a wider audience than Sayers had with her wartime BBC radio series, *The Man Born to Be King: A Play-Cycle on the Life of Our Lord and Saviour Jesus Christ*. Sayers's love of languages, history, poetry, and drama led her toward the end of her life to undertake a popular translation of Dante's *Divine Comedy*, for which she taught herself Italian. On top of that she participated with economists, sociologists, and clergy in organizing for the postwar period in Great Britain and the social revolution of the Labor government of Clement Atlee in 1945. Astonishingly, that planning took place in the war's darkest time for England, at the Malvern Conference of 1941.[14] In short, Sayers was a Christian public intellectual and activist after Eleanor Roosevelt's own heart.

Sayers was versed in the English apologetic tradition that often begins its thinking with a description of general human experience, then plots a road from unfaith to faith. The alternative in her day was the confessional theology of the Swiss theologian Karl Barth, which Walter Lowrie had introduced to America.[15] Sayers herself bridged the two camps. At times she argued by human artistic and literary analogies to theological truth, at other times she let the scriptural content dominate her thinking.[16] In the brief but highly influential essay that Johnson sent to Eleanor Roosevelt, Sayers declared that it was "the neglect of dogma that makes for dullness." The faith of the church expressed in "those amazing documents," the historic creeds, contains the "most exciting drama that ever staggered the imagination of man—and the dogma *is* the drama." She then sought by means of crisp idioms to bring the person of Jesus Christ as a human being to the attention of her readers. She did so with freshness and in close keeping with the doctrines of the incarnation and the resurrection. These she set against a dark background of sin and evil. Little wonder that she liked Kierkegaard.

Against Christian Complacency

Howard Johnson introduced just that link at his White House dinner. "You know, of course," he said, "that many moderns like Dorothy Sayers derive from Kierkegaard." No "of course" about it to Roosevelt. "Who," asked the president, "is Kierkegaard?" Johnson rose to the occasion with a lively sketch of the philosopher and his thought. He located its impact on modern thinking in its central premise of (in Frances Perkins's words) "man's natural sinfulness and his helplessness to reform himself except by the grace and help of God." This was the venerable doctrine of original sin but with a difference: not the traditional idea about a moral taint or legal guilt inherited from Adam and Eve, but the name for the existential reality that each person has assented to, or willingly takes part in—his or her fallen nature. That put the monkey on the individual's back. It was easier to ignore faraway Adam, as both Immanuel Kant and Kierkegaard recognized, than to dismiss contemporary evil in human nature. As Perkins said: "Johnson pointed out that the recent interest in Kierkegaard was chargeable to the current break-up of the humanistic illusion under which men had been laboring for a hundred years or so."[17]

What was that illusion and how did Kierkegaard bring it into disrepute? Johnson was well aware that conveying the fresh, startling character of Jesus Christ depended on answering those questions satisfactorily. While we have no transcript of what he said that evening, it is possible to piece together the general drift of his conversation from comments he made about Kierkegaard elsewhere. Some of these themes would have seemed familiar enough to Roosevelt, given his life experience, both private and public. FDR already believed, as had Kierkegaard himself, that the life of faith was a life of interaction with God's guiding, chiding, accusing, and forgiving Spirit, not a mystic reverie of one alone with the Alone. In Johnson's particular portrait of Kierkegaard as a person, Roosevelt could find plenty of points of contact as well. The Dane was "a strong spirit in a frail body, a devout communicant of the Church of Denmark. He was also wealthy and witty."[18] He wore no "hairy mantle," was not "grim or sour," but a connoisseur of fine wine and good cigars. "He was in great demand in the circles of the elite" and enjoyed the beauties of nature on country drives. But he mattered because he "was also a prophet. And he saw that society was about to come down in ruins. . . . When he warned that the skies were about to fall, his contemporaries branded him a misanthrope." To which the philosopher shot back that in the churches of Denmark "God was accorded the deference of Rector Emeritus." Kierkegaard, Johnson continued, "burnt himself out in an effort to shatter bourgeois complacency. But men were encased in the fat of self-contented, self-sufficient finitude. Not even the barbed pen could pierce the husk of self-sufficiency."[19] Johnson's remarks found a ready listener that night; a fascinated president "jotted down names of books by Kierkegaard."[20] This was all the more unusual, as the president customarily liked to do all the talking.

The issues of "humanistic illusion" and original sin stayed with FDR. "Some weeks later I happened to be reporting to Roosevelt on problems concerning the War Labor Board," wrote Secretary Perkins. "He was looking at me, nodding his head, and, I thought, following my report, but suddenly he interrupted me, 'Frances, have you ever read Kierkegaard?'" Perkins replied, "Very little—mostly reviews of his writings." "Well, you ought to read him," Roosevelt said with enthusiasm. "It will teach you something." Perkins thought the president meant that it would teach her something about the War Labor Board. But no. "It will teach you about the Nazis. Kierkegaard explains the Nazis to me as nothing else ever has."[21] How and why could that be?

Kierkegaard's books had lain unread outside of Denmark for generations after his death in 1855. But then, following the catastrophe of World War I, they bolted back to life. The liberal theology that had set the pace for all those years now came in for profound doubt, even derision. It was the establishment theology of "Christendom," an unbiblical faith acculturated to a culture of optimism about human nature and its prospects. Very quickly Kierkegaard's countervailing influence soared.[22] Despite their differences, the rising stars in Protestant theology—Karl Barth, Reinhold and H. Richard Niebuhr, Edwin Lewis, Walter M. Horton, and John C. Bennett—like Johnson himself, found in Kierkegaard a stimulus for their own work. As a result of Lowrie's translations of his works, the Dane became known in theological schools and universities. Like Johnson, many students took new life and power from his provocations. Christianity is "not a doctrine or a code or a law or a philosophy," wrote Johnson. "It is a Person. Christianity is the fact that God has existed as a particular man. It rests its whole claim on Jesus as the point where eternity has intersected time."[23] Faith's answer to that claim had to be "an unconditional yes or no," and not wait upon the deliberations of so-called reason for acceptance.[24] In the past, said Johnson, "not even God could escape the indignity of an explanation. He too had to pass before Reason's reviewing stand and report for inspection."[25] For too long the very existence of God had been more and more asserted by "proofs," "less and less proved by worship."[26] Kierkegaard prompted the generation of the 1930s and '40s to burnish their intellectual armor and sally forth to do battle.

Christian Faith as Radical Dependence

The winding path by which Kierkegaard eventually helped Roosevelt fathom collective evil started with Johnson's own recovery of faith. The doubting seminary student was intrigued upon encountering the Socratic doctrine of recollection in Kierkegaard's *Philosophical Fragments*—and Kierkegaard's critique of it. In the Socratic model, truth lies within each person all along; inquiry is a means of retrieving it. "Thus the ignorant person," wrote Kierkegaard, "merely needs to be reminded in order by himself to call to mind what he [already] knows." The teacher is the midwife to the learner, and this is "the highest [relation] one human being can sustain to another." Yet the teacher is also "accidental, an occasion, a vanishing moment," and no more. "In the Socratic view," wrote Kierkegaard, "every human being is himself the midpoint, and the whole world focuses only on him because his self-knowledge is God knowledge."[27] When self-knowledge is gained, like a baby chick pecking its way out of the shell, both the teacher and the occasion of the awakening vanish. In a key passage, Kierkegaard wrote: "The temporal point of departure is a nothing; because in the same moment I discover that I have known the truth from eternity without knowing it, in the same instant that moment is hidden in the eternal, assimilated into it in such a way that I, so to speak, cannot find it even if I were to look for it; because there is no Here and no There, but only an *ubique et nusqua* [everywhere and nowhere]."[28]

The opposite sort of universalism also bothered Kierkegaard in his day, this one denying the individual any intrinsic value. This was the system of G. W. F. Hegel, spotlighting the big picture, the unfolding of world history, and the elucidation of the emerging subterranean forces that shaped everybody's life. In this system specific individuals, historical occasions, Christianity itself were interesting largely insofar as they illustrated the inexorable movement in the grand progress of Absolute Spirit. At the end of the old regime in the late eighteenth century, Hegel declared, *Geist*—wisdom as reason, universal self-awareness, knowledge of the driving force of history—had suddenly achieved its destiny. It was now in the open and *known*. Individuals in their particular circumstances and events were no longer of significance; only the "great sweep of things" was. And Christianity? To be sure, it still had a place. It was, the Hegelians claimed, "*the* Revealed Religion, . . . the Absolute Religion in that for the first time religion realizes the *notion* of religion—i.e., of being the self-revelation of Absolute Spirit."[29] But Christianity must give up its traditional view that God is a personal, transcendent Being. There is no gulf between God and humanity; God's knowledge of humanity is also humanity's knowledge of God. As a result, people of the new age understand "reality" as never before. For the Hegelians, wrote Johnson, this meant that Christianity "was an historical phenomenon which they regarded objectively, at arm's length in order to put it into its place in the world historical scene."[30]

But for Kierkegaard, Johnson countered, "Christianity never proposed itself as a subject for speculation but as a task, as a way of life." Truth is not discovered by some collective or individual knowledge of the eternal consciousness. A point of departure in time must also be a particular moment of significance, and if it "is to acquire decisive significance, then the seeker up until that moment must not have possessed the truth." He cannot even be described as a seeker; rather, he must "be defined as being outside the truth (not coming toward it like a proselyte, but going away from it) or as untruth. He is then untruth."[31] The teacher here cannot help the learner recall what he already knows except that he is in error, and this knowledge puts him even further from the truth. "I had assumed [when I was a Socratic searcher that] I possessed intact a divine something (*nous, pneuma,* spark)," wrote Johnson after Kierkegaard, "which gave me access to the eternal *logos.* By going deep into my own soul, I could mount to the heights."[32] Christianity, on the other hand, strips the seeker "of every intellectual and moral pretension. It drives him naked and trembling to the throne of God." Thus the teacher must not only bring the truth to the person but also provide the condition necessary for understanding it. The learner lacks that necessary condition, having forfeited it himself, "and is forfeiting the condition [even now]."[33] The teacher, then, is God, who shows the learner that he is in error, and the cause of it is his own guilt. The teacher must both bring truth to the learner and give him the condition necessary to understand it.

How did such thinking translate into Johnson's work as a pastor? Consider the Ash Wednesday sermon he would deliver at St. John's Church just four days after his dinner with the Roosevelts. Fittingly for the occasion, the sermon was on sin. It drew a pointed contrast between lack of information, or inexperience, on the one hand and the Christian understanding of sin on the other. Typically, Americans and other true believers in the course of progress thought their problem was the former, a state of ignorance that the acquisition of more knowledge would correct. This approach, said the preacher, had "no place for the idea of sin." But "sin as radical error, radical mistake; sin as something essential, not just accidental; sin as something deeply engrained, not just a slip owing to inexperience," throws our condition and the evil at work in the world into sharp relief. It was not just "a little mistake" that brought Jesus to the cross. "When we look for Christ, we find him brutally impaled on a tree." His crucifixion was "a human deed" that neither time nor education can heal; the original sin that resulted in Jesus's execution was not a peccadillo or "a puppet sin" but evidence of "a basic flaw in man." Only when it is possible to confess, "I am a sinner," Johnson's sermon concluded, can anyone "know something of the forgiveness of sins"—can one know not only that God forgives one "but that *forgiveness* [itself] is the nature of God."[34]

Given the thoughtful preparation evident in Johnson's Ash Wednesday manuscript, he was quite ready to discuss the question of sin and its forgiveness at his dinner at the White House. The Kierkegaardian perspective was important—and for Roosevelt, most helpful—because it was quite different from the usual moralism that pervaded much of America's religion, Protestant and Catholic, liberal and evangelical. Sin, as Johnson presented it to the president, was arrogance, defiance of God. It began in weakness mingled with anxiety, led to the fear of losing autonomy if one gave allegiance to the person of Jesus Christ, and eventually grew into the desire to be equal with God. Sin was not vice or moral turpitude, a lack of virtue; sin was distrust, betrayal, a lack of faith. Such a view fit well with the Roosevelts' concerns with world war and power politics. Furthermore, it offered the prospect of a better understanding of the moral and ethical dimensions of the demanding roles they were called upon to play. For the individual Christian, "born beneath the Paradox" of God becoming man, "the disjunction Sin/Faith instead of Sin/Virtue becomes all the more relevant, for sin can never be cancelled out by virtue. Once again, it is faith that saves—not faith plus virtue, but faith passionate and sustained—even in the midst of his sins."[35] Since Roosevelt could admit his own sins, errors, mistakes, and wrong turns, the Kierkegaardian view of human life and faith was one that could sustain him. It was not an option for Adolf Hitler.

Fathoming Radical Evil

Since 1933, the president had been thoroughly aware of the hatred issuing out of Nazi Germany.[36] As Frank Freidel observes, "from the moment Hitler came to power, Roosevelt regarded him with a strong, almost religious dislike."[37] Once and only once, it seems, did FDR joke about the Nazis. He poked fun at the physical proportions of the "German tenor," Hermann Goering, and his "repulsive mannerisms." Wrote FDR to Ambassador William C. Bullitt, who in 1935 had observed Hitler's deputy at a state funeral: "What a grand picture that is of that Goering person! If you get a figure like his, I will order a special uniform for you and send you to all official funerals."[38] Roosevelt was not naïve about Hitler's intention, but he was shocked by Nazi brutality. In 1935 FDR noted grimly to Ambassador William E. Dodd that, "from the point of view of the group which now controls the destinies of the German people, their policy is succeeding admirably."[39] Much later, in his message to Congress on the progress of the war in 1943, he wondered whether in Hitler's case "the last trace of sanity has departed from that distorted mind."[40] The iniquity and depravity of the whole scene greatly disturbed him. Hence Roosevelt's subsequent recommendation to Secretary Perkins that she ought to read Kierkegaard. "I have never been able to make out why people who are obviously human beings could behave like that. They are human, yet they behave like demons." Kierkegaard, he declared, "gives you an understanding of what is in man that makes it possible for these Germans to be so evil. This fellow, Johnson, over at St. John's knows a lot about Kierkegaard and his theories. You'd better read him."[41]

Did the president actually *read* some of the titles he jotted down that evening in February 1944, or did his remarkable memory simply absorb what Howard Johnson told him? "Based on Perkins's careful language," writes the archivist of the Roosevelt Library, "it is possible that Roosevelt did not actually read the books but was basing his appreciation of Kierkegaard on the lengthy conversation he had had with Johnson."[42] On the other hand, Madam Perkins's remark can be read differently. Perhaps he was implying: "You'd better read him too."[43] Roosevelt was known to scan written materials accurately and retentively, and Kierkegaard lends himself to such reading. In addition, Johnson told the author that the Kierkegaard title he recommended most strongly to Roosevelt was *Sickness unto Death*, and that he, Johnson, had delivered his own copy to the White House the next day. It is hard to imagine FDR grasping the complexity of this book with its categories of Christian/Aristotelian metaphysics and their various polarities and varieties of alienation. On the other hand, there are passages in *Sickness unto Death* that would be clear to the intelligent nonspecialist. In any case, the argument about despair and sin that Johnson reconstructed from that volume helped the president understand "what it was in man that makes it possible for these Germans to be so evil."

This last statement manifests a sort of black-and-white judgmental thinking that came readily to Roosevelt. At times he could sound Manichaean. He had "a natural tendency to attribute decent motives to people"; to a significant degree he spoke "out of a bygone era of gentlemen, when certain personal things 'just weren't done'—and one man could trust another."[44] But he also knew very well the sleazy side of political life and was hardly naïve about human motives. He learned, Frances Perkins observed, that people are afraid of insecurity and that they cling to small, accustomed activities. He learned that only a few are ambitious. He became thoroughly familiar with the concept that good and evil, hope and fear, wisdom and ignorance, selfishness and sacrifice are inseparably mixed in most human beings.[45]

The key word in Perkins's testimony is "insecurity." In *Sickness unto Death*, Kierkegaard employed a nuanced psychology to describe how the Christian concept of sin arises out of just that state, and how in its extreme form it becomes despair. Kierkegaard saw despair developing by stages. At first innocence is haunted by an indefinable premonition, a dread caused by no particular discord or devil or deep evil. The alarming possibilities of freedom, of its misuses, of "what might happen next time," caused Adam to dread what will come to pass again and again. This dread is cumulative, gains momentum, and deepens so that "it surrenders the reality from which it arises—freedom."[46] Knowing they have been defrauded of what "by right" was theirs leads people to despair. In Christianity such hopelessness "becomes no longer a private matter" but stands "'before God' and in the presence of God becomes guilt."[47] Reflecting Kierkegaard, Johnson put the predicament this way: "The consciousness of guilt is man's first deep plunge into existence."[48] Thus, the progression: insecurity, haunted innocence, dread, surrender of freedom, despair, guilt, sin, spiritual hardening, and death. The line of march was written in block letters across the sky! Concluded Kierkegaard: "Sin is: before God in despair not to will to be oneself" (that is, one's true self), "or before God in despair to will to be oneself" (one's false self). And to be so, defiantly, on one's own terms.[49]

Recall Kierkegaard's discussion in *Philosophical Fragments* of "the teacher" who restores to us "the condition" needed for coming to the truth, "and along with it the truth" itself. What might we call such a teacher? Well might we call him *savior*, "for he does indeed save the learner from unfreedom, from himself. Let us call him *deliverer*, for indeed he does deliver the person who had imprisoned himself . . . and no captivity is so impossible to break out of as that in which the individual holds himself captive!" And if through his unfreedom the person is indeed guilty, then the teacher "is a *reconciler* who takes away the wrath that lay over the incurred guilt."[50] In any case, this teacher is not Socrates's incidental being who disappears upon use.

The Demon of Alienation

How does all this apply to Hitler and the Germans? Kierkegaard's book eerily anticipated the very Nazi phenomenon that so perplexed Roosevelt. In the philosopher's thought, the leader cannot find it in his heart even to will to be his true self before God. Refusing to seek help and declaring that the self "acknowledges no power over it," said Kierkegaard, this type of man "becomes an experimental god."[51] As such he is content to regard himself alone. He and the cupbearers who follow him refuse to be comforted by the true God who seeks each one out. They are not willing "to hope that an earthly distress, a temporal cross, might be removed." Instead, the leader "takes occasion to be offended at the whole of existence."[52] He wears his bitterness on his sleeve, and no one can convince him that it is wrong, for only thus can he assure himself that he is in the right. He knows that he is failing, but, in the words of one modern Kierkegaard scholar, pride and ignorance "prevent him from changing his plan."[53] He will seek help from no one, neither God nor man. To do so would mean the "humiliation of becoming nothing in the hand of the Helper for whom all things are possible."[54] Rather than seek help, "he would prefer to be himself— with all the tortures of hell, if so it must be." As a result, he and those around him move further and further not only from the truth but from awareness of that condition that might lead to an acknowledgment of error. This he indignantly refuses to do.

"His despair then has turned into defiance, and it drives him ahead with even greater determination—into non-existence."[55] He now rails against his circumstances: he alone in all the world has been unjustly treated; he and his people unjustly defrauded of what by right was theirs. "Ah, demoniac madness," cried Kierkegaard; the leader "rages most of all at the thought that eternity might get it into its head to take his misery from him." Against such an event, the deluded one evidences "inwardness with a jammed lock." At the same time, he is "alert with demoniac shrewdness to keep despair shut up in close reserve . . . locking all else out."[56] He is like an actor who dons a certain costume to play a role, but unlike the actor, he tries to be the part he is playing.

But he does not really change, and he knows it. The more the leader determines in despair to be his estranged self, "all the more does despair too potentiate itself and *become demonic*."[57] He is like the alcoholic who "steadily keeps up the intoxication from day to day, for fear of the languor which would ensue from arresting it, and the possible consequences if for one day he were to remain entirely sober—so it is with the demoniac. . . . In the consistency of evil, just for this cause he also has a totality to lose." In despair he has given up the good: "it could not help him anyway . . . but it might well disturb him, make it impossible for him ever again to acquire the full momentum of consistency, make him weak." The lock is jammed, the key either lost or thrown away. "Only in the continuation of sin," wrote Kierkegaard, can he "live and have an impression of himself"; only "the depth to which he has sunk holds him together, impiously strengthening him by consistency."[58] So with ever greater determination he plunges on into annihilation. As Johnson put it, "the golden calf has gone mad."[59]

If the results were not so frightful, the situation would be funny, wrote Kierkegaard, for the leader "bestows upon [his] undertakings infinite interest and importance." In fact, "this ruler is a king without a country, he rules really over nothing." He is "constantly building nothing but castles in the air." For a moment, wrote Kierkegaard, his musings "are enchanting like an oriental poem." His virtues make a brilliant showing. People marvel at his self-control and firmness of purpose that "border almost on the fabulous." But, says Kierkegaard, at "the bottom of it all there is nothing."[60] The emperor has no clothes; he lives in a fantasy of his own devising. Into it he carries everyone along—and the price paid is staggering.

Nowhere was that fantasy played out with greater effect than at the Nazi Party rally at Nuremberg in 1934. It was brilliantly recorded in Leni Riefenstahl's *Triumph of the Will*. "Five hundred trains carried a quarter of a million people to a specially built railway station. A vast city of tents was constructed to house the participants, and gargantuan quantities of supplies were brought in to feed and water them."[61] Banners, searchlights, speeches, choruses, march-pasts, torchlight parades, hundreds of thousands of troops shouting with outstretched right arms "*Sieg Heil!*" greeted the lone Führer. With vast columns of young men "moving and marching in unison, arranged four-square in rank and file or standing patiently in huge geometric blocks on the field," the ceremonies conveyed the "choreographed image of new-found spiritual unity."[62] That unity was solemn, humorless, and forbidding. The rituals were without reflection or substantive dialogue. His image photographed against the sky as his plane landed, or driving by in an open car in front of the buildings of Nuremberg, or against massed troops, Hitler stood, walked, and spoke alone. "At the most hushed moment," and in a kind of apostolic succession, "the 'blood-banner,' the flag carried in the beer-hall putsch of 1923, was ceremonially rededicated and touched on the new flags to pass on to them its nimbus of violent struggle and bloody sacrifice for the cause." Finally, in his major speech, Hitler worked himself and the crowd into a frenzy.[63]

In cities and towns throughout the nation, streets and plazas were named for the absolute leader. His name was everywhere. Hitler acknowledged no power over himself. The cabinet he inherited in 1933, the courts, the parliament, German art, architecture, and music, even greetings—"*Heil* Hitler"—existed only to contribute to his image and purpose. All "authority derived from his person rather than from the German state."[64] To the people the Führer was "the man from the trenches, with a common touch, not only a many-sided genius with a sense of destiny, but also a humble, even simple human being who had few needs, spurned wealth and display, was kind to children and animals and dealt compassionately with old comrades fallen on hard times."[65] In reality he held due process in contempt and inflicted unimaginable horrors on Slavs, Roma, the insane, Bolsheviks, homosexuals, and above all Jews, for whom he had a personal and pathological detestation. Women were to remain wives and mothers in the home, bearing children to realize his vision of a "pure" German race. Hitler gained unfettered command of the nation's foreign and domestic policy and maintained his control by means of private police, torture chambers, and secret prisons. Into the latter, "people disappeared without a sound" and were never heard from again.[66] He preferred acolytes to old friends and trashed his opponents unmercifully.[67] He alone expressed the will of the people of Germany.

Like Kierkegaard's "experimental god" who lived on his resentments, Hitler would not stop nursing old wounds. Time after time he invoked the torment of the Versailles Treaty. On October 14, 1933, he told the world via radio that "the deliberate degradation of Germany could no longer be tolerated."[68] She had been humiliated, plunged into economic disaster, refused equality in disarmament talks; now she wished only to correct the injustices she had borne. In the meantime, he would rid his nation and eventually, as he hoped, all Europe of the Jews whom he blamed for starting the Great War and for Germany's defeat. On the eve of World War II, his speech became confused and incoherent; he had a foreboding of his own suicide and vowed to wear the same tunic until either complete victory or defeat followed.

Finally, the events of 1933 in Germany were different from prior revolutions. What the Führer undertook and Propaganda Minister Joseph Goebbels effected was "not a social or economic revolution along the lines of the French Revolution of 1789 or the Russian Revolution of 1917. . . . It was a cultural revolution."[69] It sought to enlist the whole German population in a "spiritual mobilization," as Goebbels described it. A week after Pearl Harbor, Roosevelt spoke of Hitler's determination to destroy the Christian church by every means at his command. In its place would be "the Nazi church . . . a pagan church," he declared, quoting Hitler himself, "'absolutely and exclusively in the service of but one doctrine, one race, one Nation.'"[70]

Roosevelt was kept very well informed of developments in the 1930s by a group of able and experienced diplomats who "were not at all sanguine concerning the future."[71] Among them was William E. Dodd (at Berlin), a Virginia Jeffersonian with a *summa cum laude* doctorate from the University of Leipzig. Dodd's assessment of the Nazi regime as US ambassador to Germany from 1933 to 1937 is aptly summarized by the title of Erik Larson's best-selling account of his years in Berlin, *In the Garden of Beasts*.[72] George Earle (at Vienna) already in 1933 was reporting on instances of anti-Semitism and fascist activities and describing the Führer as "a paranoiac who had made the militaristic spirit the most intense in German history." Fellow Groton alumnus Lincoln MacVeagh (at Athens) was an invaluable diplomat who spoke six languages and wrote informative and lengthy dispatches on the "tinder box" of Europe, the Balkans.[73] Former newspaperman and Loyalist sympathizer Claude Bowers (Madrid) "warned the president that with every victory . . . the fascist powers would turn . . . without delay to some other country," and that there should be "no retreating before the gestures of bullies," the "gunmen and gangsters of Rome and Berlin."[74] The list goes on, including other Groton types: John C. Cudahy (at Warsaw), the impulsive yet valuable William C. Bullitt in Paris, the notable Joseph E. Davies in Moscow, and the irreplaceable

Arthur Sweetser of the League of Nations' Public Information Section in Switzerland from 1918 to 1942.

The president needed no special urging to adopt a strongly anti-Nazi policy. As early as May 1933, after a meeting with the German finance minister Hjalmar Schacht, Roosevelt told Secretary of the Treasury Henry Morgenthau that Germany's leaders were "a bunch of bastards."[75] He not only read their minds correctly, he also knew their language. As a boy he had been for a time at a German school at Bad Nauheim, where "we [had] German reading, German dictation, the history of Siegfried, and arithmetic." In 1890 he had a German governess, and the next year he was under the tutelage of the Swiss Jeanne Sandoz, who continued German lessons in addition to French. He spoke both languages fluently.[76] An unexpurgated edition of *Mein Kampf*, published in Germany in 1926, did not appear in English until 1939. In the meantime, the abridged versions available "gave no real sense of Hitler's Jewish obsession, nor of his frightening foreign policy goals." Roosevelt jotted in one of these: "This translation is so expurgated as to give a wholly false view of what Hitler really says—The German original would make a different story."[77] In short, Roosevelt's questions to Howard Johnson in February 1944 did not arise out of momentary curiosity; they had been brewing for a very long time.

Against Self-Righteousness

Johnson's evening at the White House was the second time he had significant contact with FDR. Sometime before that February evening he had been asked to arrange the 1944 service of commemoration for the inaugural of 1933, held every March 4. The service was held in the East Room of the White House out of wartime concerns for presidential security.[78] These commemorations were of particular importance to Roosevelt, so Johnson took great pains with the lessons, hymns, and the two prayers for the service. One, written by wartime archbishop of Canterbury William Temple, was called a "Prayer for Our Enemies": "Most loving Father, who by thy Son Jesus Christ, has taught us to love our enemies and to pray for them; we beseech thee, give to those who are now our enemies the light of thy Holy Spirit. Grant that they and we, being enlightened in conscience and cleansed from every sin, may know and do thy will, and so be changed from foes to friends united in thy service, through Jesus our Lord. *Amen.*"

Johnson was told by some clergy he had consulted that this prayer would not be acceptable. As Frances Perkins recalled it, they felt that "the White House would never authorize it in wartime; it would be misunderstood throughout the country," even by Christians. Determined to include it, Johnson "submitted his draft to the White House for approval." When the order of service came back, Johnson could read in the margin by this prayer the president's own notation: "Very good—I like it."[79]

William D. Hassett, assistant to the president, described the 1944 service in his diary: "At 10:30 a.m. in the East Room was held a religious service, commemorating the eleventh anniversary of the [1933] inauguration, a half hour service of dignity and simplicity—prayers, scripture, and hymns." Assembled were "the senior officers of the Army and Navy, the Cabinet, the Supreme Court, and all the other big wigs of officialdom with their wives." Hassett noted the role played by "the venerable Dr. Peabody, the old Groton headmaster, whose voice was full and vibrant, despite his great age. He and Mrs. Peabody arrived for the Cabinet dinner and were overnight guests."[80] It was the last time teacher and pupil met.

A year later, in 1945, with victory imminent, the service was held on January 20 following the fourth inaugural. David Lilienthal found it "more impressive than ever." The East Room was even more crowded now with military and government leaders. "I got a sense of the real point the president has in mind for these services—a family 'intercession,' except that the definition of family is broadened. The children and the grandfather were there in the row ahead—and the combination of little children and the dignity of great power and responsibility had a special overtone that 'got' me." The presence of Roosevelt's grandchildren brought home to Lilienthal how long "this man has carried this chore." Nonetheless, as he shook hands with Roosevelt afterward, he thought "he looked excellent, so much better than the depressing pictures of him we have been seeing lately."[81] Nor was Lilienthal alone in noting the importance of these services for the president. Judge Samuel Rosenman, FDR's White House counsel and speechwriter, had observed of the peacetime inauguration services, "He [Roosevelt] was deeply moved by these services, and you could see the effect of them on his face as he left the church to go to the Capitol to take his oath of office."[82]

A second prayer chosen by Howard Johnson was used in both the 1944 and 1945 services; it was a petition for victory: "O God, who seest that in this warfare we are seeking to serve thee and yet in the waging of it must do many things that are an offense against thy love; Accept we pray thee our imperfect offering. Arm us with thy Spirit that our warfare may further the victory of thy justice and truth, through Jesus Christ, our Lord. *Amen.*"[83]

With all its reservations and less than triumphant tone, this prayer also received Roosevelt's approval. St. John's curate was clear in his own mind about the evils of German totalitarianism; he was equally convinced about the dangers of self-righteousness. Both prayers allowed for the need of an enlightened mind, a cleansed conscience, the possibility of offense, and an imperfect offering on the part of those praying them. Both refused the easy option of simply declaring America's cause good and the enemy's evil. Both appealed to the love of God as found in Jesus Christ; both placed each side in the war under divine judgment. In short, Johnson reaffirmed in Kierkegaardian manner the doctrine of ongoing, universal, original sin.

Such evenhandedness was part of the theological mind-set of the time; it was derived not only from Kierkegaard but also from Reinhold Niebuhr, and from both the "neoorthodox" and the theological liberals of American Protestantism. On New Year's Day 1942, at perhaps the bleakest moment of the war, Roosevelt and Winston Churchill traveled across the Potomac to Christ Church, Alexandria. There the Reverend Edward Welles, preaching on the parable of the Good Samaritan, boldly told the president that America had behaved like the priest and the Levite in the story, passing by on the other side when other nations had been in peril. "That is not the way of Jesus Christ," Welles declared. "He endured His cross and we nationally must [now] accept our cross too." While acknowledging the evils of Nazism, Welles had tough words for the United States. The nation must be purged of its own evil; it must pray "for pardon for past shortcomings"; and it must seek "a peace built upon the only basis which can produce enduring justice and truth: the Fatherhood of God and the brotherhood of all mankind."[84] That such candor should have occurred either in wartime or subsequently at the height of the nation's power is noteworthy.

Howard Johnson's sermons at St. John's Church subsequent to his evening at the White House reiterated this view of evil. In a sermon preached in July 1944, Johnson warned the congregation of St. John's:

"Struggling men make demons out of their opponents and gods out of themselves." Every human struggle has its theological character, he claimed: "Of our opponent we say he is just plain wrong (period), which implies we are right (period). We and the truth coincide. The foe is not to be forgiven. He can only be opposed, killed." Johnson then connected self-righteousness to cruelty, declaring that to be "a problem of our immediate relationship to Germany and Japan." Where there is power, he continued, there is pride, and "that self-righteousness, self-deification conducts a nation straight into acts of cruelty and atrocity." While we can see this as an actuality in the case of Germany, the preacher declared, "Can we not also see it in ourselves as a dreadful possibility, a temptation to be shunned as we would shun the devil?" Christians in America must not use their "religion as an ego-weapon," the minister concluded.[85] Such an attitude fitted well the president's belief in the modest, supplicatory character of prayer.

A month after Roosevelt's death (April 12, 1945) and a week after Hitler had committed suicide in his Berlin bunker (April 30), Johnson again took up his theological interpretation of the war. His text was from Habakkuk 1:5–14 and 2:2–4, where the prophet explains that Israel's sin had made the ravaging, pitiless Chaldeans strong instruments of divine judgment: "This is the vision. Write it down, Habakkuk, make it plain upon tablets, so that even he who runs may read." God is neither dead nor unjust, Johnson said for the prophet: "He is turning even the wrath of men to his praise. Accept this judgment and be humbled, sobered, corrected by it. Thus will I give you the victory, not only over the Chaldeans but over your own sin as well." Johnson stated that his interest "in all this ancient history" about Israel and the Chaldeans stemmed from the relevance of the prophet's words to the present time. To a congregation in which a number of important government officials, not to mention members of the victorious Allied cause, were communicants, Johnson's words could only have been startling. "In Hitlerism a corrupt Western civilization has felt the scourge of God." The Nazis are the Chaldeans of our time. Hitler "has brought to the world a pitiless chastisement. . . . Wherever a weakness showed itself he bore down on it without scruple or mercy. The Nazi leader was made great by reason of our secret wretchedness." He did not produce the chaos of our time: "The chaos of our time produced Hitler." Those—and they were many—who claimed that Western civilization was being destroyed by the Nazis were "putting the cart before the horse," said Johnson. God was judging our civilization "as it deserved by letting us stand under this menace." Then, in a nice turnaround, Johnson concluded by saying, "Hitler brought us to our senses as no amount of preaching could. It even took Hitler to bring the preachers to their senses!"[86]

Johnson did not get light-headed over Habakkuk, however. Three years later at St. Alban's Church in Copenhagen, when the Cold War was heating up and when "the cynic cries: 'Can you think of anything *worse* than the mess we're in today?' the answer was 'Yes, I can think of something worse: the world dominated by the Nazis!'" Johnson pointed to how Germany's internal problems had been solved—"by suppression of civil liberties, by prostitution of universities, by inculcation of a lunatic religion, by liquidation of all who would not fall into step. And this was precisely the solution the Nazis had in mind for the *world's* problems." People were better off with an inept and fumbling United Nations than with life under victorious Nazis. There was no education to be had in the second kick of a mule; "better for the soul to be free to muddle through."[87]

Conclusion

Kierkegaard did not effect a major change in the thinking of Franklin Roosevelt, who retained his optimism about human improvement. But the man who carried the enormous burden of wartime leadership was helped by the priest and the philosopher to understand his ravaged world. In addition, he was reinforced in the knowledge that faith does not come from within but only from without. It is a gift that comes in the revelation constituted by the life, teaching, and person of Jesus of Nazareth. Johnson put it starkly: Christianity first "strips a person of every intellectual and moral pretension . . . [and] drives him naked and trembling to the throne of God." If in the light of the cross of Christ he "will confess that God's judgment upon him is just and will sue for mercy, here precisely is the miracle of acquittal, of forgiveness, of reconciliation. He has Christ for his clothing when he confesses himself naked, Christ for his resurrection when he acknowledges himself dead." Christianity rests its entire claim upon the fact that Jesus is the "point where eternity has intersected time."[88] The burden of Johnson's message to the president was that Hitler could admit neither such a confession nor faith. Kierkegaard informed and sustained convictions in Roosevelt's mind about the presence of the Nazi evil that he had recognized from the earliest days of his first administration. And he raised a cautionary warning against Allied self-righteousness.

So it was that, long before the study of Kierkegaard became something of a cottage industry, "Johannes Climacus" visited the White House.[89] There Howard Johnson, using Kierkegaard's categories in *Sickness unto Death*, helped the president understand how a man could be carried away by his own fantasies, refuse to recognize necessity, and become alienated from and ungrounded in the Constituting Power. And worse, diabolically try to pull others away from that Power. Those who fought against him had to take care not to mirror him.

Chapter Nine

Last Rites

After his February 1944 dinner conversation about Kierkegaard, FDR retired for the night. He likely took a moment to read his prayers and maybe a detective story as well—perhaps Dorothy Sayers. He needed the rest; people close to him had started to notice some physical decline. That picture grew ever clearer in the weeks ahead, although his physician and public-relations flacks stoutly maintained that all was well. In fact, Roosevelt had little more than a year left to live.

In that span, however, he pursued a more ambitious program than ever.[1] At home, he pushed the GI Bill as down-payment on his second Bill of Rights and campaigned for reelection to an unprecedented fourth term as president; an unusual personal dislike for his opponent, Thomas Dewey, helped fuel his energy. His agenda abroad was even more daunting. In July 1944 he traveled to Honolulu to sort out strategy in the Pacific with American military commanders. At the same time, American negotiators back home were setting up the Bretton Woods agreement with the Allied powers to prevent a repeat of the international economic chaos that had followed World War I. Keeping China in the war despite the feckless leadership of Chiang Kai-shek was a chronic worry. The greatest travail of all came in a fourteen-thousand-mile round-trip to Yalta in February 1945 for postwar planning with Churchill and Stalin. The former hoped to recover as much of the British Empire as possible; the latter wanted Soviet domination over eastern Europe to prevent another invasion from the west. Roosevelt, recalling Woodrow Wilson's ideal of national self-determination, aimed to end colonialism altogether. He invested significant hope in a United Nations that would maintain a lasting peace where Wilson's League of Nations had failed. Meanwhile, ordinary Americans were fixated on the day-to-day progress of the war, as American forces approached the Rhine in Europe and Japan in the Pacific.

Under this stress, Roosevelt's health continued to deteriorate. The essential diagnosis had come down in March 1944, a month after his Kierkegaard dinner and three months after he had returned, ailing, from a summit meeting in Tehran.[2] Roosevelt's official physician was Ross McIntire, an ear, nose, and throat specialist hired to treat the president's chronic sinusitis—and to report only good news. But now, at daughter Anna Roosevelt's insistence, the cardiologist Howard G. Bruenn was brought in, and he delivered the real news. The president was suffering severe bronchitis, hypertension, an enlarged heart, and a failing left ventricle. He was to take digitalis, lose some weight, adhere to a low-salt diet, cut down on his smoking, rest more, and avoid strain. He followed only the first two prescriptions and ignored the middle pair; the last two were out of the question until he returned from Yalta. At that point even he agreed that some serious changes were necessary. All along Roosevelt had been spending less and less time in Washington, interspersing his travels abroad with stays (kept secret for security reasons) at Hyde Park and Warm Springs. Now, in late March 1945, having reported to Congress on Yalta and caught up on paperwork, Roosevelt made one last visit to his old estate. He then went south for Easter, arriving at Warm Springs on Good Friday, March 30.[3]

In this favorite environment FDR seemed to revive. He appeared nattily dressed, right on time, for Easter morning services on April 1. Over the next days his private secretary Grace Tully and kissing cousins Laura ("Polly") Delano and Margaret ("Daisy") Suckley thought he looked better, ardent wishes perhaps being mother to the perception. He took naps and worked only five hours a day. But "work" included planning for the UN inaugural conference at San Francisco in late April, relentless bad news about China, and hard exchanges over Stalin's defiance of promises he had seemed to make at Yalta about Poland's postwar government. Thus, when Secretary of the Treasury Henry Morgenthau Jr. visited for dinner on the evening of April 11, he "was shocked at the president's appearance," at his shaking hands and mental confusion as the evening progressed.[4] The next morning, a Thursday, Roosevelt's color seemed to be better, but that was actually the harbinger of the end. Shortly before lunch, scheduled for 1:15 p.m., Roosevelt raised his hand to his forehead and exclaimed that he had "a terrific headache," then "a terrific pain in the back of my head." He was suffering a cerebral hemorrhage, a stroke, and collapsed into unconsciousness. Dr. Bruenn and others tried to help but could do nothing. At 3:35 p.m., Central War Time, the president was pronounced dead.[5]

Given the prolonged and saturated coverage that attends celebrity deaths today, the spare rites accorded so giant a figure as Roosevelt seem surprising, even insulting. His coffin was trundled onto a special train the morning after his death, Friday the 13th, for a twenty-three-hour journey to Washington, DC. It would stay in the capital for just twelve hours. The only formal rites there were a twenty-three-minute service in the East Room of the White House that Saturday; in keeping with FDR's wishes, there was no lying in state for viewing there or in the rotunda of the Capitol. But contrary to his wishes, and to the honors accorded his pitiful predecessor, Warren G. Harding, no service was held for him at the Capitol. Instead, his coffin was reloaded onto one of two special trains that departed late that night for his burial at Hyde Park the next day. There, on a crisp Sunday morning, Roosevelt's body was borne up the steep bluff of the Hudson River to the sounds of a cannon firing every fifteen seconds, in counterpoint with the tolling bell at St. James' Church; the first honored the fallen commander in chief, the second the senior warden of the vestry. Then, laden on a military caisson and escorted by an honor guard from the various armed services, Roosevelt's coffin was taken to the rose garden of his ancestral home. A short committal service followed, at the end of which a stoical Eleanor Roosevelt told the press: "The story is over." It was less than seventy-two hours since the president's death. Only two of the Roosevelts' children could attend, the other three sons being overseas at their military posts.[6]

The *New York Times* gave Roosevelt and his legacy ten full pages of coverage the morning after his death and added detailed reports of the services at the White House and at Hyde Park the next few days.[7] The press noted that the committal ceremonies, on April 15, came eighty years to the day after Abraham Lincoln's assassination, and predicted correctly that FDR would come to rank with Lincoln in the top echelon of American presidents. Much of their coverage, however, was taken up with details of ceremonial protocols, of the various dignitaries in attendance, and—increasingly—of the new president, Harry S. Truman: his person, his allies and opponents, his likely policies, his official pronouncements. All this befit the state occasion that Roosevelt's last rites entailed. But the truer measure came from the final respects he was paid by the people. Running throughout these was the "simple Christianity" that Franklin avowed and that Eleanor, Frances Perkins, Robert Sherwood, and others had seen in him all along.

The refrain began early in the train trip back to Washington, as Roosevelt's body passed by the main lodging house at Warm Springs. A tearful Chief Petty Officer Graham Jackson, an African American who had often played for FDR, sounded a soulful "Going Home" and "Nearer My God to Thee" on the accordion.[8] The latter hymn was picked up repeatedly along the funeral route, at a memorial service held at St. John the Divine in New York City, and finally one last time as the president's body was wheeled into the rose garden at Hyde Park.[9] Another favorite was "Onward, Christian Soldiers." Churchill had selected it for the Sunday morning service that sealed the Atlantic Charter off of Newfoundland in 1941; now another military band played it along the parade route from Washington's Union Station to the White House.[10] The most memorable moment for the hymn had come a few hours before. Near midnight in Charlotte, North Carolina, a few voices in the vast crowd, perhaps a Boy Scout troop, had started to sing it. It sounded a bit "ragged at first," reported UPI correspondent Merriman Smith, "but then it spread and swelled. . . . Soon eight or ten thousand voices were singing like an organ." For Smith it was "the most impressive moment" of the entire trip.[11]

As at Charlotte, so all along the train route, from country crossroads to major city stations, the people gathered. Some 25,000 at dusk that Friday in Greenville, South Carolina; 11,000 an hour later in Spartanburg; 1,500 at dawn in Charlottesville, Virginia; then 25,000 at Union Station in Washington and upwards of half a million along the route thence to the White House. The next day saw the same: 5,000 people crammed inside the Thirtieth Street Station in Philadelphia when the train pulled in at two o'clock Sunday morning; 50,000 more stood outside.[12] The mourners on the train particularly remembered the small clusters or lone individuals who stood along the tracks, day and night, as the train wound its way across the countryside: the women picking cotton in Georgia who dropped to their knees and raised clasped hands in prayer; the black man who serenaded the train at a water stop in the middle of the night with "Hand Me Down My Walking Cane," bringing other sharecroppers out of their shanties.[13] Everywhere there were silence, tears, prayers, and singing. These were FDR's real last rites, and surely the ones that he would have appreciated the most.

The formal proceedings were brief, by his own design. He wanted no eulogies and no homilies, just his old favorites: hymns, Scripture readings, and prayers. At the East Room service there were just two songs: "Eternal Father, Strong to Save" and "Faith of Our Fathers," the latter substituted at the suggestion of the presiding minister, Angus Dun, Episcopal bishop of Washington, for "America," which Eleanor had initially requested. At the Hyde Park interment there was no singing at all, only an old Episcopal hymn that the rector intoned as the coffin was lowered into the ground:

> Now the laborer's task is o'er;
> Now the battle day is past;
> Now upon the farther shore
> Lands the voyager at last.
> Father, in Thy gracious keeping
> Leave we now Thy servant sleeping.[14]

Scripture there was aplenty. The White House service began with Bishop Dun reciting Jesus's words from John 11:25–26: "I am the resurrection and the life, saith the Lord: he that believeth in me, though he were dead, yet shall he live; and whosoever believeth in me, shall never die." Then the Reverend John Magee, rector at Howard Johnson's St. John's Church, read Psalms 46 and 121. Those present could not miss the echoes of FDR's first inaugural address in the first: "God is our refuge and strength, a very present help in trouble. Therefore will not we fear, though the earth be removed, and though the mountains be carried into the midst of the sea; though the waters thereof roar and be troubled, though the mountains shake with the swelling thereof . . ." Nor, listening to Psalm 121, could they help but think of the path the president had helped chart for the country through the dangers of World War II: "I will lift up mine eyes unto the hills, from whence cometh my help. My help cometh from the Lord, which made heaven and earth. He will not suffer thy foot to be moved: he that keepeth thee will not slumber. . . . The Lord shall preserve thee from all evil: he shall preserve thy soul. The Lord shall preserve thy going out and thy coming in from this time forth, and even for evermore."

The Gospel reading, again quoting Jesus, also offered assurance against fear: "Let not your heart be troubled: ye believe in God, believe also in me. In my Father's house are many mansions: if it were not so, I would have told you, for I go to prepare a place for you" (John 14:1–2). As if the Scriptures were not clear enough, the bishop broke with the order of the Anglican Book of Common Prayer for an interpolation requested by Eleanor. It was the briefest of homilies, quoting the words by which "the President bore this testimony to his own deep faith": namely, the phrases from the first inaugural that said the only thing to be feared was fear itself. "As that was his first word to us," the bishop concluded, "I am sure he would wish it to be his last; that as we go forward to the tasks in which he has led us, we shall go forward without fear, without fear of the future, without fear of our allies or of our friends, and without fear of our own insufficiency."[15]

Bishop Dun then returned to the closing prayers from the liturgy. "Remember thy servant, Franklin Delano, O Lord, according to the favor which thou bearest unto thy people, and grant that, increasing in knowledge and love of thee, he may go from strength to strength in the life of perfect service in thy heavenly kingdom." He added words of his own crafting that turned out to sound the prevailing judgment of history upon Roosevelt down to the present: "We thank thee for the qualities of heart and mind which this thy servant brought to the service of our nation and our world. For steadfast courage in adversity; for clear vision of dangers to which many shut their eyes; for sympathy with the hungers and fears of common men; for trials met without surrender and weakness endured without defeat; for unyielding faith in the possibility of a more just and ordered world, delivered from the ancient curse of war." Not that FDR was without failings: "[We] pray for thy merciful judgment on the imperfections which he and all of us have brought to our many callings." Still, "we beseech thee to take under thy good providence the lives and causes for which he spent himself."[16] Appropriate petitions then followed for the grieving family, the nation's new leadership, and the men and women serving in the armed forces; for national unity, persistence, and responsibility; and for steadfastness on the part of all citizens, great and small, in meeting the duties of the day. The prayers ended with Hebrews 13:20–21: "Now the God of peace, that brought again from the dead our Lord Jesus, that great shepherd of the sheep . . . make you perfect in every good work to do his will, working in you that which is well pleasing in his sight, through Jesus Christ; to whom be glory for ever and ever. Amen."[17]

The East Room service did not cite FDR's favorite verses from 1 Corinthians 13 about faith, hope, and love. They were used by the minister who knew him better, the Reverend George W. Anthony, temporary rector of St. James' Church in Hyde Park, at a memorial service held there immediately after the interment.[18] Still, the Epistle reading that Bishop Dun used from the Book of Common Prayer might have been even more fitting. It came from another letter of Paul, Romans 8:14–39. The passage begins with one more note against fear: "For as many as are led by the Spirit of God, they are the sons of God. For ye have not received the spirit of bondage again to fear; but ye have received the Spirit of adoption, whereby we cry, Abba, Father." And it ends with Paul's magnificent expression of assurance equal to the one that Roosevelt had embodied his entire life: "Who shall separate us from the love of Christ? shall tribulation, or distress, or persecution, or famine, or nakedness, or peril, or sword? . . . Nay, in all these things we are more than conquerors through him that loved us. For I am persuaded, that neither death, nor life, nor angels, nor principalities, nor powers, nor things present, nor things to come, nor height, nor depth, nor any other creature, shall be able to separate us from the love of God, which is in Christ Jesus our Lord."[19]

Roosevelt's pronouncements of assurance to America were not Christian-specific. Nor did he think they should be, given the religious pluralism of the nation. However, they did not spring from the self-worship of American civil religion either. They tapped deep convictions laid in him by the Christian gospel as refracted through a confident Episcopal tradition. Roosevelt knew that "the presidency is above all a moral office," and his work in that office amounted to a translation from his Christian faith *into* terms effective across the broad range of the American people and *in* terms of some of the severest challenges the nation has ever faced.[20] In the scales of the historically possible, he accomplished that task supremely well. Perhaps he therefore deserved the plaudits the clergy awarded him. Certainly he merited, as he relished, the praise of the people. After all, he meant to be a Christian and a Democrat.

Afterword

Politics and Religion in Lincoln, Hoover, and Roosevelt

R ating presidents is a popular pastime among scholars and citizens alike. Typically, George Washington, Abraham Lincoln, and Franklin Roosevelt finish at the very top of those rankings; Herbert Hoover lands close to the bottom. Yet, comparing Lincoln, Hoover, and Roosevelt (we drop Washington because of his unique role as a founder) can help explain the various successes and failures of their presidencies, and can illuminate the character and motives of Roosevelt's in particular. Each leader faced monumental challenges and dealt with them out of a specific combination of political vision, religious conviction, and personal style. The religious element functioned in this matrix as deep background. It helped shape each president's basic identity, disposition, and style. It grounded their answers to the fundamental questions: What is politics for, and how should it be conducted?

Roosevelt and Lincoln

Lincoln's early religious experience took place in a "hard-shelled" Baptist fellowship, in which his father, Thomas, served as a sometime preacher.[1] This group was adamantly Calvinist in theology, majoring in double predestination. According to that teaching, God not only elected some people to salvation but actively damned the rest—and most—to perdition. He did so irrespective of any claims or merits that individuals might offer on their own behalf; these were virtues only by human standards, a far cry from God's. This mind-set could border on fatalism. Thus when Abraham's mother, Nancy Hanks, died or when the spring corn planting got washed away by torrential rains, there was nothing to say or do for it. As a Dutch Calvinist character in one of Peter De Vries's novels put it, "Believe in God and don't put anything past him."[2] Although Lincoln never joined his father's Baptists or any other denomination, Calvinist predestination remained a heavy religious concept in his life. His biographer Allen Guelzo concludes that, for Lincoln, "a gap yawned between himself and this mysterious God." As a boy, he had copied four lines of a Calvinist hymn by Isaac Watts:

> Time what an empty vaper tis
> and days how swift they are
> swift as an indian arr[ow] fly
> or like a shooting star.

As a man, unsparingly honest, Lincoln remained "haunted by the sense of his own foreordained inability to believe or to be content in his unbelief." He did not think that the God who decreed all things had seen fit to place a responding and reassuring religious faith in his heart. He was "only a piece of floating driftwood" that had bobbed to the top of the epochal conflict of the Civil War, an "'accidental instrument' of providence and not a beloved son."[3]

Roosevelt, by contrast, was the beloved son of wise and attentive parents. Many opportunities were his for the asking. He was given books, a pony, a stamp collection, pictures, and clothes. A series of able governesses, then an admired tutor, saw to his every need and educated him in languages and history. While Lincoln felt he could never please his father, Franklin knew from first to last that his father loved him. And his mother, Sara, doused him with close attention—perhaps too close and even overbearing, but always instilling the sense that he was God's favored one, that his was to be a noble destiny. In the long run Roosevelt was buoyed even in the hardest times by a remarkable serenity that stemmed from this nurture. He knew that there was a loving God who directed the world firmly in the direction of righteousness, that evil would not finally prosper, that good human efforts would be rewarded, that he himself was commissioned and privileged to be an unusual agent in those purposes. In short, for Franklin Roosevelt the universe made sense even if that sense could not be fully fathomed at the moment.

The early result was a young man who struck many observers as smug and callow. The great change came for him in the sudden onset of infantile paralysis at age thirty-nine, a year after his run for vice president. The disease had no cure, and upwards of 20 percent of its adult victims died. Now the question of election and reprobation struck Roosevelt. He too knew time's empty vapor; he too harbored grave doubts about his future and God's favor. Polio taught Roosevelt, as early political defeats had Lincoln, the lesson of contingency: the opportunity to power came only briefly and might be snatched away just as quickly by the tides of chance and change.

Odd as it may seem, Lincoln's severe theology steeled his commitment to democracy. If God was no respecter of persons, neither need we be. All the traditional warrants for rank and privilege were undermined; if no one was good enough for God on his or her own, no one was good enough to govern somebody else without that person's consent. From this start Lincoln followed two lines of political philosophy. The first was classic eighteenth-century appeals to liberty: the right of each individual and each community to control their own affairs without governmental, particularly British parliamentary, interference. The second was Whig economics: people should be able to do precisely what they wish with that for which they have labored and that which is exclusively their own. The Whig view had a collective dimension, too. Lincoln followed his hero Henry Clay in proposing "internal improvements"—canals, railroads, public highways—to make it possible for private industry to open new markets, thereby giving individuals the opportunity to better themselves. Other community needs would be addressed by building schools, asylums, and orphanages.[4] With those provisions, it was their own fault or a singular misfortune if individuals failed to prosper. The function of government was to do for individuals and communities what they could not do for themselves, and to punish crimes, misdemeanors, and the nonperformance of contracts. Lincoln had no interest in restraining capital, and great interest in seeing it used for the protection and expansion of opportunity and liberty for all. In this he resembled the early, progressive Herbert Hoover, not Franklin Roosevelt.

Lincoln was certainly progressive in his time, however, by extending this logic to the eradication of slavery. As flexible and politically canny as he could be, he was no ethical relativist. "I must keep some consciousness of being near right," he told his secretary John Hay. "I must keep some standard of principle fixed within myself."[5] In his debates with Stephen Douglas, he drew that standard for all to see. There was an "eternal struggle between these two principles—right and wrong—throughout the world," he proclaimed. The notion of "the divine right of kings" was the source of American slavery; the notion of "the common right of humanity" was the principle enunciated in the Declaration of Independence. If it belonged first to the United States, it belonged ultimately to the whole world.[6]

Fighting for that right required enormous political skill. As a new president, Lincoln had to deal simultaneously with secession, the border states' uncertain loyalty to the Union, insufficient enlistments, public doubts about his abilities, and the unreliability of his generals. There were tensions in his own party between Christian Republicans, Jeffersonian Republicans, and abolitionist Republicans.[7] By the summer of 1864, Democrats who wanted a negotiated peace were growing in influence. The majority of Americans North and South felt that the different races, like men and women, were in fact created unequal. But Lincoln never lost sight of his polar star of representative democracy. "I consider the central idea pervading this struggle," he said, to be "the necessity that is upon us, of proving that popular government is not an absurdity. We must settle this question now, whether in a free government the minority has the right to break up the government whenever they choose. If we fail it will go far to prove the incapability of the people to govern themselves."[8] The cost was severe—well over seven hundred thousand dead on both sides—but it was commensurate with the stakes at hand. This was the supreme test, Lincoln said in his greatest address: whether "a new nation"—in fact, *any* nation—"conceived in liberty and dedicated to the proposition that all men are created equal . . . can long endure."

As for the Great Depression, the issue was not the destruction of the Union but its internal devastation owing to economic collapse—and the collapse of people's hopes in the process. As Roosevelt put it, "the very foundation of individual life was crumbling in the spring of 1933, because of the appalling increase in suffering and destitution due to the fact of unemployment."[9] A historian suggested another metaphor: "the Depression resembled a maelstrom, a downward spiral with the near-simultaneous failures of production, employment, and consumption."[10] In March 1933, at the bottom of the Depression, some 15 million (or 30 percent) of the workforce was unemployed. If dependent families are figured in, between 40 and 50 million citizens, some 40 percent of the nation's 123 million people, were without income from full-time jobs.[11] Thus, Roosevelt may have *under*estimated when, at his second inaugural in 1937, he spoke of "one-third of a nation ill-housed, ill-clad, and ill-nourished."[12] The political stakes could not have been higher. As the journalist Lorena Hickok observed, "if someone other than FDR had been elected—someone like Huey Long—American democracy might now be coming to an end."[13] Once again as in Lincoln's day, the great experiment in popular government seemed in the eyes of many to be played out. It was, political philosopher Isaiah Berlin summarized, "a time of weakness and mounting despair in the democratic world."[14]

Facing so different a set of problems than Lincoln's, FDR had to recast the meaning of liberty for the twentieth century. The principal threat no longer lay in interference by the government but in the consequences of unbridled finance capitalism. Government "interference" was the means, perhaps the only means, of keeping the wolf from the door. It was not so much that the eighteenth century's preoccupation with liberty was out of date as that the wanton "practices of unscrupulous money changers" in a society characterized by mass industry and mass culture necessitated federal power to regulate and reform.[15] Roosevelt recognized that the primary task was to put people to work. Not slavery or laziness but a corrupted and unbalanced free-market system was the block in the road.

Personality and War

Besides religious conviction and political philosophy, the personal styles of Lincoln and Roosevelt were essential to their endurance and final success. Both of them were strong, single-minded leaders. Both knew when to act, when to put on the brakes, and when to be evasive. Both were astute, ambitious politicians, keen observers of people's skills and faults but willing to overlook mistakes. Both kept to large, long-term goals but were otherwise flexible; if one solution did not work, they went on to another. They shared an exceptional sense of political timing and kept a close watch on public opinion. If Lincoln was coolly logical, with remarkable powers of concentration in solving problems, Roosevelt was forever seeing connections. Frances Perkins judged that he "would have flashes of almost clairvoyant knowledge and understanding of a terrific variety of matters that didn't seem to have any particular relationship to each other. He couldn't always hold that or verbalize on it, but sometimes he could. Sometimes he could act on it."[16] He could connect a variety of needs, facts, and resources, first because of his phenomenal memory and, second, because he did not take his eye off his goal. Political success for Roosevelt was a matter of details, correlation, and above all direction.

Both men were outwardly affable but deeply cunning. If Lincoln, famously, played his cabinet as a "team of rivals," FDR was notorious for giving different advisers and department heads assignments that were simultaneously overlapping, competitive, and complementary. Both presidents delighted in endless real-life stories and anecdotes and used them effectively, often to avoid dealing with visitors' probing or unwelcome solicitations. Invariably petitioners left thinking the president agreed with them (Roosevelt) or that they had won the day—until it dawned on them that nothing had been finally determined (Lincoln). We have seen the importance of FDR's sense of humor; Lincoln's was a match. To his law partner, William Herndon, Lincoln "was quiet, a man of few words, although from time to time he interrupted his fits of introspection with stories and gales of laughter."[17] Once, on a bumpy carriage ride with Secretary of State William Seward, Lincoln called out to the driver, who had been cursing his horses with colorful profanity: "'Driver, my friend, are you an Episcopalian?' 'No, Mr. President, I ain't much of anything, but if I go to church at all, I go to the Methodist Church.' 'Oh, excuse me,' replied Lincoln, 'I thought you must be an Episcopalian for you swear like Secretary Seward, and he's a church-warden.'"[18] Both presidents collected a fund of anecdotes that lost nothing in the telling. What John Gunther observed of FDR applied just as well to Lincoln: "his fondness for tall tales is well known; he invented anecdotes, embellished them, and finally came to believe them himself, like a bard."[19] For both, the storytelling served a purpose: it threw assertive visitors off guard and gave the raconteur time to think, to avoid unwanted issues, and ultimately to find the right course.

Immediately for Lincoln and eventually for Roosevelt, leadership involved a war in which the nation's future lay in the balance. In these conflicts both proved unyielding as to ultimate goals. Lincoln refused to consider negotiations between "the two countries," as Jefferson Davis described South and North in late 1864, and Roosevelt demanded nothing less than the "unconditional surrender" of Germany and Japan in World War II. But grand ends required specific means, and Lincoln and Roosevelt both devoted the keenest interest to matters of strategy, the intricacies of supply, and above all the choice of commanders. Lincoln encountered years of trouble in finding adequate generals, running through the arrogant, the timid, the clueless, and the hapless until he imported Ulysses S. Grant and William T. Sherman from the western theater to settle things in the east. Roosevelt was more fortunate both in his civilian appointments and in the quality of the military leaders he chose. Eric Larrabee judges that FDR took his position as head of the armed forces "more seriously than did any other President but Lincoln, and in practice he intervened more often and to better effect than did even his battle-worn contemporaries like Churchill and Stalin." In fact, Larrabee concludes: "More than any other man, he [Roosevelt] ran the war, and ran it well enough to deserve the gratitude of his countrymen then and since, and of those from whom he lifted the yoke of the Axis tyrannies. His conduct as Commander-in-Chief . . . bears the mark of greatness."[20]

Yet, both presidents suffered from miscalculations and setbacks. At the beginning of the Civil War, Lincoln thought he knew how to win: appeal to Southern Unionists and emancipate the slaves state by state via federally funded buyouts. For his part, Roosevelt thought he could bring around Vichy France, rely on Chiang Kai-shek's China as a major ally, handle Stalin, and sideline Churchill. Both men were wrong on all counts. Lincoln could despair at his generals' defeats but especially at their only-partial victories. When, after Gettysburg, General George Gordon Meade failed to pursue Lee's Army of Northern Virginia, Lincoln exploded: "Great God! What does it mean? . . . Our Army held the war in the hollow of their hand & they would not close it." This in a letter left unsent. The words he did say lamented: "I do not believe you appreciate the magnitude of the misfortune involved in Lee's escape. He was within your easy grasp, and to have closed upon him would, in connection with your other successes, have ended the war. As it is, the war will be prolonged indefinitely."[21]

Likewise, in World War II, success came slowly. The year 1942 and the first quarter of 1943 alternated Allied victories (at Midway, El Alamein, Guadalcanal, and Stalingrad) with harrowing losses: the British fortress of Singapore with an astonishing 130,000 troops taken prisoner; Corregidor Island, the last American outpost in the Philippines; and 800,000 tons of shipping lost per month to German U-boats in the Atlantic. On Washington's birthday 1943, the president went on the radio to teach a cautionary lesson. In 1777, victory against the British at Saratoga "led thousands of Americans to throw their hats in the air, proclaiming that the war was practically won and that they should go back to their peacetime occupations—and, shall I say, 'normalcies.'" Now again, the Russian victory at Stalingrad earlier that month (February 1) had prompted similar delusions across the country. Roosevelt scolded those "among us [who] still believe in the age of miracles. They forget that there is no Joshua in our midst. We cannot count on great walls crumbling and falling down when the trumpets blow and the people shout." This was no time to throw hats in the air. "It is not enough that we have faith and that we have hope," he declared. We need to learn to "direct our thoughts and control our tongues."[22]

Both presidents applied the same cautions to themselves. Neither harbored any illusions about his own power to direct the course of history. Yet, despite the forces they could not control, the uncertainties they could not anticipate, their own blunders and those of their administrations, they did not duck accountability. In a radio address on election night 1932, Roosevelt reflected on the wisdom gained from his "many years of public life." He well knew that "when the light of favor shines" upon someone, it does not necessarily mean "that he himself is important." Rather, favor comes to a person "because for a brief moment in the great space of human change and progress some general human purpose finds in him a satisfactory embodiment." Roosevelt only wished to be the means "through which the ideals and hopes of the American people may find a greater realization." To have read correctly the aspirations of an entire people "calls for the best in any man. I seek to be only the humble element of this restoration."[23] At a similar pivotal moment amid the grimmest circumstances (December 1, 1862), Lincoln told Congress: "we cannot escape history. . . . [We] will be remembered in spite of ourselves. No personal significance, or insignificance, can spare one or another of us." Then came the warning: "The fiery trial through which we pass, will light us down, in honor or dishonor, to the last generation."[24]

Faith

At such profound moments, the presidents' religious convictions returned to the fore. Both of them thought long and hard about the providential ways of God with humankind. Lincoln was the more rationalistic of the two, having moved from his hard-shell Baptist origins along the utilitarian, skeptical lineage of the Enlightenment. Roosevelt was the heir of Protestant liberal theology and its Social Gospel. Lincoln asked the question *why*? Why the suffering? Why the terrible wartime losses of life? Roosevelt was more concerned with the *what* of providence. What was God's will for the nation and for himself? Unlike Lincoln, FDR did not ask whether or not there was a divine government. He assumed it. Lincoln did not, and increasingly wrestled with the question over the long bloody strife of the Civil War.

Lincoln asked, why did Providence take from him and Mary Todd their beloved son? Why this fearsome testing of the national foundations of liberty and equality? In his great Second Inaugural Address, Lincoln pondered how it was that both North and South "read the same Bible and pray to the same God, and each invokes his aid against the other." He was at a loss to see how "men should *dare* to ask a just God's assistance in wringing their bread from the sweat of other men's faces." On the other hand, he recalled God's admonition to "judge not, that *we* be not judged" (Luke 6:37). The logic on the ground was simple and obvious: "The prayers of both could not be answered. That of neither has been answered fully." *And Lincoln himself had no answer.* Doris Kearns Goodwin notes that Lincoln "could not condemn the South for an inability to end slavery when he himself knew of no easy solution." He turned to that harsh, familiar saying of Jesus: "Woe unto the world because of offenses; for it must needs be that offenses come, but woe to that man by whom the offense cometh" (Matt. 18:7). The promised land of democracy stood in those crosshairs: "If we shall suppose that American slavery is one of those offenses which, in the providence of God, must needs come, but which, having continued through his appointed time, He now wills to remove . . ."—*if* we shall suppose. The abhorrence of one person owning another was by no means universal, not even in the North. Were offenses themselves predestined? Why was slavery allowed to last for two and a half centuries and then rejected? On what basis did God make up his calendar, "his appointed time"?[25]

The questions remained unanswered. For Lincoln, writes Allen Guelzo, "the inevitable necessities of history" led him "to expect a victory of some sort for the Union." Lincoln's friend Leonard Swett declared that the president "believed the results to which certain causes tended, would surely follow; he did not believe that those results could be materially hastened, or impeded." But God's mills ground very slowly, and by an invisible logic. Lincoln had to admit "that providence was guided by more than mere cause and effect, that a more mysterious and unpredictable purpose guided human events." A slave society had no place in the unfolding pattern of history: "science, literacy, progress all marched irresistibly upwards over time."[26] Freedom would win out, but at what cost in human life? The Second Inaugural provided only a stark statement of fact: "The Almighty has his own purposes." The mysterious God of Calvinism who lived in his tent of darkness, the *deus absconditus* whom no man has ever seen, the *deus nudus*, the God of naked power, was directing the course of events. "Providence is carrying on this thing," said Lincoln's friend John Todd Stuart. The president responded, "Stuart, that is just my opinion." But there was little comfort to be found there; the *why* question lingered. Perhaps the Almighty "gives *to both North and South* this terrible war as the woe due to those by whom the offense came." The South, obviously, but the North? Why should both be punished together? Why should justice "bleed as freely as injustice" in the fearful losses sustained by the Union armies? The Providence of God was the only answer.[27]

In these ruminations, Mark Noll suggests, Lincoln had the courage to look "into an abyss that few of his contemporaries could bear to contemplate." In placing the blame on both sides, Lincoln saw more deeply into the contest than did his contemporaries. The whole nation was responsible for the great offense of slavery.[28] Yet, however courageous the insight, it carried little consolation. The woe due to a shared national offense had descended with a vengeance. Lincoln remembered his tough boyhood God: "Shall we discern therein any departure from those divine attributes which the believers in a living God [perhaps implying that he now was not one of them] always ascribe to him?" While they might hope and pray for a speedy end to the carnage, "if God wills that it continue until all the wealth piled by the bondsman's two hundred and fifty years of unrequited toil shall be sunk, and until every drop of blood drawn with the lash shall be paid by another drawn with the sword, as was said three thousand years ago, so still it must be said." What? The heart-sinking determination: "The judgments of the Lord are true and righteous altogether" (Ps. 19:9). Providence held redemption tight to its vest.

But then, in a stunning reversal of tone and direction, Lincoln ceased speculating and turned to the task at hand, a task the whole nation had to face: binding up the Union. In this declaration Lincoln perhaps unwittingly proclaimed the heart of the Christian gospel, the ultimately forgiving love of God. Whether or not he recognized the theological significance of his own final words, Lincoln grasped their human significance: there was work to be done, and it had to be done right. "With malice toward none, with charity for all, with firmness in the right as God gives us to see the right, let us strive to finish the work we are in, to bind up the nation's wounds, to care for him who has borne the battle and for his widow and orphan, to do all which may achieve and cherish a just and lasting peace among ourselves and with all nations."[29]

Here was his new direction, away from speculation about Providence and toward the future of the nation he had just sworn to govern. Back of the final words of the great address were echoes of Scripture, and behind those were the life, teaching, and death of the one who hung on the cross for the redemption of all humankind. While Lincoln knew his Bible, the significance of Jesus Christ remained remote to him. Divine justice stood in the foreground, and it obscured the Justifier. On such a basis, apologetic attempts to make Lincoln more Christian than he was will fall to the ground. In the final paragraph of the Second Inaugural, Lincoln showed, in the words of Ignazio Silone, "that nothing is irreparable while life lasts and that no condemnation is eternal . . . that though one should not be in love with evil, good was often born of evil."[30] The Second Inaugural was a wake-up call for all poor sinners, North as well as South. After taking into account the speculative twists and turns of divine judgment—a wholly necessary exercise—Lincoln, almost with a sigh of relief, arrived at the salient point he wished to drive home to one and all. Wounds were to be bound up, not kept open; care for the battle-weary and bereaved had to be undertaken in the name of all of them; and above all, the charity of peace must replace the malice of war. Whether Lincoln's religion guided his thinking or the words represented a conclusion wholly his own is as unknown and perhaps as unknowable as the judgments of God himself.

Franklin Roosevelt's God was not nearly as remote as Lincoln's but closer at hand, directly working in human history. The shape and character of his purpose, FDR believed, were to be found in Jesus Christ. The words of assurance about God's care spoken by Jesus were, he assumed, trustworthy. They called the believer not to speculate but to take risks, to decide, and to act in behalf of others, as Jesus himself had done. In pursuit of such ends, Roosevelt held that individuals and communities had free will. If Lincoln struggled with the predestining Calvinist God, in FDR's mind "human beings were by God's will free to choose," writes Kenneth S. Davis. "Though they worked out God's grand design, they must do so through the anguish of personal choice, guided by such signs of His will as He permitted them, human freedom being integral to God's design."[31] The questions were not *why* the economic shipwreck of the Great Depression and its human prostration occurred or *why* Hitler and the Nazis were permitted to work their evil, but rather *what* was to be done to rectify these situations and bring good out of evil.

The answers involved just as much attention to the details of manpower, command, strategy, and supply as Lincoln had given them. For Roosevelt there was also the inspiring faith in God's destiny for all. "With the unbounded determination of our people," he told the Congress on December 8, 1941, "we will gain the inevitable triumph—so help us God." Roosevelt saw trends in history: "There is a mysterious cycle in human events," he said in accepting renomination in 1936. "To some generations much is given. Of other generations much is expected. This generation of Americans has a rendezvous with destiny."[32] History remained open-ended; the play, the music, the epic poem were still being written. The lines and movements of the actors on the stage of the Almighty's improvisational theater determined the answer to how and by what methods crises would be met, but the actors were not alone, least of all Franklin Roosevelt. Like Lincoln, he too was guided by principles. They were derived both from his faith and from his citizenship in a democracy.

Lincoln's Second Inaugural quoted the Bible three times. FDR, as we have seen, frequently resorted to 1 Corinthians 13. He did so again in that radio broadcast on Washington's birthday in 1943 in which he warned the nation of difficult days still to come. He saw Saint Paul's three cardinal virtues to have been at work during Washington's harsh test in the frigid winter of 1777–1778. "It was Washington's faith—and with it his hope and his charity—which was responsible for the stamina at Valley Forge." Now in 1943, Roosevelt wanted his fellow citizens to remember how "charity" works itself out. It "suffereth long," he quoted Paul, "vaunteth not itself, is not puffed up, doth not behave itself unseemly, . . . rejoiceth not in iniquity but rejoiceth in the truth." He then went on to read to the American people the full text of the Beatitudes

(Matt. 5:3–12): "Blessed are the poor in spirit. . . . Blessed are they that mourn. . . . Blessed are the meek. . . . Blessed are they which do hunger. . . . Blessed are the merciful. . . . Blessed are the pure in heart. . . . Blessed are the peacemakers. . . . Blessed are they which are persecuted for righteousness' sake. . . . Rejoice and be exceeding glad: for great is your reward." Jesus's bracing, countercultural ethic still constituted the true north of the American people: "Today, through all the darkness that has descended upon our nation and the world," he said, "those truths are a guiding light to all."[33]

Hoover and Roosevelt

Contrary to popular fancy, Franklin Roosevelt and Herbert Hoover had a great deal in common. Both men disliked the autocrats of the Gilded Age and rejected any political or social arrangement that was (as Hoover put it) "based on the assumption of some group dominating somebody else." An economic autocracy in which "a few men through unrestrained control of property determine the welfare of great numbers" was in his view simply un-American.[34] In their university days, neither Hoover nor Roosevelt was an academic star, although Hoover eventually found his place in the Department of Geology and Mining at Stanford and Roosevelt at the editorial office of the *Harvard Crimson*. Both admired Theodore Roosevelt and were influenced by the reforms of the Progressive Era, and both became Wilsonian internationalists. Both sought to build community in America through equality of opportunity. While Hoover was a dozen years older than FDR, both entered highly visible public service at the beginning of World War I: Hoover as director of the Citizens' Relief Committee in Belgium, Roosevelt as assistant secretary of the navy. Hoover undertook a huge humanitarian effort to "contain civilian suffering brought about by war," first with massive relief projects in Belgium and later in the rest of Europe and in Russia as head of the War Food Administration.[35]

When Hoover arrived back in the United States on September 13, 1919, he had become an icon of practical American idealism. He was the "Great Engineer," always "improvising, always improving, and progressing." What is more, to the Versailles Treaty negotiations— this according to John Maynard Keynes, otherwise an acerbic critic of that conference's proceedings and product—Hoover had brought an "atmosphere of reality, knowledge, magnanimity, and disinterested-ness." He seemed the only man, Keynes continued, who could "have given us a Good Peace," and he came away with the aura of being one of the premier statesmen of his generation.[36] During the 1920s, he served in the cabinets of Presidents Harding and Coolidge as secretary of commerce. He also angled—just as ambitiously as FDR—to be president himself.

Hoover declared himself to be in favor of policies that would later rate as strongly, even radically, liberal. He sought to tax high incomes heavily and advocated "a steep graduation in inheritance taxes." He meant to redistribute the nation's wealth more evenly and to curb "unjust amassings" of money; as his biographer David Burner summarizes his view, "the rich must come to see the bearing of a heavier [tax] burden as a social duty." Hoover declared "that social injustice is the destruction of justice itself." He believed that "the American people themselves rejected Social Darwinism," adds Burner, "in favor of cooperation" to create a fairer society, and he saw the instruments of that cooperation to lie ready at hand: "the American Federation of Labor, the Chambers of Commerce, farmers' organizations, groups of engineers, lawyers, doctors."[37] The list of reforms Hoover championed is stunning. He wanted a national system of old-age pensions underwritten by the insurance companies; he "convoked the nation's first housing conference" to help those who lived in wretched dwellings; he set up a Veterans Administration to aid doughboys and others who had been broken by war; he wanted to abolish child labor and promote children's health; he canceled oil leases on public lands and added two million acres to the national forest reserves; he supported labor unions; he favored spending on public works and taking "counter-cyclical actions in a time of depression."[38] Were it not for the fact that FDR uttered the words during his 1932 campaign to take the presidency from him, Hoover might well have joined Roosevelt in scotching what would become conservative orthodoxy fifty years later, the notion "that if we make the rich richer, somehow they will let part of their prosperity trickle down to the rest of us."[39]

Yet there were huge differences between the two men—obvious differences in political philosophy and policy, crucial differences in personality and style, and deep differences in religious disposition. We take up personality and religion first. In contrast to Roosevelt's nurture in a solicitous family, Hoover was orphaned at age eleven and had to fend for himself. With his affability and lack of pretense, Roosevelt was to those around him simply the "Boss." He was expansive and ingratiating often to the point of deception. Political dexterity and a capacity for maneuver were his in abundance. He enjoyed the complexity of human relations and intuitively knew how to restore the collective energy and hope of the American people. He had confidence in their good judgment; they reciprocated by trusting him. Hoover, on the other hand, disliked the messiness of politics; he called Congress "that beer garden up there on the hill" and felt he had demeaned himself "before those Democratic swine." He was shy, austere, and blunt to the point of rudeness. He loathed the snobbishness of the fraternities at Stanford, while Roosevelt eagerly sought entry to them at Harvard. Hoover was loath to brag about himself and hid his good works. The convivial Roosevelt invented stories about his own prowess. Hoover could be aloof. "A Quaker visitor to the White House," writes David Burner, "asked the President what tenet of Quakerism was most important to him. 'Individual faithfulness,' responded Hoover." Concludes Burner: "But a President plodding faithfully along his own private uncommunicative course could not expect the public to give him its trustful support."[40] Between him and them, particularly as the Depression deepened, he built an impalpable wall of gloom.

In religion Roosevelt's low-church Anglicanism stood in sharp contrast with the Hoover family's Quaker heritage.[41] The Church of England was just that, the ultimate in a religious establishment. The Society of Friends was the ultimate antiestablishment. Born amid the English Civil War with its bloody religious animosities, the Society renounced all parties alike—Catholic, Anglican, and Puritan—and foreswore war, violence, and social conventions. Quakers held an uneasy relationship with politics, even when they became the government in colonial Pennsylvania. Some of them always suspected that political power led to compromise and corruption, and when the tension became too intense during the French and Indian War, the Quakers gave up their lead in the Pennsylvania Assembly. Business relationships, on the other hand, came easier, as they were (supposedly) carried on freely and without coercion. Above all, Quaker theology revered individual conscience, the inviolable seat of God in the soul. Governance in church matters occurred via prolonged meetings in which deliberations continued until there emerged a unanimous "sense of the meeting," forcing no one against his or her will.

At the Hoovers' home church at West Branch, Iowa, this heritage had become intertwined with the Holiness reform movement of the nineteenth century. Holiness taught Wesleyan theology, revivalist passions, and ethical crusades, in sharp contrast to traditional Quaker markers of plain living, pacifism, silent waiting, and quiet distinction from other Christians. The revivalist Friends were influenced by powerful homegrown evangelists including Herbert's great-uncle John Y. Hoover, who presided over the West Branch church. At the Iowa Yearly Meeting, writes Thomas D. Hamm, they revealed that their "first loyalty was not to the Society but to the larger community of evangelical Christians." They entered the mainstream of American Protestantism with its Bible studies, antislavery position, temperance, poor relief, and finally in 1861, enlistment in the Union army. Pacifism was put aside; according to Governor Oliver P. Morgan of Indiana, Quakers signed up at a higher rate than "any other denomination in the state."[42]

Hoover's immediate family took a moderate position in the ensuing division between the revivalists and the orthodox at West Branch. While their sympathies lay with the evangelicals, they regarded sanctification as the gradual nurturing of moral qualities, not the revivalists' instantaneous, emotionally charged release from sin. In this regard Herbert resembled FDR in having his roots among the gradualists of his tradition. Even so, he and other members of the West Branch church were increasingly free to enjoy preaching, music, and "liberation from the prying of the overseers and the frowns of the elders," writes Hamm. "In the place of silence came excitement, in the place of grimness was ecstatic joy, and all in the name of a higher vision of religious life." The Quakers' perennial humanitarianism did not disappear, however, nor did their "vision of a prosperous social order founded in self-reliance and willing cooperation."[43]

This heritage deeply shaped Hoover's character and vision. For all the official posts he held, he was never at ease with politics, in sharp contrast to Roosevelt. In both men, personality happened to match up with theory and theology. A basic difference between them lay in the contrast between technical efficiency and social adroitness, between the engineer with his infallible facts and figures and the politician with his sensitivity to tides and temperament. Religiously, they represented the two different sides of Protestant aspiration, the tension between the individual's concern for personal salvation and the communal emphasis on an ordered Christian society. In political theory, the mood of the 1930s swung toward security and collective action under the impact of the Depression. Hoover remained in the older camp of individualism, in which setbacks and difficulties were thought to improve character. Roosevelt upheld as the model citizen the one who helped his neighbor. Hoover agreed with that but insisted that charitable action come from the individual, not the government. Both presidents asked, in effect, which of the seven deadly sins most infected the body politic. For Hoover it was *sloth*, carelessness and ignorance. For Roosevelt it was *avarice*, covetousness and greed.

The Quaker Individualist

In 1922 Hoover published a manifesto entitled *American Individualism*. It espoused something of a Great Man view of history and envisioned the good society as a hierarchy based on merit. Material and spiritual advancement, Hoover declared, depended on a constantly renewable supply of leaders who would rise from the mass of people. "Our social, economic, and intellectual progress is almost solely dependent upon the creative minds of those individuals with imaginative and administrative intelligence who create or who carry discoveries to widespread application." To be sure, he wanted equal opportunity: one of the nation's "great ideals" was "that we keep the social solution free from [the] frozen strata of classes." Only by such flexibility could individual "salvation" become a reality. Hoover saw Europe as hopelessly locked into classes, castes, and stratification, but in America the "free-running mills of competition" had produced "rare individuals" who "are able to spread their influence over so enlarged a number of lesser capable minds as to have increased their [the leaders'] potency a million-fold." The description was a little scary; it was also autobiographical. Hoover inveighed against the indolence of "rich or impecunious loafers" as well as "timorous mediocrities." He disparaged the "mind of the crowd." "The crowd only feels: it has no mind of its own which can plan. The crowd is credulous, it destroys, it consumes, it hates, and it dreams—but it never builds." To keep them at bay, it was necessary to groom individual greatness with just the right preparation. On the one hand, each rising individual "must stand up to the emery wheel of competition." Likewise, it would be foolish as well as sentimental to "abandon self-interest as a motive force to leadership and to production." But the winners in the competition also needed to cultivate "an enlarging sense of responsibility and understanding."[44]

Roosevelt agreed with Hoover about "rich loafers," but for him the aggressive ambition in Hoover's formula had utterly drowned any sense of social responsibility. He inveighed against "a generation of self-seekers," unscrupulous "money changers," "the existence of un-fair methods of competition, of cut-throat prices," "unfair wages," and "improper working conditions." In his May 1933 address to the US Chamber of Commerce, Roosevelt warned that when "the lone wolf, the unethical competitor, the reckless promoter . . . whose hand is against every man's, declines to join in achieving an end recognized as being for the public welfare . . . the government may properly be asked to apply restraint." In his first fireside chat, right after his inau-guration, he declared that "selfish victory is always destined to be an ultimate defeat."[45] Roosevelt's attitude toward the unsuccessful poor, so different from Hoover's, reflected one of his favorite passages from the Book of Common Prayer, the so-called forgotten man's prayer: "Re-member in pity such as are this day destitute, homeless or forgotten of their fellow men." As Frances Perkins remembered it, that line lay at the source of the New Deal: "as Roosevelt described it, 'new deal' meant that the forgotten man, the little man, the man nobody knew much about, was going to be dealt better cards to play with." The term "forgotten man" found its way into a campaign speech of April 7, 1932, and thereafter the address carried that title.[46] Furthermore, FDR em-braced the crowd that Hoover despised. From East Coast to West Coast he addressed masses of citizens with his familiar "My friends." The greeting was not inconsequential. No politician had ever spoken that way before. It was not only good politics; it was also good social ethics. It implied that all men and women were part of a community and that the government had responsibility for it.

For Hoover, government had no such role to play. Not that people should be left to starve. Far from it. Private philanthropy in the hearts and hands of caring individuals would clothe the naked, shelter the exposed, and feed the hungry, just as Hoover himself had done when, through his Commission for Relief in Belgium, he commandeered rail-ways, factories, warehouses, and hundreds of canal boats in the face of the kaiser's armies to provide relief to war-torn civilian populations. In the early 1920s, his American Relief Administration provided food to sustain fifteen million people daily in the Soviet Union. At home and abroad, people were thunderstruck by what American efficiency could accomplish. These extraordinary efforts involved large-scale bureaucracies and technical sophistication, but to explain them Hoover invoked the myth of the untrammeled individual. "The American pioneer," he wrote, "is the epic expression" of American individualism, "and the pioneer spirit is the response to the challenge of opportunity, to the challenge of nature, to the challenge of life, to the call of the frontier." That spirit, he said, built roads, bridges, railways, and cities, and created new states; it "carried every attribute of high civilization over a continent. The days of the pioneer are not over," he continued, and he seemed validated when Charles Lindbergh flew the Atlantic in 1927. In America, contentions and jealousies were primarily over the division of "comforts and luxuries," Hoover claimed, "for none of us is either hungry or cold or without a place to lay his head." He was wrong when he wrote those words in the 1920s; the words would prove even more wrong in the early '30s.[47]

Hoover's Quaker religion played out in his diagnosis of what threatened America and what constituted its sure defense. World War I, said this heir of pacifism, had instilled a dangerous spiritual reaction: "many men came to believe that salvation lay in mass and group action." War not only destroyed human life but also submerged the individual in "the struggle of the race." The continuance of that mass capitulation in peacetime would "destroy the foundations of our civilization." Doom could come via socialism, which would obliterate "the economic stimulation of each member" of society. Or it might come from the corrupt machine of Tammany Hall. It could be the "Bolshevist party, or some other form of tyranny." It could even be "capitalism in the sense that a few men through unrestrained control of property determine the welfare of great numbers"; that too was "far apart from the rightful expression of American individualism."[48]

Of all these threats, the most looming was government interference. "The perpetual howl of radicalism is that it is the sole voice of liberalism . . . that all reform and human advance must come through government." Hoover's Quaker sense of the meeting and the divine touch in every individual led him to trust instead in voluntary cooperation, in "the widespread aspiration for mutual advancement, self-expression, and neighborly helpfulness," and in "a rising vision of service." He put great trust in "chambers of commerce, trade associations, labor unions, bankers, farmers, propaganda associations, and what not." He argued that the "moral standards of business and commerce are improving, vicious city governments are less in number; invisible government [the domain of lobbyists] has greatly diminished; public conscience is penetrating deeper and deeper, . . . and above all is the growing sense of service." This sort of public spirit would take care of sloth, radicalism, and the infatuated mind of the crowd. But when government interfered with the free workings of society, it simply multiplied the sins of the slothful.[49]

The combination in Hoover's mind of the Quaker belief in the individual as the repository of the Holy Spirit and the presence of the American hero on the stage of history goes far to explain his insistence on laissez-faire economics in the Depression. He took the Quaker sense of the meeting and applied it to national politics. He was confident that by appointing commissions to make surveys and gather information on national needs of every sort, advanced solutions would commend themselves objectively to the enterprising. The trouble was that, with all their technical efficiency, the commissions were not only slow but also lacked the power to implement their conclusions in statutes and laws. That suited Hoover. He himself was averse to compulsion. In the Quaker tradition, "for government to coerce was to violate the respect and freedom that are required if the Spirit within is to develop."[50] His vision left out the sin of covetousness and the abuses of liberty committed in the name of personal gain that occurred in all too many places. Roosevelt knew better. Whether the covetous were Northern ward heelers, graduates of Groton and Harvard, or Southern populist demagogues, FDR knew their minds. The greedy must be coerced to toe the line of fairness and give opportunity to vastly more people. Manipulation was a necessary good.

The Spirit of Interdependence

As it happened, Roosevelt outlined his own big picture of things in the 1920s in a little-noticed speech at Milton Academy, a private school in Milton, Massachusetts. The occasion, in 1926, was to commemorate the school's twenty-two alumni who had died in World War I. But instead of using the address to retreat into an outmoded mythology, as had Hoover, Roosevelt launched into a consideration of the future. His title was *Whither Bound?*, and the question was meant to challenge the students to take the progressive side in responding to the rapid changes that would inevitably unfold in the years ahead. In taking that side, Roosevelt said, they would be harvesting the best of Christianity for the preservation and extension of democracy.[51]

Roosevelt showed himself to be an avid diagnostician of technological development. The "great inventions of yesterday—steam, telegraph, telephone, electric light and power, and industrial machinery"—had taken some time to have their effect. Only in the past fifty years had real change gone forward on a mass level, so that one could "truly say that the lives of the great majority of the people are more different from the lives of 1875 than were our grandfathers' lives from those of the year 1500." The pace of change had especially accelerated in the past decade and was only going to quicken in the future. Leaders in "scientific thought and research" were saying that "investigation and experimentation will not, cannot, cease, but that they are adding, day by day, in startling manner, to the results already obtained." The speaker drew students' attention to recent advances in medicine, hygiene, physiology, psychology, transportation, and agriculture, and showed particular interest in the question of energy supply. "Only a few years ago we were worrying about the day, soon to arrive, when there would be no more coal, and, therefore, no more power or light," but that had become a moot point with the development of hydroelectric power. Now the worry was "that if the present increase in the need for power continues, all the water available in the world will be insufficient." The visionary of the Tennessee Valley Authority was already looking beyond that to "that time [when] the natural heat of the sun and of the earth's interior will be serving mankind."

Roosevelt was just as current with advances in the field of telecommunications. In the future, he told the students, "by a twist of a knob or the push of a button you [will be able to] see and talk with some true friend half the world away." In fact, "every trend of modern science is toward the greater unification of mankind." Isolation by nation, race, or class was a luxury none could any longer afford. "Economic progress—social, financial, industrial, agricultural—is forcing the issue." Scientists were working along international lines. "Laws and governments in each national unit are influenced by experiments in other units." Consequently, the mandate for the students gathered in front of him was to "lend helping hands to people we do not like, people who do not 'belong to our crowd,' people whom we subconsciously hope we may never see again." Theirs was the call to bring democracy to all social relationships. "Class consciousness" was still "an ancient disease" that need to be cured. Roosevelt hoped "we are coming to accept people for what they are, not for what they appear or claim to be, not for what their parents were." For this to be accomplished, the name of Christ and the Christian concept of the neighbor were essential: "Do not forget that Christ's greatest teaching was, 'Thou shalt love thy neighbor as thyself.'" Unlike Hoover's forebodings about the crowd, Roosevelt held out hope; the goal was being approached little by little. "The necessity of greater cooperation will put every individual into closer touch with every other. More and more we become interdependent."

Roosevelt built his vision of the future upon a detailed look at the past. It was a bracing draft of the Whig view of progress, from the fall of the Roman Empire to the dawn of the twentieth century. Across the Dark Ages and reign of superstition, across the Renaissance and Reformation, the struggles for freedom of inquiry and freedom of conscience, wars of religion and monarchical reaction, the history of the West was a story of real battles. Yet, no matter what calamities were encountered, "civilization and Christianity were not blotted out." The "Bible has been called upon to justify repression of liberal thought," but true religion survived anyway and was thriving: "Christianity is great enough and broad enough to throw off the control of dead hands and to march forward in step with the progress of mankind." Accordingly, Roosevelt scotched "those radicals who tell you that our religion is dead." Quite the contrary, "churches to-day are beginning to go along with the new scientific growth and are opening the way to a simpler faith, a deeper faith, a *happier* faith, than ever our forefathers held." Nor was progress just scientific and material: "I see something spiritual coming to [those of] you who will take part." That spiritual something had to do with "service to mankind." True, the idea was "still in its infancy of development. True service will not come until all the world recognizes all the rest of the world as one big family." In its historical reputation, the Social Gospel ran into rough sledding in the 1920s. Nonetheless, Roosevelt remained its happy warrior.

This fuller picture of progress entailed politics as well. Here real change had begun to occur only at the end of the eighteenth century, Roosevelt said. In the Europe of 1500, "less than five per cent of all people could fairly be graded above the rank of serfs." Most were "devoid of even what we would call the rudiments of any education at all." Only in the nineteenth century had the average person "obtained at least some hope and possibility of acquiring knowledge." Thus, if the American and French Revolutions "marked a new epoch" in human history, their leaven "has worked so slowly that the processes of acquiring representative government are still going on." Here came FDR's altar call. When liberals "come to power, they translate the constantly working leaven of progress into law or custom or use." But "measured by years, the actual control of human affairs is in the hands of conservatives for longer periods than in those of liberals or radicals." Accordingly, America's "national danger" was that it might "suffer from too long a period of the do-nothing or reactionary standards."

In this situation there was no time to wallow in Hooverian fears for the future, lamenting that "the Nation cannot endure—I will flee from Sodom—the time is out of joint." Such attitudes reflected "a Victorian atmosphere of gloomy religion, of copybook sentiment, of life by precept." They thought the "accepted social structure of the world was becoming demoralized" and were appalled when the course of democratic change came to gender roles as well. "Women—think of it, Women!"—Roosevelt jibed, "were commencing to take positions in offices and industrial plants and demanding—a very few of them—things called political rights."

Likewise, in returning to his political career, Roosevelt ignored the trumpeters of individualism, and for two reasons. The first was his paralysis and his ever-present need for physical assistance in the simplest routines of daily life. He was unable even to dress himself each morning. He knew firsthand the necessity of help. Polio brought home to him the interconnectedness of daily life. As there had been no possibility in his own case of "letting things alone," so in the national paralysis caused by the Depression, talk of individualism jangled out of tune. Second, as David M. Kennedy notes, the deadening reality of the Depression "revealed one of the perverse implications of American society's vaunted celebration of individualism. In the culture that ascribed all success to individual striving, it seemed to follow axiomatically that failure was due to individual inadequacy." The twin thunderheads of defeat and shame had paralyzed the white middle class. It was "dumb with misery."[52] Thus, Roosevelt opened his presidential campaign of 1932 with a direct attack on the "old . . . philosophy of 'letting things alone.'" Laissez-faire capitalism was in critical condition; the nation needed government intervention to revive, and then to thrive.[53]

In the 1932 campaign, President Hoover gave speeches that created "logical structures, anchored firmly in the bedrock of the earlier economic theories," and strove for "an overall pattern of a certain consistency." He introduced "people into his orderly scheme of things"; he did not begin by imagining their lives and then drawing conclusions.[54] By contrast, Roosevelt's speeches could appear to be blithe and general. To Hoover, well informed, disciplined, and dour, FDR was lacking in knowledge, a lightweight and an opportunist. For his part, Roosevelt observed that the thirty-first president had "accomplished many great tasks where he was the sole boss, and relating to some specific object." He doubted whether Hoover's "type of ability could coordinate all of the one hundred and one simultaneous tasks that fall to the lot of a President."[55] Nor did Roosevelt's own thinking lack substance. It lay there just beneath his optimistic surface, but its lineaments were clear. In the "Forgotten Man" speech, he acclaimed those who "build from the bottom up and not from the top down, that put their faith once more in the forgotten man at the bottom of the economic pyramid."[56] The poor had suffered in every collapse of the American economy from the Panic of 1819 onward. It was time to end that pattern and achieve a new reach in the promise of democracy.

There is a final irony to this comparison. Roosevelt was to be attacked by his opponents and enemies, including Hoover, as wanting to be a dictator. It was a charge he constantly had to deny during his administrations. Hoover, the Quaker who sought in Friends' meetings and in endless conferences a common mind and spirit, was never so accused by the media. Yet in his consistent move to the right in the late 1920s, he displayed many signs of a dictatorial nature. William E. Leuchtenburg draws attention not only to Hoover's ambition—of which he had no less than Roosevelt—but also to his being "unable to understand how anyone could disagree with him" and his tendency to throw tantrums when someone did. Often condescending toward FDR, often self-delusory, he told his secretary in January 1933, "I'll have my way with Roosevelt yet."[57] He never did, and never forgot or forgave what he considered the affront of his defeat. Over the subsequent decades, many have joined him. But Roosevelt's is still the achievement that sets the mark.

Notes

Introduction

1. Robert E. Sherwood, *Roosevelt and Hopkins* (New York: Harper and Brothers, 1948), 9.

2. James Roosevelt, "Lecture on Work," Roosevelt Family Papers, Container 52, 8, Franklin D. Roosevelt Library, Hyde Park, New York (hereafter Roosevelt Library); Frank Wilson Correspondence, Container 1, President's Personal File, 918, Roosevelt Library, and President's Secretary's File, 139, Roosevelt Library; State of the Union address, January 1939, *The Public Papers and Addresses of Franklin D. Roosevelt*, ed. Samuel I. Rosenman, 13 vols. (New York: Random House, 1938–c. 1950), 8:1–3; D-Day prayer, President's Statements File, Roosevelt Library.

3. For valuable detail and analysis of this topic, see Peter W. Williams's *Religion, Art, and Money: Episcopalians and American Culture from the Civil War to the Great Depression* (Chapel Hill: University of North Carolina Press, 2016).

4. James D. G. Dunn, *Beginning from Jerusalem* (Grand Rapids: Eerdmans, 2009), 821.

5. John T. Noonan Jr., *The Lustre of Our Country: The American Experience of Religious Freedom* (Berkeley: University of California Press, 1998), 213–16.

6. Benjamin M. Friedman, "FDR & the Depression: The Big Debate," *New York Review of Books*, November 8, 2007, 29; Friedman reviews Amity Shlaes's *The Forgotten Man: A New History of the Great Depression* and Robert D. Leighninger Jr.'s *Long-Range Public Investment: The Forgotten Legacy of the New Deal*.

Chapter 1

1. Weston to Early, July 10, 1944; Early to Weston, July 17, 1944, President's Personal File, 918, Franklin D. Roosevelt Library, Hyde Park, New York (hereafter Roosevelt Library).

2. E. A. White and I. A. Jackson, *Annotated Constitution and Canons for the Government of the Protestant Episcopal Church*, 2 vols. (New York: Seabury, 1982), 1:364. For the exception, see Minutes of the Vestry Meeting, St. James' Episcopal Church, Hyde Park, NY, July 4, 1943, 49. Wilson's successor, George W. Anthony, presided thereafter as "temporary rector": Minutes, February 27, 1944, 51.

3. These linkages have been explored in many studies. The most relevant titles here include Robert Kelley, *The Cultural Pattern in American Politics: The First Century* (New York: Knopf, 1979); Mark A. Noll and Luke E. Harlow, eds., *Religion and American Politics: From the Colonial Period to the Present*, 2nd ed. (New York: Oxford University Press, 2007); and Daniel Walker Howe, *The Political Culture of the American Whigs* (Chicago: University of Chicago Press, 1984).

4. Franklin D. Roosevelt, "The Roosevelt Family of New Amsterdam before the Revolution" (unpublished sophomore thesis, Harvard College, 1901), 16, and notes, 17. (Notes are paginated separately from the text.)

5. On Delano family history, see Kenneth S. Davis, *FDR: The Beckoning of Destiny* (New York: Putnam, 1972), 36–42, and Geoffrey C. Ward, *Before the Trumpet: Young Franklin Roosevelt, 1882–1905* (New York: Vintage Books, 1985), 65–102.

6. Davis, *FDR: The Beckoning of Destiny*, 35–36; Ward, *Before the Trumpet*, 64–65. The Roosevelts had plenty of company in moving from other fellowships to the Episcopal Church. The church grew over sixfold between 1870 and 1930, mostly among the prosperous, urban, and better educated. See Peter W. Williams, *Religion, Art, and Money: Episcopalians and American Culture from the Civil War to the Great Depression* (Chapel Hill: University of North Carolina Press, 2016), 215.

7. Frank Freidel, *Franklin D. Roosevelt: The Apprenticeship* (Boston: Little, Brown, 1952), 24.

8. Freidel, *Franklin D. Roosevelt*, 31; Rita Halle Kleeman, *Gracious Lady: The Life of Sara Delano Roosevelt* (New York: Appleton-Century, 1935), 154.

9. Colleen McDannell, *The Christian Home in Victorian America, 1840–1900* (Bloomington: Indiana University Press, 1986), 100–101.

10. "I shall always count myself fortunate in having met Mark Twain when I was a boy & a devotee of his works then as I am now," FDR recalled. A devotee at age five? Samuel's nephew, Cyril Clemens, gave an equally flawed but detailed account of the visit: "The great man with his snow-white hair, his white flannel suit, and his characteristic drawl made a profound impression on the little visitor and on the spot became his hero." Alas, in 1887 Mark Twain's hair was not white! See Cyril Clemens, *The Literary Education of Franklin D. Roosevelt* (Webster Groves, MO: International Mark Twain Society, 1935), 15. For the FDR quote, see Cyril Clemens, facing 27; see also Ron Powers, *Mark Twain: A Life* (New York: Free Press, 2005), illustration 38.

11. Powers, *Mark Twain*, 490, quoting the *St. Louis Globe-Democrat*, March 17, 1885.

12. The genre of nondevotional lives of Christ had boomed in the nineteenth century. The Hyde Park library's holdings thereof run from Thomas Jefferson's *The Life and Morals of Jesus of Nazareth* to Henry Van Dyke's *The Story of the Other Wise Man* (1895). Authors mined this vein in the twentieth century, too, with such offerings as *The Man Nobody Knows* (1925), written by business booster, advertising executive, and future mortal enemy of FDR, Bruce Barton; the fundamentalist response, Arno C. Gaebelein, *The Christ We Know* (1927); Roman Catholic Richard Charles Beam's *Jesus of Nazareth, the Divine Lord* (1925); Russian Orthodox Vladimir Simkovitch's *Toward the Understanding of Jesus* (1933); French Catholic Francois Mauriac's *Vie de Jesus* (1936); a Jewish take in Sholem Asch's *The Nazarene* (1939); and liberal Protestant lion Harry Emerson Fosdick's *The Complete Sayings of Jesus* (1942). Beside these stood Charles F. May's *Our Book of Books* (1938) and Virgilius H. Krull, *A Prophetic Biography of Jesus* (1942). All

these are in the catalogue of the FDR Presidential Library and Museum, http://www
.fdrlibrary.marist.edu/archives/. Absent from the collection are two prominent lives
of Jesus: the Protestant modernist Shirley Jackson Case's *Jesus: A New Biography* (Chicago: University of Chicago Press, 1927) and Maurice Goguel, *La vie de Jesus* (Paris:
Payot, 1932). Whatever their scholarly limitations, the titles show FDR's remarkably
ecumenical taste.

Roosevelt's appetite for both reading and collecting books was voracious. The 252
titles he chose to hold at "Top Cottage" measure either his affection, reference priorities, or both: 20 volumes on trees, 16 on fishing, 15 on plants and gardens, 15 on
exploration, 7 on birds, 4 on the Hudson River valley, 2 each on oceans and animals.
The shelves of literature included 8 volumes of English poetry, 6 of English novelists,
15 of American literature, 8 of fantasy, theater, and humor. He had works by J. B. Bury,
Carlyle, Darwin, John Dewey, the great Russian authors, as well as Freud and Marx.
They were alongside the perennial King James Bible and the Book of Common Prayer.

More generally, FDR favored the works of Lewis Carroll, Rudyard Kipling, Francis Parkman, Nathaniel Hawthorne, Herman Melville, and James Fenimore Cooper,
among them Cooper's *History of the Navy of the United States of America* (1847). These
rested beside Aesop's Fables, the sagas of Homer, Aeschylus, Dante's *The Divine Comedy*,
and a surprising number of books for young people in both French and German. His
love of naval history registered in such volumes as Isaac Taylor's *The Ship, or Sketches of
the Vessels of Various Countries* (1867). Later in life he himself chose for the "President's
Room" at Hyde Park the works of Kipling and Hawthorne, Dickens's *A Christmas Carol*,
selections from the psalms of David, and Francis Thompson's *The Hound of Heaven*
(1907).

As a youth he read biographies of military and naval figures such as Gustavus
Adolphus, Lord Nelson, Lafayette, Napoleon, and Admiral Dewey. Travel and geography fascinated him. At age nine he was given the large stamp collection of his uncle, Frederic A. Delano, who had in turn received it from Sara. Simultaneously and no
doubt used in tandem with the stamps were numerous geography books by American
authors J. A. Cummings and W. C. Woodbridge; Jesse Olney's standard text, *A Practical
System of Modern Geography* (1834); and S. August Mitchell's *School Geography* (1846).
These stood together with *Cast Up by the Sea* (1869) by the British explorer of India and
Africa, Sir Samuel White Baker, and Harriet Beecher Stowe's informative, lively, and
neglected book on Florida, *Palmetto-Leaves* (1873). Both Baker's and Stowe's books went
into special cabinets in the President's Room. They contributed to the boy's growing
interest in other places at home and abroad and in world affairs. And he read them with
astonishing speed and retention.

13. Quoted in Freidel, *Franklin D. Roosevelt: The Apprenticeship*, 30–31.

14. Adam L. P. Smith, "Interchange," in "Abraham Lincoln at 200," special issue,
Journal of American History, September 2009, 464; Carlo Levi, *Christ Stopped at Eboli*
(New York: Farrar, Straus, 1947), 122.

15. Kleeman, *Gracious Lady*, 134–35.

16. The historical studies of this phenomenon are far too numerous to be listed
here. A good recent overview is available in Daniel Walker Howe, *What Hath God
Wrought: The Transformation of America, 1815–1848* (New York: Oxford University Press,
2007), 164–202, 285–327.

17. Davis, *FDR: The Beckoning of Destiny*, 26–27; Ward, *Before the Trumpet*, 25–30. On Nott's long career and reformist endeavors, see Codman Mislop, *Eliphalet Nott* (Middletown, CT: Wesleyan University Press, 1971).

18. Davis, *FDR: The Beckoning of Destiny*, 29.

19. Kleeman, *Gracious Lady*, 145.

20. James Roosevelt, "Summary of My Life," n.d., c. 1890s, Isaac Roosevelt to James Roosevelt, October 2, 1848, Franklin D. Roosevelt Family Papers, Container 52, Roosevelt Library. Both Edward Pearsons Newton, *Historical Notes on Saint James Parish: Hyde Park-on-Hudson, New York* (Poughkeepsie, NY: A. V. Haight, 1913), 44, and Davis, *FDR: The Beckoning of Destiny*, 32, attest to James's constant care for the public school and the local hospital.

21. This is contrary to Kenneth S. Davis, who claims that on the trip the newlyweds "did nothing but enjoy themselves as they journeyed leisurely through Italy, Spain, France, Holland, Germany, Switzerland, and across the Channel into England and Scotland . . . nowhere did they have meaningful contacts with classes of people whose discontents were developing dangerous pressures in every continent." See Davis, *FDR: The Beckoning of Destiny*, 48–49, after Clara and Hardy Steeholm, *The House at Hyde Park* (New York: Viking, 1950), 72, and Kleeman, *Gracious Lady*, 132.

22. James Roosevelt, "Lecture on Work," Roosevelt Family Papers, Container 52, 8, Roosevelt Library. All quotations in the next six paragraphs come from this source unless otherwise noted.

23. Quoted in John Morton Blum, *From the Morgenthau Diaries: Years of Crisis, 1928–1938* (Boston: Houghton Mifflin, 1959), 243.

24. Howe, *What Hath God Wrought*, 573, 581. For James Roosevelt's Whig convictions, see Isaac Roosevelt to James Roosevelt, February 7, February 25, and May 29, 1848, Roosevelt Family Papers, Container 52, Roosevelt Library.

25. For the reformist element in the post–Civil War democracy that attracted James Roosevelt, see Eric Foner, *Reconstruction: America's Unfinished Revolution, 1863–1877* (New York: Harper & Row, 1988), especially 499–500, 506, 523, 568, 586, and 609.

26. Blum, *From the Morgenthau Diaries*, 33.

27. See *F.D.R.: His Personal Letters*, ed. Elliott Roosevelt, 4 vols. (New York: Duell, Sloan & Pearce, 1947–1950), 1:22, 42, 46, 48, 533 (Rogers); 35n, 884 (Morgan).

28. [Genevieve M. Spratt, comp.], *Historical Notes on Saint James' Parish, Hyde Park-on-Hudson, New York, 1911–1961* (privately printed, 1961), 38. Length of service as vestrymen and wardens is regulated by the New York Corporations Law, para. 43; otherwise there are no diocesan regulations pertaining to parish vestries from 1900 to 1946. See "Canons," *Journal of the . . . Convention* (New York: J. J. Little, 1900), and *Diocese of New York: Constitution, Canons, Rules of Order, and Statutes* (New York: EDNY, 1946). Recently, parishes in the Diocese of New York have been encouraged in their parochial bylaws to provide term limits (Vice Chancellor Charles Banks to Archivist Wayne Kempton, August 23, 2009). The Episcopal Church in the state of New York was subject to state law because of the Ministry Act of 1693, confirmed by Governor Benjamin Fletcher in 1697.

29. Morgan to FDR, August 12 and August 29, 1940, President's Secretary's File, 139, Roosevelt Library. Like FDR, Morgan was a graduate of Groton School, class of 1897. He had been diagnosed with cancer in the 1930s and received encouraging counsel from

FDR that had a profound impact on his life (Gerald Morgan Jr. interview with author, September 14, 2009).

30. FDR to Bowie, April 27, 1911, 2. After Bowie demurred, Roosevelt wrote to his older half brother, James Roosevelt Roosevelt, on May 6, 1911: "I fear we aimed too high" (Business and Personal File: St. James' Church, Container 23, Roosevelt Library). From 1931 through 1942, St. James's parochial reports show an average of 155 adult communicants; 306 baptized persons, including children; and a Sunday school average of 73 children (Parochial Statistics, Journals of the Convention of the Diocese of New York, 1931–1941, and file cards, Stewardship Department, 1941–1942, Archives, Diocese of New York).

31. Edmund P. Rogers to FDR, April 29, 1929, Container 23, Roosevelt Library.

32. FDR to Rogers, March 4, 1929, and also March 26, March 27, March 29, May 1, and June 8; FDR to Frank R. Wilson, July 1, 1929; FDR to Peabody, February 27, 1929; Peabody to Rogers, February 22, 1929; Peabody to FDR, October 4, 1929; Rogers to FDR, October 8, 1929, November 13, Container 23, Roosevelt Library.

33. Rogers to FDR, April 29, 1929, Container 23, Roosevelt Library.

34. Sara Delano Roosevelt to Frank Wilson, February 26, 1933, Wilson Correspondence, Container 1; see also FDR to Frank Wilson, March 1, 1938; Stephen T. Early to Frank Wilson, February 19, 1940; William D. Hassett to Frank Wilson, March 1, 1940, Container 1; Florence Wilson to Eleanor Roosevelt, March 9, 1943; Florence Wilson to Stephen T. Early, January 25, 1945, File 918, all in Roosevelt Library.

35. With its Southern and urban Northern constituencies, the Democratic Party was divided in the 1920s over the twin issues of the Klan and Prohibition. Roosevelt wanted to emphasize what Democrats had in common and not what divided them, hence opening himself to the false charge that he was a friend of the Klan. See H. W. Brands, *Traitor to His Class: The Privileged Life and Radical Presidency of Franklin Delano Roosevelt* (New York: Anchor Books, 2008), 198.

36. Frank Wilson to FDR, February 6, 1936, President's Secretary's File, Container 139, Roosevelt Library. The quotation is from the popular radio program *Amos and Andy*. For the Court's invalidations and their significance, see William E. Leuchtenburg, *The Supreme Court Reborn: The Constitutional Revolution in the Age of Roosevelt* (New York: Oxford University Press, 1995), 85–96, 214–16.

37. Interviews with Robert Wilson, July 11 and August 15, 2009; obituary, *Washington Post*, December 5, 1960.

38. Frank Wilson to FDR, November 10, 1933 (on local Hyde Park election); February 26, 1937 (on mission outreach); Container 139, Roosevelt Library. Chapel Corners is a small community along Route 9G, 6 miles north of the Hudson River State Hospital and 1.3 miles south of the entrance to the Val-Kill Handicraft Center; Alicia J. Vivona to the author, September 3, 2009.

39. FDR to Frederick L. Barry, February 1, 1937, President's Personal File, 918, Roosevelt Library.

40. FDR to Frank Wilson, February 14, 1940, "Hyde Park—St. James' Church 1940–1944," President's Secretary's Files, Roosevelt Library.

41. FDR to Frank Wilson, May 10, 1939, File 918, Roosevelt Library. Conversation with Robert Wilson, August 11, 2009. When the king and queen wrote FDR that they wished to present St. James' Church with either a Bible or candlesticks, Roosevelt asked

Wilson which they needed most or "would be most appropriate for the church"; FDR to Frank Wilson, July 14, 1939, File 918, Roosevelt Library.

42. Untitled speech by Frank Wilson, President's Personal File, 918, Roosevelt Library; FDR to Frank Wilson, June 9, 1942, Container 1, Roosevelt Library.

43. FDR to Frank Wilson, September 26, 1942; FDR to the Navy Department, November 5, 1942, President's Personal File, 918, Roosevelt Library.

44. FDR to Frank Wilson, February 5, 1943, President's Personal File, 918, Roosevelt Library. See also Walter Russell Bowie to FDR, January 9, 1943; FDR to Frank Wilson, January 30, 1943, and Florence Wilson to Eleanor Roosevelt, March 9, 1943.

45. FDR to Frank Wilson, February 4, 1938 (sexton); November 10, 1933 (brass plate); Frank Wilson to FDR, February 6, 1936, and FDR to Frank Wilson, December 18, 1936 (organ overhaul); FDR to Henry K. Brant, June 25, 1943 (fire insurance); FDR to Halpin, February 19, 1937, February 26, 1937, December 30, 1938; Morgan to FDR, January 14, 1939 (purchase of bonds); Halpin to FDR, January 22, 1941, January 14, 1942 (the budget deficit was, respectively, $675.30 and $58.49); Frank Wilson to FDR, May 18, 1938, June 23, 1942 (strawberry festival); LeHand to Taylor, November 2, 1939, to Evelyn Paul, June 23, 1942; Tully to Taylor, October 19, 1943. FDR to Taylor, March 15, 1943 (carpet), President's Secretary's File, 139, Roosevelt Library.

46. FDR to Morgan, January 10, 1938, File 918, Roosevelt Library.

47. The number of vestry meetings per year was as follows: 1, 1935; 2, 1936; 2, 1937; 3, 1939; 1, 1940; 2, 1941; 2, 1942; 2, 1943; 3, 1944; Gloria Golden, St. James' Church archivist, to the author, October 8, 2009.

48. Williams, *Religion, Art, and Money*, 85–95, provides the details as well as the larger history and intentions behind the project.

49. William H. Owen, *I Remember* ([New York]: privately printed, 1939), 147–49; copy in the St. Mark's Library of the General Theological Seminary, New York City.

50. Eleanor Roosevelt to Sara Delano Roosevelt, July 5, 1905, 27 and 66; see also 20, 50, 59–61.

51. FDR to Manning, March 1, 1922, Manning Papers, Box 3, File 17, Archives, Diocese of New York, New York City.

52. Quoted in Geoffrey C. Ward, ed., *Closest Companion: The Unknown Story of the Intimate Relationship between Franklin Roosevelt and Margaret Suckley* (Boston: Houghton Mifflin, 1995), 67. The Cathedral of St. John the Divine was begun in 1892 and is in fact still unfinished as of this writing, earning it the sobriquet "St. John the Unfinished." The Washington National Cathedral was begun in 1907 and completed in 1990; for more detail, see Williams, *Religion, Art, and Money*, 95–101.

53. P. Brussee, *Grote- of St. Laurenskerk* (Rotterdam: Stichting Grote- of St. Laurenskerk, 1981). FDR had J. R. Callenbach's *The Cathedral of Rotterdam* (1939) in the President's Room at Hyde Park.

54. For these themes, see Williams, *Religion, Art, and Money*, 85, 90–94, 212–14.

55. Quoted in George DeMille, *A History of the Diocese of Albany* (Philadelphia: Church Historical Society, 1948), 92.

56. Williams, *Religion, Art, and Money*, 8, 81, 89–90.

57. William T. Manning, "The Protestant Episcopal Church and Christian Unity," *Constructive Quarterly* 3 (March–December 1915): 684–86.

58. Manning to FDR, February 20, 1937, Manning Papers, Box 3, File 23. By this

time the indefatigable bishop had become a notable person in New York. In 1934 he rated a line in Cole Porter's song "You're the Top" from the hit musical *Anything Goes*: "You're the boats that glide on the sleepy Zuider Zee, / You're Nathan panning, / You're Bishop Manning, / You're broccoli." "Nathan panning" refers to the acerbic theater critic George Jean Nathan; see Robert Kimball, ed., *The Complete Lyrics of Cole Porter* (New York: Knopf, 1983).

59. Watson to Manning, May 24, 1939, Manning Papers, Box 3, File 20.

60. Manning to FDR, September 25, 1941, Manning Papers, Box 3, File 20.

61. *New York Times*, February 22, 1933; *Diocesan Bulletin* (Diocese of New York) 10, no. 1 (January 1933): 1.

62. William T. Manning, *The Bishop's Address* (New York: Printed by Order of the Convention, 1933), Tuesday, May 9, 1933.

63. Manning to FDR, May 22, 1933, Manning Papers, Box 3, File 20.

64. Sara Delano Roosevelt to Elinor Morgenthau, June 21, 1941, St. Paul's Church Eastchester Papers, Box 8, File 57. Archives of the Diocese of New York.

65. Harry M. Dunkak, "A Colonial and Revolutionary Parish in New York: St. Paul's Church, Eastchester," *Anglican and Episcopal History* 57, no. 4 (1988): 398, 400.

66. Franklin D. Roosevelt, "Governor Roosevelt's Address at Descendants Day Ceremonies," St. Paul's Episcopal Church–Eastchester *Monthly Bulletin* 3 (May and June 1931): 5–7. The line of march from Anne Hutchinson to the Bill of Rights was hardly direct, however. It passed through John Locke's *The Reasonableness of Christianity* (1695), to the Whig policy of toleration after 1689, to Scottish commonsense philosophy and other products of the Enlightenment, such as scientific epistemology. Hutchinson was no more interested in certifying Christianity because of its "reasonableness" than in tolerating the Massachusetts Puritan establishment's suggestion that (to her mind) one could please God by works rather than by faith. As for common sense or even inductive reasoning, she relied on scriptural and personal mystic revelations. While she hesitated to unchurch anyone, at least until the second coming of Christ, Hutchinson cast a very doleful eye on Boston's claim to be a godly society. Nor was she interested in "America." Nonetheless, Hutchinson unwittingly opened the door to democracy—or more accurately, to freedom of religion—a crack.

67. FDR to Weigle, November 28, 1940, President's Personal File, 2033, Roosevelt Library.

Chapter 2

1. Quotations from Nathan Miller, *FDR: An Intimate History* (Garden City, NY: Doubleday, 1983), 24–25; Geoffrey C. Ward, *Before the Trumpet: Young Franklin Roosevelt, 1882–1905* (New York: Harper & Row, 1985), 182; Arthur M. Schlesinger Jr., *The Crisis of the Old Order, 1919–1933* (Boston: Houghton Mifflin, 1957), 321; Kenneth S. Davis, *FDR: The Beckoning of Destiny* (New York: Putnam, 1972), 104. On Roosevelt's Groton more generally, see Jean Edward Smith, *FDR* (New York: Random House, 2007), 26–29; Frank Freidel, *Franklin D. Roosevelt: The Apprenticeship* (Boston: Little, Brown, 1952), 35–37, and Davis, *FDR*, 101–5.

2. FDR to *New York Times*, June 3, 1934, quoted in Freidel, *Franklin D. Roosevelt: The Apprenticeship*, 34.

3. Frank D. Ashburn, *Peabody of Groton: A Portrait* (New York: Coward McCann, 1944), gives a detailed chronicle of Peabody's life, including copious quotations from letters and papers. Peter W. Williams, in *Religion, Art, and Money: Episcopalians and American Culture from the Civil War to the Great Depression* (Chapel Hill: University of North Carolina Press, 2016), explores the Episcopal prep-school phenomenon, 151–74, and Peabody, 161–69. More briefly, see Freidel, *Franklin D. Roosevelt: The Apprenticeship*, 36–40, and Davis, *FDR: The Beckoning of Destiny*, 105–7.

4. Ashburn, *Peabody of Groton*, 69–77. See, further, James McLachlan, *American Boarding Schools: A Historical Study* (New York: Scribner's Sons, 1970), 281; Thomas Dixon, *The Invention of Altruism* (Oxford: Oxford University Press, 2009), passim.

5. Endicott Peabody, "First Sunday in the New Chapel," October 14, 1900, Peabody Papers, Groton School Archives, Groton, Massachusetts.

6. Ashburn, *Peabody of Groton*, 13–33; J. R. de S. Honey, *Tom Brown's Universe: The Development of the English Public School in the Nineteenth Century* (London: Millington Books, 1977). Among the other newer schools, Marlborough attracted sons of clergy; Epsom, sons of doctors. For the reform of English education, see Jonathan Gathorne-Hardy, *The Old School Tie: The Phenomenon of the English Public School* (New York: Viking, 1978), 124, 193–95. On the newer schools' function in middle-class formation, see A. N. Wilson, *The Victorians* (New York: Norton, 2003), 280, 294.

7. Gathorne-Hardy, *The Old School Tie*, 148; Honey, *Tom Brown's Universe*, 34–36, 47, 151.

8. John P. Nagler, "Baptism in Helldorado: Endicott Peabody in Tombstone, 1882" (unpublished BA thesis, Brown University, 2007), 16.

9. Peabody, "Recollections," c. 1944, in Ashburn, *Peabody of Groton*, 38.

10. Wilson, *The Victorians*, 41–47; Margaret Ferrand Thorp, *Charles Kingsley, 1819–1875* (New York: Octagon Books, 1969), 61.

11. Thorp, *Charles Kingsley*, 59.

12. Quoted in Ashburn, *Peabody of Groton*, 38.

13. On Peabody's Tombstone years, see Ashburn, *Peabody of Groton*, 45–59, and Nagler, "Baptism in Helldorado," passim.

14. Nagler, "Baptism in Helldorado," 23.

15. William M. Beakenridge, *Helldorado: Bringing the Law to the Mesquite* (Boston: Houghton Mifflin, 1928), 126–27.

16. Richard Slotkin, *The Fatal Environment: The Myth of the Frontier in the Age of Industrialization, 1800–1890* (New York: Atheneum, 1985), 499. The Greenbackers were a minor political party named after western farmers' demand that the government print additional paper money ("greenbacks") to keep prices up for their goods. They also sought an eight-hour day and a graduated income tax and were opposed to railroad land grants. They merged in 1884 with the Anti-Monopoly Party.

17. Ashburn, *Peabody of Groton*, 181. Williams explains Brooks's career and import in *Religion, Art, and Money*, 27–50.

18. *The Public Papers and Addresses of Franklin Delano Roosevelt*, ed. Samuel I. Rosenman, 13 vols. (New York: Random House, 1938–c. 1950), 7:513, address at Denton, Maryland, September 5, 1938.

19. C. G. Brown, "Christocentric Liberalism in the Episcopal Church," *Historical Magazine of the Protestant Episcopal Church* 38, no. 1 (1968): 8, 16.

20. The classic study is C. Howard Hopkins and Ronald C. White, *The Social Gospel: Religion and Reform in a Changing America* (Philadelphia: Temple University Press, 1976). A revisionist view is provided in Susan Curtis, *A Consuming Faith: The Social Gospel and Modern America* (Baltimore: Johns Hopkins University Press, 1991).

21. See the concluding, millenarian pages of the work that launched the Social Gospel as a movement: Walter Rauschenbusch's *Christianity and the Social Crisis* (New York: Macmillan, 1907). Curtis, *A Consuming Faith*, brings out this theme throughout.

22. The three most distinguished recent treatments of the movement emphasize these tensions: Michael McGerr, *A Fierce Discontent: The Rise and Fall of the Progressive Movement in America, 1870–1920* (New York: Free Press, 2003); Nell Irvin Painter, *Standing at Armageddon: A Grassroots History of the Progressive Era, 1877–1919* (New York: Norton, 2008); and Jackson Lears, *Rebirth of a Nation: The Making of Modern America, 1877–1920* (New York: Harper, 2009). Equally illuminating is the classic work of Robert H. Wiebe, *The Search for Order, 1877–1920* (New York: Macmillan, 1967).

23. George W. Martin, "Preface to a Schoolmaster's Biography," in *Views from the Circle: Seventy-Five Years of Groton School* (Groton, MA: Trustees of Groton School, 1960), 144. The biblical reference is to Gen. 3:8. For a critique of Martin's article, see John F. Woolverton, *The Skeptical Vestryman and Plato's Heavenly Way of Justice* (Plymouth, NH: Colophon, 1977), 29–31.

24. David C. Acheson, '39, C. Douglas Dillon, '27, in "Stories of the Rector," *Groton School Quarterly* 8, no. 1 (April 1991): 6.

25. Harriman, quoted in Ward, *Before the Trumpet*, 189; Biddle, quoted in Ward, 190.

26. McGeorge Bundy, '36, quoted in "Stories of the Rector."

27. Ellery Sedgwick, "Three Men of Groton," in *Views from the Circle*, 20. Sedgwick was owner and editor of the *Atlantic Monthly* from 1908 to 1939.

28. Davis, *FDR: The Beckoning of Destiny*, 105–6.

29. From 1890 to 2005, Riis's book went through forty-five editions.

30. Kathleen Dalton, *Theodore Roosevelt: A Strenuous Life* (New York: Knopf, 2002), 123, 151–53, 271; quotation, 150.

31. Ashburn, *Peabody of Groton*, 66.

32. Dalton, *Theodore Roosevelt*, 406.

33. Jacob Riis, *The Making of an American* (New York: Macmillan, 1902), 436.

34. FDR to his parents, January 21, 1900, in *F.D.R.: His Personal Letters*, ed. Elliott Roosevelt, 4 vols. (New York: Duell, Sloan & Pearce, 1947–1950) (hereafter *FDRPL*), 1:378, 379.

35. Riis to Endicott Peabody, October 22, 1900; see also Riis's letters of Spring (April?) 1893, September 17, 1898, October 1900; James B. Lane, *Jacob A. Riis and the American City* (Port Washington, NY: Kennikat, 1974), 220.

36. William Anthony Avery, "The Story of Thomas C. Walker" (typed document, n.d.); see also Thomas C. Walker, "How Things Look to a Negro Lawyer and Teacher," *Southern Workman* 19, no. 7 (1890): 79. Courtesy of Hampton University Archives.

37. FDR to his parents, May 14, 1897, in *FDRPL*, 1:97.

38. For Peabody as a supporter of ameliorative reforms, see MacLachlan, *American Boarding Schools*, 287–88. For Perkins's role in particular, see George W. Martin Jr., *Madam Secretary: Frances Perkins* (Boston: Houghton Mifflin, 1976), chap. 8, especially 76–81.

39. Endicott Peabody, "Consumers' Leagues" (typescript, November 30, 1897), 2, Peabody Papers. Unless otherwise noted, all quotations in the next three paragraphs are from this source.

40. Rainsford to Endicott Peabody, January 29, 1888, Peabody Papers.

41. In a single year, 1894, the City Mission recorded an aggregate of 10,865 home, hospital, and prison visits, while 28,192 sailors passed through the doors of the Sailors' Home. See John F. Woolverton, *Robert H. Gardiner and the Reunification of Worldwide Christianity in the Progressive Era* (Columbia: University of Missouri Press, 2005), 58–59.

42. *Grotonian*, January 1892, 46, 54; November 1892, 20; February 1894, 80; see also May 1890 for a speech by Fulton Cutting about similar work in New York City; Groton School Archives.

43. Allan Nevins, *Grover Cleveland: A Study in Courage* (New York: Dodd, Mead, 1966), 665.

44. Endicott Peabody to Atwood, January 5, 1896, quoted in Ashburn, *Peabody of Groton*, 117.

45. The reference here is to the immensely popular *Cassell's Book of Sports and Pastimes* (London and New York: Cassell, Petter, Galpin, 1881), the first of eight editions.

46. Endicott Peabody, "The Sunday Problem," November 1896, Peabody Papers.

47. Sedgwick, "Three Men of Groton," 20.

48. Richards to Floyd Tomkins, March 4, 1965, Tomkins Papers, Archives of the Episcopal Church, Austin, Texas.

49. Endicott Peabody, sermon preached on October 15, 1899, Peabody Papers. Unless otherwise noted, all quotations in the following four paragraphs are from this source.

50. William Lawrence, *Fifty Years* (Boston: Houghton Mifflin, 1923), 15–16.

51. [Endicott Peabody], "Battles Won by Faith," in *Talks to Boys in the Chapel of Groton School*, ed. Sherrard Billings (Boston: Houghton Mifflin, 1928), 18.

52. Endicott Peabody, "A Republic's Aim," in Billings, *Talks to Boys in the Chapel of Groton School*, 59–60.

53. Endicott Peabody, "Last Sunday, Year 1899–1900," Peabody Papers.

54. Eleanor's life at Allenswood is covered in Joseph P. Lash, *Eleanor and Franklin: The Story of Their Relationship, Based on Eleanor Roosevelt's Private Papers* (New York: Norton, 1971), 117–31. On religion, see 126–27.

55. Lash, *Eleanor and Franklin*, 145–49.

56. Lash, *Eleanor and Franklin*, 183 (quotation), 220.

57. Lash, *Eleanor and Franklin*, 287–301, 352–58, 378–85.

58. Lash, *Eleanor and Franklin*, 352–58, 378–85.

59. Lash, *Eleanor and Franklin*, 385, 333, 466, 517–18.

60. The best recent study of Perkins is Kirstin Downey, *The Woman behind the New Deal: The Life of Frances Perkins, FDR's Secretary of Labor and His Moral Conscience* (New York: Doubleday, 2009). See also the detailed study by Martin, *Madam Secretary*.

61. Downey recounts Perkins's childhood in *Woman behind the New Deal*, 6–11; her college years, 11–13. On Riis, 10; on Kelley, 12–13.

62. In Downey, *Woman behind the New Deal*: on Chicago, 16–21; on Philadelphia, 21–24; early years in New York, 25–36; Triangle fire, 33–36.

63. Downey, *Woman behind the New Deal*: for Perkins's early involvement in politics, see 37–53; on her relationship with Smith, 75–95; with FDR, from Albany to Washington, 96–125. Her role in the administration thereafter is covered in close detail, 149–340.

64. See Downey, *Woman behind the New Deal*, 17–18; quotation, 20.

65. Martin, *Madam Secretary*, 279–83; quotations, 281.

66. Martin, *Madam Secretary*, 280–81; Downey, *Woman behind the New Deal*, 279–80. Perkins's valuable account is *The Roosevelt I Knew* (New York: Viking, 1946).

67. This contra Clyde Griffen, "Reconstructing Masculinity from the Evangelical Revival to the Waning of Progressivism: A Speculative Synthesis," in *Meanings for Manhood: Constructions of Masculinity in Victorian America*, ed. Mark C. Carnes and Clyde Griffen (Chicago: University of Chicago Press, 1990), 195. Griffen places these characteristics in opposition.

68. John Higham discusses *fin de siècle* pessimism in his marvelous portrait of the 1890s, "The Reorientation of Culture in the 1890s," in *Hanging Together: Unity and Diversity in American Culture*, ed. Carl J. Guarneri (New Haven: Yale University Press, 2001), 185–90.

69. Quoted in Ralph Barton Perry, *The Thought and Character of William James*, 2 vols. (Boston: Little, Brown, 1935), 2:251.

70. Kurt A. Klingbeil, "Franklin D. Roosevelt and American Religious Leaders" (PhD diss., School of Education, New York University, 1972), 292; Endicott Peabody to FDR, February 13, 1935, President's Personal File, 398, Franklin D. Roosevelt Library, Hyde Park, New York.

71. Quoted in Geoffrey C. Ward, *A First-Class Temperament: The Emergence of Franklin Roosevelt* (New York: Harper & Row, 1989), 202. Brown served in the Sixty-Third Congress, 1913–1915; he was then appointed a special assistant to the secretary of the interior, 1917–1918. See *Biographical Directory of the United States Congress, 1774–1989* (Washington, DC: United States Government Printing Office, 1989), 684.

72. Gary Scott Smith, *Faith and the Presidency* (New York: Oxford University Press, 2006), 199. "Judging by the length and tone of their letters most [pastors] thought their advice would be taken very seriously." It was. Though evangelicals and fundamentalists did not share the positive reaction of liberal Christians, all were pleased with the opportunity to give their views.

73. Quoted in Ashburn, *Peabody of Groton*, 342–43.

74. Endicott Peabody to FDR, October 5, 1937, Peabody Papers.

75. FDR to Endicott Peabody, October 16, 1937, Peabody Papers.

76. Endicott Peabody to FDR, January 4, 1941, quoted in Ashburn, *Peabody of Groton*, 348.

77. FDR to Endicott Peabody, January 11, 1941, quoted in Ashburn, *Peabody of Groton*, 349.

78. Endicott Peabody to FDR, December 11, 1941, and March 20, 1942, quoted in Ashburn, *Peabody of Groton*, 349–50.

79. Quoted in Ashburn, *Peabody of Groton*, 343.

80. Ackland to Elizabeth Peabody, November 18, 1944, Peabody Papers.

81. White House to Mrs. Endicott Peabody, Western Union, November 18, 1944, Peabody Papers.

Chapter 3

1. Groton School in Roosevelt's years is described in Kenneth S. Davis, *FDR: The Beckoning of Destiny* (New York: Putnam, 1972), 102–10; James MacGregor Burns, *Roosevelt: The Lion and the Fox* (New York: Harcourt, Brace & World, 1956), 10–14; Frank Freidel, *Franklin D. Roosevelt: The Apprenticeship* (Boston: Little, Brown, 1952), 35–36, 40–51; and Jean Edward Smith, *FDR* (New York: Random House, 2007), 26–29. For particulars, see FDR to James and Sara Delano Roosevelt, September 1896–June 1897, in *F.D.R.: His Personal Letters*, ed. Elliott Roosevelt, 4 vols. (New York: Duell, Sloan & Pearce, 1947–1950) (hereafter *FDRPL*), vol. 1: Mrs. Peabody's parlor, 35, 36, 38; choir, 37, 38, 40, 42, 45, 46, 60, 78, 84, 96, 97, 109, 112, 113, 115; Glee Club, 53; Debating Society, 68–78; reading to boys, 40, 60, 66; chapel decorations, 59, 102; noncompulsory sports, 66, 67, 87, 89, 91, 93. On the *Grotonian*, see William Amory Gardner, *Groton Myths and Memories* (Concord, NH: Rumford, 1928), 101.

2. *FDRPL*, 1:405.

3. FDR to his parents, May 16, 1899, in *FDRPL*, 1:310; Gardner, *Groton Myths and Memories*, 56.

4. Geoffrey C. Ward, *Before the Trumpet: Young Franklin Roosevelt, 1882–1905* (New York: Vintage Books, 1985), 249.

5. Geoffrey C. Ward, ed., *Closest Companion: The Unknown Story of the Intimate Friendship between Franklin Roosevelt and Margaret Suckley* (Boston: Houghton Mifflin, 1995), 172.

6. Douglas Brown related an example to the author (June 7, 2008) of FDR's being turned down for the post of prefect in favor of the rector's nephew.

7. Ward, *Closest Companion*, 193.

8. George Biddle, "As I Remember Groton School," in *Views from the Circle: Seventy-Five Years of Groton School* (Groton, MA: Trustees of Groton School, 1959), 112.

9. Roosevelt letters, September 20 and September 27, 1896, in *FDRPL*, 1:37, 40.

10. Ward, *Before the Trumpet*, 182.

11. Ward, *Before the Trumpet*, 194.

12. There are discrepancies between Peabody's notebooks and the higher grades recorded in the volume of FDR's personal letters edited by his son, Elliott Roosevelt. In his entry for "F. Roosevelt" in Notebook 1896, Peabody Papers, Groton School Archives, Groton, Massachusetts, Peabody records "poor English," while in *FDRPL* 1 he receives an 8.50 on a decimal scale of 10.00.

13. See *FDRPL*, 1:48, 60, 182, 187–88, 209, 223, 233, 279, 319, 323, 325–26, 353–54, 364–65, 386, 399, 405, 411. The graduation number comes from Douglas Brown, "To: Anyone Interested," a single page comparing Dean Acheson's standing with Franklin Roosevelt's, Groton School Archives. Though he was "a fairly decent scholar," Acheson graduated twenty-fourth out of a class of twenty-four.

14. See "F. Roosevelt" entry in Peabody's Notebook of the respective years, Peabody Papers.

15. *FDRPL*, 1:119, 122, 141, 169, 251, 302, 386, 407.

16. *FDRPL*, 1:201–5. On scarlet fever at the time, see *Encyclopedia Britannica*, 11th ed., 24:304. At the end of the nineteenth century, long before the advent of many vaccinations, not to mention antibiotics, diseases concerned people more immediately. The ranks of infants, young children, and adolescents in the 1890s were regularly winnowed by diphtheria, scarlet fever, typhoid, measles, and whooping cough. Chloromycetin was not available as a remedy for typhoid until the 1940s, and only with the availability of the antibiotic penicillin in 1944 was the treatment of scarlet fever revolutionized.

17. Grace Tully, *FDR: My Boss* (New York: Scribner's Sons, 1949), 135. For more or less regular mention of illnesses at the school, see also *FDRPL*, 1:48, 349, 382, 396, 438–39.

18. Tully, *FDR*, 273.

19. T. J. Jackson Lears, *No Place of Grace: Anti-Modernism and the Transformation of American Culture, 1880–1920* (New York: Pantheon, 1981), 110; Clyde Griffen, "Reconstructing Masculinity," in *Meanings for Manhood: Constructions of Masculinity in Victorian America*, ed. Mark C. Carnes and Clyde Griffen (Chicago: University of Chicago Press, 1990), 186.

20. Less obviously military figures represented were Demosthenes, Dante, Newton, Shakespeare, Milton, Goethe, Franklin, Hawthorne, Emerson, Hamilton (but not Jefferson), Lincoln, and Socrates.

21. Carmina Grotonia (1910), *Groton School Sing-Song Book* (1912, 1916, and 1926), variously.

22. Endicott Peabody, "The Relation of Religion and Life in a Boarding School," quoted in Frank D. Ashburn, *Peabody of Groton: A Portrait* (New York: Coward McCann, 1944), 193; see *FDRPL*, 1:278.

23. Lears, *No Place of Grace*, 108.

24. The classic presentation is Richard Hofstadter, *Social Darwinism in American Thought* (Boston: Beacon, 1955). For a more nuanced view, see Robert C. Bannister, *Social Darwinism: Science and Myth in American Social Thought*, new ed. (Philadelphia: Temple University Press, 1988).

25. For the founding of numerous patriotic and ancestral organizations at the time, see Michael Kammen, *Mystic Chords of Memory: The Transformation of Tradition in American Culture* (New York: Knopf, 1991), 217–21.

26. Kammen, *Mystic Chords of Memory*, 218–23.

27. E. Anthony Rotundo, "Boy Culture," in Carnes and Griffen, *Meanings for Manhood*, 17.

28. John Higham, *Hanging Together: Unity and Diversity in American Culture*, ed. Carl J. Guarneri (New Haven: Yale University Press, 2001), 176, 181, and 190 (first quotation); see also Lears, *No Place of Grace*, 109–13. For the second quotation, see Christopher Lasch, "The Moral and Intellectual Rehabilitation of the Ruling Class," in *The World of Nations: Reflections on American History, Politics, and Culture* (New York: Vintage Books, 1974), 80–99.

29. See, for instance, Richard Slotkin, *The Fatal Environment: The Myth of the Frontier in the Age of Industrialization, 1800–1890* (New York: Atheneum, 1985), chaps. 18, 19, and 20; Henry F. May, *Protestant Churches and Industrial America* (New York: Harper & Row, 1967), 91–111; Matthew Fry Jacobson, *Whiteness of a Different Color: European*

Immigrants and the Alchemy of Race (Cambridge, MA: Harvard University Press, 1998), chaps. 2 and 5; quotation, 42. Andrew Delbanco, in *The Death of Satan: How Americans Have Lost the Sense of Evil* (New York: Farrar, Straus & Giroux, 1995), 321, clarifies that while it had never been absent from American life, racism emerged "*as an ideology*" in the 1890s and "as a developed theory had all the appeal of a hot new fashion."

30. David W. Blight, *Race and Reunion: The Civil War in American Memory* (Cambridge, MA: Belknap Press of Harvard University Press, 2001), 346.

31. *FDRPL*, 1:215; "mickey," of course, is an anti-Irish slur.

32. *FDRPL*, 1:254.

33. Higham, *Hanging Together*, 212.

34. Kevin J. McMahon, *Reconsidering Roosevelt on Race: How the Presidency Paved the Road to Brown* (Chicago: University of Chicago Press, 2004), 17.

35. *FDRPL*, 1:17, 39, 43, 46, 73, 80, 232, 249, 338.

36. *FDRPL*, 1:136.

37. *FDRPL*, 1:160–64. The manuscript is carefully written, with paragraphs marked by stars; students had to declaim their materials and were not permitted to read from a text.

38. Eric Larrabee, *Commander in Chief: Franklin Delano Roosevelt, His Lieutenants, and Their War* (New York: Harper & Row, 1987), 634. Mahan's example was Britain between 1660 and 1783.

39. *FDRPL*, 1:358.

40. *FDRPL*, 1:378.

41. See *FDRPL*, 1:379, for the parallel between Filipino insurgency under the command of Emilio Aguinaldo and Boer guerrilla resistance under Louis Botha, Jacobus Delarey, and Christian de Wet.

42. *FDRPL*, 1:40, 41, 42, 45–46, 60, 108, 112–13, 115, 179, 271, 301, 336, 395.

43. Brent was an electrifying speaker; he later became a famous Episcopal bishop in the Philippine Islands and then in western New York. St. Stephen's Mission Church, where Brent was assistant priest, was in 1897 one of the city's most famous Social Gospel centers. See John F. Woolverton, *Robert H. Gardiner and the Reunification of Worldwide Christianity in the Progressive Era* (Columbia: University of Missouri Press, 2005), chap. 2 and variously.

44. *FDRPL*, 1:111, 98, 180, 410. On other preachers, see 183, 318, and 303; for comments on confirmation services, 251, 276.

45. *FDRPL*, 1:259.

46. *FDRPL*, 1:285.

47. *FDRPL*, 1:182, 185, and 241. Batt was minister of a nondenominational Union Church in West Concord.

48. "The Missionary Society," *Grotonian*, January 1894, 57–58.

49. *Grotonian*, November 1899, 26–27; May 1900, 150; Minutes of the Missionary Society meetings, September 22, 1901, 1; October [n.d.] 1901, 3; November [n.d.] 1901, 5, Groton School Archives.

50. *FDRPL*, 1:282, 286. See also 285 and 349.

51. Sarah Hamill, "St. Andrew's Church, Ayer," in *The Episcopal Diocese of Massachusetts, 1784–1984*, ed. Mark J. Duffy (n.p.: Episcopal Diocese of Massachusetts, 1984), 126–29.

52. Frank Ashburn, *Fifty Years On: Groton School, 1884–1934* (New York: privately printed, 1934), 62.

53. *FDRPL*, 1:367–68, 377.

54. Ward, *Before the Trumpet*, 187.

55. *FDRPL*, 1:61; see also 349.

56. *FDRPL*, 1:413.

57. Quoted in Joseph P. Lash, *Eleanor and Franklin: The Story of Their Relationship, Based on Eleanor Roosevelt's Private Papers* (New York: Norton, 1971), 137.

58. *FDRPL*, 3:291.

59. Gardner, *Groton Myths and Memories*, 106.

60. *FDRPL*, 1:411.

61. Ward, *Closest Companion*, 282.

62. Archivist Alycia Vivona, Franklin D. Roosevelt Library, Hyde Park, New York (hereafter Roosevelt Library), to the author, January 30, 2008.

63. FDR to his parents, November 23, 1900, in *FDRPL*, 1:435.

64. Smith, *FDR*, 36–37. For FDR's views of the young ladies, see *FDRPL*, 1:8, 435–37, 453, 463 (re: Eleanor Roosevelt), 467–68 (re: Alice Roosevelt), 477, 523; and Ward, *Before the Trumpet*, 249–55.

65. Quoted in Robert H. Gardiner to Endicott Peabody, March 11, 1902, May 4, 1905; see also Peabody to Gardiner, October 13, 1915, Peabody Papers, Groton School Archives.

66. FDR to his parents, October 5, 1900, in *FDRPL*, 1:425. FDR visited Groton School on October 14, 1900, November 18, 1900, January 20, 1901, February 23, 1901, October 15, 1901, November 28, 1901, May 4, 1902, May 26, 1902, and October 1, 1903, among other occasions.

67. Freidel, *Franklin D. Roosevelt: The Apprenticeship*, 52.

68. FDR to his mother, January 21, 1901, in *FDRPL*, 1:463; May 12, 1902, 473.

69. FDR to his mother, October 8, 1902, in *FDRPL*, 1:477.

70. Eustace Hale Ball, "Roosevelt at Harvard," *New York Times*, July 18, 1920, 10; FDR: Family, Business, and Personal Papers, Box 19, Roosevelt Library.

71. John F. Woolverton, "Walter Russell Bowie," in *Dictionary of Virginia Biography*, ed. Sara B. Bearss et al. (Richmond: Library of Virginia, 2001), 2:138–40. Bowie claimed that FDR dealt easily and effectively with paid workers for the *Crimson*; see Bowie to Frank Gilbert, March 11, 1950, Box 19, Roosevelt Library.

72. Ruhl to Gilbert, April 17, 1950, Box 19, Roosevelt Library. See also Ward, *Before the Trumpet*, 240.

73. Editorial, *Harvard Crimson*, September 30, 1903, in *FDRPL*, 1:503; for his other activities in order, see 427, 443, 446, 456, and 509.

74. C. R. D. Meier to Gilbert, April 19, 1950, Box 19, Roosevelt Library. In 1904, after Roosevelt had left the editorship, the publication of students' names was discontinued.

75. Freidel, *Franklin D. Roosevelt: The Apprenticeship*, 65; for James Roosevelt's membership in Porcellian, see Ward, *Before the Trumpet*, 235. The quotation is also from *Before the Trumpet*, 236.

76. Ward, *Before the Trumpet*, 236.

77. Ward, *Before the Trumpet*, 238.

78. *FDRPL*, 1:434–36; see also FDR to his parents, November 23, 1900, November

27, 1900, December 3, 1900; and the Minutes of the Groton Missionary Society, October 1901, December 1901, June 1902, Groton School Archives.

79. Social Service Committee, Records and Reports, 1902–1905, Pusey Library, Harvard University, Cambridge, Massachusetts, 034–H–4; "Radio Address before the White House Conference on Children in a Democracy," January 19, 1940, *The Public Papers and Addresses of Franklin D. Roosevelt*, ed. Samuel I. Rosenman, 13 vols. (New York: Random House, 1938–c. 1950), 9:52.

80. L. LeRoy Cowperthwaite, "Franklin Roosevelt at Harvard," *Quarterly Journal of Speech*, February 1952, 37; I have supplied information from various dictionaries about FDR's courses as well as about the historians themselves.

81. Rollo Walter Brown, *Harvard in the Golden Age* (New York: Current Books, 1948), 131.

82. Roosevelt received a C plus in both Latin and French, Cs in history, government, and geology; archivist Alycia Vivona of the Roosevelt Library to the author, July 2, 2008.

83. FDR's editions were *Lessings Werke. Mit einleitungen und Lessings lebensbeschreibung* (Stuttgart: G. J. Goschen, 1874), and John R. Effinger Jr., ed., *Selected Essays from Sainte-Beuve* (Boston: Ginn, 1895). For Sainte-Beuve's involvement with nineteenth-century literary circles in France, see Curtis Cate, *George Sand: A Biography* (Boston: Houghton Mifflin, 1975), passim.

84. Peter N. Stearns, *Priest and Revolutionary: Lamennais and the Dilemma of French Catholicism* (New York: Harper & Row, 1967), 40, 59, 71, 92, and 101; for the reference to Christ, see Cate, *George Sand*, 363. On Chateaubriand, see Christopher Prendergast, *The Classic: Sainte-Beuve and the Nineteenth-Century Culture Wars* (New York: Oxford University Press, 2007), 275. The leading ideas of *L'Avenir* were condemned on August 15, 1832, by the papal encyclical *Mirari Vos*.

85. Gotthold Ephraim Lessing, "Gegensatze des Herausgebers," quoted in Hans W. Frei, *The Eclipse of Biblical Narrative* (New Haven: Yale University Press, 1974), 115.

86. "I go back to a day in particular when several miles behind the actual line of contact between the two armies [in World War I] I passed through wheat fields, wheat fields with ripened grain uncut; wheat fields in which there were patches, little patches of color, something in the wheat, and some of those patches wore a dark grey uniform and others of those patches wore an olive drab uniform. As we went through these fields there were American boys carrying stretchers, and on those stretchers were German boys and Austrian boys and American boys being carried to the rear. . . . If any man or woman, after thinking about that, can bear in his heart any motive in this year which will lead him to cast his ballot in the interest of intolerance and of a violation of the spirit of the Constitution of the United States, then I say solemnly to that man or woman, 'May God have mercy on your miserable soul.'" Quoted in H. W. Brands, *Traitor to His Class: The Privileged Life and Radical Presidency of Franklin Delano Roosevelt* (New York: Anchor Books, 2008), 214–15.

87. Frei, *Eclipse*, 172.

Chapter 4

1. Stephen Early to the Reverend James Appleby, August 27, 1943, President's Personal File, Container 1, Box 90, Franklin D. Roosevelt Library, Hyde Park, New York (hereafter Roosevelt Library). See also *F.D.R.: His Personal Letters*, ed. Elliott Roosevelt, 4 vols. (New York: Duell, Sloan & Pearce, 1947–1950) (hereafter *FDRPL*), 3:331–32; Jon Meacham, *American Gospel: God, the Founding Fathers, and the Making of a Nation* (New York: Random House, 2006), 270; and Frank Freidel, *Franklin D. Roosevelt: Launching the New Deal* (Boston: Little, Brown, 1973), 202.

2. Edmund Fuller and David E. Green, *God in the White House* (New York: Crown, 1963), 206.

3. "Address at the Fiftieth Anniversary of the Statue of Liberty," October 28, 1936, *The Public Papers and Addresses of Franklin D. Roosevelt*, ed. Samuel I. Rosenman, 13 vols. (New York: Random House, 1938–c. 1950) (hereafter *FDRPPA*), 5:543.

4. John Calvin, *Institutes of the Christian Religion*, ed. John T. McNeill, trans. Ford Lewis Battles, 2 vols. (Philadelphia: Westminster, 1977), 3.2.42; 1:590.

5. On FDR's contracting polio, see Frank Freidel, *Franklin Delano Roosevelt: The Ordeal* (Boston: Little, Brown, 1954), 97–101; Kenneth S. Davis, *FDR: The Beckoning of Destiny* (New York: Putnam, 1972), 645–59; and Julie M. Fenster, *FDR's Shadow: Louis Howe, the Force That Shaped Franklin and Eleanor Roosevelt* (New York: Palgrave Macmillan, 2009), 133–38. Quotations from David M. Oshinsky, *Polio: An American Story* (New York: Oxford University Press, 2005), 26; Lovett to Dr. E. H. Bennett, September 2, 1921, FDR: Papers Pertaining to Family Business, Container 23, Roosevelt Library; and Linda Gordon, *Dorothea Lange* (New York: Norton, 2009), 11. See also Peabody to Eleanor Roosevelt, September 5, 1921, Roosevelt Family Papers, Roosevelt Library, 30–125.

6. Richard Thayer Goldberg, *The Making of Franklin D. Roosevelt: Triumph over Disability* (Cambridge, MA: Abt Books, 1981), 206, 33.

7. Quotations, Endicott Peabody to Eleanor Roosevelt, September 5, 1921, Roosevelt Family Papers, 30–125; and Goldberg, *The Making of Franklin D. Roosevelt*, 34, 166. Jonas Klein, *Beloved Island: Franklin & Eleanor and the Legacy of Campobello* (Forest Dale, VT: Paul S. Eriksson, 2007), 108–16.

8. Delano to FDR, September 4, 1921, FDR: Papers Pertaining to Family Business, Container 23. On Delano's later roles, see Patrick D. Reagan, *Designing a New America* (Amherst: University of Massachusetts Press, 1999), 28, and Glenn C. Altschuler and Stuart M. Blumin, *The GI Bill: A New Deal for Veterans* (New York: Oxford University Press, 2009), 40–41.

9. *FDRPPA*, 13:62.

10. Interview with Gerald Morgan Jr., September 14, 2009.

11. Goldberg, *The Making of Franklin D. Roosevelt*, 206 (biblical reference is to Gal. 1:17b), 5, 52–54, 67, 84, 100, 165; *FDRPPA*, 7:151.

12. Hugh Gregory Gallagher, *FDR's Splendid Deception* (Arlington, VA: Vandamere, 1994), 54–57; quotation, 57.

13. Marc Shell, *Polio and Its Aftermath: The Paralysis of Culture* (Cambridge, MA: Harvard University Press, 2005), 184; Kenneth S. Davis, *FDR: The New York Years* (New York: Random House, 1976, 1985), 292–95; quotation, 294.

14. Gallagher, *FDR's Splendid Deception*, 214.

15. Frances Perkins, *The Roosevelt I Knew* (New York: Viking, 1946), 30, 29; more generally, Shell, *Polio and Its Aftermath*, 190–95.

16. Perkins, *The Roosevelt I Knew*, 45.

17. Goldberg, *The Making of Franklin D. Roosevelt*, 165; Joseph P. Lash, *Eleanor and Franklin: The Story of Their Relationship, Based on Eleanor Roosevelt's Private Papers* (New York: Norton, 1971), 424.

18. *FDRPL*, 2:635.

19. Freidel, *Franklin D. Roosevelt: Launching the New Deal*, 4; James Roosevelt and Sidney Shalett, *Affectionately, FDR* (New York: Harcourt Brace, 1959), 232.

20. Michael Beschloss, *Presidential Courage* (New York: Simon & Schuster, 2007), 175–76, 190, 194.

21. H. W. Brands, *Traitor to His Class: The Privileged Life and Radical Presidency of Franklin Delano Roosevelt* (New York: Anchor Books, 2008), 194–97; quotation, 197.

22. Davis, *FDR: The New York Years*, 16.

23. Gallagher, *FDR's Splendid Deception*, 207.

24. Quoted in Bernard Bellush, *Franklin D. Roosevelt as Governor of New York* (New York: AMS, 1955), 12–13.

25. *FDRPPA*, 1:40–41.

26. Perkins to FDR, December 25, 1932, quoted in Freidel, *Franklin D. Roosevelt: Launching the New Deal*, 4.

27. John Gunther, *Roosevelt in Retrospect* (New York: Harper & Brothers, 1950), 278; Kenneth S. Davis, *FDR: The New Deal Years, 1933–1937; A History* (New York: Random House, 1986), 34; Freidel, *Franklin D. Roosevelt: Launching the New Deal*, 207; James R. McGovern, *And a Time for Hope: Americans in the Great Depression* (Westport, CT: Praeger, 2000), 22; Ronald Isetti, "The Moneychangers of the Temple: FDR, American Civil Religion, and the New Deal," *Presidential Studies Quarterly* 26 (Summer 1996): 689.

28. All primary source citations in this and the next two paragraphs are from *FDRPPA*, 2:11–16.

29. Goldberg, *The Making of Franklin D. Roosevelt*, 168.

30. Isetti, "The Moneychangers of the Temple," 685.

31. Anne O'Hare McCormick, "A Man of the World and the World's Man," in *Franklin Delano Roosevelt: A Memorial*, ed. Donald Porter Geddes (New York: Pocket Books, 1945), 87. McCormick was the only newspaper person to whom FDR gave exclusive interviews or, as she called them, "tea and conversation."

32. Arthur M. Schlesinger Jr., *The Coming of the New Deal* (Boston: Houghton Mifflin, 1959), 572.

33. Jonathan Alter, *The Defining Moment: FDR's First Hundred Days and the Triumph of Hope* (New York: Simon & Schuster, 2006), 189.

34. In this way FDR put himself in the august American tradition that Christopher Lasch sets forth in *The True and Only Heaven: Progress and Its Critics* (New York: Norton, 1991).

35. *FDRPPA*, 11:373. "Fireside Chat on the Cost of Living," September 7, 1942.

36. McGovern, *And a Time for Hope*, 45.

37. Stuart Hampshire, "Morality and Pessimism," in *Public and Private Morality*, ed. Stuart Hampshire (Cambridge: Cambridge University Press, 1978), 9. See also

Amartya Sen, *The Idea of Justice* (Cambridge, MA: Belknap Press of Harvard University Press, 2009), 19 and chaps. 11–13.

38. Of Berlin's many writings, the most relevant to this point are those collected in *The Crooked Timber of Humanity: Chapters in the History of Ideas*, ed. Henry Hardy (New York: Random House, 1992), and *Concepts and Categories: Philosophical Essays*, ed. Henry Hardy (New York: Viking, 1978). See especially "Joseph de Maistre and the Origins of Fascism" and "The Pursuit of the Ideal," in *The Crooked Timber of Humanity*, and "From Hope and Fear Set Free," in *Concepts and Categories*. Quotations are from *The Crooked Timber of Humanity*, 97, 5; and Alasdair MacIntyre, *After Virtue* (Notre Dame: University of Notre Dame Press, 1984), 142–43.

39. Isaiah Berlin, "Roosevelt through European Eyes," *Atlantic* 196 (July 1955): 67–71.

40. Berlin, *The Crooked Timber of Humanity*, 19.

41. Berlin, *Concepts and Categories*, 198.

42. *FDRPPA*, 13:62.

43. A. Bartlett Giamatti, *Take Time for Paradise: Americans and Their Games* (New York: Summit Books, 1989), 33–34.

44. Apocalyptic thought in the Christian tradition has been premillennial, that is, expecting Christ to return before the thousand-year rule of the saints could begin. Utopianism is postmillennial, expecting the thousand-year rule of the saints before the second coming of Christ. Two mid-nineteenth-century Episcopalians, Henry Dana Ward and Joshua Himes, were influential in the founding of the Millerite Adventist movement, which exemplified the first category. Both later became Episcopal priests without giving up their apocalyptic views.

45. Thomas H. Greer, *What Roosevelt Thought: The Social and Political Ideas of Franklin D. Roosevelt* (East Lansing: Michigan State University Press, 2000), 7, quoting Roosevelt's campaign address of October 28, 1936.

46. Charles H. Lippy, "Social Christianity," in *Encyclopedia of the American Religious Experience*, ed. Charles H. Lippy and Peter W. Williams, 3 vols. (New York: Scribner's Sons, 1988), 2:927; William McGuire King, "Liberalism," in *Encyclopedia of the American Religious Experience*, 2:1138, quoting Newman Smyth, *Old Faiths in New Lights* (1879), 291–93.

47. Paul Boyer, *When Time Shall Be No More: Prophecy Belief in Modern American Culture* (Cambridge, MA: Harvard University Press, 1992), 107. For thorough detail, see Matthew A. Sutton, *American Apocalypse: A History of Modern Evangelicalism* (Cambridge, MA: Harvard University Press, 2014), 232–62.

48. *FDRPPA*, 13:524.

49. Edward Bellamy, *Looking Backward, 2000–1887* (New York: Vanguard, 1887, 1927). Mark Twain's anti-utopian *A Connecticut Yankee in King Arthur's Court* (1889), published almost simultaneously with Bellamy's book, is its obverse. It too is in the Roosevelt library. Frederic Cople Jaher, in *Doubters and Dissenters* (New York: Free Press, 1964), explores the heavy wave of utopian/dystopian fiction published in the generation on either side of 1900.

50. Walter Rauschenbusch, *For God and the People: Prayers of the Social Gospel Awakening* (Boston: Pilgrim, 1910). Rauschenbusch's definitive books are *Christianity and the Social Crisis* (New York: Macmillan, 1907); *Christianizing the Social Order* (New

York: Macmillan, 1912); and *A Theology for the Social Gospel* (New York: Macmillan, 1917).

51. FDR to Avery, May 5, 1931, Accession Record, Roosevelt Library. Myra Avery was a member of the Board of Visitors of the Hudson River State Hospital. For FDR's purchase of books of prayers, see *FDRPL*, 2:47.

52. Rauschenbusch, *For God and the People*, 9–10; James C. Livingston, *Modern Christian Thought from the Enlightenment to Vatican II* (New York: Macmillan, 1971), 267.

53. Rauschenbusch, *Christianizing the Social Order*, 69; Rauschenbusch, *A Theology for the Social Gospel*, 178.

54. Rauschenbusch, *For God and the People*, 125–26.

55. *FDRPPA*, 7:513; address at Denton, Maryland, September 5, 1938, *FDRPPA*, 4:272.

56. Robert D. Leighninger Jr., *Long-Range Public Investment: The Forgotten Legacy of the New Deal* (Columbia: University of South Carolina Press, 2007), 11, 18, 25, 20–21; Jean Edward Smith, *FDR* (New York: Random House, 2007), 319, 322; Davis, *FDR: The New Deal Years*, 77.

57. Leighninger, *Long-Range Public Investment*, 27, 30–31.

58. Smith, *FDR*, 322.

59. Leighninger, *Long-Range Public Investment*, 80–101, 129, and 83.

60. Henry Steele Commager, *The American Mind* (New Haven: Yale University Press, 1950), 344–45.

61. Sarah T. Phillips, *This Land, This Nation: Conservation, Rural America, and the New Deal* (Cambridge: Cambridge University Press, 2007), 102 and 107; see also Davis, *FDR: The New Deal Years*, 490.

62. Wallace's article in the *New York Times Magazine*, January 3, 1937, quoted in Davis, *FDR: The New Deal Years*, 490.

63. Erskine Caldwell, *You Have Seen Their Faces* (New York: Modern Age Books, 1937).

64. Smith, *FDR*, 357; William E. Leuchtenberg, *Franklin D. Roosevelt and the Era of the New Deal, 1932–1940* (Cambridge, MA: Da Capo, 1972), 157.

65. Davis, *FDR: The New Deal Years*, 491–92.

66. David M. Kennedy, *Freedom from Fear: The American People in Depression and War, 1929–1945* (New York: Oxford University Press, 1999), 175–77.

67. Kennedy, *Freedom from Fear*, 247.

68. Harry L. Hopkins and Dorris A. Westall, *Maine: A Guide "Down East"* (Cambridge, MA: Riverside, 1937), v and vii.

69. George T. McJimsey, *The Presidency of Franklin Delano Roosevelt* (Lawrence: University Press of Kansas, 2000), 104.

70. McJimsey, *The Presidency of Franklin Delano Roosevelt*, 74, 66, 57, 94, and 99.

71. Gallagher, *FDR's Splendid Deception*, 43.

72. Kenneth S. Davis, *FDR: Into the Storm, 1937–1940* (New York: Random House, 1993), 226–29.

73. FDR, "Second Inaugural Address," *FDRPPA*, 6:1-6, quotation, 4.

Chapter 5

1. Thomas H. Greer, *What Roosevelt Thought: The Social and Political Ideas of Franklin D. Roosevelt* (East Lansing: Michigan State University Press, 2000), 29.

2. See, for instance, *The Teacher's Prayer Book* (New York: Thomas Nelson & Sons, 1898), 84; J. R. Dummelow, ed., *A Commentary on the Holy Bible* (London: Macmillan, 1909), 913.

3. "First Inaugural Address," March 4, 1933, *The Public Papers and Addresses of Franklin D. Roosevelt*, ed. Samuel I. Rosenman, 13 vols. (New York: Random House, 1938–c. 1950) (hereafter *FDRPPA*), 2:15.

4. *FDRPPA*, 4:419. Roosevelt's admiration of Jefferson is seen in many places—for instance, in Franklin D. Roosevelt, *Looking Forward* (New York: John Day, 1933), 11–13, and in Roosevelt's sponsorship of the construction of the Jefferson Memorial on the Tidal Basin in Washington, DC.

5. Hans W. Frei, "Saint, Sinner, and Pilgrim: Three Paths in Quest of Christ's Presence" (unpublished, typed manuscript, n.d., c. 1957, Archives, Virginia Theological Seminary), 6.

6. Eleanor Roosevelt, *This Is My Story* (New York: Harper and Brothers, 1937), 188.

7. H. D. M. Spence, Joseph S. Exell, F. W. Farrar, et al., eds., *The Pulpit Commentary: I Corinthians* (New York: Funk & Wagnalls, 1883), 423.

8. H. L. Gouge, *The First Epistle to the Corinthians* (London: Methuen, 1903), 117.

9. Gouge, *The First Epistle to the Corinthians*, 121; Charles J. Ellicott, *St. Paul's First Epistle to the Corinthians* (London: Longmans, Green, 1887), 257; Hermann Olshausen, *Biblical Commentary on St. Paul's First and Second Epistles to the Corinthians*, trans. J. E. Cox (Edinburgh: T&T Clark, 1855), 213.

10. Thomas Charles Edwards, *A Commentary on the First Epistle to the Corinthians* (New York: A. C. Armstrong, 1886), 339, 343, 342; Spence, Exell, and Farrar, *The Pulpit Commentary*, 452.

11. Spence, Exell, and Farrar, *The Pulpit Commentary*, 426.

12. *FDRPPA*, 2:366–67: "Extemporaneous Speech at Hyde Park Methodist Episcopal Church," September 29, 1933.

13. *FDRPPA*, 5:85; *FDRPPA*, 9:9: "Annual Message to Congress," January 3, 1940.

14. *FDRPPA*, 9:10: "Annual Message to Congress," January 3, 1940.

15. *FDRPPA*, 9:29: "Address at Jackson Day Dinner," January 8, 1940; also *FDRPPA*, 10:87.

16. *FDRPPA*, 7:75.

17. *FDRPPA*, 9:469: "Mobilization for Human Needs," October 13, 1940.

18. *FDRPPA*, 7:56.

19. Gary Scott Smith, *Faith and the Presidency* (New York: Oxford University Press, 2006), 194; Greer, *What Roosevelt Thought*, 4.

20. Nicholas Wolterstorff, *Justice: Rights and Wrongs* (Princeton: Princeton University Press, 2008), 110–12.

21. Raymond Clapper, *Watching the World* (New York: McGraw-Hill, 1944), 86–87, quoted in Jean Edward Smith, *FDR* (New York: Random House, 2007), 366–67. According to Eleanor Roosevelt, "My Day," June 29, 1936, Pons also sang "The Star-Spangled Banner."

22. Smith, *FDR*, 367.

23. All quotations in the following paragraphs come from *FDRPPA*, 5:234ff., except for that from Cass R. Sunstein, *The Second Bill of Rights* (New York: Basic Books, 2004), 76.

24. Aylicia Vivona, archivist, Roosevelt Library, to the author, June 5, 2008.

25. *The Secret Diaries of Harold L. Ickes: The First Thousand Days, 1933–1936* (New York: Simon & Schuster, 1953), 626.

26. Sunstein, *The Second Bill of Rights*, quotations, 77–78, 2.

27. *FDRPPA*, 3:287ff., 312ff., 325ff., and 247; David M. Kennedy, *Freedom from Fear: The American People in Depression and War, 1929–1945* (New York: Oxford University Press, 1999), 246; internal quotations from FDR adviser Raymond Moley. On FDR's personal stake in security, see Jonathan Alter, *The Defining Moment: FDR's First Hundred Days and the Triumph of Hope* (New York: Simon & Schuster, 2006), 13–15.

28. Frances Perkins, *The Roosevelt I Knew* (New York: Viking, 1946), 113.

29. *FDRPPA*, 4:337, 340, 341.

30. Smith, *FDR*, 332.

31. Smith, *FDR*, 326, and Alter, *The Defining Moment*, 284.

32. Kenneth S. Davis, *FDR: The New Deal Years, 1933–1937; A History* (New York: Random House, 1986), 437.

33. *FDRPPA*, 2:11–12, 14, 15, and 155; 3:125, 126–27, 128.

34. See, for instance, *FDRPPA*, 1:631, 773; 2:12, 595; 3:8, 125, 195, 291–92, 315, 374, 395, 411, 436; 4:272; 5:13, 404, 636; 5:189, 350–51, 636; 6:5, 290, 331, 431.

35. *FDRPPA*, 7:167, 237.

36. *FDRPPA*, 1:626 and 5:180; 2:156, 3:127, 195; 5:636; 6:214.

37. *FDRPPA*, 2:157.

38. *FDRPPA*, 3:274; 5:350–51; 6:361, 493.

39. Quoted in Perkins, *The Roosevelt I Knew*, 295.

40. *FDRPPA*, 5:389.

41. Davis, *FDR: The New Deal Years*, 441, 452.

42. The cartoon appeared in the *New Yorker* of September 26, 1936. The Trans-Lux was a newsreel movie house between Fifty-Ninth and Sixtieth Streets, west of Madison Avenue.

43. *FDRPPA*, 4:272, 275.

44. *FDRPPA*, 7:276.

45. *FDRPPA*, 6:331. See also Jim Senter, "'Dreams as Old as Roanoke': Franklin Roosevelt's 1937 Lost Colony Speech," *North Carolina Historical Review* 84, no. 3 (2007): 277–99.

46. *FDRPPA*, 6:5, "Second Inaugural Address," January 20, 1937.

47. *FDRPPA*, 7:9–11.

48. John Gunther, *Roosevelt in Retrospect* (New York: Harper & Brothers, 1950), 118.

49. *FDRPPA*, 6:332, "Address at Roanoke Island, NC," August 18, 1937. The Bentham title that FDR actually chose for his personal study was his *Theory of Legislation* (Boston: Weeks, Jordan, 1840), a work originally composed by Etienne Dumont, a "friend and disciple of Bentham's who examined the master's manuscripts and treatises and arranged, compiled, condensed, and translated them into French. R. Hildreth then translated this compilation back into English. Dumont's preface indicates that much of

his work is derived from Bentham's *Principles and Morals of Legislation*." Robert Clark, supervisory archivist, Roosevelt Library, to the author, March 24, 2008.

50. Jeremy Bentham, *Manual of Political Economy*, chap. 1, quoted in John Herman Randall, *The Making of the Modern Mind* (Boston: Houghton Mifflin, 1926), 361.

51. Henry Sturt, "Utilitarianism," in *Encyclopedia Britannica* (1911), 27:821.

52. John Rawls, *A Theory of Justice*, rev. ed. (Cambridge, MA: Belknap Press of Harvard University Press, 1999), 19–30, 160–68. Quotations, 20, 24–25, 167; emphasis added 167.

53. The three-faith consensus was assumed, for instance, in *FDRPPA*, 7:75, "Informal, Extemporaneous Remarks to . . . Visiting Protestant Ministers," January 31, 1938; also 9:509, "Campaign Address," October 28, 1940. For FDR's popularization of "Judeo-Christian," see Gene Zubovich, "The Strange, Short Career of Judeo-Christianity," *Aeon*, March 22, 2016, https://aeon.co/ideas/the-strange-short-career-of-judeo-christianity. Will Herberg famously analyzed the syndrome in a landmark 1950s work of sociology, *Protestant-Catholic-Jew: An Essay in American Religious Sociology* (Garden City, NY: Doubleday, 1955).

54. *FDRPPA*, 1:777, "The Philosophy of Social Justice through Social Action," campaign address at Detroit, October 2, 1932.

55. *FDRPPA*, 10:440.

56. *FDRPPA*, 2:366–67, "Extemporaneous Speech at Hyde Park Methodist Episcopal Church," September 29, 1933.

57. *FDRPPA*, 9:10, "Annual Message to the Congress," January 3, 1940.

58. Perkins, *The Roosevelt I Knew*, 324–25.

59. Roosevelt, *Looking Forward*, 256.

60. *FDRPPA*, 5:359, "Address to the Conference on the Mobilization for Human Needs," September 16, 1936.

61. George T. McJimsey, *The Presidency of Franklin Delano Roosevelt* (Lawrence: University Press of Kansas, 2000), 73.

62. *FDRPPA*, 2:340, 342; see also *FDRPPA*, 5:148, "'New Approaches to Old Problems': Address at Rollins College," March 23, 1936.

63. *FDRPPA*, 9:31.

64. *FDRPPA*, 5:148–49, "'New Approaches to Old Problems': Address at Rollins College, Florida," March 23, 1936.

65. *FDRPPA*, 2:216.

66. Greer, *What Roosevelt Thought*, 110.

67. *FDRPPA*, 1:756.

68. *FDRPPA*, 4:236–37; see also 3:288, 291.

69. Perkins, *The Roosevelt I Knew*, 18.

70. Greer, *What Roosevelt Thought*, 9.

71. *FDRPPA*, 7:431.

72. McJimsey, *The Presidency of Franklin Delano Roosevelt*, xii.

Chapter 6

1. In the 1938 election, the Republicans gained eighty-one seats in the House of Representatives and eight in the Senate. Roosevelt specifically targeted Congressman

John O'Connor of New York and Senators Walter George of Georgia, Millard Tydings of Maryland, Pat McCarran of Nevada, and Ellison D. ("Cotton Ed") Smith of South Carolina.

2. John A. Garraty, *The Great Depression* (New York: Doubleday, 1987), 396; see also Kenneth S. Davis, *FDR: Into the Storm, 1937–1940* (New York: Random House, 1993), 9–10, 137–46, 205–11, 221–32.

3. Frances Perkins, *The Roosevelt I Knew* (New York: Viking, 1946), 140–41.

4. Eleanor Roosevelt, *This I Remember* (New York: Harper & Row, 1949), 69–70.

5. John Rawls, *A Brief Inquiry into the Meaning of Sin and Faith* (Cambridge, MA: Harvard University Press, 2009), 124.

6. All citations in the following paragraphs are from this address. *The Public Papers and Addresses of Franklin D. Roosevelt*, ed. Samuel I. Rosenman, 13 vols. (New York: Random House, 1938–c. 1950) (hereafter *FDRPPA*), 8:1–3.

7. *FDRPPA*, 8:153.

8. Davis, *FDR: Into the Storm*, 345, 329.

9. Quoted in Davis, *FDR: Into the Storm*, 365.

10. Robert N. Rosen, *Saving the Jews: Franklin D. Roosevelt and the Holocaust* (New York: Thunder's Mouth, 2006), 62–66.

11. Susan Welch, "American Opinion toward Jews during the Nazi Era: Results from Quota Sample Polling during the 1930s and 1940s," *Social Science Quarterly* 95, no. 3 (September 2014): 615–35.

12. Press conference of November 15, 1938, quoted in Jean Edward Smith, *FDR* (New York: Random House, 2007), 426.

13. Rosen, *Saving the Jews*, 85.

14. George T. McJimsey, *The Presidency of Franklin Delano Roosevelt* (Lawrence: University Press of Kansas, 2000), 262. FDR actually extended quotas and was responsible for enabling twenty-seven thousand German and Austrian refugees to remain in the United States; see Robert Dallek, *Franklin D. Roosevelt and American Foreign Policy, 1932–1945*, 2nd ed. (New York: Oxford University Press, 1995), 167–68.

15. David M. Kennedy, *Freedom from Fear: The American People in Depression and War, 1929–1945* (New York: Oxford University Press, 1999), 417.

16. Rosen, *Saving the Jews*, 428.

17. FDR to Suckley, September 11 to 26, 1938, in Geoffrey C. Ward, ed., *Closest Companion: The Unknown Story of the Intimate Friendship between Franklin Roosevelt and Margaret Suckley* (Boston: Houghton Mifflin, 1995), 124–25.

18. Leo Ribuffo, *The Old Christian Right: The Protestant Far Right from the Depression to the Cold War* (Philadelphia: Temple University Press, 1983), 181 and 102. Ironically Winrod reproduced pro-Nazi materials in the *Defender*, his journal with a monthly circulation of one hundred thousand. Other populist religious demagogues in the 1930s, some with national followings, included the radio priest Father Charles E. Coughlin; Klansman George Christians of the Crusader White Shirts; pantheistic socialist William Dudley Pelley, with his "Comrade Christ"; Elizabeth Dilling; and Gerald L. K. Smith. Ribuffo, 101–3, 136–39, 178–89, 194–97, 329–31.

19. Justus D. Doenecke, *The New Deal* (Malabar, FL: Krieger, 2003), 72.

20. Patrick J. O'Brien, "Jouett Shouse," in *American National Biography* (New York: Oxford University Press, 1999), 19:890–92.

21. George Wolfskill, *The Revolt of the Conservatives: A History of the American Liberty League, 1934–1940* (Boston: Houghton Mifflin, 1962).

22. On the NAM, see Wendy L. Wall, *Inventing the "American Way": The Politics of Consensus from the New Deal to the Civil Rights Movement* (New York: Oxford University Press, 2008), 48–62. The organization's own archives attest to "57,000 businessmen—12,000 manufacture-members, . . . 40,000 members of 307 regional, state and local manufacturing or trade groups affiliated with the National Industrial Council, and 6,300 subscribers to the National Industrial Committee." #1411, Box 40, Corporate Records, 1931–1959 folder, Hagley Library, Wilmington, DE.

23. Yanek Mieczkowski, "Henning W. Prentis, Jr.," in *American National Biography*, 17:829–30. Quotations from Wall, *Inventing the "American Way,"* 59.

24. Garraty, *The Great Depression*, 184–85, 186–87, 197, 199–200, and 203–4.

25. William C. Placher, *Narratives of a Vulnerable God: Christ, Theology, and Scripture* (Louisville: Westminster John Knox, 1994), 17.

26. Kennedy, *Freedom from Fear*, 157; oath quoted in Adam Nagorski, *Hitlerland: American Eyewitnesses to the Nazi Rise to Power* (New York: Simon & Schuster, 2012), 162.

27. US Army Center of Military History, www.history.army.mil. Members of the military swear allegiance to the nation and to observing the orders of the president of the United States and "the officers appointed over me." For those entering civilian office, whether in the several states or in the national government, see the Constitution of the United States, Article VI.

28. Report of a Deputation to the White House by Henry St. George Tucker, April 6, 1943, President's Personal File 7211 and 21.

29. Sixty-eighth press conference, November 10, 1933, *FDRPPA*, 2:464.

30. Nagorski, *Hitlerland*, 157–66.

31. Richard E. White Jr., *Kingfish: The Reign of Huey P. Long* (New York: Random House, 2006), 168–71, 231; quoted in Alan Brinkley, *Voices of Protest: Huey Long, Father Coughlin, and the Great Depression* (New York: Knopf, 1982), 58. Long's enumeration of senators reflects the total of ninety-six from the forty-eight states at the time.

32. William E. Leuchtenburg, *The FDR Years: On Roosevelt and His Legacy* (New York: Columbia University Press, 1995), 80.

33. Brinkley, *Voices of Protest*, 72–73, 80.

34. Sinclair Lewis, *It Can't Happen Here* (New York: New American Library, 2005); Mark Schorer, *Sinclair Lewis: An American Life* (New York: McGraw-Hill, 1961), 623.

35. Geoffrey Perret, *Old Soldiers Never Die: The Life of Douglas MacArthur* (New York: Random House, 1966), 113–14, 116–20, 163–64, 172–73, 185, 480, 482–83, 548.

36. Quoted in Rexford G. Tugwell, *The Brains Trust* (New York: Viking, 1968), 428.

37. In order, Carlo D'Este, *Eisenhower: A Soldier's Life* (New York: Holt, 2002), 226; Perret, *Old Soldiers Never Die*, 214; Eric Larrabee, *Commander in Chief: Franklin Delano Roosevelt, His Lieutenants, and Their War* (New York: Harper & Row, 1987), 333, 329.

38. Quoted in Smith, *FDR*, 285.

39. D'Este, *Eisenhower*, 218–24, 226; Perret, *Old Soldiers Never Die*, 212, 481; Larrabee, *Commander in Chief*, 329.

40. Larrabee, *Commander in Chief*, 351.

41. Donald G. Jones, "Civil and Public Religion," in *Encyclopedia of the American*

Religious Experience, ed. Charles H. Lippy and Peter W. Williams, 3 vols. (New York: Scribner's Sons, 1988), 3:1395–96. Civil religion exists, writes Jones, "whenever a majority of the people of the nation . . . ascribe ultimacy to aspects of their political society such as social ideals, when they envision a transcendent goal to the political process, when they believe that a sacred reality is the source of meaning for their history and social order, and when these convictions are expressed through public rituals."

42. Davis, *FDR: Into the Storm*, 382. Davis's hope that history will supply the wisdom and cautionary instruction classically afforded by religion is manifestly contradicted by history itself, inasmuch as historians are no safer or more reliable oracles than clergy.

43. John T. Noonan Jr., *The Lustre of Our Country: The American Experience of Religious Freedom* (Berkeley: University of California Press, 1998), 1.

44. Hans W. Frei, *Types of Christian Theology* (New Haven: Yale University Press, 1992), 12. Durkheim was a pioneer of the hermeneutics of suspicion that accords the intelligent outsider—the anthropologist, the Freudian analyst, the Marxist economist, etc.—the power to objectively analyze what religion "really" is or does. Possessing privileged rational approaches that "explain" texts and liturgies, they command the high ground. Frei also draws attention to a variant on this approach, the "hermeneutics of restoration" propounded by Clifford Geertz, in which the outsider attempts to see the culture from the agent's point of view without going native or mimicking him. See Geertz, *The Interpretation of Cultures* (New York: Basic Books, 1973), 3–30.

45. Noonan, *Lustre of Our Country*, 213–16; quotations, 244, 246–47.

46. Robert N. Bellah, "Civil Religion in America," in *Religion in America*, ed. William G. McLoughlin and Robert N. Bellah (Boston: Houghton Mifflin, 1968), passim.

47. Noonan, *Lustre of Our Country*, 244.

48. Ronald Isetti, "The Moneychangers in the Temple: FDR, American Civil Religion, and the New Deal," *Presidential Studies Quarterly* 26 (Summer 1996): 683.

49. Noonan, *Lustre of Our Country*, 246–47.

50. Grace Tully, *FDR: My Boss* (New York: Scribner's Sons, 1949), 264–65; Robert E. Sherwood, *Roosevelt and Hopkins* (New York: Harper and Brothers, 1948), 212–13.

51. The President's D-Day Prayer, June 6, 1944, Statements File, Franklin D. Roosevelt Library. Corrections and parentheses appear in the draft of the prayer. For the text see also *FDRPPL*, 13:152–53.

52. Cf. John Bunyan, *The Pilgrim's Progress* (London: Oxford University Press, 1932), 78: "And ever and anon the flame and smoke would come out in such abundance, with sparks and hideous noises." See also Joel 2:5, 2 Pet. 3:10, and William Shakespeare, *Macbeth* (New Haven: Yale University Press, 1949), II/3, 60–67.

53. Cf. Prov. 3:17, Wisdom's "ways are ways of pleasantness and all her paths are peace."

54. Tully, *FDR*, 265. Proof that Tully was part of the company at Watson's home that weekend rests on her observation regarding the "tightly contained state of his nerves" while awaiting news of the landing. For reasons of secrecy, Tully was also the only person permitted to type FDR's speeches; see Sherwood, *Roosevelt and Hopkins*, 296.

55. As the rector of the parish began with prayer, Perkins recounted, "I opened an eye and stole a look around the circle of bowed heads and said to myself, 'I think I know

what each one of you is praying for.' And, John," she continued, "you must never tell anyone." Author's conversation with Frances Perkins.

56. Book of Common Prayer (1928), 36; (1979), 820.

57. Brad R. Braxton, "Martin Luther King, Jr.: Heir of the African American Interpretive Legacy," *A.M.E. Church Review* 117, no. 379–380 (Fall 2000): 60, quoted in Dennis C. Dickerson, "African American Religious Intellectuals and the Theological Foundations of the Civil Rights Movement, 1930–55," *Church History* 74, no. 2 (June 2005): 217.

58. George Steiner, *Real Presences* (Chicago: University of Chicago Press, 1989), 190–91.

59. Bunyan, *Pilgrim's Progress*, 78. For Bunyan's influence, see Paul Fussell, *The Great War in Modern Memory* (New York: Oxford University Press, 1975), 137–44.

60. John Bunyan, *Grace Abounding to the Chief of Sinners* (Oxford: Oxford University Press, 1962), 14–15, quoted in Geoffrey Nuttall, "The Heart of *The Pilgrim's Progress*," in *Reformation Principle and Practice*, ed. Peter Brooks (London: Scolar, 1980), 232.

61. Gary Scott Smith, *Faith and the Presidency* (New York: Oxford University Press, 2006), 197–98. FDR was paraphrasing the 1932 Oxford University Press edition, 69, 76–77, 78, 81, and 140.

62. *FDRPPA*, 5:165, April 13, 1936.

63. *FDRPPA*, 5:579, November 2, 1936.

64. Smith, *Faith and the Presidency*, 219.

65. *FDRPPA*, 7:381–82.

66. Quoted in Merlin Gustafson and Jerry Rosenberg, "The Faith of Franklin Roosevelt," *Presidential Studies Quarterly* 19 (Summer 1989): 561.

67. All quotations in this paragraph are from Arthur M. Schlesinger Jr., *The Coming of the New Deal* (Boston: Houghton Mifflin, 1959), 586.

Chapter 7

1. *The Public Papers and Addresses of Franklin D. Roosevelt*, ed. Samuel I. Rosenman, 13 vols. (New York: Random House, 1938–c. 1950) (hereafter *FDRPPA*), 6:408. Kenneth S. Davis, *FDR: Into the Storm, 1937–1940* (New York: Random House, 1993), 130–36.

2. The speech is quoted in Robert E. Sherwood, *Roosevelt and Hopkins* (New York: Harper and Brothers, 1948), 124.

3. *FDRPPA*, 9:187. See also FDR's address to the Pan-American Union, April 15, 1940, especially 160–61, for references to "moral order." Likewise, his acceptance of a third term, particularly 299, with its reference to "human decency"; his address at Ottawa, Canada, *FDRPPA*, 12:368, referring to "the fundamentals of decent human conduct"; and his annual appeal for polio victims on January 29, 1944, 13:61, with its reference to "the eternal principle of kindness."

4. Robert Dallek, *Franklin D. Roosevelt and American Foreign Policy, 1932–1945*, 2nd ed. (New York: Oxford University Press, 1995), 266. "Radio Address Announcing Unlimited National Emergency," May 27, 1941, *FDRPPA*, 10:180–95. On the very night of the speech, the Royal Navy sank the *Bismarck*.

5. *FDRPPA*, 10:183, 187.

6. *FDRPPA*, 10:191.

7. Charles A. Lindbergh, "Address Delivered at an America First Committee Meeting in New York City on April 23, 1941," http://www.charleslindbergh.com/american first/speech2.asp, 1–2.

8. Wayne S. Cole, *Roosevelt and the Isolationists, 1932–1945* (Lincoln: University of Nebraska Press, 1983), 280–83, 410; quotation, 280.

9. Richard J. Evans, *The Third Reich at War* (New York: Penguin Press, 2009), 140–41; William K. Klingaman, *1941: Our Lives in a World on the Edge* (New York: Harper & Row, 1988), 96.

10. Lindbergh, "Address," 4–5.

11. Quoted in Cole, *Roosevelt and the Isolationists*, 435.

12. Cited in Sherwood, *Roosevelt and Hopkins*, 128.

13. George W. Martin, *CCB: The Life and Century of Charles C. Burlingham, New York's First Citizen* (New York: Hill & Wang, 2005), 112–17, 169.

14. Dallek, *Franklin D. Roosevelt*, 267.

15. Sources on the non-/anti-interventionist front are multiple and varied. See especially three works by Justus D. Doenecke: *Storm on the Horizon: The Challenge to American Intervention, 1939–1941* (London: Rowman & Littlefield, 2000), a comprehensive survey; *The Battle against Intervention, 1939–1941* (Malabar, FL: Krieger, 1996), a brief survey; and *In Danger Undaunted* (Palo Alto, CA: Hoover Institution Press, 1990), an annotated anthology of important primary sources. See also relevant entries in the *Dictionary of American Biography* and the *American Biographical Dictionary*.

16. Regarding the group Clark assembled in favor of rearmament, see Davis, *FDR: Into the Storm*, 568–75.

17. Quoted in David Levering Lewis, *W. E. B. Du Bois: The Fight for Equality and the American Century, 1919–1963* (New York: Holt, 2000), 463. *Time* magazine's description of Muste quoted in Kurt A. Klingbeil, "FDR and American Religious Leaders" (PhD diss., New York University, 1972), 243.

18. Doenecke, *Storm on the Horizon*, 11.

19. All quotations taken from Charles Lindbergh's Des Moines speech, September 11, 1941, http://www.charleslindbergh.com/americanfirst/speech.asp.

20. See documents 118 and 121 in Doenecke, *In Danger Undaunted*, 391–401; quotations, 395, 401.

21. Quoted in James Reston, *Deadline: A Memoir* (New York: Random House, 1991), 69.

22. Reston, *Deadline*, 51.

23. Quoted in Richard W. Fox, *Reinhold Niebuhr: A Biography* (New York: Pantheon, 1985), 185, 176.

24. Fox, *Reinhold Niebuhr*, 189–91; Harvey Cox, "Theology, Politics, and Friendship," *Christianity & Crisis* 46, no. 1 (1986): 16.

25. Rexford G. Tugwell, *The Democratic Roosevelt* (Garden City, NY: Doubleday, 1957), 97.

26. Hobson to Wood, October 21, 1941, in Doenecke, *In Danger Undaunted*, 388–89. Once the United States had entered the war, these two groups, pro- and anti-intervention, came together in March 1942 in what became known as the "Delaware Conference" on the campus of Ohio Wesleyan University. There, writes David A.

Hollinger, the formidably powerful pacifist persuasion joined the "Protestant realists"—Reinhold Niebuhr, John Foster Dulles, and others—"to advance liberal politics with a measure of unity and confidence that would not survive, but that sustained the 'Protestant Establishment' during the years of its greatest public authority." David A. Hollinger, "The Realist-Pacifist Summit Meeting of March 1942 and the Political Reorientation of Ecumenical Protestantism in the United States," *Church History* 9, no. 3 (2010): 657, 677.

27. All quotations from Doenecke, *In Danger Undaunted*: Flynn to Wood, November 11, 1941, 138–39; Judson to James B. Conant, February 3, 1941, 123–24; Stuart to Hutchins, October 29, 1941, 136–38; Castle to Stuart, February 14, 1941, 125–27.

28. "Washington News Letter #16" (June 4, 1941), in Doenecke, *In Danger Undaunted*, 264–66. Quotation, Richard Parker, *John Kenneth Galbraith: His Life, His Politics, His Economics* (New York: Farrar, Straus & Giroux, 2005), 141.

29. All quotations from Doenecke, *In Danger Undaunted*: "Washington News Letter #16" and "Union Now?," 265–66, 240–43; Bowles to Stuart, July 15, 1941, 279. For a similar point of view about communism versus Nazism, see "Statement of the New York Chapter," June 23, 1941, in Doenecke, 290–91.

30. Doenecke, *In Danger Undaunted*, 49.

31. Doenecke, *Storm on the Horizon*, 323.

32. Sherwood, *Roosevelt and Hopkins*, 435.

33. Frances Perkins, *The Roosevelt I Knew* (New York: Viking, 1946), 379; Sherwood, *Roosevelt and Hopkins*, 435. George T. McJimsey, *Harry Hopkins: Ally of the Poor and Defender of Democracy* (Cambridge, MA: Harvard University Press, 1987), 208, disagrees with Sherwood's characterization of other officials, especially with reference to secretaries Henry Stimson and Frank Knox, and General George Marshall.

34. James MacGregor Burns, *Roosevelt: The Soldier of Freedom* (New York: Harcourt Brace Jovanovich, 1970), 164–67. For Roosevelt's words to the cabinet, see Jean Edward Smith, *FDR* (New York: Random House, 2007), 537.

35. Perkins, *The Roosevelt I Knew*, 368.

36. Sherwood, *Roosevelt and Hopkins*, 435–37.

37. H. W. Brands, *Traitor to His Class: The Privileged Life and Radical Presidency of Franklin Delano Roosevelt* (New York: Anchor Books, 2008), 648.

38. See Perkins, *The Roosevelt I Knew*, 380–85.

39. *FDRPPA*, 11:78.

40. Joseph P. Lash, *Eleanor and Franklin: The Story of Their Relationship, Based on Eleanor Roosevelt's Private Papers* (New York: Norton, 1971), 654. Burns, *Roosevelt: Soldier of Freedom*, 177.

41. James Roosevelt and Sidney Shalett, *Affectionately, FDR* (New York: Harcourt Brace, 1959), 339–46. For Elliott Roosevelt, see FDR to Eleanor Roosevelt, November 21, 1943, in *F.D.R.: His Personal Letters*, ed. Elliott Roosevelt, 4 vols. (New York: Duell, Sloan & Pearce, 1947–1950) (hereafter *FDRPL*), 3:1470.

42. *FDRPPA*, 11:251.

43. *FDRPPA*, 11:410, October 7, 1942.

44. Kenneth S. Davis, *FDR: The War President, 1940–1943* (New York: Random House, 2000), 10.

45. Perkins, *The Roosevelt I Knew*, 64, 66.

46. Don Handleman, "Clowns," in *Encyclopedia of Religion*, ed. Mircea Eliade (New York: Macmillan, 1987), 3:548.

47. Joseph W. Bastien, "Humor and Satire," in *Encyclopedia of Religion*, 6:526.

48. Conrad Hyers, *And God Created Laughter: The Bible as Divine Comedy* (Atlanta: John Knox, 1987), 45.

49. Erich Auerbach, *Mimesis: The Representation of Reality in Western Literature* (Princeton: Princeton University Press, 1953), 12, 14–15, 17–18.

50. "The Budget Seminar," January 6, 1942, *FDRPPA*, 11:20–21.

51. Press conference, February 18, 1941, *FDRPPA*, 10:24, and April 15, 1941, 10:116.

52. Press conference, July 9, 1942, *FDRPPA*, 11:302.

53. FDR to Patton, August 4, 1943, in *FDRPL*, 2:1437. Despite his bravado, Patton admitted his mistakes—unlike Eisenhower and, even more, British general Bernard Montgomery. He admitted to being frightened, was a strict adherent to the Geneva Convention, and was horrified at the "sadistic bombing" of enemy cities. See George S. Patton Jr., *War as I Knew It* (Boston: Houghton Mifflin, 1947): admission of mistakes, 181, 185, 201, 213, 267; fear, 157, 239; Geneva Convention, 253; bombing cities, 288. Cf. Russell F. Weigley, *Eisenhower's Lieutenants: The Campaign of France and Germany, 1944–1945* (Bloomington: Indiana University Press, 1990), 566.

54. "Address to the Teamsters," September 23, 1944, quoted in Brands, *Traitor to His Class*, 783.

55. Final radio speech of the 1940 presidential campaign, November 4, 1940, *FDRPPA*, 9:554–55.

56. "Eight Hundred and Forty-Eighth Press Conference," October 1, 1942; "The President Reports on the Home Front," October 12, 1942, *FDRPPA*, 11:395, 422–23, respectively.

57. State of the Union address, January 6, 1942, *FDRPPA*, 11:29.

58. "Fireside Chat Opening the Third War Loan Drive," September 8, 1943, *FDRPPA*, 12:377.

59. "The President Sends Greetings to Yank on the Publication of Its First Issue," May 28, 1942, *FDRPPA*, 11:255; see also "Address to International Student Assembly," September 3, 1942, *FDRPPA*, 11:351.

60. *FDRPL*, 3:1443–44.

61. *FDRPPA*, 12:89

62. Robert H. Ferrell, *The Dying President: Franklin D. Roosevelt, 1944–1945* (Columbia: University of Missouri Press, 1998), 79–80.

63. Sherwood, *Roosevelt and Hopkins*, 843.

64. "Christmas Eve Address to the Nation," December 24, 1944, *FDRPPA*, 13:444.

65. *FDRPPA*, 13:181.

66. Edward Humes, *Over Here: How the G.I. Bill Transformed the American Dream* (Orlando: Harcourt, 2006), 29, 34.

67. Glenn C. Altschuler and Stuart M. Blumin, *The GI Bill: A New Deal for Veterans* (New York: Oxford University Press, 2009), 40, 41, and 44.

68. Humes, *Over Here*, 31, 33.

69. Altschuler and Blumin, *The GI Bill*, 147; James T. Patterson, *Grand Expectations: The United States, 1945–1974* (New York: Oxford University Press, 1997), 68–69; for statistics, see 66–68.

70. Humes, *Over Here*, notes the key roles played in the shaping of the bill by Harry Colmery of the American Legion and by Senators Elbert D. Thomas (D-UT) and John Gibson (D-GA), as well as by Rankin. Samuel I. Rosenman, *Working with Roosevelt* (New York: Harper and Brothers, 1952), 394–95, shows how early exposure to poor, rural schools in Georgia made FDR critical of regional and local controls. See also Alan Brinkley, *The End of Reform: New Deal Liberalism in Recession and War* (New York: Knopf, 1995), 259.

71. Altschuler and Blumin, *The GI Bill*, 58; John Morton Blum, *V Was for Victory: Politics and American Culture during World War II* (San Diego: Harcourt Brace, 1976), 248–49.

72. Examples abound for 1943 alone; see, for instance, *FDRPPA*, 12:32–33, 87, 99, 133, 163, 341, 405, 449, 450.

73. All quotations in this and the next paragraph are from *FDRPPA*, 13:32–42, "Message on the State of the Union," January 11, 1944; quotations, 40, 41, 32 (emphases added). Clearly Roosevelt had been thinking along these lines as early as the end of 1942; in his January 7, 1943, State of the Union address, he mentions many of these economic rights, though not in such formal style; see *FDRPPA*, 12:31.

74. Quoted in Perkins, *The Roosevelt I Knew*, 88.

75. State of the Union address, 1942: *FDRPPA*, 11: 41.

76. Sherwood, *Roosevelt and Hopkins*, 843.

77. "Radio Address in Connection with the Christian Foreign Service," March 16, 1940, *FDRPPA*, 9:103; "Acceptance of a Third Term Nomination," July 19, 1940, *FDRPPA*, 9:297; "Radio Address for the 1940 Mobilization for Human Need," October 13, 1940, *FDRPPA*, 9:468; fireside chat, September 8, 1943, *FDRPPA*, 12:377; "Address at the White House Correspondents' Association," February 12, 1943, *FDRPPA*, 12:74; "Fourth Inaugural Address," January 20, 1945, *FDRPPA*, 13:523; State of the Union address, January 7, 1943, *FDRPPA*, 12:32.

78. "Radio Address Announcing Unlimited National Emergency," May 27, 1941, *FDRPPA*, 10:188–92.

79. "Acceptance of a Third Term Nomination," July 19, 1940, *FDRPPA*, 9:302.

80. Sherwood, *Roosevelt and Hopkins*, 872; David M. Kennedy, *Freedom from Fear: The American People in Depression and War, 1929–1945* (New York: Oxford University Press, 1999), 806; FDR to James M. Landis, January 11, 1945, in *FDRPL*, 4:1564–65.

81. FDR to Thomas, May 14, 1941, in *FDRPL*, 4:1156.

82. Marcus Graeser, "World History in a Nation-State: The Transnational Disposition of Historical Writing in the United States," *Journal of American History* 95, no. 4 (2009): 1050 and 1049. In Turner's course Roosevelt read *The Frontier in American History*; see *FDRPL*, 1:n.505.

83. John Milton Cooper Jr., *The Warrior and the Priest: Woodrow Wilson and Theodore Roosevelt* (Cambridge, MA: Belknap Press of Harvard University Press, 1983), 358, 361.

84. About his private prayers there is little doubt. FDR kept a well-worn copy of the Book of Common Prayer at his bedside in the White House. In 1933 he even urged the Jewish Russian ambassador, Maxim Litvinoff, to say his prayers: Perkins, *The Roosevelt I Knew*, 143–45.

85. "Christmas Eve Message to the Nation," December 24, 1941, *FDRPPA*, 10:594–95.

86. Christine Wicker, *The Simple Faith of Franklin Delano Roosevelt* (Washington, DC: Smithsonian Books, 2017), 67, 120.

87. *The Journals of David E. Lilienthal: The TVA Years* (New York: Harper & Row, 1964), 593.

88. Jon Meecham, *American Gospel: God, the Founding Fathers, and the Making of a Nation* (New York: Random House, 2006), 160–62. For more detail, see Jon Meecham, *Franklin and Winston: An Intimate Portrait of an Epic Friendship* (New York: Random House, 2004), 113–16.

89. Jim Bishop, *FDR's Last Year: April 1944–April 1945* (New York: William Morrow, 1974), 655.

Chapter 8

1. Frances Perkins, *The Roosevelt I Knew* (New York: Viking, 1946), 146. This chapter is based on the account in Perkins's book and on the vivid recollections my wife and I have of our evening in 1966 with Johnson when he recounted the story of dining with the Roosevelts. Madam Perkins was a guest at our home in Virginia on April 4, 1952, in connection with a lecture she gave that night at the Virginia Theological Seminary. From that visit and from this portion of her study of Roosevelt, it is clear that she too talked with Johnson about his dinner at the White House. For additional detail, see the White House records provided by the Franklin D. Roosevelt Library, Hyde Park, New York.

2. Quoted in Johnson's obituary, *New York Times*, June 17, 1974, 34. Johnson went on to edit the English translation of Kierkegaard's *Either/Or* (New York: Doubleday, 1959).

3. The best recent biography is Joakim Garff, *Søren Kierkegaard: A Biography*, trans. Bruce H. Kirmmse (Princeton: Princeton University Press, 2005).

4. Johnson to Lowrie, September 6, 1943, Walter Lowrie Papers, Princeton University Library, Princeton, New Jersey.

5. Johnson to Mrs. Franklin D. Roosevelt, January 17, 1944, Papers of Eleanor Roosevelt, Franklin D. Roosevelt Library.

6. Eleanor Roosevelt to Johnson, January 21, 1944, Papers of Eleanor Roosevelt.

7. Johnson to Lowrie, March 31, 1944, Walter Lowrie Papers. Instead of writing an account of the evening, however, Johnson added—tantalizingly for the historian—"Perhaps you would like to hear about this when I see you." Fortunately the author of this book did hear about it.

8. Johnson, conversation with the author, May 22, 1966.

9. Perkins, *The Roosevelt I Knew*, 147.

10. James Cochrane Agey was with the 535 Fighter Squadron at Camp Springs, Andrews Air Force Base, in Maryland, outside of Washington, DC. Agey had apparently been working on a biography of his aunt, Elizabeth Cochrane, a journalist popularly known as "Nellie Bly" who had been a strong supporter of women's rights; she was married to Robert Livingston Seamans, with whom Eleanor Roosevelt possibly shared a common ancestor. Later in the evening the party was joined by two houseguests: Hildur Coon of the United States Student Assembly and her sister, Jean. As Perkins

shows in *The Roosevelt I Knew*, 75, such an assemblage of people was not unusual at the Roosevelt White House.

11. Johnson to Eleanor Roosevelt, February 22, 1944, Papers of Eleanor Roosevelt.

12. Eleanor Roosevelt, "My Day," Thursday, February 24, 1944, United Feature Syndicate.

13. Nancy M. Tischler, "Dorothy L. Sayers," in *Dictionary of Literary Biography* (Detroit: Gale Research, 1983), 10:124.

14. F. A. Iremonger, *William Temple, Archbishop of Canterbury: His Life and Letters* (London: Oxford University Press, 1948), 428–53.

15. Walter Lowrie, *Our Concern with the Theology of Crisis* (New York: Meador, 1932).

16. See Claude Welch, *In This Name: The Doctrine of the Trinity in Contemporary Theology* (New York: Scribner's Sons, 1952), 85–92, 248–52.

17. Perkins, *The Roosevelt I Knew*, 147. For Kant's contribution to the turn away from the sense of inherited, Adamic sin, see the chapter "On the Radical Evil in Human Nature" in his *Religion within the Limits of Reason Alone* (1793).

18. Howard A. Johnson, "For St. John's College, Annapolis," n.d., RG97-1-13, Howard A. Johnson Papers, Archives of the Episcopal Church, Austin, Texas.

19. Howard A. Johnson, *Kierkegaard: An Introduction* (Cincinnati: Forward Movement, 1965), 5.

20. Perkins, *The Roosevelt I Knew*, 148.

21. Perkins, *The Roosevelt I Knew*, 148.

22. James C. Livingston, *Modern Christian Thought from the Enlightenment to Vatican II* (New York: Macmillan, 1971), 311–24. Livingston's survey of the extraordinary half century (1920 to 1970) of theological work by such eminences as Karl Barth, Emil Brunner, Rudolf Bultmann, Paul Tillich, H. Richard Niebuhr, and Reinhold Niebuhr shows that Kierkegaard exerted an epochal influence on all of them. This tradition continues in the work of recent scholars, particularly Joakim Garff, Christine Battersby, Jurgen K. Burkdahl, David J. Gouwens, Carol Meyers, Robert C. Roberts, D. Anthony Storm, and Jean Wahl. For one taste, see William C. Placher, *Narratives of Vulnerability* (Louisville: Westminster John Knox, 1994), 177–79.

23. Johnson, *Kierkegaard*, 28.

24. In the Christian lexicon, the opposite of faith is not reason, of course, but sin. Christianity itself is rational in keeping with its intention and principles. Thus the opposite of reason is not faith but *imago* in the Latin, daydreaming and woolgathering.

25. Johnson, "For St. John's College," 2.

26. Kierkegaard would have called recent battles between the Christian Right (Jerry Falwell and James Dobson) and equally humorless "new atheists" such as Richard Dawkins, Christopher Hitchens, and Daniel Dennett a Tweedledum-Tweedledee contest over proofs for the existence of God. In fact, the two sides share common assumptions that an "objective orientation is the way of truth." Both demand certainty; both ignore contingency as well as the individual's venture in faith. That venture is not based on the ontological—or any other—proof for the existence of God but on the appropriation of Jesus Christ on the cross and in the resurrection for the forgiveness of sins. Kierkegaard lays this out in his greatest philosophical work, *Concluding Unscientific Postscript to Philosophical Fragments*, ed. H. V. Hong and E. H. Hong, 2 vols. (Princeton: Princeton University Press, 1992), 1:369–431. But he would also claim that liberal scholars who

search for the "historical Jesus" in the Jesus Seminar and like ventures also make Jesus Christ and Christianity objects to be studied. All three groups concern themselves with the what of Christianity, not the how of faith.

27. Kierkegaard, *Philosophical Fragments* (Princeton: Princeton University Press, 1985), 9, 11, and 12.

28. Kierkegaard, *Philosophical Fragments*, 13. Jungian psychology offers a more recent version of this notion. Here the individual is like a little chick pecking its way out of the prison that walls it in and keeps it from knowing and welcoming itself. Knowledge (*gnosis*) of the self alone is elevated, deified to become one with the collective unconscious, that is, with God. Such awareness comes at a price: "life realized in terms of the self rather than in terms of others." Finally, for Jung, too, particular occasions, objects, "even particular persons are important only insofar as they help to illustrate the already familiar ultimate and eternal consciousness."

29. Livingston, *Modern Christian Thought*, 156.

30. Johnson, "For St. John's College," 3.

31. Kierkegaard, *Philosophical Fragments*, 13.

32. Johnson, *Kierkegaard*, 26.

33. Kierkegaard, *Philosophical Fragments*, 15.

34. Howard A. Johnson, "Too Much Purple," sermon for Ash Wednesday, February 23, 1944, St. John's Church, Washington, DC, typescript, Howard A. Johnson Papers, 3, 5, 10, and 11.

35. George Price, *The Narrow Passage: A Study of Kierkegaard's Concept of Man* (New York: McGraw-Hill, 1963), 203.

36. For starters, see FDR to William C. Bullitt, April 21, 1935, and June 21, 1935, in *F.D.R.: His Personal Letters*, ed. Elliott Roosevelt, 4 vols. (New York: Duell, Sloan & Pearce, 1947–1950) (hereafter *FDRPL*), 3:476, 488; FDR to William E. Dodd, December 2, 1935, and August 5, 1936, 530–31, 605–6. See also Robert Edwin Herzstein, *Roosevelt and Hitler: Prelude to War* (New York: Paragon House, 1989), particularly xiv–xvi, 78–79, 82, 230, and 238–39.

37. Frank Freidel, *Franklin D. Roosevelt: Launching the New Deal* (Boston: Little, Brown, 1973), 123.

38. FDR to Bullitt, June 21, 1935, in *FDRPL*, 2:488. Bullitt and Goering had represented America and Germany, respectively, at the funeral of Polish leader Marshal Jozef Pilsudski.

39. *FDRPL*, 2:530.

40. *The Public Papers and Addresses of Franklin D. Roosevelt*, ed. Samuel I. Rosenman, 13 vols. (New York: Random House, 1938–c. 1950) (hereafter *FDRPPA*), 12:392–93, "Message to the Congress on the Progress of the War," September 7, 1943.

41. Quoted in Perkins, *The Roosevelt I Knew*, 148; see also 156 for further comments regarding FDR's puzzlement at and rejection of dictators and their concentrated power and responsibility.

42. Robert Clark to the author, January 27, 2005. There are no books by Søren Kierkegaard in President Roosevelt's personal book collection; likewise, while the president could order any book he wanted from the Library of Congress, after 1927 there are no records of books borrowed by either presidents or White House staffs (librarian Cheryl L. Fox to the author, February 6, 2007).

276

43. This is the conclusion of Merlin Gustafson and Jerry Rosenberg in "The Faith of Franklin Roosevelt," *Presidential Studies Quarterly* 19 (Summer 1989): 564.

44. Thomas H. Greer, *What Roosevelt Thought: The Social and Political Ideas of Franklin D. Roosevelt* (East Lansing: Michigan State University Press, 2000), 41, 43.

45. Perkins, *The Roosevelt I Knew*, 44.

46. Price, *The Narrow Passage*, 46.

47. Price, *The Narrow Passage*, 58.

48. Johnson, *Kierkegaard*, 16.

49. Søren Kierkegaard, *Sickness unto Death* (Princeton: Princeton University Press, 1941), 130. For a discussion of this point, see Robert C. Roberts, "The Grammar of Sin and the Conceptual Unity of *The Sickness unto Death*," in *International Kierkegaard Commentary: "The Sickness unto Death,"* ed. Robert L. Perkins (Macon, GA: Mercer University Press, 1987), 49, 131–56. See also Livingston, *Modern Christian Thought*, 314.

50. Kierkegaard, *Philosophical Fragments*, 17.

51. Kierkegaard, *Sickness unto Death*, 110.

52. Kierkegaard, *Sickness unto Death*, 113.

53. Price, *The Narrow Passage*, 57.

54. Kierkegaard, *Sickness unto Death*, 114.

55. Price, *The Narrow Passage*, 57.

56. Kierkegaard, *Sickness unto Death*, 116, 117.

57. Kierkegaard, *Sickness unto Death*, 115 (emphasis added).

58. Kierkegaard, *Sickness unto Death*, 176, 177.

59. Johnson, *Kierkegaard*, 6.

60. Kierkegaard, *Sickness unto Death*, 110, 111.

61. Richard J. Evans, *The Third Reich in Power, 1933–1939* (New York: Penguin Press, 2005), 123–24.

62. Evans, *The Third Reich*, 125.

63. Evans, *The Third Reich*, 124. There is no reference to this film in Official File 73: Motion Pictures at the Roosevelt Library at Hyde Park. This does not mean that Roosevelt never viewed it, for not every film he saw is documented in the file.

64. Evans, *The Third Reich*, 44; see also 701 with reference to Hitler's speech on September 1, 1939, at the start of World War II, with its personal commitment to victory or death.

65. Evans, *The Third Reich*, 122–23.

66. Robert Gellately, *Backing Hitler: Consent and Coercion in Nazi Germany* (New York: Oxford University Press, 2001), 18.

67. Evans, *The Third Reich*, 645; Gellately, *Backing Hitler*, 12.

68. Evans, *The Third Reich*, 618.

69. Evans, *The Third Reich*, 120.

70. *FDRPPA*, 10:556, "Address Commemorating the 150th Anniversary of the Ratification of the Bill of Rights," December 15, 1941.

71. William E. Kinsella, "Assessment of Hitler before World War II," in *Franklin D. Roosevelt: The Man, the Myth, and the Era, 1882–1945*, ed. Herbert D. Rosenbaum and Elizabeth Bartelme (New York: Greenwood, 1987), 74.

72. Erik Larson, *In the Garden of Beasts* (New York: Crown, 2011).

73. MacVeagh delivered his ambassadorial credentials with a speech in classical Greek, which, though none of them could understand it, delighted his listeners.

74. Larson, *In the Garden of Beasts*, 76. Roosevelt had closely read and was influenced by Claude Bowers, *Jefferson and Hamilton* (Boston: Houghton Mifflin, 1925).

75. Quoted in Jonathan Alter, *The Defining Moment: FDR's First Hundred Days and the Triumph of Hope* (New York: Simon & Schuster, 2006), 286; see also FDR to Jesse I. Straus, February 13, 1936, in *FDRPL*, 3:555, for corroboration of the date May 1933.

76. See Geoffrey C. Ward, *Before the Trumpet: Young Franklin Roosevelt, 1882–1905* (New York: Vintage Books, 1985), 149–52, for a thorough discussion of Roosevelt's earliest exposure to the German language.

77. Hertzstein, *Roosevelt and Hitler*, both quotations, 78. Occasionally FDR, listening to Hitler's speeches on the radio, would translate sentences for others in the room; see FDR to Josephus Daniels, July 26, 1932, in *FDRPL*, 2:289, as well as Freidel, *Franklin D. Roosevelt: Launching the New Deal*, 403.

78. Hayden G. Bryan, executive director, St. John's Church, to the author, February 17, 2007. This contra Perkins, *The Roosevelt I Knew*, 148, who said the service was held at St. John's Church.

79. Perkins, *The Roosevelt I Knew*, 148–49.

80. William D. Hassett, "Record," William D. Hassett Papers, MMC-3002, Library of Congress, Washington, DC.

81. *The Journals of David E. Lilienthal: The TVA Years* (New York: Harper & Row, 1964), 676.

82. Samuel I. Rosenman, *Working with Roosevelt* (New York: Da Capo, 1972), 433.

83. "In Time of War," in *A Prayer Book for Soldiers and Sailors* (New York: Church Pension Fund, for the Army and Navy Commission of the Protestant Episcopal Church, 1941).

84. Quoted in Jon Meecham, *American Gospel: God, the Founding Fathers, and the Making of a Nation* (New York: Random House, 2006), 163–64.

85. Howard A. Johnson, "Sons of Thunder," a sermon preached at St. John's Church, July 23, 1944, Howard A. Johnson Papers.

86. Howard A. Johnson, "God's Work in Our Day," a sermon preached at St. John's Church, May 6, 1945, Howard A. Johnson Papers.

87. Howard A. Johnson, "Remembrance Sunday," a sermon preached at St. Alban's Church, Copenhagen, Denmark, November 9, 1947, Howard A. Johnson Papers.

88. Howard A. Johnson, "The Divine Incognito," Howard A. Johnson Papers, AR 1983.65, Box 15.

89. Johannes Climacus was Kierkegaard's pseudonym.

Chapter 9

1. A recent definitive study of Roosevelt's last year is Joseph Lelyveld, *His Final Battle: The Last Months of Franklin Roosevelt* (New York: Vintage Books, 2016). For an equally insightful close-up of the last three months, see David B. Woolner, *The Last Hundred Days: FDR at War and at Peace* (New York: Basic Books, 2017). Jim Bishop's

earlier account, *FDR's Last Year, April 1944–April 1945* (New York: Morrow, 1974), remains of value.

2. The closest study is Robert Ferrell, *The Dying President: Franklin D. Roosevelt, 1944–1945* (Columbia: University of Missouri Press, 1998).

3. For a concise overview of Roosevelt's days after Yalta, see Jean Edward Smith, *FDR* (New York: Random House, 2007), 756–64. Much greater detail is available in Woolner, *The Last Hundred Days*; on the trip to Warm Springs, 239ff.

4. Smith, *FDR*, 762.

5. Smith, *FDR*, 763–64; quotations, 763.

6. Despite its sensationalistic subtitle, Robert Klara's *FDR's Funeral Train: A Betrayed Widow, a Soviet Spy, and a Presidency in the Balance* (New York: St. Martin's, 2010) gives a valuable overview of the events from FDR's death to his interment. The present account relies, along with it, on "Comparison of the Requests of Franklin D. Roosevelt as to His Funeral and Burial, dated December 26, 1937, with the Actual Occurrences," Franklin D. Roosevelt Library, Hyde Park, New York. Eleanor Roosevelt quoted in Bishop, *FDR's Last Year*, 669.

7. See *New York Times*, April 13–16, 1945.

8. William D. Hassett, *Off the Record with FDR: 1942–1945* (New Brunswick, NJ: Rutgers University Press, 1958), 340; Grace Tully, *F.D.R.: My Boss* (New York: Scribner's Sons, 1949), 369.

9. *New York Times*, April 15, 1945, 5; Bernard Asbell, *When FDR Died* (New York: Holt, Rinehart & Winston, 1961), 194.

10. Bishop, *FDR's Last Year*, 650.

11. Asbell, *When FDR Died*, 158 (source of quotation); Klara, *FDR's Funeral Train*, 61–62.

12. Statistics from Klara, *FDR's Funeral Train*, 57–68.

13. Klara, *FDR's Funeral Train*, 65.

14. "Comparison of the Requests of Franklin D. Roosevelt," 8, 9, 22.

15. "Comparison of the Requests of Franklin D. Roosevelt," 8, 9, 11. Full texts of the passages alluded to come from the King James Version of the Bible and the 1928 Book of Common Prayer.

16. "Comparison of the Requests of Franklin D. Roosevelt," 9, 10.

17. "Comparison of the Requests of Franklin D. Roosevelt," 10, 11.

18. *New York Times*, April 16, 1945, 5.

19. "Comparison of the Requests of Franklin D. Roosevelt," 9.

20. Quotation from H. W. Brands, *Traitor to His Class: The Privileged Life and Radical Presidency of Franklin Delano Roosevelt* (New York: Anchor Books, 2008), 818.

Afterword

1. Of the writing of Lincoln biographies there is no end. Particularly relevant to the issues treated here are Stephen B. Oates, *With Malice toward None: A Biography of Abraham Lincoln* (New York: Harper Perennial, [1977] 2011), and Allen C. Guelzo, *Abraham Lincoln: Redeemer President* (Grand Rapids: Eerdmans, 1999).

2. Peter De Vries, *The Blood of the Lamb* (Boston: Little, Brown, 1961), 25.

3. Guelzo, *Abraham Lincoln*, 38, 328–29.

4. Daniel Walker Howe, *What Hath God Wrought: The Transformation of America, 1815–1848* (New York: Oxford University Press, 2007), chap. 15. Howe points out that Americans in the twenty-first century will note with surprise "that the party of the business community should be the party most sympathetic to central planning and governmental intervention in the economy, the reverse of the usual pattern in our day" (583).

5. Quoted in David Herbert Donald, *"We Are Lincoln Men": Abraham Lincoln and His Friends* (New York: Simon & Schuster, 2003), 74.

6. Lincoln, in the seventh debate with Stephen Douglas, Alton, Illinois, October 15, 1858; see Rodney O. Davis and Douglas L. Wilson, eds., *The Lincoln-Douglas Debates* (Urbana and Chicago: University of Illinois Press and the Knox College Lincoln Studies Center, 2008), 285.

7. Harry S. Stout, *Upon the Altar of the Nation: A Moral History of the Civil War* (New York: Viking, 2006), referred to, in order, 205-6, 170, 71–72.

8. Lincoln to Hay, May 1861, quoted in Doris Kearns Goodwin, *Team of Rivals: The Political Genius of Abraham Lincoln* (New York: Simon & Schuster, 2005), 356.

9. *The Public Papers and Addresses of Franklin D. Roosevelt*, ed. Samuel I. Rosenman, 13 vols. (New York: Random House, 1938–c. 1950) (hereafter *FDRPPA*), 6:5.

10. James R. McGovern, *And a Time for Hope: Americans in the Great Depression* (Westport, CT: Praeger, 2000), 4.

11. For varied estimates of the situation, see John A. Garrity, *The Great Depression* (Garden City, NY: Anchor Books, 1987), 100–101; William E. Leuchtenburg, *Franklin D. Roosevelt and the New Deal* (New York: Harper & Row, 1963), 18–40; Kenneth S. Davis, *FDR: The New York Years, 1928–1933* (New York: Random House, [1979] 1985), 379; and George T. McJimsey, *The Presidency of Franklin Delano Roosevelt* (Lawrence: University Press of Kansas, 2000), 62.

12. *FDRPPA*, 6:5.

13. Quoted in Jonathan Alter, *The Defining Moment: FDR's First Hundred Days and the Triumph of Hope* (New York: Simon & Schuster, 2006), 222.

14. Isaiah Berlin, *Personal Impressions* (Princeton: Princeton University Press, 2001), 24.

15. Roosevelt, "First Inaugural Address," March 4, 1933, *FDRPPA* 2.

16. Quoted in George W. Martin, *Madam Secretary: Frances Perkins* (Boston: Houghton Mifflin, 1976), 435.

17. Donald, *"We Are Lincoln Men,"* 74.

18. Donald, *"We Are Lincoln Men,"* 171.

19. John Gunther, *Roosevelt in Retrospect* (New York: Harper & Brothers, 1950), 67.

20. Eric Larrabee, *Commander in Chief: Franklin Delano Roosevelt, His Lieutenants, and Their War* (New York: Harper & Row, 1987), 1, 644.

21. Quoted in James M. McPherson, *Battle Cry of Freedom: The Civil War Era* (New York: Oxford University Press, 1988), 667.

22. "Address on Washington's Birthday," February 22, 1943, *FDRPPA*, 12:113–14.

23. Raymond Moley, *After Seven Years* (New York: Harper & Brothers, 1939), 401–2. Moley prints the full text of this talk, noting in a footnote on p. 65 that it is "conspicuous by its absence" from *FDRPPA* 1.

24. Quoted in Edmund Wilson, *Patriotic Gore* (New York: Oxford University Press, 1962), 103.

25. All quotations come from Lincoln's Second Inaugural Address, except for Goodwin, *Team of Rivals*, 256. Emphasis added.

26. Guelzo, *Abraham Lincoln*, 326.

27. Guelzo, *Abraham Lincoln*, 416–17, 325–26. Emphasis added.

28. Mark A. Noll, *America's God: From Jonathan Edwards to Abraham Lincoln* (New York: Oxford University Press, 2002), 430–32.

29. Lincoln was using Matt. 18:7 ("With malice toward none"); Eph. 4:31; 1 Pet. 2:1; Col. 3:14; and FDR's favorite, 1 Cor. 13:1–13 ("with charity for all"); Ps. 147:3 and Luke 10:34 ("bind up the nation's wounds"); and Zech. 7:10 and James 1:27 ("care for his [the dead soldier's] widow and his orphan").

30. Ignazio Silone, *Bread and Wine* (New York: Harper & Brothers, 1937), 264.

31. Kenneth Sydney Davis, *FDR: The War President, 1940–1943* (New York: Random House, 2000), 247.

32. *FDRPPA*, 10:515; 5:235.

33. "Address on Washington's Birthday," *FDRPPA*, 5:113–14.

34. Herbert Hoover, *American Individualism* (Garden City, NY: Doubleday, 1922), 12, 18.

35. Quotation, David Burner, *Herbert Hoover: A Public Life* (New York: Knopf, 1979), 74. For detail on Belgian relief, see 79–95; on post–World War I relief, 114–37. On the paradox between Hoover's activist reputation and his final fatalism about relieving the effects of the Great Depression, see William E. Leuchtenburg, *The FDR Years: On Roosevelt and His Legacy* (New York: Columbia University Press, 1995), 213.

36. Burner, *Herbert Hoover*, 138–39; Keynes's quotation, 138.

37. Quotations, Burner, *Herbert Hoover*, 146, 139; Hoover, *American Individualism*, 11.

38. William E. Leuchtenburg, *Herbert Hoover, 1929–1933: The American Presidents* (New York: Times Books, 2009), 86ff.

39. *FDRPPA*, 1:771.

40. Leuchtenburg, *Herbert Hoover*, 93; Burner, *Herbert Hoover*, 253.

41. While Burner, *Herbert Hoover*, shows the Quaker side of Hoover's religion, George Nash denies any such influence: George Nash, *The Life of Herbert Hoover: The Engineer, 1874–1914* (New York: Norton, 1983), 573.

42. Thomas D. Hamm, *The Transformation of American Quakerism: Orthodox Friends, 1800–1907* (Bloomington: Indiana University Press, 1988); quotations, 88, 68. See 24–28 for reform activities; 106–11 for Holiness Quakers.

43. On the moderate party, see Hamm, *Transformation of American Quakerism*, 110–20; for quotations, see 88; Burner, *Herbert Hoover*, 69.

44. Hoover, *American Individualism*, 22, 9, 20, 23, 61, 43, 24, 10, 17.

45. "First Inaugural Address," March 4, 1933, *FDRPPA*, 2:14; "Address to the United States Chamber of Commerce," May 4, 1933, 156–57; first fireside chat, March 12, 1933, 186.

46. The Book of Common Prayer (1928), 599; *F.D.R.: His Personal Letters*, ed. Elliott Roosevelt, 4 vols. (New York: Duell, Sloan & Pearce, 1947–1950) (hereafter *FDRPL*), 1:259; Frances Perkins, *The Roosevelt I Knew* (New York: Viking, 1946), 166; Thomas H.

Greer, *What Roosevelt Thought: The Social and Political Ideas of Franklin D. Roosevelt* (East Lansing: Michigan State University Press, 2000), 50.

47. Hoover, *American Individualism*, 63, 64, 33.

48. Hoover, *American Individualism*, 30, 50, 17–18.

49. Hoover, *American Individualism*, 67, 28–29, 42, 58.

50. Burner, *Herbert Hoover*, 326, 339; quotation, 161.

51. Franklin D. Roosevelt, *Whither Bound? A Lecture at Milton Academy on the Alumni War Memorial Foundation*, May 18, 1926 (Boston: Houghton Mifflin, 1926). All quotations in the next few paragraphs come from this document.

52. David M. Kennedy, *Freedom from Fear: The American People in Depression and War, 1929–1945* (New York: Oxford University Press, 1999), 174–75; Kennedy attributes "dumb with misery" to newspaperwoman Lorena Hickok.

53. Roosevelt recalled the 1932 campaign in his "Address at the Dedication of the Triborough Bridge," New York City, July 11, 1936, *FDRPPA*, 5:257.

54. Frank Freidel, *Franklin D. Roosevelt: Launching the New Deal* (Boston: Little, Brown, 1973), 15.

55. FDR to Charles H. Betts, December 21, 1928, in *FDRPL*, 2:20.

56. *FDRPPA*, 1:624, 626.

57. Quotations from Leuchtenburg, *Herbert Hoover*, 4, and Alter, *The Defining Moment*, 147.

Index

Titles published in the

LIBRARY OF RELIGIOUS BIOGRAPHY SERIES

Thomas Merton and the Monastic Vision
by Lawrence S. Cunningham

God's Strange Work: William Miller and the End of the World
by David L. Rowe

Blaise Pascal: Reasons of the Heart
by Marvin R. O'Connell

Occupy Until I Come: A. T. Pierson and the Evangelization of the World
by Dana L. Robert

The Kingdom Is Always but Coming: A Life of Walter Rauschenbusch
by Christopher H. Evans

A Christian and a Democrat: A Religious Biography of Franklin D. Roosevelt
by John F. Woolverton with James D. Bratt

Francis Schaeffer and the Shaping of Evangelical America
by Barry Hankins

Harriet Beecher Stowe: A Spiritual Life
by Nancy Koester

Billy Sunday and the Redemption of Urban America
by Lyle W. Dorsett

Assist Me to Proclaim: The Life and Hymns of Charles Wesley
by John R. Tyson

Prophetess of Health: A Study of Ellen G. White
by Ronald L. Numbers

George Whitefield: Evangelist for God and Empire
by Peter Y. Choi

*The Divine Dramatist: George Whitefield and
the Rise of Modern Evangelicalism* by Harry S. Stout

Liberty of Conscience: Roger Williams in America
by Edwin S. Gaustad